AQA
A-level

Business

2 **Fifth Edition**

Malcolm Surridge and
Andrew Gillespie

Approval message from AQA

This textbook has been approved by AQA for use with our qualification. This means that we have checked that it broadly covers the specification and we are satisfied with the overall quality. Full details of our approval process can be found on our website.

We approve textbooks because we know how important it is for teachers and students to have the right resources to support their teaching and learning. However, the publisher is ultimately responsible for the editorial control and quality of this book.

Please note that when teaching the *AQA A-level Business* course, you must refer to AQA's specification as your definitive source of information. While this book has been written to match the specification, it cannot provide complete coverage of every aspect of the course.

A wide range of other useful resources can be found on the relevant subject pages of our website: aqa.org.uk.

Every effort has been made to trace all copyright holders, but if any have been inadvertently overlooked the Publishers will be pleased to make the necessary arrangements at the first opportunity.

Although every effort has been made to ensure that website addresses are correct at time of going to press, Hodder Education cannot be held responsible for the content of any website mentioned in this book. It is sometimes possible to find a relocated web page by typing in the address of the home page for a website in the URL window of your browser.

Hachette UK's policy is to use papers that are natural, renewable and recyclable products and made from wood grown in sustainable forests. The logging and manufacturing processes are expected to conform to the environmental regulations of the country of origin.

Orders: please contact Bookpoint Ltd, 130 Milton Park, Abingdon, Oxon OX14 4SB. Telephone: +44 (0)1235 827720. Fax: +44 (0)1235 400454. Lines are open 9.00a.m.–5.00p.m., Monday to Saturday, with a 24-hour message answering service. Visit our website at www.hoddereducation.co.uk

© Malcolm Surridge and Andrew Gillespie 2015

First published in 2015 by
Hodder Education
An Hachette UK Company
Carmelite House
50 Victoria Embankment
London EC4Y 0DZ

Impression number   10 9 8 7 6 5 4 3 2

Year   2019 2018 2017 2016

Cover photo peshkov – Fotolia

Illustrations by Integra Software Services Pvt. Ltd, Pondicherry, India

Typeset in ITC Berkeley Oldstyle Std Book 11/14pt by Integra Software Services Pvt. Ltd, Pondicherry, India

Printed in Italy

A catalogue record for this title is available from the British Library

ISBN 978 147183578 0

Contents

Introduction

Welcome to your A-level course in Business. This book has been written to meet the precise requirements of Year 2 of AQA's A-level specification and to build on its AS specification.

Book structure

This book is divided into chapters that match exactly the content and structure of the AQA specification which will help you to understand where you are in terms of covering the relevant material. The Year 2 A-level course is divided into four units of study, each comprising between two and eight chapters. The book develops and extends the knowledge that you acquired during Year 1 of studying Business, but focuses on long-term strategic decision making throughout. At the start of each chapter we give an overview of issues that will be covered and a list of the topics that you will need to make sure that you have understood by the end.

Decision making is a key theme for this specification and therefore for this book, as it was for the Year 1 book. The entire Year 2 specification has been written around the theme of decision making. Thus the first unit of study entails analysing the current strategic position of a business (where are we now?), while later units look at strategic direction (where do we want to go?), strategic methods and managing change (how do we get there?) Understanding this from the outset will help you to see the wider picture and how the topics that you study are interrelated.

Book features

As you read the book you will study a range of different models and theories. Mastering these will help you to understand situations which businesses and managers encounter. They also give you a framework to analyse the issues involved in a specific situation and can guide you in making relevant judgements and in justifying them.

Within each chapter, we have included a number of features to support you in studying the material. These are:

Business in focus

This feature should help to bring a topic to life by showing it in action in a real context. We hope to show you how theories and models can be applied to real businesses, and used to help understand and analyse the decisions that managers, and others associated with businesses, have to make. Each Business in focus feature will have two questions at the end to encourage you to think further about the topic.

What do you think?

This feature is designed to encourage you to reflect on what has been covered in a particular part of the book. It may ask you to relate an idea or concept to other topics in the book or to your own experience, or to consider what you might decide to do in a specific situation.

Maths moment

This feature offers you an opportunity to apply your numerical skills to a topic and to interpret the meaning of business-related data.

Study tip

This feature helps you to think about the material in relation to the examinations that you will take at the end of the course. It might, for example, advise you on how to revise a particular topic.

These will give you links to important sites where you can get more information on a particular story or topic and allow you to carry out further research to deepen your understanding.

ASSESSMENT ACTIVITIES

At the end of each chapter we provide a series of A-level assessment activities. Answering these will help you to develop the skills necessary to tackle examination questions. The features we have included are:

Knowledge check questions

These are questions intended to test your knowledge and understanding of the material set out in the chapter.

Short answer questions

These require you to develop relatively brief responses to a variety of questions, some of which will be calculations.

Data response question

These provide a business scenario and ask you to answer three questions by using your knowledge and understanding of the material in the chapter and relating it to the scenario provided.

Essays

These are intended to help you develop the skills needed to write effective answers to relatively open questions which have higher mark allocations.

Case study

In addition, at the end of each unit we have written a case study which covers all the material within that unit and also may draw on topics covered in earlier units. Each end-of-unit case study has a set of questions carefully designed to reflect the examinations that you will take at the end of your course.

AQA's A-level examination in Business

All those studying AQA A-level Business have to take three examinations at the end of their second year of study. It is important for you to remember that these A-level examinations will cover the Year 1 material set out in the companion volume to this book as well as the Year 2 material covered in the following pages. In other words, all three examinations assess the entire content of the A-level specification.

The details of the three examinations are set out below.

Paper One

This paper is worth 33.3 per cent of the total A-level marks and its duration is 2 hours. It carries 100 marks in total and has four compulsory sections:

- Section A – 15 multiple-choice questions each worth one mark
- Section B – short-answer questions totalling 35 marks
- Sections C and D – each comprising two essays from which you must choose one (that is one essay from Section C and one from Section D).

Paper Two

This paper is also worth 33.3 per cent of the total A-level marks and also lasts for 2 hours. It carries 100 marks in total. The paper comprises three compulsory data-response questions each carrying approximately 33 marks and made up of three or four individual questions. One of these data-responses questions will have mainly numerical or graphical data.

Paper Three

This paper is also worth 33.3 per cent of the total A-level marks and lasts for 2 hours. It carries 100 marks in total. The paper consists of a case study and approximately six compulsory questions.

Wider study

This book will guide you through the AQA Year 2 A-level Business programme of study, although it is important for you to supplement this with research and wider reading. You are fortunate in that there is an immense amount of information available about businesses, their behaviour, their decision making and the environments in which they operate. The internet is an enormous and valuable resource: for example, the websites of public limited companies provide links to their annual reports and accounts which contain much information about their finances and their strategies. You will also find much relevant information in magazines, newspapers and on TV programmes.

Wider study brings a number of benefits. It allows you to see some of the models and theories that you have studied (such as Ansoff's matrix) in operation which will help to deepen your understanding. It will also provide a wealth of real-world examples for you to use to support your arguments when responding to examination questions.

Business is an exciting, relevant and topical subject. We hope that you enjoy your second year of study and wish you good fortune in your examinations.

Malcolm Surridge and *Andrew Gillespie*

Unit 7

Analysing the strategic position of a business

Chapter 1

Mission, corporate objectives and strategy

Introduction

The purpose of this chapter is to set the scene for you to study how managers and other interested stakeholders analyse the strategic position of a business. It is important to know what a business hopes to achieve in the long term when making an assessment of its strategic position. Therefore, we start by considering what the business is attempting to achieve by looking at its reason for existing and its corporate objectives. We also consider what influences the choice of mission and corporate objectives made by businesses. We examine how a business's strategy relates to its mission and its corporate objectives and how decisions on its strategy impact on decisions made within the business's functions, such as finance and marketing. Finally, we investigate how SWOT analysis can assist in the process of setting corporate objectives and in implementing strategy, and assess its value to managers.

What you need to know by the end of this chapter:

- the factors that can influence a business's mission
- the internal and external influences on corporate objectives and decisions
- the links between mission, corporate objectives and strategy
- the distinction between strategy and tactics
- the impact of strategic decision making on functional decision making
- the value of SWOT analysis.

Study tip

This chapter builds on material you studied in Year 1 of your A-level Business course. This material is covered in Chapter 1 of the Year 1 companion volume to this book. You may wish to re-read this material to refresh your memory before continuing with this chapter.

Mission statements

A **mission statement** sets out the purpose of an organisation and thus gives its reason for existing. Mission statements commonly focus on:

- what the business wants to be
- the values of the business
- the range of the firm's activities
- the importance of different groups, such as employees, customers and investors.

The John Lewis Partnership operates 31 department stores and 336 Waitrose supermarkets across the UK. It is owned by its 90,000 employees, who are called partners. It is not surprising that its mission statement focuses on its staff:

'The happiness of all our members, through their worthwhile, satisfying employment in a successful business.'

The BBC's mission statement reflects its role as the UK's major public service broadcaster and considers its customers:

'To enrich people's lives with programmes and services that inform, educate and entertain.'

By setting out a mission, everyone within the business knows what they should ultimately be trying to do. All of their actions should be directed towards the same thing. This should make decision making easier: when faced with a series of options managers can compare them in relation to the business's mission statement; in this way the mission statement acts as an anchor. Mission statements can also motivate people: they know why they are employed and what the business is trying to achieve.

Mission statements and vision statements

Some companies operate with mission statements, whilst others prefer to have a **vision statement**. Some businesses draw up both mission and vision statements.

What is the difference? A mission statement states a business's purpose – why it exists. A vision statement sets out what it wants to do or be in the future. Thus, a mission statement relates to the business's current position and is intended to provide information to stakeholders. Vision statements tend to be longer term as they look to the future and can be a source of inspiration to stakeholders such as employees and suppliers.

Oxfam and Tate & Lyle have two quite different vision statements.

Oxfam, a globally renowned charity, has a vision statement that reflects the values that the organisation wishes to project:

'Our vision is a just world without poverty. We want a world where people are valued and treated equally, enjoy their rights as full citizens, and can influence decisions affecting their lives.'

Figure 1.1 Oxfam's work deals with extreme poverty daily

In contrast, Tate & Lyle, a multinational supplier of food, industrial chemicals and animal feed, bases its vision statement around satisfying its customers – across the world. It is:

'To be a leading global provider of speciality food ingredients and solutions.'

Vision statements, because they are forward looking, should dovetail with a business's corporate objectives. In other words, achieving the targets embedded in its corporate objectives should enable the business to fulfill its vision.

Figure 1.2 shows how mission statements, vision statements, a business's strategy and its corporate or strategic objectives fit together to provide a framework for senior managers to work within. They also play an important role in communicating an organisation's purpose, intentions, plans and progress to a range of stakeholders, including shareholders or other owners, customers, employees, investors and suppliers.

Key terms

A **mission statement** sets out a business's overall purpose to direct and stimulate the entire organisation.

A **vision statement** sets out a business's aspirations for the future.

Influences on a business's mission

The mission of a business will be influenced by a range of factors, including the following:

● the values of the founders of the business
● the values of the business's employees
● the industry of which the business is part
● society's views
● the ownership of the business.

The values of the founders of the business

The founders of a business can instil certain values in a business which are fundamental in determining why the business exists. These values are expressed in its mission statement. Some founders of businesses can remain hugely influential

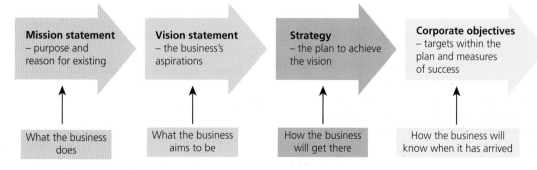

Figure 1.2 The roles of mission, vision, strategy and corporate objectives

Mission statement – purpose and reason for existing

Vision statement – the business's aspirations

Strategy – the plan to achieve the vision

Corporate objectives – targets within the plan and measures of success

What the business does

What the business aims to be

How the business will get there

How the business will know when it has arrived

long after they cease to be involved with the organisation that they created and their principles live on in the business's mission.

Johnson & Johnson supplies medical and pharmaceutical products and is still guided by the values of its founders. These values were shaped in the 1940s by the Johnson family and are fundamental to decision making throughout the company today. The company publicises that it puts 'the needs and well-being of the people we serve first'.

The values of the business's employees

Employees may be hired initially because there is some significant overlap between their values and the values of the organisation that recruits them. For example, the Bristow Group, which provides helicopter services to other businesses such as oil and gas companies, emphasises its values in its recruitment processes. It believes it is critically important for all employees to understand and embrace its vision and mission.

However, over time, the values of employees may begin to change that of the organisation and this is likely to be reflected in its mission statement as well as in its vision statement. The more senior employees are likely to have greater influence on the business's mission because they may take decisions that directly influence it. This influence may be more significant when a business experiences a higher rate of labour turnover over a sustained period or in businesses in which employees play a dominant role in the production process.

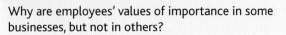

What do you think?

Why are employees' values of importance in some businesses, but not in others?

The industry of which the business is part

In some industries businesses are much more likely to be successful if they operate with certain values and this will be reflected in their mission statement. Businesses that are part of the fashion industry, for example, are likely to operate with mission statements that emphasise creativity and uniqueness. Chanel, a company that specialises in clothing, other luxury goods and fashion accessories, is an example and this is reflected in its mission statement:

'To be the Ultimate House of Luxury, defining style and creating desire, now and forever.'

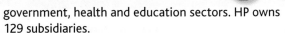

Business in focus: Hewlett Packard

Hewlett Packard (or HP as it is called today) was founded by Bill Hewlett and Dave Packard who met in the 1930s when they were engineering students at Stanford University in California. From the outset they believed in designing and manufacturing products that would make a difference to their customers' lives. HP's mission statement still places the customer at the centre of the business's activities and reflects the values of the founders:

'To provide products, services and solutions of the highest quality and deliver more value to our customers that earns their respect and loyalty.'

HP began in a small garage on 1 January 1939 and has grown rapidly since. In 2014 it employed 317,500 employees and generated revenues in excess of $111 billion. It manufactures a wide range of products, including printers, scanners, computers and digital cameras. The company sells its products to individuals, all types of business as well as customers in the government, health and education sectors. HP owns 129 subsidiaries.

HP also has a vision statement:

'To view change in the market as an opportunity to grow; to use our profits and our ability to develop and produce innovative products, services and solutions that satisfy emerging customer needs.'

HP has announced it is to divide its existing business into two separate companies by autumn 2015. HP Inc. will be the company responsible for producing PCs and printers, while its enterprise products and services business will be supplied by Hewlett-Packard Enterprise.

Questions

1. Explain why having a mission statement is of value to HP.

2. Does a business benefit from using a mission statement that is based on values that were considered important over 75 years ago?

In contrast, companies in the pharmaceutical industry could be expected to operate with long-term horizons and to place value on innovation. AstraZeneca is an Anglo-Swedish pharmaceutical company that employs over 11,000 people in its research division and spends £2.86 billion annually on research and development. Its vision statement reflects the industry in which it trades:

'To be a global biopharmaceutical business delivering great medicines to patients through innovative science and excellence in development and commercialisation.'

Society's views

What is acceptable, or better still, appealing and desirable, depends on the views held by society. At the time of writing there is considerable concern for the physical environment and a desire to protect it as far as possible. This has led to many businesses, notably those in industries with the potential to damage the environment, to address environmental protection within their mission or vision statements. Companies such as Shell (oil exploration and refining) and Rio Tinto (mining) have included environmental protection within their mission or values.

The ownership of the business

An enterprise that is owned by the state (and is therefore part of the public sector) may have a mission that shows concern for social values. Figure 1.3 shows the vision and mission statements of the National Health Service (NHS) in England as well as its purpose, behaviour and values. These statements are highly inclusive throughout and recognise that the organisation is publicly funded.

This contrasts with the mission statement of Ripple hedge Fund, an investment business based in San Francisco. It is a privately-owned company and its mission is to maximise returns for its investors. Its mission focuses on short-term profits for its relatively small number of investors. The NHS in England is expected, as a publicly-owned organisation, to provide its services to all over the long term.

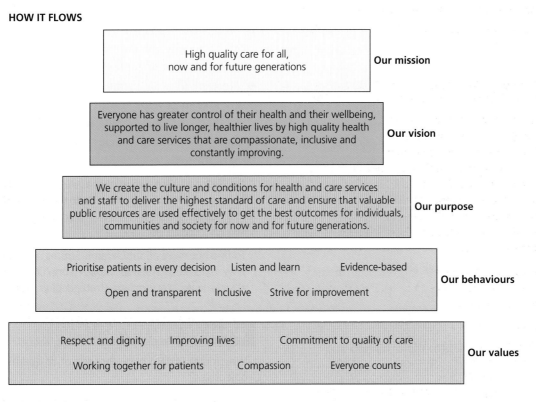

Figure 1.3 Mission, vision and other statements for England's National Health Service
Source: NHS England

Corporate objectives and strategic decisions

Corporate objectives

Once a firm has established its mission it can set its corporate objectives. These objectives are sometimes referred to as strategic objectives and they turn the mission statement into something which is more quantifiable. Rather than simply being a statement of intent, an objective sets out clearly what has to be achieved. Corporate objectives are medium- to long-term goals established to coordinate the business. Objectives are frequently quantified and have a stated timescale, such as to increase market share by 15 per cent within two years. However, this is not always the case as some corporate objectives, such as those that relate to social responsibility, may not be easy to measure.

Corporate objectives relate to the entire business, and not merely to a specific function such as finance or operations. They are more general and are set by senior managers within the organisation. Corporate objectives provide guidance for more junior managers responsible for setting objectives lower down the organisational structure and for the setting of functional objectives.

Businesses pursue a wide range of corporate objectives. Peter Drucker, a management guru, argued in *The Practice of Management* in 1954 that eight areas of business activity existed where businesses could usefully set corporate or strategic objectives.

- **Market position**. This could be the share of sales in a specific new or existing market or a growth rate for sales in a market.
- **Innovation**. This refers to the invention and development of new goods and services, as well as new processes and methods of producing and supplying products.
- **Financial resources**. These objectives could relate to the amount of capital available to a business and its sources, and how it might be used.

- **Physical resources**. This refers to the buildings, land, equipment and technological resources available to the business.
- **Human resources**. Objectives in this area may relate to motivation or engagement amongst employees.
- **Productivity**. This refers to the efficient use of resources to gain the maximum output from minimal inputs.
- **Social responsibility**. This is an area in which setting objectives has become more common as businesses have responded more fully and openly to stakeholders' needs.
- **Profits**. These objectives could relate to an overall level of profits or to profit measured against other factors such as revenue or the amount of capital invested.

Oxfam has set itself a range of corporate objectives which it expects to be achieved by 2019. One of Oxfam's aims is to promote the development of sustainable food supplies and this gives rise to three objectives.

- More small-scale and marginal producers will intensify their production sustainably, adapt to climate change and increase their resilience to shocks and stresses.
- More rural women living in poverty are economically empowered and able to influence the decisions that affect them.
- More small-scale producers, both women and men, are able to develop resilient livelihoods, with greater food security, participate in agricultural markets, and prosper from policies that promote small-scale agriculture.

Source: The Power of People Against Poverty: Oxfam Strategic Plan, 2013–2019

What do you think?

Why might Oxfam have chosen not to quantify these objectives?

Tate & Lyle plc's corporate objectives arise from the notion of growth which underpins its mission statement. They include developing a deeper understanding of its customers' needs, improving its ability to be innovative, increasing its share in emerging markets such as India and generating a stable cash flow.

Strategic decisions

Management involves making many decisions. What to do, how to do it, who will do it and when to do it all have to be decided. Clive Boddy, a writer on management, has defined a decision as 'involving a specific commitment to action'. Managers have to take a range of decisions in businesses but, for the moment, we will focus on strategic decisions.

Influences on corporate objectives and decisions

Organisations are subject to a range of influences when setting corporate objectives and taking strategic decisions. Some of these arise externally, whilst others occur within the organisation.

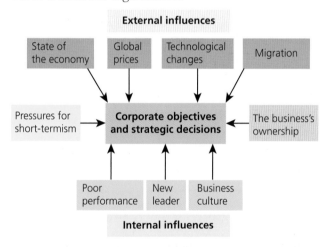

Figure 1.4 Factors influencing corporate objectives and decisions

The business's ownership

Internal influences on decisions regarding a business's corporate objectives will include the business's ownership.

Some privately-owned companies (whether private or public companies) may be under pressure to deliver high levels of **shareholder returns**. This means that they may decide to set corporate objectives which are intended to generate high levels of profits for shareholders in the form of **dividends** as well as driving up the business's share price. If such objectives are reached successfully, this is likely to be an attractive option for potential and existing shareholders, especially if they are seeking short-term gains.

Key terms

Shareholder returns are the financial benefits derived by shareholders from buying a company's shares and are the combination of an appreciating share price and dividends paid.

Dividends are that part of a company's profits that are paid to shareholders in proportion to the number of shares that they own.

Senior managers may be encouraged to set corporate objectives and make strategic decisions intended to drive up the company's share price by using share options as a form of financial motivation. Under a share option scheme a company's senior managers may be offered the opportunity (or option) to buy an agreed number of the company's shares at a specific future date and at an agreed price. This will encourage the managers concerned to set objectives and take decisions to increase the company's share price beyond that set out in the share option. If they are successful in meeting these objectives, they can take the option of buying the shares and then sell them immediately at a profit.

In contrast, businesses which have different ownership structures may set very different corporate objectives and take different strategic decisions. The John Lewis Partnership, which we mentioned earlier in this chapter on page 2, is a business that is owned by all its employees, known as partners. Andy Street, John Lewis's managing director, has described the purpose of this partnership as 'the happiness of members through their worthwhile and satisfying employment in a successful business'. There are no external shareholders involved. This means that John Lewis can do what is best for all its partners and the long-term health of the business. In addition, there is no conflict of interest between the various parts of the business. Through an elected council, management are held to account across the company and the common good is upheld. This can result in very different objectives and decisions. Certainly, senior managers at John Lewis do not have to worry about the company's share price. The retailer's corporate objectives centre on sustainable growth and delivering a reasonable profit to its partners (employees).

Small businesses such as sole traders and mutual, non-profit making businesses could operate with very different corporate objectives, perhaps focusing on providing excellent levels of service or fulfilling a social need – possibly providing jobs in an area of high unemployment. These can result in the setting of corporate objectives relating to customer needs or providing secure employment.

Pressures for short-termism

Short-termism is a significant issue for UK businesses. The term refers to an excessive focus on short-term results, for example maximising profits in a financial year, at the expense of long-term interests. A review in 2013 by Sir George Cox into short-termism revealed that 60 per cent of business leaders and 86 per cent of trades union representatives judged it to be a major or significant impediment to growth and development of business in the UK.

Short-termism can prevent senior managers thinking in the long term and may act as a disincentive to setting corporate objectives which encourage strategic decisions like research into new products and processes, training of employees to provide high level skills and creating new production facilities which may only break-even in the long term. Instead, it encourages decisions which

frequently involve cost-cutting and loss of jobs. Critics of short-termism argue that it prevents the UK developing businesses that are internationally competitive and are essential to the future success of the economy.

Key term

Short-termism is the pressure to deliver quick results to the potential detriment of the longer term development of a company.

Study tip

Short-termism is a topical issue in politics as well as business. These two aspects of short-termism intertwine and together lead to an important debate. Do some research to find out more about this debate. The website below provides a link to a report by Oxford University into the impact of short-termism and how to combat it.

Weblink

To find out more about the report by Oxford University visit: www.oxfordmartin.ox.ac.uk/downloads/commission/ Oxford_Martin_Now_for_the_Long_Term.pdf

Business in focus: BHP Billiton cuts its capital expenditure

BHP Billiton, the world's largest mining conglomerate, announced its intention to cut $600m (£381m) from its capital expenditure in the financial year ending 2015, reducing its investment to $14.2 billion. The company plans to reduce the following year's capital expenditure by $1 billion to $13 billion by 2016.

Cutting its capital expenditure could impact on the company's ability to mine its products. It believes that its capital equipment will become more productive which will offset the effects of reducing expenditure in this area.

The company's managers are concerned to maintain dividend payments to the company's shareholders and to ensure high levels of profits, allowing it to be regarded as an attractive place for investors to place their money.

The company is facing difficult trading conditions. Prices for commodities have fallen substantially recently. Iron ore prices, for example, have fallen by about 50 per cent to around $60 per tonne since January 2014.

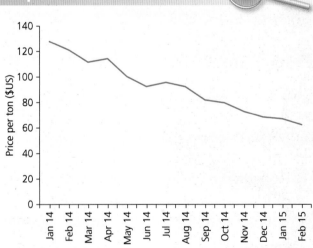

Figure 1.5 The price of iron ore, January 2014–February 2015

Source: Data from The Steel Index (TSI) via the International Monetary Fund (IMF)

Questions

1. Explain why BHP Billiton may have taken strategic decisions to cut its capital expenditure.

2. Do you think that short-termism is always a bad thing?

The business's internal environment

A number of factors may arise from within the business that can have a significant influence on the objectives that are established and the decisions that are taken.

Poor performance

A period of poor performance, indicated by a decline in sales and revenue and a loss of market share, may provoke a change in a business's strategy and in the corporate objectives it uses to guide and measure its performance.

Several businesses within the UK's supermarket industry have experienced poor performance recently. Tesco plc, once the UK's most successful and admired retailer, has suffered a range of problems. The company has seen its revenue fall and its profits slump and has experienced a major accountancy error that resulted in it overstating its profits by £250 million in 2014. As a consequence, its share price has fallen by 50 per cent over a year. Its new Chief Executive is developing a new strategy to repair some of the damage and has taken a number of strategic decisions including closing 43 stores, selling surplus land and increasing the number of staff working in the remaining stores to remedy the situation.

A new leader

Similarly, a new leader in a business may have a major influence on the objectives set and the strategic decisions that are taken in pursuit of those objectives. Harriet Green was appointed CEO of the travel company Thomas Cook in 2012 when it was performing very poorly. She was given the task of turning it around. She set tough objectives in terms of reducing costs and in reducing the number of the company's outlets as she implemented a strategy to make the company more dependent upon internet sales. The strategic decisions she oversaw reduced the number of jobs at the company, but improved its profitability significantly.

The business's culture

A business's workforce may have a particular set of values, attitudes and beliefs – these are described as the business's **culture**. Businesses can operate with a range of cultures as we shall see in Chapter 16. We can use two examples to show how a business's culture may influence the corporate objectives that are established and the strategic decisions that are made. For example, a business may be entrepreneurial and encourage ideas and employees' initiatives. This may entail the setting of corporate objectives to decentralise the organisation and delegate authority to more junior employees. On the other hand, a different business may operate with a customer-focused culture where customers are highly valued. This may result in corporate objectives and strategic decisions related to product development and employee training (to place customers first).

Key term

Culture encompasses the values, attitudes and beliefs of those who work for a business.

Figure 1.6 Tesco plc's corporate objectives are influenced by Dave Lewis, the company's newly appointed Chief Executive, as well as its poor financial performance.

The business's external environment

A business's external environment has a major influence on management decision making, not least in relation to strategic decisions and setting corporate objectives. A number of elements of the external environment can be particularly influential.

The state of the economy

The UK's economy is still feeling the effects of the financial crisis and the deep recession of 2008–9. A report in 2014 by the National Institute of Economic and Social Research warned 'that real consumer wages (that is adjusted for the effects of inflation) were still at 2004 levels, and would not rise above their 2009 peak until 'around 2019 or 2020.' This has implications for businesses. As shown in Figure 1.7, consumer spending has held up, even after inflation has been taken into account, but this has been supported by consumers increasing their borrowing.

This means that the ability of consumers to spend money is curtailed and they seek value for money and competitive prices. Businesses have had to adjust their corporate objectives to reflect this. For example, many retailers in the UK have revised corporate objectives in terms of sales and the number of shops or stores required. A recent study by the Centre for Retail Research estimated that UK retail store numbers could fall by 22 per cent by 2018 as strategic decisions to close stores continue.

Figure 1.7 below shows that consumer spending in the UK has shown substantial changes in its pattern over a period of just one year. Spending on recreation and culture has risen strongly, as has spending on transport, clothing and footwear. At the same time, expenditure on food and drink has declined. These figures will help to shape strategic decision making across a range of manufacturing and service industries.

What do you think?

Is the state of the economy the most important influence on the setting of corporate objectives for all businesses?

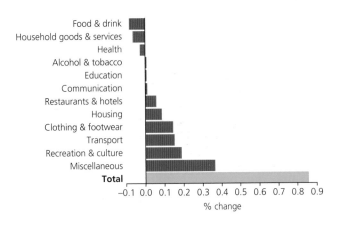

Figure 1.7 Changes in consumer expenditure in real terms between 2013 and 2014

Source: Office for National Statistics (ONS)

Prices on global markets

The prices of commodities such as wheat and oil which are traded globally have received a lot of attention recently. Changes in global prices impact heavily on objective setting and strategic decision making in many industries.

For example, at the time of writing (February 2015) oil prices have fallen by around 50 per cent to approximately $52 a barrel over the last 12 months. This affects the costs of many firms and may encourage expansion, but the greatest effects are felt in the oil industry. Falling prices have resulted in strategic decisions in this industry to cut exploration activity as well as to reduce day-to-day operations. In response to the falling price of oil, BP announced a $1 billion restructuring programme, which is expected to result in the loss of hundreds of jobs across its UK and US operations. A report, *Fuelling the Next Generation*, commissioned by industry body Oil and Gas UK, revealed that the UK could suffer 35,000 job losses as firms set objectives based on reducing costs.

Technological changes

Technology impacts on the setting of objectives and the making of strategic decisions in many ways. It may encourage firms to adopt objectives based on capital-intensive production and to use robots and other forms of technology to replace labour in production. This can be seen in the use of automated check-outs in many shops. It can have an even more dramatic impact on business models as retail firms use the potential of the internet to reach customers and to supply products 24 hours a day.

Many banks in the UK are setting corporate objectives based on changing consumer behaviour reflected in greater use of the internet. For example, Barclays Bank has announced its objective to close approximately 25 per cent of its 1,515 bank branches across its UK network. This will have huge implications for the business's operations.

BMW has set itself the objective of a large-scale expansion of the use of robots on its car manufacturing production lines. The company plans to design additional tasks for collaborative robots (which can work alongside humans on a wide range of relatively small-scale production activities) as they are progressively introduced in five of its factories. The installation of these robots will have significant implications for the company's strategic decisions, not least those on training and recruitment.

Figure 1.8 Robots involved in car production

Patterns of migration

The UK has been subject to high levels of migration for the last 20 years. Figure 1.9 illustrates this. The numbers leaving the UK (emigration) have varied between 200,000 and 400,000 annually, but have been significantly below the numbers entering the UK (immigration). As a consequence, there have been high positive levels of net migration – the balance between emigration and immigration. More people have entered the UK than have left.

This has had profound implications for the objectives and strategic decisions of a range of businesses in the UK because immigration affects the workforce that is available, as well as providing additional consumers for the products of many firms. The effects are more significant in certain areas. For example, universities in the UK attract over 400,000 students from overseas which impacts on their corporate objectives in terms

of scale of operations and range of courses. Another example is agriculture, particularly in locations such as East Anglia, because it is dependent on migrant labour as a low-cost alternative to greater mechanisation.

The difference between strategy and tactics

A corporate **strategy** is a long-term plan to achieve the business's vision through attaining its corporate objectives. For example, if a firm's vision was to become the market leader, it might decide to achieve this through a strategy based on low prices. This may entail setting corporate objectives relating to controlling or reducing costs and increasing sales.

Strategies tend to involve a major commitment of resources and are difficult to reverse. For example, the decision to invest in new product development is likely to involve a high level of finance and take several years. Strategic decisions also tend to involve a high level of uncertainty. Over time, market conditions often change significantly and so firms must change their strategies to cope with these unfamiliar conditions.

The value of producing a clear strategy is that it sets out the firm's overall plan; this helps employees develop their own plans to implement the strategy. If employees know that the firm wants to diversify, for example, they know that it is realistic to consider market opportunities in new segments of the market. In contrast, if they are aware that the strategy is to boost the firm's market presence in a particular region, they are likely to focus on putting more resources into this area.

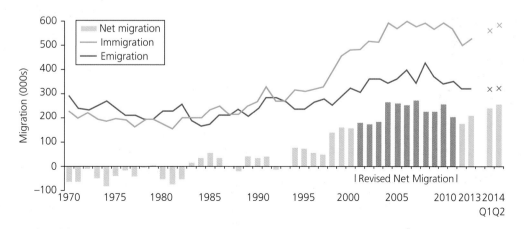

Figure 1.9 Emigration, immigration and net migration for the UK, 1970–2014

Source: Office for National Statistics (ONS)

Tactical decisions

The decisions made about how to implement a business's strategy are called 'tactical decisions' or **tactics**. Tactical decisions tend to be short term, to involve fewer resources and involve less uncertainty. These types of decisions, such as temporary increases in production or a change of supplier, are made regularly by relatively junior managers who may only be responsible for a small element of the business's activities. However, in making these decisions the junior managers are guided by the business's strategy – their decisions should be an integral part of this plan to achieve the business's objectives.

Strategic decisions	Tactical decisions
Long-term	Short-term
Involve high commitment of resources	Fewer resources involved
Difficult to reverse	Easier to reverse
Usually taken by senior management	Normally taken by junior management

Table 1.1 The differences between strategic and tactical decisions

Key terms

A **strategy** is the long-term plan to achieve the business's vision through attaining its corporate objectives.

Tactics are short-term decisions, usually involving relatively few resources, that are made to implement a strategy.

The links between mission, corporate objectives and strategy

A successful business is likely to have a clearly stated mission and vision which acts as a broad guide to its managers. A sound awareness of the business's mission and vision will enable senior managers to develop corporate objectives which, if achieved, will fulfil the mission and vision. The next piece in the jigsaw is the development of a plan or strategy by which the managers intend to achieve the business's corporate objectives. Junior managers will take relatively minor decisions to support this plan. Good communication

between managers at all levels in the organisation is essential for this to operate effectively.

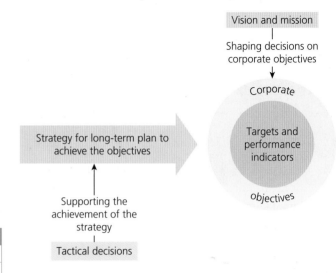

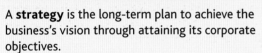

Figure 1.10 Mission and vision, corporate objectives, strategy and tactics

Taylor Wimpey plc is one of the UK's largest house builders. It expresses its mission in terms of what it does as follows:

'*We provide high-quality places to live with appropriate facilities, an attractive environment and a sense of place.*'

Its vision is 'to become the UK's leading residential developer for creating value and delivering quality for all our stakeholders'. The company has set itself three strategic objectives relating to profitability and growth – for example, targeting an average profit figure equal to 15 per cent of the value of capital invested into the business. These are supported by other objectives relating to customers, employees and the environment. Its strategy, or plan, to achieve these objectives has a number of key elements or drivers including: investing in its employees, using assets with maximum efficiency and a philosophy of continually improving the way the business is run.

Weblink

To find out more about Taylor Wimpey plc's objectives and strategy visit:
www.taylorwimpey.co.uk/corporate

Strategic decision making and functional decision making

We saw earlier in this chapter on pages 11–12 that strategic decisions are judgements made by senior managers that are long term, involve a major commitment of resources and are difficult to reverse. They are taken in pursuit of the business's corporate objectives. Strategic decisions have great implications for those responsible for taking decisions within a business's functions. A business's functions are the departments or areas that comprise a business, such as operations, finance, marketing and human resources. Decisions taken in these areas will be intended to support strategic decision making and the achievement of the business's corporate objectives.

Strategic decisions are taken first with subsequent **functional decisions** acting to support them. For example, a business that has set itself corporate objectives relating to growth may take a strategic decision to enter new markets. This will have significant consequences for functional decision making.

- Marketing may need to take decisions about researching into consumers' needs in different markets and launching new products or adapting existing ones.

- Financial decisions could relate to raising capital to fund the expansion or seeking more effective ways to manage cash flow at a time of rapid growth.
- Human resource decisions could include preparing new workforce plans to meet the expected increase in the scale of production.
- Operations could take decisions regarding the most efficient locations and the increased use of technology in production to gain price competitiveness in the new markets.

These functional decisions have to be coordinated to ensure that the different functions work effectively together to support the strategic decision – joined-up thinking is required. For example, if managers responsible for operations take decisions to use more capital intensive methods of production, this will need to be coordinated with decisions in human resources to ensure that the right number of employees are available in the right place and with the right skills.

Key term

A **functional decision** is a judgement taken by managers responsible for one aspect of a business's activities, such as marketing or human resources.

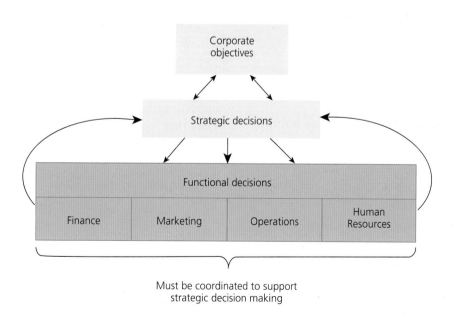

Figure 1.11 Functional and strategic decision making

Business in focus: BT buys EE

BT has revealed that it intends to buy EE, the largest of the UK's mobile telephone companies, in a takeover that is valued at £12.5 billion. EE is a tempting target for BT as it has over 24 million customers and a highly developed 4G network. If the takeover is completed BT will increase the number of customers it has by more than 200% and will target them with its other communication and media products.

EE is currently owned by Deutsche Telekom and Orange, who will be offered shares in the new and enlarged company as well as a reported £6.2 billion in cash. Although this is a costly deal, BT is expected to reduce EE's operating costs by up to £360 million to achieve higher profit margins.

It has been apparent that BT has been eager, as a central part of its business strategy, to re-enter the mobile phone market (it sold its previous company in 2001). In doing so, BT's managers are seeking to create a business that offers a broad range of products to its customers, therefore allowing them to purchase products which they can access on a diverse spectrum of devices including televisions, landlines, tablets and smartphones.

BT's takeover of EE will increase the competitive pressures faced by its competitors and is likely to result in consumers buying from fewer, larger businesses. This trend may only be in the best interests of sole stakeholders.

Source: Adapted from an article in *The Independent*, 5 February 2015

Questions

1. Explain the possible ways in which the takeover decision by BT's board of directors might affect its functional decisions.

2. Do all stakeholders benefit when markets are made up of fewer, larger businesses?

SWOT analysis

SWOT analysis is a method of strategic analysis which considers the internal and external environments of a business. SWOT is an acronym: S and W stand for 'strengths' and 'weaknesses' and these look at the internal position of a business at the present time.

A business's current strengths may include:

- a high level of cash
- a strong brand name
- a good distribution network
- highly skilled and loyal staff.

The following are examples of weaknesses a business may have:

- large amounts of long-term borrowing
- under utilised capacity
- a low net profit margin
- a lack of new products under development.

The letters O and T represent 'opportunities' and 'threats'. This part of SWOT analysis refers to external factors and looks to the future. Opportunities offer positive chances for the business, whilst threats are factors which might be damaging.

A business may benefit from opportunities in the future such as:

- growth in a major market
- an alliance with a competitor to develop new technology
- rising income levels amongst target consumer groups.

On the other hand, its future threats may include:

- being taken over by a larger competitor
- a change in consumer tastes leading to a significant fall in demand
- new laws increasing the business's costs of production.

Managers try to identify strengths, weaknesses, opportunities and threats as accurately as possible. They then rank these in order of their significance – for example, what is the most significant threat?

Key term

SWOT analysis is a management technique used to identify a business's strengths and weaknesses, as well as the opportunities and threats to which it will be exposed.

Using the information in a SWOT analysis

Once a SWOT analysis has been undertaken managers should have a clearer view of what the business is good at, what its weaknesses are, what it could be doing and against what it should protect itself.

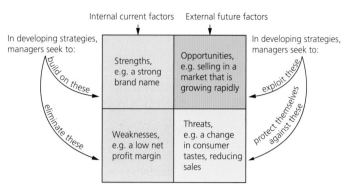

Figure 1.12 SWOT analysis

From this, managers can develop a strategy, or range of strategies, that seek to:

- build on strengths to exploit opportunities
- reduce or eliminate their weaknesses
- protect the business against threats.

A SWOT analysis is not a one-off exercise. Given that a business is subject to constant change in its internal and external environment, this should be constantly monitored and analysed and strategies should be adjusted accordingly. For example, a strategy of growth may be appropriate in an economy that is expanding rapidly, but in a recession it may be necessary to focus on protecting market share.

Business in focus: Toyota

Toyota is a large, multinational Japanese car manufacturer. In 2014 it manufactured 10.2 million cars and employed nearly 340,000 people globally. It is the twelfth largest company in the world, when ranked according to sales revenue. It produces a range of environmentally-friendly vehicles including hybrid electric cars such as the best-selling Prius and all-electric vehicles, for example the RAV4 EV or the iQ EV.

Figure 1.13 Toyota manufactures environmentally-friendly vehicles

Strengths	Opportunities
● Achieved record profits of £15 billion in 2015 ● World's largest car manufacturer in terms of volume (2014) ● Successful research and development ● Effective use of lean production ● Holds large stakes in other businesses, e.g. Daihatsu and Fuji	● Increasing demand for environmentally-friendly vehicles ● Strong growth in demand for cars in emerging markets such as China and Brazil ● Oil prices have fallen by 50% and are forecast to remain low ● Interest rates in many key developed markets are at a historic low
Weaknesses	**Threats**
● Has had to recall a large number of vehicles to repair faults, damaging brand image ● Fined $1.2 billion in the USA over concealment of faults with some of its cars ● Sales in home market (Japan) declined by 7% during 2014–15 ● Sales currently relatively low in emerging markets	● Global car manufacturers have more productive capacity than needed ● A rival car manufacturer is enjoying a more rapid sales growth ● Tightening emissions standards in many countries is increasing cost and complexity of production ● Intense competition in the environmentally-friendly vehicles market from Nissan

Table 1.2 A SWOT analysis for Toyota

Questions

1. Explain one way in which the information in this SWOT analysis might influence strategic decisions made by the management team at Toyota.

2. The car manufacturing market is changing very quickly. Does this mean this SWOT analysis is of little value?

The value of SWOT analysis

SWOT analysis offers a range of benefits to managers when devising strategies:

- SWOT analysis is a low-cost and straightforward technique that can be used by managers in all types of businesses and may be very suitable to assist managers of small businesses in devising strategy.
- It can assist managers to think in a structured way and focus on both the internal operations of the business and its external environment.
- Its use encourages management teams to develop plans that are logical in the context of the business's current position, whilst actively promoting a forward-looking approach which should be a central element of business planning.
- SWOT analysis, and especially the 'threat' part of the analysis, can help managers to recognise and assess risk which is an important part of making strategic decisions.
- SWOT analysis can be combined effectively with other management techniques, such as PEST-C analysis to help to develop a business's strategy.

- SWOT analysis can be used within a business's functions, for example, as an important part of developing a marketing strategy.

Naturally, SWOT analysis has a range of limitations to balance its benefits:

- A SWOT analysis only covers issues that can be classified as a strength, weakness, opportunity or threat. It can be difficult to address uncertain or two-sided factors, such as factors that could either be a strength, a weakness or both.
- It can provide a lot of information, but is unlikely to offer any solutions and its results will require further analysis by managers. Any benefit from the analysis will depend on the quality of the interpretation – if this is poor, then the analysis is likely to be of little value.
- The analysis offers no assistance to managers in judging the relative importance of strengths, weaknesses, opportunities and threats in contributing to the development of a strategy. As a consequence, managers may underestimate the importance of one or more of the four elements.
- Decisions on a business's strategy should be based on reliable, relevant and comparable data. However, SWOT analysis can be subjective depending on the opinions and positions of those collecting and analysing the data.
- A SWOT analysis is only as good as the data on which it is based – if the data used is poor, the analysis is unlikely to be useful. Also, the data on which SWOT analysis is based can become outdated quickly. For example, in Table 1.2, Toyota's profit levels and market position could be quite different a year later.

ASSESSMENT ACTIVITIES

(a) Knowledge check questions

1 State two likely components of a business's mission statement.

2 What is the difference between a business's mission statement and its vision statement?

3 Define the term 'corporate objective'.

4 State three areas of business activity, identified by Peter Drucker, where businesses can usefully set corporate objectives.

5 What is meant by the term 'strategic decision'?

6 State two disadvantages that may result from managers taking decisions that are influenced by short-termism.

7 State two internal factors that might influence the setting of corporate objectives and the strategic decision making within a business.

8 State two external factors that might influence the setting of corporate objectives and the strategic decision making within a business.

9 Distinguish between strategy and tactics.

10 What is meant by the term 'SWOT analysis'?

(b) Short answer questions

1 Explain how the industry of which a business is part might influence its mission statement. (4 marks)

2 Explain the relationship between a business's mission and its corporate objectives. (5 marks)

3 Explain how the type of ownership of a business may influence the corporate objectives that it sets itself. (5 marks)

4 Explain why a small business facing competition from larger rivals should engage in a SWOT analysis before making strategic decisions. (9 marks)

(c) Data response question

Ford is a multinational car manufacturer. In 2013 it sold 6.33 million cars in the highly competitive global market and generated revenues of over $7 billion. Ford says its philosophy means it goes further to make its cars better, its employees happier and the planet a better place to be. This is reflected in its mission statement:

One Team.

People working together as a lean, global enterprise for automotive leadership, as measured by: Customer, Employee, Dealer, Investor, Supplier, Union/Council, and Community Satisfaction.

The Ford Motor Company enjoyed a very successful year in 2013. It achieved record profits in North America and the Asia-Pacific-Africa region and doubled its dividend for shareholders. It is setting itself ambitious objectives:

● Its largest manufacturing expansion in the last 50 years. It will increase capacity in six factories in the USA, open two new plants in Asia, one in South America and one in Europe.

● A focus on producing vehicles that are best-in-class in quality, safety and innovative technology.

● The launch of a record number of new vehicles over the coming year.

● The pursuit of other objectives including increased global sales and market share, and an ongoing commitment to reducing the environmental impact of its vehicles.

Source: Ford website, www.gusjohnsonford.com/our-mission-statement/

Strengths	Opportunities
● Strong position in US market ● Sound financial performance ● Significant growth in China	● Rising demand for environmentally-friendly vehicles, notably in the USA and Europe ● New emission standards ● Growth through takeovers and mergers
Weaknesses	**Threats**
● Poor environmental record ● High cost structure ● Unprofitable European operations	● Rising raw material prices ● Intense competition ● Fluctuating exchange rates

Table 1.3 SWOT analysis for Ford Motor Company

Source: Adapted from Strategic Management Insight website, www.strategicmanagementinsight.com/

1 Explain the possible influences on Ford's mission statement.   (6 marks)

2 Analyse the ways in which the use of its SWOT analysis might help Ford to make more effective decisions in the future.   (9 marks)

3 Do you agree that factors from its external environment were the most important influence on Ford's choice of corporate objectives and its strategic decisions? Justify your opinion.
    (15 marks)

(d) Essays

1 To what extent do you think that short-termism is the most important influence on setting corporate objectives for public limited companies in the UK?   (25 marks)

2 'SWOT analysis is simple and inexpensive and therefore only of value to small businesses.' To what extent do you agree with this statement?   (25 marks)

Chapter 2

Analysing internal position: financial ratio analysis

Introduction

This chapter investigates how stakeholders can assess the strengths and weaknesses of a business's existing financial position by analysing financial statements such as balance sheets and income statements. We examine the structure and components of balance sheets and income statements and the key indicators of financial performance that can be seen within them. We also consider how a range of financial ratios can be used to assess business performance. Finally, we discuss the value of financial ratios in judging a business's performance.

What you need to know by the end of this chapter:

- how to assess the financial performance of a business using balance sheets, income statements and financial ratios, including profitability, liquidity, gearing and efficiency ratios
- the value of financial ratios when assessing a business's performance over time or in comparison with other businesses.

Financial statements

Businesses in the UK produce a range of financial information to assist stakeholders in assessing their performance and to inform decision making. This information is presented in a range of financial statements of which we shall consider two:

- **balance sheets**
- income statements.

The information these contain is important for stakeholders when judging the performance of a business.

Key term

A **balance sheet** is a financial statement recording the assets and liabilities of a business on a particular day at the end of an accounting period. The balance sheet represents a picture of a business's assets and liabilities at a particular moment in time.

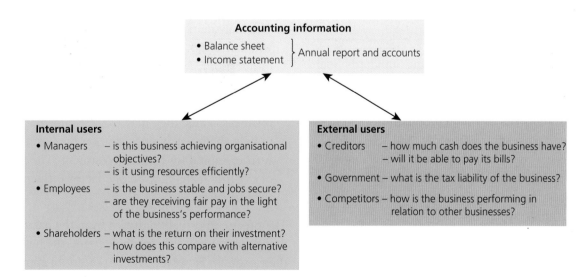

Figure 2.1 Stakeholders and financial information

How to analyse balance sheets

What is a balance sheet?

A balance sheet is a financial statement recording the **assets** (possessions) and **liabilities** (debts) of a business on a particular day at the end of an accounting period. The balance sheet represents a picture of a business's assets and liabilities at a moment in time: it is commonly described as a 'snapshot' of the financial position of an organisation. Because of this, balance sheets always carry a date, the day on which the valuation of assets and liabilities took place.

In 2009 the International Accounting Standards Board (IASB) – the organisation which oversees accounting practices worldwide – proposed renaming balance sheets as '**statements of financial position**'. Unlike many other changes introduced by the IASB, this change has not really proved popular. Many major UK public companies continue to use the term 'balance sheet' in their annual accounts and we shall use it throughout this chapter.

By recording assets and liabilities the balance sheet sets out the ways in which the business has raised its capital and the uses to which this capital has been put. The balance sheet provides a great deal of information for those with an interest in a business, and is the primary financial document published by businesses.

Balance sheets can relate to a single enterprise or to several, in which case they are referred to as **consolidated balance sheets**. Balance sheets are an essential source of information for a variety of business decisions and for a number of stakeholders.

- **Shareholders** (and potential shareholders) may use balance sheets to assess a business's potential to generate good returns in the future. Thus, they may examine the extent and type of assets available to a business. A high proportion of assets, such as machinery and property, may signify a potential for profit, depending upon the type of business.
- **Suppliers** are more likely to use a balance sheet to investigate the short-term position of the company. Thus, they may consider cash and other liquid assets a business holds and make a judgement about whether the business is likely to be able to pay its bills over the coming months. This may help a supplier reach a decision on whether or not to offer credit to the business in question.
- **Managers** will be interested in a balance sheet as an indication of the performance of the business. Thus, they may extract information to help them reach a decision on how to raise further capital for future investment. The amount of existing loans may be one factor influencing this decision.

The precise information drawn from the balance sheet will depend upon the stakeholder and the nature of their enquiry. However, it is important to appreciate that this particular financial statement contains a great deal of information.

Assets

An asset is something that a business owns. Assets are what a business uses its capital to purchase. There are two main categories of assets that appear on a business's balance sheet. The distinction between the two categories is based upon the time the assets are held within the business.

1. **Non-current assets**. These are assets owned by a business that it expects to retain for one year or more. Such assets are used regularly by a business and are not purchased for the purpose of resale. Examples of non-current assets include land, property, production equipment and vehicles.

2. **Current assets**. This category of asset is likely to be converted into cash before the next balance sheet is drawn up. Therefore, cash and inventories are examples of current assets as they are only retained by the business for a relatively short period of time. Another category of current asset is receivables (sometimes termed 'trade and other receivables' to indicate different types of debtors). These are debts owed to the business in question due for payment within 12 months and so will become cash within one year.

There is another way to classify assets which, although it does not affect the balance sheet directly, is still important to understand.

1. **Tangible assets**. These are assets that have a physical existence and have been traditionally included on a balance sheet. Tangible assets include:
    - land and property, which are frequently the most valuable assets owned by a business
    - machinery and equipment, a tangible asset that is likely to be of importance to manufacturing industries.

2. **Intangible assets**. These assets do not take a physical form. Examples include:
    - Patents and other rights. Apple held $4.14 billion of intangible assets on its balance sheet in 2014 of which a proportion would represent the value of its patents.
    - Goodwill. This is the value of established custom and a good name to a business.

- Brands. These can be included on a balance sheet if they were purchased or can be separately valued. It has been estimated that 80 per cent of the worth of companies such as Coca-Cola and Marlboro comprises intangible assets. However, the value of brands can fluctuate.

Intangible assets are only recorded on the balance sheet if they can be separately identified and money was spent upon their acquisition. For example, it would be appropriate for mobile phone companies to present their licences to supply services (sold to them by the government) as intangible assets.

Liabilities

A liability is a debt owed by the business to organisations or individuals. Another way of thinking of a liability is that it shows the sources of capital the business has raised in order to purchase its assets. As with assets, there are a number of categories of liabilities:

1. **Current liabilities**. In many senses these are the equivalent of current assets and are payments due within a relatively short period of time, normally one year. They represent debts owed by the business due for payment within one year or less. Examples of such short-term debt are overdrafts and tax due for payment. Trade and other payables (which is money owed to suppliers and other organisations) are another category of payments that will be made within 12 months.

2. **Non-current liabilities**. These are debts that a business does not expect to repay within the period of one year. Mortgages and bank loans repayable over several years are common examples of this type of liability.

3. **Total equity**. It may seem strange that the money invested into the business by its owners (shareholders in the case of a company) is a liability. However, if the company ceases trading, shareholders would hope for the repayment of their investment. Thus, these funds (called total equity or total shareholders' equity) are liabilities.

Business in focus: Household balance sheets

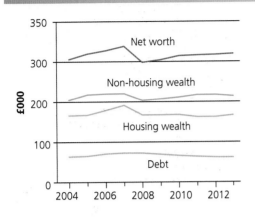

Figure 2.2a Average household finances, 2004–13

Source: Office for National Statistics (ONS)

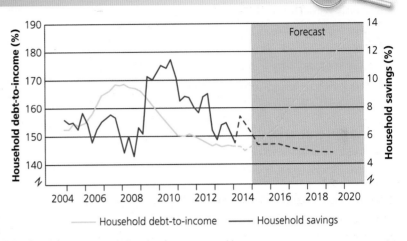

Figure 2.2b Debt-to-income and savings for households in the UK, 2004–19

Source: Office for Budget Responsibility (OBR)

Decisions on spending taken by households in the UK are crucial for the country's economy. After paying back debts to strengthen their balance sheets in the years after the financial crisis of 2008–9, consumers are spending again. Yet the value of their assets, like wages, remains lower in 2014 than in 2007.

Economists forecast that many households (their term for families or other groups who share finances) will start to borrow more heavily to finance spending. This will increase their levels of debt and could make household balance sheets look weaker once again.

Source: Text adapted from an article in *The Economist*, 3 January 2015

Questions

1. Describe the major assets and liabilities that a household in the UK might have.

2. Do you think it matters if households in the UK increase the amount of borrowing (or debt) they have in relation to their incomes as forecast in Figure 2.2b?

Net assets

It is possible to calculate a business's net assets (sometimes called 'net assets employed') by totalling the business's assets and subtracting the business's total liabilities. Thus:

Net assets = (non-current assets + current assets) − (non-current liabilities + current liabilities)

This is one way of calculating the value of a business. Net assets represent what would be left to the owners of a business if all its assets were sold and all its liabilities were paid.

Why does a balance sheet always balance?

The balance sheet is well named as at all times the assets held by a business must match its liabilities (including capital borrowed from its owners). Why is this the case?

First, there exists what accountants call the 'dual aspect' of constructing a balance sheet. Thus, any transaction that is recorded on the balance sheet has two effects that cancel out each other. The following examples highlight this point:

- If a business borrows £575,000 to purchase vehicles, the loan will appear as a liability as it is owed by the business to a bank or other financial institution. However, at the same time, the business will have additional assets recorded on its balance sheet (in this case vehicles initially valued at £575,000). Thus, this transaction will not cause the balance sheet to become unbalanced.

- Alternatively, the business might sell a non-current asset for cash. In this case the business will have non-current assets of a lower value, but its holdings of cash will rise by the same amount. In these circumstances the value of total assets is unchanged and the balance sheet still balances.

Another feature of the balance sheet that ensures that it continues to balance is reserves. Reserves are simply profit accumulated during previous years' trading and not paid out to the owners of the business. This accumulated profit is not held in the form of cash but is invested into a range of assets that are useful to the business and hopefully generate further profits. If a business is successful, purchases more assets and grows, then its value will increase and so will the value of the assets. It may borrow money to achieve this growth; if it does, liabilities will grow at the same rate. However, if it funds its growth through profits, then the matching liability will be recorded as reserves, indicating that the owners' stake in the business has risen in value. Remember that the total equity on the balance sheet represents money lent to the organisation.

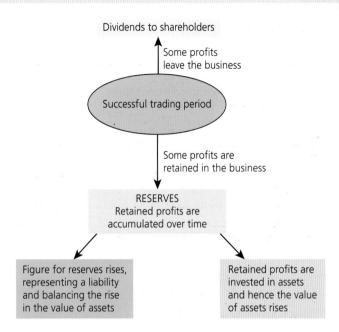

Figure 2.3 Assets, liabilities and reserves

The structure of a balance sheet

The precise layout of balance sheets can vary a little according to the type of business, although the structure is similar for all businesses. All balance sheets list assets first – non-current followed by current assets. Next, current liabilities are normally recorded, allowing a firm to calculate its working capital (simply current assets less current liabilities). Finally, the last section records the sources of finance both borrowed and provided by the owners.

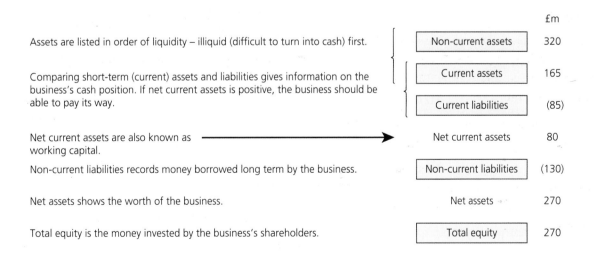

Figure 2.4 The basic structure of a public company's balance sheet

Study tip

Remember that the AQA A-level Business specification only requires you to be able to read and interpret balance sheets and not to construct them.

Reading and interpreting balance sheets

Professional managers, potential investors and accountants can gain a great deal of information about a company from reading its balance sheet. In this section we consider two balance sheets of Ted Baker plc to illustrate the uses of this financial statement. Ted Baker plc is a fashion retailer which sells clothing and accessories for men and women through its own shops and concessions in other stores.

	2014 £000s	2013 £000s
Non-current assets		
Intangible non-current assets	6,080	983
Tangible non-current assets	51,121	51,302
	57,201	**52,285**
Current assets		
Inventories	80,432	67,673
Trade and other receivables	34,793	34,124
Cash and other current assets	29,184	10,592
	144,409	**112,389**
Current liabilities		
Trade and other payables	(45,289)	(40,793)
Overdraft	(37,282)	(19,862)
Tax payable	(3,857)	(4,360)
Other current liabilities	(3,118)	(269)
	(89,546)	**(65,284)**
Net current assets	**54,863**	**47,105**
Non-current liabilities		
Payments due in over 1 year	0	(497)
	0	**(497)**
Net assets	**112,064**	**98,893**
Equity		
Share capital	11,333	11,297
Reserves and retained earnings	100,731	87,596
Total equity	**112,064**	**98,893**

Table 2.1 Ted Baker plc balance sheet as at 25 January 2014 and 26 January 2013 (summarised)

Source: Adapted from Ted Baker plc's Annual Report & Accounts, 2013–14

Weblink

To find out more about Ted Baker plc visit: www.tedbakerplc.com/

There are a number of features on the balance sheet that are worth examining when assessing the performance of the business in question. It is possible to make some assessment of the short-term financial position of the business as well as its longer term strategy from reading the balance sheet.

The short term

Assessing a business's short-term situation entails examining its ability to pay its bills over the next 12 months. The balance sheet sets out a business's short-term debts (current liabilities) and also the current assets it has available to pay these creditors. The net position of these two factors is recorded as net current assets/liabilities. If assets are greater than liabilities, the figure resulting will be referred to as net current assets. It will be called net current liabilities if current liabilities are greater.

The balance between current assets and current liabilities is also known as working capital. If a business has more current assets than current liabilities, it has a positive figure for working capital and should be able to pay its debts in the short term. However, if current liabilities exceed current assets, this may cause liquidity or cash problems, depending upon the type of business.

Maths moment

$$\frac{1+b}{c}=3$$

Assume that in 2014 Ted Baker plc's balance sheet revealed a net current liability figure of £5,500,000 and that its total current assets were unchanged at £144,409,000. Calculate the level of current liabilities that would be necessary to create this situation.

The long term

A business's balance sheet can be examined in a number of ways:

- Movement of non-current assets: a sudden increase in non-current assets may indicate a rapidly growing company, which may mean that the company's financial performance might improve over the medium term.
- Considering how a business has raised its capital may also be valuable. As we shall see in Chapter 3, it is risky for a company to borrow too much. Thus, a company raising more through borrowing (non-current liabilities) than through share capital and reserves might be vulnerable to rises in interest rates.

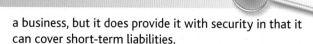

Business in focus: Ted Baker plc (1)

Table 2.1 shows Ted Baker plc's balance sheet. The latest year (2014) is shown in the left-hand column. This method of presenting the latest data on the left is common in company's financial statements. Negative figures are shown in brackets.

We can see from the company's balance sheet that it operates with net current assets in both trading years. However, 2014 has a larger figure for net current assets than 2013 – £54.86 million compared to £47.10 million. This shows us that Ted Baker plc's current assets exceeded its current liabilities by a greater amount in 2014. The company not only had sufficient short-term assets to cover its short-term liabilities, but it held an increasing surplus of short-term assets. This is relatively unusual for retailers. They can rely on customers spending large amounts of cash daily in their shops, thus providing funds to settle short-term liabilities. Hence some only hold relatively small amounts of current assets. It is noticeable that the amount of cash held by the company has nearly trebled to £29.18 million. This is a major reason for the growth in current assets. Holding large amounts of cash is unlikely to earn much return for

a business, but it does provide it with security in that it can cover short-term liabilities.

Another noteworthy feature of Ted Baker plc's balance sheet is that the company has very low levels of long-term borrowing, less than £0.5 million in 2013 and zero in 2014. This is shown by the fall in non-current liabilities to zero. The company's profits rose strongly in 2014 providing it with the opportunity to repay long-term debt. At the same time, the company's value has increased substantially, primarily because of a rise in the value of the company's intangible assets. This was the result of the company developing computer systems for use in its forthcoming e-commerce operations that have considerable value.

Questions

1. Do you think that Ted Baker plc's balance sheet was stronger in 2013 or 2014? Explain your reasoning.
2. What other information might a shareholder interested in investing in the company need to make an informed decision?

- Reserves provide an indication of the profits earned by the business. A rapid increase in reserves is likely to reflect a healthy position with regard to profits.
- The overall value of the business. It may be a good sign if the business's value – measured for example by its net assets – has increased. If the business has achieved this without borrowing heavily, it may be regarded as a positive development.

Working capital

What is working capital?

Working capital measures the amount of money available to a business to pay its day-to-day expenses, such as bills for fuel and raw materials, wages and business rates. Much attention is given to the **capital** firms choose to invest in non-current assets, but of equal importance to the success of a business is the capital set aside to finance regular transactions.

Working capital is what remains of a business's short-term assets once it has settled all its immediate debts. It is possible to calculate the working capital of a business from its balance sheet by using the following formula:

Working capital = current assets – current liabilities

Key terms

Working capital is current assets minus current liabilities.

Capital is the money invested into a business and is used to purchase a range of assets including machinery and inventories.

Inventories are the raw materials and other items necessary for production to take place. They also include finished products that have not yet been sold.

Mortgages are long-term loans, repaid over periods of up to 50 years, used to purchase property.

Debentures are loans with fixed interest rates which are long term and may not even have a repayment date.

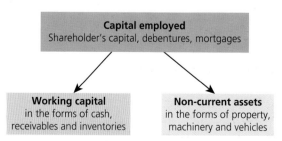

Figure 2.5 A business's capital

On a balance sheet working capital may be labelled as net current assets, as would be the case for Ted Baker plc in 2013 and 2014. However, if current liabilities are greater than current assets, then it will be labelled as net current liabilities and the figure will be in brackets.

The right amount of working capital

It is simple to argue that a business should hold large amounts of working capital to ensure it can always pay its debts in the short term and has spare assets in a liquid form (cash and trade and other receivables, for example). However, holding excessive amounts of working capital is not wise. The nature of liquid assets, such as cash and trade and other receivables, means that they earn little or no return for the business. Therefore, a well-managed business will hold sufficient liquid assets to meet its need for working capital, but will avoid having too many assets in such an unprofitable form.

A number of factors can influence the amount of working capital a firm needs to hold.

- **The volume of sales**. A firm with a high level of sales will need to purchase more raw materials, pay a greater amount of wages and so on. Therefore, its need for working capital will be correspondingly higher.
- **The amount of trade credit offered by the business**. If a firm offers customers a lengthy period of time before they are required to pay, this increases the business's requirement for working capital. In effect, companies allowing trade credit offer their customers an interest-free loan.
- **Whether or not the firm is growing**. In a period of growth, working capital requirements are likely to rise as the business purchases more fuel and raw materials. If a business expands without arranging the necessary working capital, it is described as overtrading.
- **The length of the operating cycle**. The operating cycle is the amount of time that elapses between the firm first paying for raw materials and receiving payment from customers. Some manufacturing industries (e.g. shipbuilding) have long operating cycles and a correspondingly greater need for working capital.
- **The rate of inflation**. When prices rise rapidly, firms require greater amounts of working capital to fund the increased costs of wages, components and raw materials.

As a rough guide, a firm holding current assets of twice the value of current liabilities would normally have sufficient working capital, although in recent years it has become common for businesses to operate with fewer current assets. It is also important for a business to have a significant proportion of its working capital in the form of cash. Cash, the most liquid of assets, is essential to pay the most immediate of bills.

Depreciation

It is important for stakeholders analysing a business's balance sheet (as well as its income statement) to understand the meaning and implications of **depreciation**.

What is depreciation?

Depreciation is the reduction of the value of an asset over a period of time. Thus, a company may purchase production line equipment at a cost of £80,000 in January 2015 and expect that this equipment will last

| **Working capital** Essential to pay for day-to-day expenses and keep the business operating | = | **Current assets** • Cash in the bank • Trade and other receivables due to settle their accounts soon • Inventories – raw materials and components, unsold finished products | less | **Current liabilities** (Debts payable in the short term) • Debts repayable to the bank, e.g. overdraft • Trade and other payables who expect to be paid in the near future • Tax due to HM Revenue and Customs NB An overdraft only represents a current liability if the bank calls for it to be repaid. |

Figure 2.6 Working capital

for four years and have no resale value. Therefore, the value of the asset falls by £20,000 each year, reflecting its decline in value. The amount of the decline in value (i.e. depreciation) is shown as an expense on the company's income statement. The process over the four years of the asset's life is shown in Table 2.2.

Year	Value of asset recorded on balance sheet at end of financial year (31 December)	Amount depreciated annually
2015	£60,000	£20,000
2016	£40,000	£20,000
2017	£20,000	£20,000
2018	£0	£20,000

Table 2.2 An example of depreciating assets

Figure 2.7 Depreciation – a link between the balance sheet and the income statement

Why do firms depreciate assets?

Firms have to depreciate their non-current assets for a number of reasons. One of these is to spread the cost of an asset over its useful life. In the case of the company investing £80,000 in production line equipment, it would have been incorrect to show the value of the equipment as £80,000 throughout its life. Its resale value would decline for a number of reasons:

● the equipment would lose value as a result of wear and tear
● the availability of more modern equipment would mean that the desirability of this 'older' style equipment would lessen
● poor or inadequate maintenance of the equipment may mean expensive repairs are necessary, further reducing the equipment's value.

Thus, reducing the value of an asset in line with these factors ensures that the value of the business recorded on the balance sheet is a relatively accurate indication of the true worth of the business.

Depreciation also allows firms to calculate the true cost of production during any financial year. The company in Table 2.2 would have overstated its costs in 2015 if it had allocated the entire cost of its new production line equipment to that particular financial year. By depreciating the equipment by £20,000 each year for four years, one-quarter of the cost of the equipment is recorded each year as an expense on the company's income statement. This helps to gain an accurate view of the profitability (or otherwise) of the business over the lifetime of the production line equipment.

Key term

Depreciation is the reduction of the value of an asset over a period of time.

How to analyse income statements

The role of profit

At its simplest, **profit** is what remains from revenue once costs have been deducted. Profit is one of the most commonly used words in business and is important for a number of reasons. It acts as a signal to attract new businesses into a market and to encourage an existing business to grow. The pursuit of profit is an important business objective.

However, some businesses (e.g. charities and mutual organisations) do not aim to make profits and profits that impose high social costs on others may not be highly valued. Businesses that generate high profits through polluting the environment or hiring sweatshop labour in less-developed countries may attract criticism and lose sales in the long run.

Due to increased public awareness of ethical and environmental issues, many businesses are taking a long-term view of profit. They may be prepared to incur higher costs in the short term (through using more expensive materials from sustainable sources, for example) to maintain a positive corporate image and higher profits in the long term.

Profits and the income statement

However, in the construction of the **income statement** there are two main types of profit identified:

- **Gross profit**. This form of profit is calculated by deducting direct costs (such as materials and shop-floor labour) from a business's sales revenue. This gives a broad indication of the financial performance of the business without taking into account other costs such as overheads.
- **Net profit**. This is a further refinement of the concept of profit and is revenue less direct costs and indirect costs (or overheads) such as rent and rates, as well as interest payments and depreciation. This gives a better indication of the performance of a business over a period of time as it takes into account all costs incurred by a firm over a trading period.

Net profit can take a number of forms.

- Trading or operating profit. This type of profit takes into account all earnings from regular trading activities and all the costs associated with those activities. However, this form of profit excludes any income received from, or costs incurred by, activities that are unlikely to be repeated in future financial years.
- Net profit before tax. This is a business's trading or operating profit plus any profits from one-off activities.
- Net profit after tax. This is the amount left to the business once corporation tax (or income tax in the case of a sole trader or partnership) has been deducted. This is an important form of profit. There are no more charges on this profit and the managers of the business can decide what to do with it.

The quality of profit

It may seem strange, but some profits are better than others. Firms regard profit that is likely to continue into the future as high-quality profit. Thus, if a business introduces a new product onto the market and it immediately begins to generate a surplus and looks to have a promising future, then this will be high-quality profit. In contrast profits may be poor quality. Total, the French oil company, announced in 2015 that it intends to sell non-current assets valued at $5 billion. If sold at a profit, this may have added to the company's overall net profit figure for the year. However, this form of profit will not continue into the future and is therefore low-quality profit.

The amount of trading or operating profit earned by a firm is more likely to represent high-quality profit as it excludes any one-off items. This level of profit might reasonably be expected to continue into the future, depending upon market conditions. Shareholders are interested in profit quality as it gives some indication of the company's potential to pay dividends in the future.

Business in focus: Tesco's profit scandal

Tesco plc, the world's third biggest retailer, is involved in a scandal resulting from its misreporting of profits. An investigation has revealed that the company overstated its profits by £263 million in 2014. An investigation by the accountancy firm Deloitte found that Tesco had been including the revenues received from sales promotions too early in its accounts and pushing back the date at which costs were recorded. The net effect was to increase the company's profits – on paper.

The company made a statement to the London Stock Exchange in which said it had 'identified an overstatement of its expected profit for the half year, principally due to the accelerated recognition of commercial income and delayed accrual of costs'. One outcome of the scandal has been a sharp fall in the company's share price. Tesco's shares fell by almost 9 per cent in value to 209p, their lowest figure since 2003.

Tesco has suspended eight of its senior managers while an enquiry is held into the company's accountancy practices. Meanwhile the scandal has posed another threat to the company at a time when it is losing share in the highly competitive UK grocery market to price discounters such as Aldi.

Questions

1. Explain why is it important for Tesco to report its profits accurately.
2. Will all of Tesco's shareholders suffer as a consequence of this misreporting of its profits?

The structure of the income statement

Figure 2.8 provides an initial guide to the structure of the income statement as presented by most companies.

The income statement comprises calculations involving four stages:

1. First, 'gross profit' is calculated. This is the difference between the revenue figure (this can be called sales revenue or turnover) and the cost of the goods that have been sold. The latter is normally expressed simply as 'cost of sales'. This element of the income statement is sometimes called the trading account.
2. Second, 'operating profit' is calculated by deducting the main types of overheads such as distribution costs and administration costs.
3. Next, profit before taxation is calculated, which is arrived at by including interest received by the business and interest paid by it. These are normally shown together as a net figure labelled 'financing costs'.

4. The final stage of the income statement is to calculate profit after taxation. This is arrived at by deducting the amount of tax payable for the year, and shows the net amount that has been earned for the shareholders. At this stage the company may indicate which profits are from continuing operations (those parts of the business that will be trading in the future) and which are from discontinuing operations.

Group income statements

During the last 25 years many companies have been taken over by other companies to form groups. Each company within such a group retains its separate legal identity, but the group is also legally obliged to produce a group income statement (and balance sheet). A group income statement simply records the aggregated position of the group as a whole.

Examples of organisations producing consolidated accounts include The Kingfisher Group (which owns companies such as B&Q and Screwfix) and the Tui Group (which owns a range of companies including Thomson Airways and Thomson Cruises). It is quite likely that the accounts of any large organisations you examine will be group accounts, including Ted Baker plc (see Table 2.3).

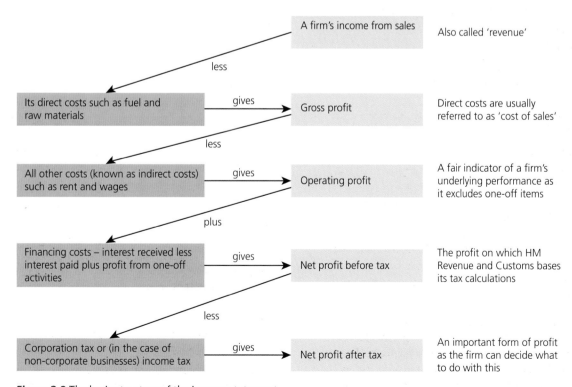

Figure 2.8 The basic structure of the income statement

Income statements and the law

The legal requirements relating to income statements are set out in the Companies Act 2006. This legislation demands the production of financial statements, including an income statement. It also specifies the information to be included in these accounts. Companies do not seek to reveal more information about themselves than they need to.

Public limited companies provide information on earnings per share on their income statements. Earnings per share are simply the company's profits after tax divided by the number of shares the company has. Diluted earnings per share gives a slightly lower figure as it takes into account all possible shares that could be issued by the company at that time, that is those issued plus those due to be issued as part of a share option scheme, for example.

The income statement does not have to detail every expense incurred by the firm, but summarises the main items under standard headings. The Act sets out acceptable formats for presentation of the relevant data. A summarised form of one of these is shown for Ted Baker plc in Table 2.3.

The notes to the income statements must disclose details of:

- auditor's fees paid for verifying the accuracy of the accounts
- depreciation amounts
- the total of directors' emoluments (earnings)
- the average number of employees, together with details of the cost of wages and salaries, national insurance and pensions payments.

Companies must disclose the following:

- **Exceptional items** are large (usually one-off) financial transactions arising from ordinary trading activities. However, they may be so large as to risk distorting the company's income statement. Ted Baker plc's income statement in Table 2.3 contains an example of an exceptional cost. These one-off costs relate to the company's stores in Liverpool, Paris and New York and set-up costs for the company's expansion into China.
- **Extraordinary items** are large transactions outside the normal trading activities of a business. As a result they are not expected to recur. A typical example is the closure of a factory or division of a business. These items have only been included in income statements over recent years.

	52 weeks ended 25th January 2014 £000s	52 weeks ended 26th January 2013 £000s
Revenue	321 921	254 466
Cost of sales	(123 451)	(95 740)
Gross profit	**198 470**	**158 726**
Administrative & other expenses	(166 724)	(134 107)
Exceptional costs	(1 046)	(2 614)
Licence income	8 888	7 509
Operating profit	**39 588**	**29 514**
Profit from joint ventures	331	198
Finance income	316	34
Finance expenses	(1 312)	(824)
Profit before tax	**38 923**	**28 922**
Taxation	(10 071)	(7 325)
Profit for the year	**28 852**	**21 597**
Earnings per share (pence)		
Basic	67.2	51.5
Diluted	66.3	49.9

Table 2.3 Summarised group income statement for Ted Baker plc

Source: Adapted from Ted Baker plc's Annual Report & Accounts, 2013–14

There is no single format for a limited company's income statement. The Companies Act of 2006 sets out the minimum amount of information that must be included, though some modification can be made to ensure a 'true and fair view' of the business's performance.

Interpreting income statements

A number of groups are likely to have an interest in a business's income statement. These stakeholders are illustrated in Figure 2.9.

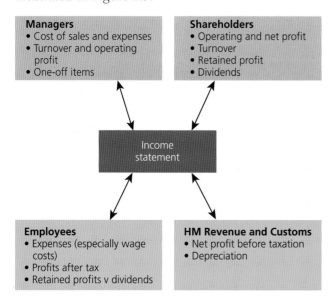

Managers
- Cost of sales and expenses
- Turnover and operating profit
- One-off items

Shareholders
- Operating and net profit
- Turnover
- Retained profit
- Dividends

Income statement

Employees
- Expenses (especially wage costs)
- Profits after tax
- Retained profits v dividends

HM Revenue and Customs
- Net profit before taxation
- Depreciation

Figure 2.9 Some groups with an interest in income statements

- **Shareholders** are perhaps the most obvious group with an interest in the income statement. Shareholders will be interested in a business's sales revenue and operating or net profit. This will provide some guidance as to the performance of the enterprise, especially when compared with previous years. Shareholders will also be likely to examine how profits have been utilised. Some may seek the maximum dividend possible (an example of short-termism), while others may be interested in a longer term return and welcome substantial reinvestment in the expectation of future profits.
- **Managers** use the income statement as an important source of information regarding the performance of the business. Managers are, of course, able to see the income statement in much more detail than that provided in the annual report and accounts. (Published accounts contain the minimum amount of information required under law to avoid giving competitors any advantage.)

Managers will monitor sales performance through turnover figures and judge costs against sales revenue. If expenses and cost of sales rise by a greater amount than revenue, action may be necessary. Managers will also consider carefully the effects of one-off items on the account.

- **Employees** may be interested in profits after tax if their pay is related to company performance through a profit-related pay scheme. They may also be interested in the level of dividends if they are shareholders. The level of profits after taxation may also be an indication of the company's ability to fund a pay increase or, alternatively, of the security of their employment.
- **HM Revenue and Customs** is the organisation responsible for collecting corporation tax from companies on the government's behalf. HMRC will therefore scrutinise company accounts and use net profit before tax as the basis for their calculation of tax liability (the amount of tax to be paid). They may also check that the income statement meets all necessary standards (for example the basis upon which non-current assets have been depreciated).

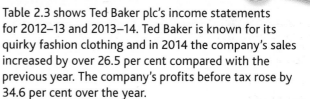

Business in focus: Ted Baker plc (2)

Table 2.3 shows Ted Baker plc's income statements for 2012–13 and 2013–14. Ted Baker is known for its quirky fashion clothing and in 2014 the company's sales increased by over 26.5 per cent compared with the previous year. The company's profits before tax rose by 34.6 per cent over the year.

The company's sales were boosted by rapidly increasing sales on the internet. Its e-commerce business increased by 55.7 per cent to £23.2 million (in 2013 it was £14.9 million). In November 2013, it launched an improved website for its customers in the UK. This was followed, in August 2014, by the launch of a further website targeted at customers in the USA. The US site extends the facilities available on its UK website. It offers men and women separate routes through the website. It has been designed to be relevant to the needs of individual customers and to help browsing of particular products.

Questions

1. Explain the likely reactions of two of Ted Baker plc's stakeholders to the information in its income statement for 2013–14.

2. Is effective use of e-commerce and the internet likely to be the most important factor determining the success of retailers in the future?

Window dressing balance sheets and income statements

Most businesses, and especially public limited companies, are under pressure to present their financial performance in the most favourable terms possible. There are a number of methods by which a company can improve the look of its balance sheet – these processes are called **window dressing**.

- Some companies borrow money for a short period of time to improve their cash position just before the date on which the balance sheet is drawn up. This action may enhance the company's apparent ability to pay its short-term debts.
- An alternative method of improving a company's cash or liquidity position is through the use of sale and leaseback. This entails the sale of major non-current assets and then leasing them back. Many retailers have negotiated sale and leaseback deals on their high-street properties.
- Businesses may maintain the value of intangible assets on the balance sheet at what might be excessive levels to increase the overall value of the organisation. This tactic is only possible when the assets in question (for example goodwill or brands) have been purchased.
- Capitalising expenditure, which means including as non-current assets items that might otherwise have simply been regarded as an expense and not included on the balance sheet. Thus, a firm might spend heavily on computer software and include this as a fixed asset on the basis that it will have a useful life of several years. This action will increase the value of the business.
- On income statements businesses may bring forward sales to an earlier period and thereby boost revenue for a particular financial year. This does result, however, in a lower figure in the next financial year. This was part of the issue involved in the financial scandal faced by Tesco and covered on page 28.

There is a fine line between presenting accounts as favourably as possible and misrepresenting the performance of the firm, which is illegal. The authorities have made several adjustments to accountancy procedures in order to restrict the extent of window dressing.

covered on page 28.

Key term

Window dressing is the preparation of financial statements to present the company's performance in the best possible light.

Using financial ratios to assess the internal position of a business

We have considered how stakeholders might analyse a business's financial statements to judge its performance. Ratio analysis allows stakeholders to take this analysis a step further.

Key term

Ratio analysis is a technique for analysing a business's financial performance by comparing one piece of accounting information with another.

What is a ratio?

The key feature of **ratio analysis** is that it compares two pieces of financial information. By comparing two pieces of data in this way it is possible to make more informed judgements about a business's performance.

A comparison of the financial performance of two companies in 2014 can illustrate the advantages of using two pieces of data to make more in-depth and informed judgements. Unilever is an Anglo-Dutch multinational consumer goods company which owns over 400 brands, including Dove, Knorr and Sunsilk. In 2014 it announced an operating profit of £1,803 million for the year. In comparison, easyJet, one of the UK's best-known budget airlines, turned in an operating profit of £318 million in 2014. A simple judgement would therefore suggest that Unilever plc had performed more successfully. However, if we took into account the value of sales achieved by the two companies (their revenue), a more meaningful judgement could be made.

Table 2.4 shows that when we compare profit for the year with revenue, easyJet's performance could be judged superior to that of Unilever. easyJet earned over 22.51 pence of profit from each £1 of sales, while Unilever only made 14.82 pence of profit on each £1 of sales. Using this ratio (which is called the operating profit margin and was studied in Year 1) it is possible to make a more accurate judgement than simply comparing levels of profit.

Company	Operating profit (£m)	Revenue (£m)	Operating profit as a % of revenue
Unilever plc	1,803	12,169	14.82
easyJet plc	318	1,413	22.51

Table 2.4 Comparing the financial performance of two companies by using a simple ratio

Source: Unilever and easyJet's annual reports

Ratio analysis allows managers, directors, shareholders and other interested parties to place key figures such as profits and turnover in context. The use of ratio analysis does not guarantee that a manager or shareholder will make a correct decision. The results of ratio analysis do, however, give decision makers more information and make a good quality decision more likely.

Types of ratio

There are a number of ways of classifying ratios. One approach is to identify four main categories of ratio.

1. **Profitability ratios** assess the amount of profit made by the business in relation to the capital available to it or to other figures such as its revenue.
2. **Liquidity ratios**, also known as solvency ratios, measure the ability of the business to settle its debts in the short term.
3. **Gearing** examines the relationship between internal and external sources of finance. It is therefore concerned with the long-term financial position of the company.
4. **Efficiency ratios** measure the effectiveness with which an enterprise uses the resources available to it. These are also termed internal control ratios.

Type of ratio	Profitability ratios	Liquidity ratios	Gearing	Efficiency ratios
Ratios used:	Return on capital employed Profit margins (studied in Year 1)	Current ratio	Gearing – long-term loans: capital employed	Payables days Receivables days Inventory turnover ratio
Purpose of ratios:	To provide a fundamental measure of the success of the business	To assess the ability of the business to pay its immediate debts	To assess the extent to which the business is based on borrowed money	To provide evidence on how well the managers have controlled the business
Interested stakeholders:	Shareholders Creditors Managers Competitors Employees	Creditors Suppliers Managers	Shareholders Managers Creditors	Shareholders Managers Employees Competitors

Table 2.5 Types of ratio, when they are used, to what purpose and by whom

Sources of information for ratio analysis

The most obvious sources are the published accounts of the business or businesses concerned. In particular, ratio analysis requires access to a business's balance sheet and income statement. However, although this might be essential information, it is not all that is required to conduct an in-depth ratio analysis of a business.

Other possible sources of information include the following:

- **The performance of the business over recent years**. Having an understanding of the trends of ratios over time can assist in making judgements. Thus, a profitability ratio might appear fairly low, but if it represents a continuation of a steadily rising trend, then the figure may be more acceptable to stakeholders.
- **Norms or benchmarks for the industry**. The results of ratio calculations should be judged against what is normal for the industry. Thus, an investor might calculate that a company's receivables day ratio is 35 days (the number of days, on average, that customers take to settle their bills). This might be acceptable for a manufacturing business, but not for a fast-food business.
- **The economic environment**. A decline in profit ratios might appear to reflect an unsuccessful business. However, this might be more acceptable in the context of a severe economic recession in which sales and prices have declined.

Expressing ratios

Ratios are normally expressed in one of three forms:

1. As a proper ratio – for example, the current ratio is 1.6:1.
2. As a percentage – return on capital employed (ROCE) expresses operating profit as a percentage of capital employed by the business.
3. As a multiple – inventories are turned over (or sold) five times a year.

Profitability ratios

A business's profits are the surplus of revenue over total costs for a trading period. **Profitability** has a subtly different meaning: it compares a business's level of profits to some other factor such as the amount of capital used within the business or its sales revenue. These ratios compare the profits earned by a business with other key variables, such as the level of sales achieved or the capital available to the managers of the business.

In Chapter 17 of the Year 1 (or AS) book, we introduced the idea of **profit margins** and covered three types of profit margin:

- gross profit margin
- operating profit margin
- profit for the year margin.

This section builds on your understanding of these profit margins or profit ratios.

Key terms

Profitability is a measure of financial performance that compares a business's profits to some other factors such as capital employed or revenue.

A **profit margin** is a ratio that expresses a business's profit as a percentage of its revenue over a trading period.

Study tip

If you are unsure about these profit margins, please review Chapter 17 in *AQA A-level Business 1*.

Return on capital employed (ROCE)

This is an important ratio comparing the operating profit earned with the amount of capital employed by the business. The capital employed by the business is measured by its total equity plus its non-current liabilities.

The importance of this ratio is reflected in the fact that it is also termed 'the primary efficiency ratio'. The result of this ratio, which is expressed as a percentage, allows an assessment to be made of the overall financial performance of the business. A fundamental comparison can be made between the prevailing rate of interest and the ROCE generated by a business.

$$\text{Return on capital employed (ROCE)} = \frac{\text{operating profit} \times 100}{\text{total equity} + \text{non-current liabilities (capital employed)}}$$

Using this ratio

A typical ROCE may be expected to be in the range of 20–30 per cent. It is particularly important to compare the results from calculating this ratio with the business's ROCE in previous years and also those achieved by its competitors.

A business may improve its ROCE by increasing its operating profit without raising further capital or by reducing the amount of capital employed, perhaps by repaying some of its long-term borrowing, for example its mortgage.

Company	Type of business	Date of accounts	Operating profit (loss)	Total equity + non-current assets	ROCE
Betfair Group plc	Online gambling	30/04/2014	£61.6m	£171.4m	35.94%
Sage Group plc	Computer software	30/09/2014	£298.4m	£1,235.1m	24.16%
GlaxoSmithKline plc	Pharmaceuticals	31/12/2014	£4,936m	£27,356m	18.04%
Tullow Oil	Oil and gas exploration	31/12/2014	($1,965m)	$10,083m	−19.49%

Notes to Table 2.6: The returns here vary enormously. The most eyecatching figure is that of Tullow Oil. The company's financial position has been severely affected by unsuccessful exploration projects and a substantial fall in the price of oil. The high profit level of the Betfair Group may be partly due to its increased marketing aiming its products at a wider target audience.

Table 2.6 ROCE data for a selection of companies

Source: Companies' annual reports

Maths moment

What level of operating profit would GlaxoSmithKline plc have needed to make during 2014 to achieve a ROCE figure to match that of the Sage Group plc?

Liquidity ratios

Liquidity ratios allow managers and other interested parties to monitor a business's cash position. Even profitable businesses can experience problems with liquidity and may be unable to pay their bills as they fall due. Liquidity ratios measure the liquid assets held by a firm (cash and other assets such as receivables that are easily convertible into cash). The value of these assets is then compared with the short-term debts or liabilities the business will incur. In this way, stakeholders may evaluate whether the business's performance may be harmed as a result of liquidity problems. Managers can use a number of ratios to measure liquidity; we shall just consider one, the current ratio.

Current ratio

This measures the ability of a business to meet its liabilities or debts over the next year or so.

The formula to calculate this ratio is:

$$\text{Current ratio} = \frac{\text{current assets}}{\text{current liabilities}}$$

The current ratio is expressed in the form of a ratio, for example 2:1. This example would mean that the firm in question possessed £2 of current assets (cash,

receivables and inventories) for each £1 of current liabilities (payables, taxation and proposed dividends, for example). In these circumstances, it is probable that the business would be able to meet its current liabilities without needing to sell non-current assets or raise long-term finance.

Using this ratio

For years, holding current assets twice the value of current liabilities was recommended. This is no longer accepted, partly due to the use of computers in inventory control and the widespread use of just-in-time (JIT) systems of production. A more typical figure might now be 1.6:1.

In spite of this, the 'normal' figure for this ratio varies according to the type of business and the state of the market. Fast-food outlets and banks typically operate with lower ratios, whereas some manufacturing firms may have higher ratios.

Firms with high current ratio values (say, 3:1) are not necessarily managing their finances effectively. It may be that they are holding too much cash and not investing in non-current assets to generate income. Alternatively, they may have large holdings of inventories, some of which might be obsolete.

Firms can improve the current ratio by raising more cash through the sale of non-current assets or the negotiation of long-term loans. (NB: raising more cash through short-term borrowing will increase current liabilities, having little effect on the current ratio.)

Company	Type of business	Date of balance sheet	Current asset	Current liabilities	Current ratio
J Sainsbury plc	Grocery retailing	15/03/2014	£4,362m	£6,765m	0.64:1
Rolls Royce	Manufacturing engines	31/12/2014	£11,188m	£7,685m	1.46:1
Rio Tinto plc	Mining	04/05/2014	£328.8m	£514.9m	0.64:1

Notes to Table 2.7: J Sainsbury, a supermarket which can rely on many customers paying cash or using debit cards, is able to operate successfully with lower levels of liquidity than Rolls-Royce, a manufacturer. The results for Rio Tinto illustrate two trends. Firstly, many businesses, even those engaged in mining, operate with much lower levels of liquidity than might have been the case 20 years ago. However, since the financial crisis of 2008–9 some businesses have operated with slightly higher liquidity ratios: Rio Tinto plc's current ratio was 1.46:1 in 2009.

Table 2.7 Current ratios for a selection of companies

Source: Companies' annual reports

Business in focus: easyJet's performance

easyJet reported an impressive financial performance in September 2014. The company has benefited, along with other airlines, from increased numbers of people travelling overseas from the UK. It has reduced prices as the cost of oil has fallen in global markets and, with increased passenger numbers, its planes are fuller. In late 2014, its planes operated with capacity utilisation averaging 89.7 per cent. Its business model is heavily based on internet bookings with customers paying at the time they book.

The airline has impressed analysts with its cost savings and the use of larger planes to reduce the cost per passenger on its flights.

At the end of the 2013–2014 financial year easyJet held cash totalling £985 million. This was despite the company paying a special dividend of £175 million to shareholders during the year, as well as making payments for new aircraft and repaying some of its borrowing.

Item	2014	2013	2012	2011
Revenue (£m)	4,527	4,258	3,854	3,452
Operating profit (£m)	581	497	331	269
Current assets (£m)	1,261	1,448	1,327	1,738
Current liabilities (£m)	1,420	1,379	1,264	1,177

Table 2.8 Summary of easyJet's financial performance, 2011–14

Source: easyJet's annual reports

Questions

1. Do you think that easyJet's liquidity position has strengthened or weakened between 2011 and 2014? Explain your reasoning.
2. Is liquidity the most important measure of a business's financial performance?

Gearing

Gearing measures the long-term liquidity of a business. Under some classifications gearing is included as a liquidity ratio. There are a number of methods of measuring gearing; we shall consider the simplest form of the ratio. The gearing ratio analyses how firms have raised their long-term capital. The result of this calculation is expressed as a percentage.

There are two main forms of long-term finance available to businesses:

1. **Non-current liabilities**. This includes preference shares and debentures (both have fixed interest payments) as well as long-term loans. This category of finance comprises long-term borrowing and may be called loan capital.
2. **Total equity**. This arises from selling shares and increases in the value of the business.

The capital employed by a business is simply the total of these two. So the gearing ratio measures the percentage of a firm's capital that is borrowed.

$$\text{Gearing} = \frac{\text{non-current liabilities} \times 100}{\text{total equity} + \text{non-current liabilities}}$$

This measure of a business's performance is important because, by raising too high a proportion of capital through fixed interest capital, firms become vulnerable to increases in interest rates. Shareholders are also unlikely to be attracted to a business with a high gearing ratio as their returns might be lower because of the high level of interest payments to which the enterprise is already committed.

- A highly geared business has more than 50 per cent of its capital in the form of loans.
- A low-geared business has less long-term borrowing and a gearing figure below 50 per cent.

Much attention tends to be given to businesses that have high gearing and are vulnerable to increases in interest rates. However, this may be considered acceptable in a business that is growing quickly and generating high profits. Furthermore, a low-geared business may be considered too cautious and not expanding as quickly as possible.

Using this ratio

The key yardstick is whether a business's long-term borrowing is more than 50 per cent of capital employed.

Companies with secure cash flows may raise more loan capital because they are confident of being able to meet interest payments. Equally, a business with well-known brands may be able to borrow heavily against these brands to increase long-term borrowing.

Firms can improve their gearing by repaying long-term loans, issuing more ordinary shares or redeeming debentures.

Company	Type of business	Date of balance sheet	Non-current liabilities	Total equity + non-current liabilities	Gearing
Sky plc	TV broadcaster	30/06/2014	£2,858m	£3,930m	72.72%
Babcock International plc	Support services	31/03/2014	£1,051m	£2,077m	50.60%
Vodafone plc	Telecommunications	31/03/2014	£25,020m	£96,801m	25.85%

Notes to Table 2.9: These three companies are operating with a range of gearing ratios. Sky is highly geared following two successful takeover bids, while Vodafone's gearing is significantly below 50 per cent offering significant opportunities for further long-term borrowing. Babcock International, however, has little scope for further long-term borrowing as it is just over the 50 per cent guideline.

Table 2.9 Gearing ratios of some leading companies

Source: Companies' annual reports

Efficiency ratios

This group of ratios measures the effectiveness with which management controls the internal operation of the business. They consider a number of aspects of the management of an enterprise, including the following:

- How well inventories are managed.
- The efficiency of creditor control (how long before customers settle their accounts).
- The time taken by a business to settle its own debts.

There are a large number of ratios that fall under this heading, but we shall concentrate on just three: inventory turnover ratio, receivables days and payables days.

Inventory turnover ratio

This ratio measures a company's success in converting inventories into sales. The ratio compares the value of inventories with sales achieved, valued at cost. This permits an effective comparison with inventories, which are always valued at cost. If the company makes a profit on each sale, then the faster it sells its inventories, the greater the profits it earns. This ratio is only of relevance to manufacturing businesses, as firms providing services do not hold significant quantities of inventories.

$$\text{Inventory turnover ratio} = \frac{\text{cost of goods sold}}{\text{average inventories held}}$$

In this form the results of calculating this ratio are expressed as a number of times a year – in this case the number of times a business's entire inventory is sold in a year. On 22 February 2014 Tesco held inventories valued at £3,576 million. During the company's financial year, which ended on that day, the company's cost of sales (that is, the cost of buying its inventories) was £59,547 million. The company's inventories turnover ratio was therefore 16.65 times.

The inventory turnover formula can be reorganised to express the number of days taken on average to sell the business's inventories.

$$\text{Inventory turnover ratio} = \frac{\text{inventories} \times 365}{\text{cost of sales}}$$

Our Tesco calculation would then become £3,576 million × 365 ÷ £59 547 million, giving an answer of 21.92 days. Thus, if Tesco sells its entire inventories every 22 days, it will sell its inventories approximately 16.6 times during a year.

Using this ratio

The standard figure for this ratio varies hugely according to the type of business. A market trader selling fruit and vegetables might expect to sell their entire inventories every two or three days – about a hundred times a year. At the other extreme, an antiques shop might only sell its stock every six months – or twice a year.

A low figure for inventory turnover could be due to obsolete inventories. A high figure can indicate an efficient business, although selling out of inventories results in customer dissatisfaction.

Improving the inventory or stock turnover ratio requires a business to hold lower levels of inventories or to achieve higher sales without increasing levels of inventories.

Receivables days

This ratio (also referred to as receivables or debtors' collection period) calculates the time typically taken by a business to collect the money that it is owed. This is an important ratio, as granting customers lengthy periods of credit may result in a business experiencing liquidity problems. If a company has substantial cash sales, these should be excluded from the calculation.

$$\text{Receivables days} = \frac{\text{receivables} \times 365}{\text{revenue}}$$

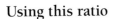
Using this ratio

There is no standard figure for this ratio. In general, a lower figure is preferred as the business in question receives the inflow of cash more quickly. However, it can be an important part of a business's marketing strategy to offer customers a period of trade credit of perhaps 30 or 60 days.

A rise in this ratio may be due to a number of causes. A period of expansion may mean that a business has to offer improved credit terms to attract new customers, or a 'buy now pay later' offer may have been introduced.

This ratio may be improved by reducing the credit period on offer to customers or by insisting on cash payment. A more focused approach is to conduct an aged debtors' analysis. This technique ranks a business's debtors (the persons or businesses owing money to the organisation) according to the period of credit taken. This allows managers to concentrate on persuading the slowest payers to settle their accounts.

Payables days

This ratio (also referred to as payables or creditors' collection period) calculates the time typically taken by a business to pay the money it owes to its suppliers and other creditors. This is an important ratio, as delaying payment for as long as possible can help a business to avoid liquidity problems.

$$\text{Payables days} = \frac{\text{payables} \times 365}{\text{cost of sales}}$$

Using this ratio

Businesses can improve their liquidity position by delaying payment, but this may result in poor relationships with suppliers who may themselves suffer liquidity problems as a result of the delay in payment.

Businesses may be charged interest on delayed payments, which can add to costs and weaken a business's liquidity position.

Using receivable and payable days together

By comparing payable days and receivable days a business can assess its liquidity position. If payable days is a lower figure, then it is more likely that the business will experience liquidity problems as, on average, it is paying suppliers and other creditors more quickly than it is receiving payment from its customers.

Item	WM Morrison plc 02/02/2014	Glencore plc 31/12/2013
Receivables	£316m	£24,536m
Revenue	£17,680m	£232,694m
Receivables days	6.52 days	38.49 days
Payables	£2,272m	£26,041m
Cost of sales	£16,606m	£227,145m
Payables days	49.94 days	41.85 days

Notes to Table 2.10: Morrison plc's balance between payable and receivable days is healthy from the company's point of view as its customers pay within 6.5 days (most will pay cash), while the supermarket takes nearly 50 days to pay its own debts. Glencore plc, a multinational mining company, has similar payable and receivable days. However, the balance is slightly in the company's favour as may be expected of a large company with considerable negotiating power.

Table 2.10 Receivable days and payable days for two leading companies

Source: Companies' annual reports

The value and limitations of ratio analysis in assessing performance

Ratio analysis provides stakeholders with an insight into the performance of a business. However, to offer the maximum amount of information, the details gained from ratio analysis need to be compared with other data, such as that outlined below:

- **The results for the same business over previous years**. This allows stakeholders to appreciate the trend of the data. Thus, a low but steadily increasing figure for ROCE might be reassuring to investors.
- **The results of ratio analysis for other firms in the same industry**. We have seen that results expected from various ratios vary according to the type of business under investigation. Thus, the inventory turnover ratio will be much higher for a retailer selling perishable products than for a manufacturer. By comparing like-with-like a more informed judgement on the business's performance may be made.
- **The results of ratios from firms in other industries**. Stakeholders can compare the ratios

of a particular business with those from a wide range of businesses. This might allow, for example, a comparison between two businesses experiencing rapid growth. The Centre for Inter-Firm Comparisons offers anonymous data on the financial ratios of many UK firms.

A significant weakness of ratio analysis is that it only considers the financial aspects of a business's performance. While this is undeniably important, other elements of a business should be taken into account when evaluating performance.

- **The market in which the business is trading**. A business that is operating in a highly competitive market might experience relatively low profits, reducing the results of ratios such as the return on capital employed (ROCE).
- **The position of the firm within the market**. A market leader might be expected to provide better returns than a small firm struggling to establish itself. However, the small struggling firm may be investing heavily in developing new products and establishing a brand identity. The struggling firm may generate large profits in the future.
- **The quality of the workforce and management team**. These are important factors in assessing a business, but not ones that will be revealed directly through ratio analysis. Indeed, a business that invests heavily in its human resources may appear to be performing relatively poorly through the use of ratio analysis.
- **The economic environment**. In general, businesses might be expected to perform better during periods of prosperity and to produce better results from ratio analysis. As the UK economy has enjoyed strong rates of economic growth (over 2.5 per cent annually) since the start of 2014, it is reasonable to expect the financial performance of many (but not all) businesses to improve.

Business in focus: Imperial Tobacco Group plc

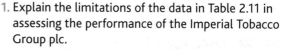

The Imperial Tobacco Group plc is one of the world's largest tobacco groups. It employs more than 35,000 people and sells a range of tobacco products, such as cigars and cigarettes, in 160 countries.

The company's strategy is based on sustainable sales and careful control of costs and cash. The company plans to close factories in the UK and France and move production to new locations in Eastern Europe in 2015.

Ratio	2014	2013
Gearing	69.90%	67.40%
Return on capital employed (ROCE)	11.34%	11.29%
Current ratio	0.94:1	0.76:1

Table 2.11 Key ratios for Imperial Tobacco Group plc, 2013 and 2014

Source: Imperial Tobacco Annual Report, 2014

Questions

1. Explain the limitations of the data in Table 2.11 in assessing the performance of the Imperial Tobacco Group plc.
2. Do the limitations of ratio analysis mean that this data is of little value to the company's stakeholders?

ASSESSMENT ACTIVITIES

(a) Knowledge check questions

1 What is the difference between an income statement and a balance sheet?

2 State two examples of current assets and two examples of current liabilities.

3 What is meant by the term 'non-current liability'?

4 A business has the following information on its balance sheet:

Non-current assets = £250 million

Current assets = £30 million

Non-current liabilities = £180 million

Current liabilities = £20 million

Which of the following is its working capital?

(a) £10 million   (c) £80 million

(b) £70 million   (d) £100 million

5 A business has the following information on its income statement:

Revenue = £155,000

Taxation = £3,000

Operating profit = £14,500

Cost of sales = £95,000

Which of the following is its gross profit?

(a) £152,000   (c) £71,500

(b) £57,000   (d) £60,000

6 What is the difference between an exceptional item and an extraordinary item on a business's income statement?

7 State two examples of efficiency ratios.

The following information is about XYZ Ltd and relates to questions 8 and 9.

Operating profit = £845,000

Total equity = £3,250,000

Current assets = £375,000

Revenue = £3 450,000

Current liabilities = £290,000

Non-current liabilities = £2,500,000

8 Which of the following is XYZ Ltd's ROCE figure?

(a) 26.00%   (c) 24.49%

(b) 14.70%   (d) 33.80%

9 Which of the following is XYZ Ltd's gearing figure?

(a) 72.46%   (c) 230.00%

(b) 56.52%   (d) 43.48%

10 State two items of data with which the results of ratio analysis can be usefully compared.

(b) Short answer questions

1 Explain the difference between the net current assets and the net assets of a public limited company.   (4 marks)

2 Explain two possible external factors that need to be taken into account when conducting ratio analysis.   (5 marks)

3 Explain the possible benefits to a public limited company's shareholders if it earns 'high quality profit' regularly.   (5 marks)

4 Explain why an investor considering buying shares worth £100,000 in one of the UK's major supermarkets might benefit from conducting ratio analysis before making a decision to buy. (9 marks)

(c) Data response question

Royal Mail

Royal Mail plc provides postal services throughout the UK and in Europe. The company was privatised (that is sold from the public sector to the private sector) in October 2013.

Royal Mail operates in an increasingly competitive postal services market in the UK and overseas. However, it has benefited from the rising popularity of online retailing as this has resulted in rising demand for parcel delivery services. Some of its competitors in the parcels market have faced financial problems: rival City Link announced it was going into administration on Christmas Day, 2014. Royal Mail has also had significant success in cutting its costs which has pleased shareholders.

Royal Mail is required by law to maintain the universal service. This guarantees that letters can be sent to any location within the United Kingdom for a fixed price. Royal Mail is legally obliged to continue to provide the universal service until at least 2021. Some of its competitors can opt to operate in more profitable areas, especially large cities. Amazon, the global online retailer, is launching its own parcels delivery service in the UK soon.

Item	31/03/2014(£m)	31/03/2013(£m)
Revenue	9,456	9,279
Operating profit	1,643	383
Profit for the year	1,280	600
Balance sheet		
Non-current assets	4,156	3,225
Current assets	1,320	1,391
Current liabilities	1,938	1,825
Non-current liabilities	1,137	1,386
Total equity	**2,401**	**1,405**

Table 2.12 A selection of financial data for Royal Mail plc, 2013–2014

Source: Royal Mail's annual report, 2014

Questions

1 Explain why the income statement is an important document for a stakeholder wishing to assess the financial performance of Royal Mail plc. (6 marks)

2 Use relevant financial ratios to analyse the strengths and weaknesses of Royal Mail plc's performance in 2013 and 2014. (9 marks)

3 Is it possible to assess Royal Mail plc's likely future performance on the basis of the results of financial ratio analysis? Justify your opinion. (15 marks)

(d) Essays

1 To what extent do you think that profitability is the most important measure of performance for the directors of a public company in the UK? (25 marks)

2 'The results of financial ratio analysis are historical and therefore of little use to a business's stakeholders.' To what extent do you agree with this statement? (25 marks)

Chapter 3

Analysing internal position: overall position

Introduction

This chapter is a natural development from Chapter 2 which investigated how financial data may be analysed to assess a business. This chapter considers a range of non-financial information that can be analysed by stakeholders to assess the existing internal position of a business. We consider the operations, human resource and marketing data that is available to interested parties, how it can be analysed over time, or in comparison to other businesses, and what it can reveal about the performance of a business in both the short and long term. The chapter also investigates the nature and importance of core competences to managers and other stakeholders and the value of Kaplan and Norton's Balanced Scorecard and Elkington's Triple Bottom Line in assessing the performance of businesses.

What you need to know by the end of this chapter:

- how to analyse data other than financial statements to assess the strengths and weaknesses of a business
- the importance of core competences
- how to assess short- and long-term business performance
- the value of different measures of assessing a business's performance, including Kaplan and Norton's balanced scorecard model and Elkington's triple bottom line.

Using non-financial data to assess strengths and weaknesses

We saw in Chapter 1 that businesses can conduct SWOT analyses to identify their strengths and weaknesses, as well as the future opportunities open to the business and the threats it may face. Assessing strengths and weaknesses within a SWOT analysis considers a business's current position at the current time. Managers conducting SWOT analyses can consider a range of internal evidence.

The analysis of big data is currently receiving a lot of attention in the media. 'Big data' is a term used to describe large and complex sets of data that were not previously available to managers. This data is increasingly used to help businesses devise strategies by enabling them to spot trends, for example in consumer behaviour, that may not have been apparent previously. However, the increasing volume and variety of data available to managers can assist with other aspects of decision making, including assessing a business's strengths and weaknesses. This data can relate to the business's internal functions such as operations and marketing.

Operations data

Operations management (often termed 'operations') is an area of management concerned with planning and controlling the production process within a business. A management team could use a range of operations data to assess a business's strengths and weaknesses. This data could measure a number of aspects of a business's operational performance including the following:

- productivity of labour and capital used in production
- measures of quality
- capacity utilisation.

Productivity as a measure of operational performance

Analysing a business's **productivity** data allows stakeholders to measure the efficiency with which an organisation converts inputs (of resources such as labour and capital) into outputs of goods and services. Highly productive businesses use fewer inputs to produce a unit of output. This is likely to allow it to produce a unit of output more cheaply, assuming it doesn't pay comparatively high costs for its inputs. As a consequence, its **unit costs** of production may be lower than those of its rivals. This can represent a considerable competitive advantage for businesses selling in price competitive markets and may be an important strength for such a business.

Much productivity data relates to a single input or resource – this is known as a single productivity measure – and only measures output in terms of labour or productivity. Fuller measures of productivity measure output against all the inputs or resources used by the business and are called multifactor productivity measures. This distinction is illustrated in Figure 3.1.

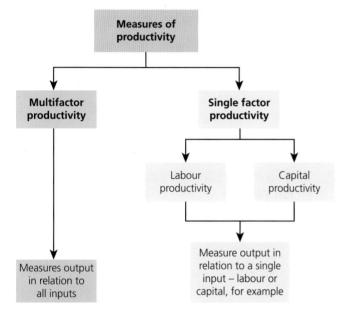

Figure 3.1 Measures of productivity

When measuring productivity to assess the strengths of a business's operational performance, it is important to bear a number of factors in mind.

- Multifactor productivity measures are preferable as they take into account all factors used in production. Multifactor productivity measures the efficiency with which all factors of production are used in the production process. Thus it compares the volume of output over a time period with the quantity of all factors used in production – that is capital and land, as well as labour. It is relatively straightforward for managers to improve single factor productivity by using less of it in production. For example, a manufacturing business could replace 50 per cent of

its labour with capital equipment in the production process. If output is unchanged, the effect of this action will be to double labour productivity, but operational performance may not have improved.

- Productivity data ignores costs. Rising productivity may be achieved alongside increased costs of resources and the higher costs will offset the benefits of the productivity gains. For this reason labour costs per unit may provide a better measure of operational performance.

Study tip

As with most measures of business performance, it is not possible to judge whether a business's productivity figures represent a strength or a weakness without comparing them to something else. The most obvious, and telling, comparison is with productivity data for competitors. It is also worth considering such data over time to judge whether or not operational performance is improving.

Key terms

Productivity measures the quantity of inputs required to produce a unit of output.

Unit costs measure the cost per unit of output produced.

Quality measures the extent to which a product meets customers' requirements.

Measuring quality

Quality can be a tricky concept to measure, though businesses do collect much data on customer satisfaction. Quality may be judged by:

- measuring customer loyalty through the number of repeat customers
- measuring customer satisfaction rates through questionnaires or surveys
- measuring specific elements of operational performance such as the number of faulty products (for manufacturers) or response times to customer queries (in service industries).

For example, companies engaged in supplying train services in the UK produce operational data relating to punctuality as shown in Figure 3.2.

Business in focus: The operational performance of UK train companies

Network Rail Ltd is the owner and operator of most of Britain's railway infrastructure – that is its rail track, power supply, signals and stations. It produces data on the overall operational performance of the rail industry in Britain as well as individual companies.

It uses a public performance measure (PPM), which shows the percentage of trains that arrive at their terminating station on time. PPM combines figures for punctuality and reliability into a single performance measure.

Network Rail itself causes some delays as some are due to infrastructure faults. However, the PPM figure also includes external factors such as weather, trespass, vandalism, cable theft, etc. These account for approximately 20 per cent of all delays in UK train services.

Performance for 4 January to 31 January 2015
- The national PPM is 87.9 per cent.
- This compares to 89.2 per cent for the same period in 2014.
- The moving annual average (MAA) is 89.5 per cent. (Using a moving average smoothes out short-term fluctuations in the data.)

Performance by train company

Table 3.1 below shows the average PPM for Britain as a whole and for a selection of train operating companies.

Train company	PPM January 2015	PPM January 2014
East Coast	91.6%	86.4%
Virgin Trains	89.2%	78.7%
Southern	75.0%	79.2%
Abellio Greater Anglia	91.9%	91.6%

Table 3.1 Performance data for a selection of Britain's train operating companies

Figure 3.2 Public performance data for the Britain's rail industry, 2002–15
Source: Adapted from Network Rail's website, www.networkrail.co.uk/

Questions
1. Explain the possible value to Network Rail Ltd resulting from collecting and analysing this data.
2. Do you think that the data in Table 3.1 is a good measure of the performance of train companies?

Capacity utilisation

The capacity of a business is the maximum amount it can produce using its existing resources. **Capacity utilisation** measures existing output relative to the maximum figure. Using capacity fully helps a business to produce its products as cheaply as possible and to offer competitive prices.

This can be a vital measure of operational and, ultimately, overall performance for two reasons.

1. For some businesses (for example, cinemas) attracting additional customers involves few or no additional costs but generates extra revenue. Thus, the impact on profits of high-capacity utilisation is significant and this can be an important measure.

2. In price competitive industries (i.e. where demand is price elastic) operating at high levels of capacity utilisation is a means of keeping unit costs low, enabling the business to maintain acceptable profit margins whilst selling at low prices. The budget airline easyJet carried 65,348,876 passengers and achieved a capacity utilisation figure of 90.8 per cent on its aircraft during 2014. The importance of this operations data to the company is shown by the decision to make it available to its investors (and potential investors) via its website.

Key term

Capacity utilisation measures the extent to which a business uses the resources available to it.

Maths moment

Assume that easyJet's capacity utilisation in 2014 was 95 per cent. How many passengers would it have carried during the year?

However, as with most operational data, capacity utilisation has its weaknesses. For example, it reveals nothing about the costs that a company is paying for its resources; it simply measures the efficiency with which they are used. Thus, an airline such as easyJet may struggle to maintain low prices, even with high levels of capacity utilisation on its planes, if other costs rise.

Other operational data

The operational data that stakeholders analyse to assess a business's strengths or weaknesses will vary according to the type of business under scrutiny. Key data for businesses, such as insurance companies, which provide services might relate to customer satisfaction as measured, for example, by speed of responding to and processing claims. In contrast, oil exploration companies (BP, for example) will set great store by data on employee safety given the dangers of the working environment for employees.

Figure 3.3 An offshore oil platform, a potentially dangerous working environment

One way in which businesses use technology, which is known as operational intelligence (OI), is the extraction of data from operational activities and its rapid analysis. The results are used in decision making to improve the organisation's operational performance. The use of OI can assist businesses in identifying and developing their operational strengths.

Human resources data

It is becoming increasingly important for human resources (HR) to use data, numbers and statistics to show trends in a range of HR issues, such as employee efficiency and engagement. Businesses have a range of HR data which can be analysed by interested parties to help make a judgement about the strengths and performance of this particular function. This can provide some insight into the business's overall strengths, especially for labour intensive businesses. HR data can take a number of forms including the following:

- labour productivity
- **absenteeism** rates
- health and safety data
- labour cost per unit of production
- costs associated with employees, such as average wages and recruitment costs
- labour turnover and retention.

Financial measures of HR performance

Financial measures of HR performance are perhaps the most easily analysed and can provide data in a form that is readily comparable. A business's managers can normally calculate labour cost per unit of output relatively easily and this is more informative than labour productivity data. Labour productivity data measures the quantity produced per employee per time period, but excludes the cost of labour, for example the hourly wage rate. **Unit labour cost** includes wage cost and productivity.

Key terms

Absenteeism occurs when an employee is not present at his or her place of work.

Unit labour costs measure the labour cost per unit of output produced.

It is perfectly possible for managers and other interested parties to analyse labour cost per unit of output over time and to make judgements about performance. Equally, comparisons can be made between different divisions of a business (or different businesses if the data is available) using this type of data to gain some idea of relative performance and to make judgements about apparent strengths and weaknesses within the HR function. However, it is important to appreciate that labour cost per unit is affected by factors outside a business's HR function, such as the amount and productivity of capital equipment used in production.

If such data reveals declining performance, management may take strategic decisions to rectify it. Since 2012 a number of Chinese clothing manufacturers have transferred their operations to Bangladesh to take advantage of lower wage costs: £45–65 per worker per month as compared with £215–350 in China. The implications of these different wage rates for the unit labour costs of firms selling in price competitive global markets is apparent.

What do you think?

What other factors apart from wage costs might global manufacturers take into account when assessing the strengths of their workforces?

Non-financial measures of HR performance

This category includes absenteeism, **labour turnover** and data relating to health and safety of a business's workforce. These measures are not directly financial and can be difficult to quantify in monetary terms. However, most have an impact on financial measures of HR performance.

High rates of absenteeism can indicate a workforce that lacks engagement and motivation and this can damage competitiveness. Research by the Confederation of British Industry (CBI), a UK employers' organisation, has shown that average days of absenteeism per employee has fallen from 9 in 1990 to 5.3 in 2012. Interestingly, absenteeism rates are higher for larger businesses. In the UK in 2012, firms with over 250 employees lost an average of 5.8 days per employee to absenteeism; the equivalent figure for firms with fewer than 250 employees was 4.3 days.

Labour turnover data provides a useful means of assessing a business's HR performance. Businesses with higher than average labour turnover face additional costs to recruit and train new employees, as well as a potential short-term decline in productivity. On the other hand, businesses with high levels of **labour** or **employee retention** avoid many recruitment costs and can benefit in other ways as they may have more motivated and engaged employees achieving higher levels of labour productivity. This may apply particularly to those businesses that manage to retain their most talented employees.

Other factors that may indicate that a business's workforce may represent a strength include the extent to which a specific workforce is diverse and inclusive. Creating a diverse workforce through an inclusive approach to recruitment and selection allows a business to benefit from the different qualities and attributes that it possesses and can improve overall performance. Health and safety data can play an important part in some industries in measuring the extent to which the workforce is protected and can help the business to develop a strong employer brand. Possessing a strong employer brand (that is, being seen as a good business to work for) assists organisations in recruiting the most talented, creative and productive employees. Health and safety data could be an important factor for companies in the oil and gas industry, such as BP plc (see the Business in focus on page 47).

Key terms

Labour turnover is the percentage of a business's employees who leave the business over some period of time (normally a year).

Labour or **employee retention** is the extent to which a business holds onto its employees.

Other issues in using HR data

Businesses are increasingly analysing their own HR data to identify strengths and weaknesses. Human resources analytics is the application of sophisticated data mining techniques to HR data. The objective of human resources analytics is to provide an organisation with insights for effectively managing employees to build on strengths and to eliminate weaknesses.

Business in focus: BP's workforce

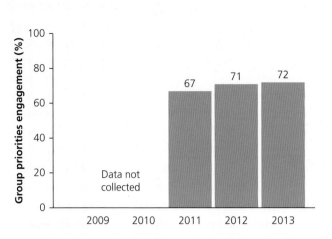

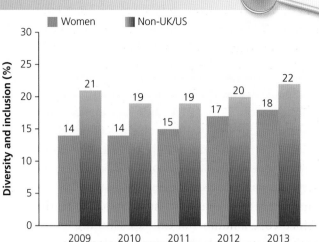

We track how engaged our employees are with our strategic priorities for building long-term value. The measure is derived from answers to 12 questions about BP as a company and how it is managed in terms of leadership and standards.

Each year we report the percentage of women and individuals from countries other than the UK and US among BP's group leaders. This means we can track progress in building a diverse and well-balanced leadership team, helping to create a sustainable pipeline of diverse talent for the future.

Figure 3.4 HR data on engagement and diversity and inclusion for BP plc, 2009–13

Source: BP Strategic Report, 2013

BP plc is a British multinational oil and gas company which extracts, refines, distributes and retails oil and gas products throughout the world. It is one of the world's six major companies in this industry. At the start of 2014, BP employed 83,900 people in locations across the globe, down slightly from 86,400 the previous year.

The increasing demand for energy products and the complexity of BP's operations means that attracting and retaining skilled and talented people is vital to the achievement of its strategy. BP plc seeks to develop the skills it needs from within its existing workforce and complements this with targeted external recruitment. The company conducts external assessments for all external recruitment into BP at senior levels, as well as for internal promotions to senior level and group leader level roles. These assessments help to achieve rigour and objectivity in its hiring and talent processes.

	2013	2012	2011
Injuries recorded – incidents per 200,000 working days	0.31	0.35	0.36
Days absent from work following injury – incidents per 200,000 working days	0.070	0.076	0.090

Table 3.2 BP plc safety data, 2011–2013

Source: BP Strategic Report, 2013

Questions

1. What other data might BP's stakeholders require about the performance of the company's human resources other than that shown in the graphs in Figure 3.4?

2. Why do you think BP's directors choose engagement and diversity and inclusion as its performance indicators relating to its HR function?

Marketing data

There is a wide range of marketing data available to stakeholders seeking to assess a business's performance in relation to that of its competitors in a particular market. The importance of marketing data in decision making by managers and other stakeholders is reflected in the work of major global marketing intelligence agencies such as Mintel. Companies such as Mintel can provide a variety of data related to marketing and sell their services to a variety of customers.

Weblink

To find out more about Mintel visit:
www.mintel.com/about-mintel

Marketing data that may help to assess a business's strengths or weaknesses can relate to the business itself as well as the market or markets in which it trades. This may include the following:

● Historic and forecast data on specific markets: company shares, overall size and growth rates, segmentation. This will include information such as product life cycles. Research shows that apps relating to entertainment have remarkably short product life cycles: an estimated 40 per cent of these apps are deleted from devices within three weeks. At the other extreme, Cadbury's Dairy Milk is a chocolate brand that has been in existence for over 100 years and is still selling very well.

● Information on the key forces driving change in the market which have strategic implications. This may include the development of new products, entry of new suppliers or government activity which is expected to alter sales.

● Data on important issues affecting consumer behaviour in particular markets. This could be important in influencing consumers' buying decisions as well as decision making by other stakeholders. Data relating to a company's products which may be available online and especially through social media may also be important. Research in 2012 (by Yubo Chen, Yong Liu and Jurui Zhang and published in the American *Journal of Marketing*) reports that consumer reviews on products posted on social media play significant roles as investors update and adapt their expectations about a new product's sales potential. Thus, online reviews may provide valuable data on a business's strengths. Online reviews also affect decisions made by consumers on whether or not to purchase products.

● Information relating to sales figures, brand recognition and expenditure on advertising and other marketing activities. Although this is likely to be historic, it provides a basis for stakeholders to judge expected future performance.

Data relating to entire markets

It is important to consider information on the market when analysing the strengths and weaknesses of a business's marketing activities. This enables the firm's

performance and prospects to be placed in a context. Figure 3.5 shows data relating to the UK market for organic products – mainly food products. It reveals that sales revenue grew by 4 per cent in 2014, which is a notable achievement when food prices in the UK fell by 1.9 per cent, and spending by consumers of food declined by 1.1 per cent.

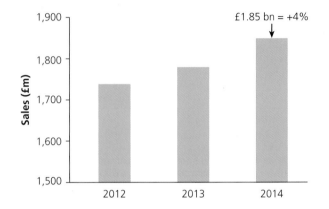

Figure 3.5 UK sales of organic products, 2012–14

Source: The Soil Association website, www.soilassociation.org/

This information on the UK organic market is useful and suggests that businesses operating in this market may have considerable potential. However, this information would need to be supplemented by other data to make a full assessment of the market and its potential and to analyse the likely consequences for a firm operating in this market.

Analysts may require a range of further information:

● The ease with which products can be distributed to consumers. In the case of organic products in the UK: what is the attitude of major retailers (particularly supermarkets) to selling organic products? Is it a range they are seeking to promote?

● The share of organic products in the wider market. The figures for organic products for 2014 look encouraging, but how do these relate to a longer term trend? What are the sales projections for this market? The UK is increasingly part of a global market, so data on global markets for organic products would be important to assess the likely extent of overseas competition and possible opportunities in foreign markets.

- Data on the other firms operating in the market when considering a particular business. For the organic market this might include those firms who are producing food and other organic products, their size and product ranges and their capacity to produce this type of product in the future.
- The attitudes and motivations of relevant consumer groups. Organic products are sold in a niche market in the UK and any analysis of businesses selling organic products would need to examine who the consumers of organic products are, why they buy these products, their income levels and likely future patterns of expenditure. This would also include the importance of price in the buying decision – is demand for organic food relatively price inelastic that is, an increase in price does not result in a directly proportional decrease in sales, because consumers place a high value on products supplied without the use of chemicals?

Weblink

To find out more about The Soil Association visit: www.soilassociation.org/

Understanding what has happened in a market and judging (as far as is possible) what is likely to happen in the future are important elements of assessing marketing data and a firm's strengths or weaknesses in this area. For example, data may reveal that the market in which a specific firm is operating is likely to exhibit strong sales growth over the next few years. This is important as it is easier for a firm to increase its sales in a growing market – it does not have to take customers from rivals as new ones are appearing – but will need to be ready to capitalise on this opportunity. However, some businesses sell in markets which are getting smaller which means sales figures have to be judged differently. British American Tobacco (a British multinational tobacco company) announced in 2015 that its sales had fallen by just 1 per cent over the first nine months of 2014: a performance which analysts considered impressive given that smoking rates in wealthy developed countries are falling sharply.

Marketing data for specific businesses

Using relevant information to analyse the marketing environment in which a business operates is only part of the analysis of marketing data. It is also important to acquire information about the specific firm in question and to use this in conjunction with data illustrating the broader picture.

Analysts would require varied data relating to a firm's marketing activities:

- Details on its product range, including some assessment on its forecast future sales (this may link to product life cycles). This might also include product development, sales figures, including historic and forecast figures, as well as data on market share.
- The results of marketing research, for example consumers' perceptions of the business's products, its brands and reputation.
- Information on the firm's marketing activities including product development and its marketing budgets.

Mothercare plc's sales data 2013–14

Mothercare plc is a UK-based multinational retailer. It operates two brands:

- Mothercare. This is a specialist retailer of products designed to meet the needs of mothers-to-be, babies and children up to eight years.
- Early Learning Centre. A retailer that sells toys for children up to eight years.

	2014 £m	2013 £m	2012 £m
UK sales			
Sales through stores	295.5	340.5	398.7
Direct sales, e.g. online	134.1	127.7	130.0
Wholesale sales, e.g. through partners such as Boots	29.7	31.5	31.3
International sales			
Sales through stores	721.9	677.7	606.2
Wholesale sales, e.g. through partners such as Boots	7.3	7.7	6.9
Total sales	**1,188.5**	**1,185.1**	**1,173.1**

Table 3.3 Mothercare plc UK and international sales figures, financial years ending 2012–14

Source: Mothercare plc Annual report, 2014

Table 3.3 states Mothercare's UK and international sales for three years. The initial impression is that the company's sales have been relatively poor – growing by only £15.4 million (or 1.3 per cent) between 2012 and 2014. Once inflation is taken into account the value of the company's sales have fallen in real terms.

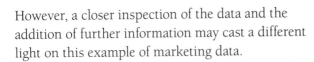

However, a closer inspection of the data and the addition of further information may cast a different light on this example of marketing data.

Its international division is performing strongly and it was here that the bulk of the company's sales were achieved. Between 2012 and 2014 international sales increased by £116.1 million (or 18.9 per cent), a much more impressive figure.

The board of directors of the company were implementing a strategy to reduce the company's losses by reducing the number of stores operating in the UK. Although UK sales fell 7.5 per cent in 2014 to £462.3 million, much of this was the result of closing shops. Comparing sales in the shops that survived with the figures for the same shops a year earlier (known as a like-for-like comparison) reveals that sales only declined by 1.9 per cent. This strategy appears to be having some success and in a trading update in 2015 the company announced that UK like-for-like sales had risen by 1.1 per cent over a year.

This marketing data for Mothercare plc is very limited. It excludes much important information such as sales forecasts, information about product ranges and, of course, data relating to the markets in which Mothercare operates.

Marketing data can reveal a great deal about a business but it can be misleading. It does need to be placed in context of the business's wider activities and the markets in which it trades. It is frequently valuable to compare marketing data for a specific business with that for other businesses in the same industry as well as for the business in earlier years.

Study tip

This section of the chapter has considered functional data that may be used to analyse a business's strengths or weaknesses. However, data that suggests, for example, that one function is performing poorly is likely to have implications for the entire business and may have been caused by poor management in other functions. Be prepared to look for evidence of this when analysing data.

Environmental data

Environmental factors are becoming increasingly important for the managers of businesses.

Management of energy, natural resources or waste will affect the current performance of many businesses. Equally, failure to plan for a future in which environmental factors are likely to be increasingly significant may risk the long-term future of a business.

Simultaneously, interest from stakeholders in businesses' environmental performance is at an all-time high. This is reflected in the decisions of 89 per cent of the UK's largest 100 companies to report on environmental issues in their annual report and accounts. The UK government recommends that businesses report on their environmental performance in four main areas which incorporate 22 separate measures, although only a small proportion of these are relevant to any single business. The four areas are:

1. Emissions to air, including greenhouse gases, dust and particles.
2. Emissions to water, such as metals and organic pollutants.
3. Emissions to land, which encompasses fertilisers, pesticides and waste, for example landfill.
4. Use of scarce and non-renewable resources, such as water and oil.

Key issues in interpreting environmental data are that it should be relevant to the business and in a form suitable for comparison with that provided by similar businesses or to official guidelines or regulatory limits. The ways in which environmental performance is measured and reported varies hugely between industries. For example, businesses engaged in agriculture might focus strongly on emissions to land, specifically the use of pesticides and fertilisers. In contrast, airlines would be likely to focus on emissions to air and use of non-renewable oil products.

Study tip

We will look at the collecting, analysis and reporting of environmental data in more detail in Chapter 6 when we cover corporate social reports.

Business in focus: Environmental performance at Rio Tinto

Rio Tinto plc is one of the world's largest mining companies. It extracts iron ore, copper, aluminium, diamonds and other minerals and employs 60,000 in 40 countries across six continents. The company's businesses include open-pit and underground mines, mills, refineries, smelters and power stations.

Environmental indicator	2014	2013	2012	2011
Significant environmental incidents	12	15	7	11
Greenhouse gas emissions (million tonnes CO_2)	33.9	37.2	40.7	43.2
Waste disposal or storage (million tonnes)	1,742	1,922	1,854	1,536
Land disturbed through company's activities (km²)	3,592	3,556	3,530	3,485

Table 3.4 A selection of environmental data for Rio Tinto plc, 2011–14

The company reports on its environmental performance (an extract is shown in Table 3.4) and seeks to minimise its impact on the environment:

'We have a responsibility to all our stakeholders and to the wider world, and so we endeavour to integrate sustainable development into everything we do.'

Despite this, the company has faced considerable criticism for the environmental consequences of its mining activities. The government of Norway has been a high-profile critic and sold all its shares in the company (valued at $500 million) in protest at its environmental and ethical performance.

Source: Rio Tinto's annual reports and website, www.riotinto.com/

Questions

1. For what reasons might the management team at Rio Tinto plc have decided to report extensively on the company's environmental performance?
2. Is environmental data the most important measure of a firm's performance nowadays?

The importance of core competencies

What are core competencies?

The term '**core competencies**' was first used in a series of articles in the *Harvard Business Review* in 1990. Core competencies were described as '… the collective learning in the organization, especially how to coordinate diverse production skills and integrate multiple streams of technologies'. The authors, Coimbatore Prahalad and Gary Hamal, argued that a business's core competencies arise from a combination of its collective learning and its technical skills, and give the firm a source of **competitive advantage**.

Prahalad and Hamal's work demonstrated that core competencies can provide a business with uniqueness: things that it can do exceptionally well and that competitors cannot easily copy. The two writers painted a picture of a business as a tree whose roots represent its competencies. These roots grow and nourish the organisation's 'core products' which create a number of subsidiary businesses. These subsidiary businesses sell 'end products' to consumers. These relationships are illustrated in Figure 3.6.

Prahalad and Hamal used examples of highly successful companies in the 1980s (such as Honda and Canon) to show how their enviable performances were the result of focusing on the things at which they excelled. These companies concentrated on identifying their core competencies to build and reinforce unique areas of expertise and devoted resources to these areas and not those in which they were relatively weak. The development and use of core competencies assisted a business in developing core products which could be used to provide end products for consumers. Sony's core competencies have allowed it to produce core products related to miniaturised technology – this has helped it to supply global markets with a range of desirable electronic products.

Key terms

Core competencies are the unique abilities that a business possesses that provide it with competitive advantage.

Competitive advantage is a superiority that a business possesses over its rivals that may allow it to achieve objectives, such as increased market share or profitability.

Outsourcing occurs when an organisation uses a separate business or businesses to complete part of its work – for example, a business may outsource cleaning its premises.

Core competencies can take diverse forms depending on the business and the products that it sells. Apple, the American technology company, has core competencies that relate to the design of its products when integrated effectively with its other business functions. Some business analysts believe Apple compromises everything to design, but this helps it to sell huge volumes of its products at premium prices. It sold 74.5 million iPhones in the last three months of 2014 alone.

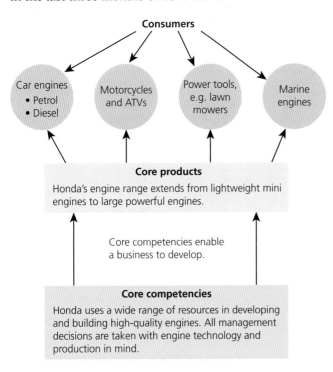

Figure 3.6 How core competencies work, using Honda as an example

Developing core competencies

Prahalad and Hamal argued that core competencies are the combination of the organisation's knowledge, its production skills and multiple streams of technologies. They suggested three factors could be used to test whether an organisation's attributes are truly core competencies.

Do they provide access to a wide range of markets?

This test of core competence assesses whether a business's attributes enable it to create desirable new products. We mentioned earlier that Apple's designs represent a core competency and this has been used to create products (such as the iPad and iPhone) with great success, enabling it to enter new markets. However, design alone will not provide Apple with a core competence: it is the deployment of unique design knowledge and skills in coordination with the other functions within the business (such as marketing) that are involved in bringing a product to the market.

Do they contribute significantly to the end-product benefits received by the customer?

Customers are strongly attracted to certain products which offer benefits that they believe are not available elsewhere. As a result, they are willing to pay higher prices for certain products. Goods and services supplied by firms who possess core competencies will fall into this category – our example of the distinctiveness of the design of Apple's products passes this test too. The John Lewis Partnership is another example where its highly regarded quality of customer service provides its customers with tangible benefits and gives the company a clear competitive advantage.

Are they difficult for competitors to imitate?

A core competence should not be easy to replicate otherwise it is not sustainable. It should be something that is highly desirable to competitors but is difficult to acquire. For example, Microsoft has expertise in many IT products and this is not easy for its rivals to copy. Similarly, Dropbox (which provides computing storage solutions) has developed core competencies based on agile use of technology and a good understanding of customer needs to continually develop innovative products which its rivals are struggling to match.

Why are core competencies important?

Core competencies can allow businesses to take full advantage of opportunities to enhance performance and provide competitive advantage with the potential of market leadership. The development and strengthening of core competencies can show that a business is using the right amount of resources and in the right areas of its operations. Many managers believe that businesses should outsource all non-core activities, i.e. require another organisation to carry them out. This can streamline a business's operations and encourage employees to focus on its competencies.

Core competencies are powerful as they give a business something that helps it to add value. The business's customers should believe that a business has attributes that enable it to supply distinctive and unique goods and services. If it achieves this, its competitiveness increases and, along with it, its market power. Apple is currently a phenomenal example of the effectiveness of core competencies in operation.

If businesses can match core competencies with market opportunities, then this can form the basis for creating new businesses. It brings together a business's strengths with a gap in the market in which a considerable potential for sales exists. As an example, Honda was able to take advantage of rising consumer incomes which led to increasing demand for power tools in a number of countries. This resulted in it establishing a business selling lawn mowers using its successful engines to power them.

Business in focus: Google's core competencies

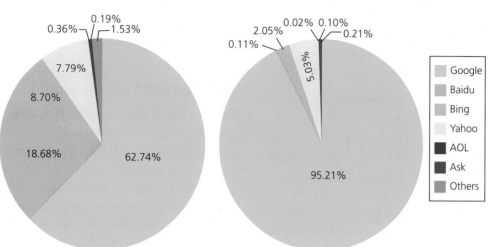

Figure 3.7 Global market share for search engines, January 2015

Source: Data from Netmarketshare, www.netmarketshare.com/

Google's hugely popular search engine service dominates its markets, and especially that relating to mobile phones and tablets. This is evidence of a considerable and sustainable competitive advantage.

Google's employees solve complex problems everyday pursuing the company's core mission to organise the world's information and make it universally accessible to its users. Google aims to bring together smart, talented people from a diversity of backgrounds. However, Google believes that what makes working at Google truly unique is the workplace culture that encourages innovation and a healthy disregard for the impossible.

Source: Text adapted from the Google website, www.google.co.uk/about/careers/lifeatgoogle/

Questions

1. Explain how Google's employees can help the company to establish core competences.

2. Do you think it is possible for a company to sustain core competences in the technology industry over a long period of time?

Figure 3.8 Over 95 per cent of internet searches on mobile devices use Google Search.

Core competencies – criticisms

There are some criticisms of Prahalad and Hamal's model of core competencies. One area of criticism centres on the weaknesses that develop in a business that outsources a number of its operations. **Outsourcing** is a common technique used by managers to allow them to focus resources on key elements of the business. As parts of the business are outsourced, the critics argue, the workforce becomes more fragmented. People work for different organisations with different goals and objectives, and different business cultures. This can result in a lack of harmony and unity of purpose, and a below par performance from the workforce.

Another area of criticism of the theory relating to core competencies is based on the notion that it is out of date. One such critic is Mark Parker, the CEO of the multinational clothing company Nike. Parker argues that in a world which is experiencing rapid change, having core competencies (in the form of certain strengths designed to succeed in a range of markets) is unlikely to help managers meet customers' evolving demands. He uses his company's development of digital products such as electronic wristbands designed to measure energy usage as an example of how successful companies need to make major strategic moves into different industries.

Some may believe, however, that even a diverse move from the clothing to the digital market could be more successful if the company concerned is able to rely on certain transferable strengths to underpin its development of new products.

Assessing short- and long-term performance

In Chapter 1 on page 8 we encountered the issue of short-termism. Short-termism can prevent senior managers thinking about the long term. This may act as a disincentive to setting corporate objectives which encourage long-term strategic decisions. Examples of such long-term decisions include investing in research into new products and processes, training of employees to provide high-level skills and creating new production facilities which may only break-even in the long term. Instead, it encourages decisions which frequently involve cost-cutting and loss of jobs.

It is possible to consider various aspects of the internal position of a business to assess its short-term and long-term performance, and gain some insight into whether the management team are avoiding the pressures for short-termism.

Research and development activities

Research and development (R&D) is part of the process of innovation. It entails using human, financial and other resources to develop new products or new, and more efficient, methods of production. This can result in businesses selling highly desirable products at premium prices. Apple is an example of a company that has benefited from its investment in R&D.

However, in some industries such as aerospace, pharmaceuticals and biotechnology, R&D can be very expensive and it may take many years before a business receives a return on its investment. Figure 3.9 shows that certain industries invest more heavily in R&D and that they are more likely to be implementing long-term strategies.

Thus, one way in which a business's potential short- and long-term performance can be judged is by considering the extent of its investment in R&D, particularly in comparison to other firms in the same industry. A firm that invests relatively little may generate higher short-term returns but at the expense of its long-term performance. Clearly, a firm that invests more heavily than its direct competitors may not achieve a better long-term performance. Its R&D may not be successful or it may encounter problems protecting its ideas. However, it is a statement of intention.

Huawei is a Chinese multinational IT company. It produces and sells telecommunications equipment, IT products and smart devices. The company invests particularly heavily in R&D. Huawei has over 70,000 product and solution R&D employees, comprising more

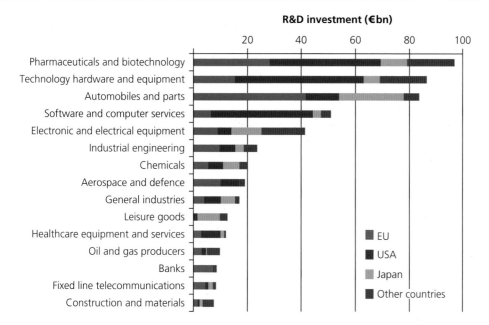

R&D investment (€bn)

Figure 3.9 R&D investment by industrial sector based on the world's top 2,500 companies, 2013

Source: European Commission fact sheet, World trends in R&D private investment – Facts and figures, Brussels, 4 December 2014, http://europa.eu/rapid/press-release_MEMO-14-2347_en.htm

than 45 per cent of its total workforce. It operates 16 R&D facilities in countries that include Germany, Sweden, the USA, France, Italy, Russia, India and China. The company's R&D investment amounted to $4,815 million in 2012, accounting for 13.7 per cent of the company's annual revenue. Huawei has cumulatively spent more than $20,800 million on R&D since 2003. This is heavy investment in R&D even by the standards of this industry and may generate high returns in the long term.

Weblink

To find out more about Huawei visit: www.huawei.com/en/

Profit quality

Profit is a major financial measure of performance, but it is possible to look beyond the amount of profit to its nature in judging the likely performance of a business in the short- and long-term. Firms regard profit that is likely to continue into the future as high-quality profit. In contrast, that which is unlikely to be repeated, for example a profit generated from the sale of a non-current asset, is classified as low-quality profit.

Thus, a business that is generating a high proportion of its profits in ways which are not sustainable may be considered to be more likely to perform better in the short term. Procter and Gamble is an

American consumer products company that owns many well-known global brands. The company has taken the decision to sell 100 brands during 2015 including Duracell (batteries) and Braun electrical appliances. These sales may generate high profits for the company in the short term, but the quality of the profit will be low as this strategy is not sustainable. The company's long-term performance will, however, be shaped by the use to which it puts the revenue that it receives from these sales.

Employee engagement

Key term

Employee engagement describes the connection between a business's employees and its mission, goals and objectives.

Employee engagement is receiving a great deal of attention currently. The Chartered Institute of Personnel and Development (CIPD) believes that engaged employees willingly contribute intellectual effort, experience positive emotions and meaningful connections to others in the workplace. Businesses frequently seek to measure employee engagement, usually through workplace surveys.

Businesses that seek to promote employee engagement are more likely to seek a long-term relationship with employees, as they tend to believe that employees are the most valuable asset a business has and they should be developed to maximise their value to the organisation. This makes a long-term approach essential. Employees are seen as a resource to be valued and developed over time and in response to changing market conditions. Positive data on employee engagement may be valuable evidence regarding a business's long-term performance, though many other factors will affect the organisation's future performance.

Customer satisfaction

A business's performance in terms of customer satisfaction is relatively easy to measure through the use of surveys and questionnaires. For example, Ofcom, the organisation that regulates the telecommunications industry, publishes the results of customer satisfaction surveys for businesses operating in the industry. In 2014, O2 received the highest customer service ratings for mobile telephone services.

High scores for customer satisfaction can represent evidence that a business is aiming to develop customer loyalty and to increase market share by providing consumers with a good experience. This may translate into a strong overall performance by the business in the longer term. Equally, it may be that achieving high levels of customer service is costly (for example, in terms of staff training) which may detract from a business's short-term financial performance.

Energy company	Customer satisfaction score (%)
Ecotricity	83
Good energy	82
Ebico	81
Ovo Energy	80
Utility Warehouse	76
Flow energy	73
Cooperative Energy	61
M&S Energy	57
Sainsbury's Energy	57
First Utility	54
Extra Energy	52
SSE	50
E.ON	50
Spark Energy	50
British Gas	49
EDF Energy	49
Scottish Power	41
Npower	35

Table 3.5 Customer satisfaction ratings for the UK's gas and electricity suppliers

Source: Adapted from an article in the *Independent*, 21 January 2015; data from Which?

Table 3.5 shows that the UK's major suppliers of energy (gas and electricity) such as EDF Energy, Npower and British Gas (highlighted) receive comparatively low ratings for customer satisfaction. Smaller rivals such as Ecotricity and Good Energy perform much better in this regard. This may indicate that these small and relatively new businesses are intent on capturing market share over the longer term and, thus, it may provide an indication of likely long-term performance. However, this contrast between small new suppliers and large established businesses may also reflect the nature of the energy supply market, particularly that customers are quite reluctant to change suppliers and that large businesses rely on this inertia.

What do you think?

Is achieving high levels of customer satisfaction less important for a large, well-established business?

Brand image and reputation

Key term

A **brand** is a name, sign, symbol or design used to differentiate a good or service from those supplied by competitors.

A business that is committed to maximising its long-term performance can be expected to take decisions that will protect and enhance its **brand**. It will ensure that it takes decisions that avoid damaging the brand and that are appropriate to the brand's position within the market.

In 2014 the American car manufacturer, GM, faced legal action alleging that it had deliberately concealed safety problems in hundreds of thousands of American consumers' cars to avoid the cost of recalling the vehicles and replacing the defective parts. This, allied to adverse publicity surrounding other acknowledged faults in the company's products, has severely damaged the firm's reputation and its brand image. This apparent desire to protect short-term profits is highly likely to impact negatively on the company's long-term performance.

Business in focus: Ryanair seeks to strengthen brand image

Ryanair, the UK's most popular budget airline, has continued its impressive recent financial performance. In December 2014 it flew 6.02 million passengers, an increase of 20 per cent on the 2013 figure. Over the whole of 2013 the airline attracted 86.4 million passengers, a rise of 6 per cent when compared to the previous year. The airline's success follows a decision to improve the quality of its customer service with the intention of improving its brand image.

Alongside improvements in its customer services, Ryanair has increased its capacity by launching new routes and new services targeted at business passengers. At the same time it has increased the frequency of flights to its existing popular destinations. Despite increasing its capacity, and the highly competitive nature of the European airline market, its capacity utilisation also increased by 7 per cent to 88 per cent in December 2014.

These figures represent a significant turnaround for the airline which issued two profit warnings in 2013 and reflect the early success of the airline's new strategy. Kenny Jacobs, Ryanair's Chief Marketing Officer, said: 'With our new routes, increased frequencies, improving customer experience and Business Plus service, Ryanair continues to deliver so much more than the lowest fares in every market we operate in.'

Source: Adapted from an article in the *Financial Times*, 5 January 2015

Questions

1. Explain the possible reasons why Ryanair's performance appears to have responded quickly to its decision to improve its brand image.
2. Does brand image matter to businesses that sell products at low prices?

Other businesses seek to enhance their brand images, even though they incur additional costs, as they believe it will help to develop brand loyalty and increase market share. Ultimately, it is expected to improve the business's long-term performance including financial returns. Vodafone plc, one of the world's leading telecommunications companies, publicises its desire to create 'long-term value' by taking decisions that protect and enhance its reputation and brand image with its stakeholders. It is perhaps no coincidence that Vodafone is the UK's most valuable brand with an estimated worth of £17.92 billion in 2014.

Sustainability

A sustainable approach to business is one that can be conducted in the long term. It entails using a business's resources, as well as natural resources, in such ways as to avoid damaging or compromising future use and business activity. 'Sustainability' is a much used term in business at the present time, but businesses that genuinely seek to operate sustainable business models are focusing squarely on long-term performance even at the expense of short-term costs.

As an example, there are forecasts of severe shortages of cocoa beans within ten years because production in Ghana and Cote d'Ivoire (which supply 60 per cent of the world's cocoa beans) is forecast to slump. This is due to insufficient investment by farmers as well as the effects of climate change and farming

practices in reducing the supply of suitable land. The implications for chocolate manufacturers such as Nestlé are significant as the price of cocoa is likely to rise sharply as its availability declines. This may require the company, along with other chocolate producers, to invest heavily to support the activities of Africa's cocoa farmers and prevent them switching to supply other crops that are easier to grow. Although this is potentially costly in the short-term for chocolate manufacturers, investing in sustainable sources of supply is likely to enhance their long-term performance.

The value of other measures of assessing business performance

We saw in Chapter 2 that financial measures of performance are used extensively to assess the performance of a business. However, relying simply on financial measures of performance may result in a business failing to judge its performance accurately or fully. Financial measures of performance may be important for some stakeholder groups, but not for all. Furthermore, financial measures of performance tend to measure the consequences of past decisions and actions rather than providing an indication of future performance. As a consequence, managers have increasingly used more than one set of measures to judge a business's performance.

To broaden how they measure the performance of their organisations, some management teams have opted to use different frameworks to assess performance. There are a range of models available that provide different ways of measuring performance. We shall consider two models of performance measurement:

- Kaplan and Norton's balanced scorecard
- Elkington's triple bottom line.

Kaplan and Norton's balanced scorecard

Key term

The **balanced scorecard** is a planning and management strategy designed to match business activities to the aspirations set out in the organisation's vision statement.

In Chapter 1 on page 3 we encountered the concept of the vision statement in which a business states what it hopes to achieve in the future. Businesses do not normally state their visions in financial terms and, thus, it is not appropriate to assess their achievements against their vision by use of financial measures of performance. Kaplan and Norton's **balanced scorecard** approach is based on the premise that financial data is inadequate on its own as a measure of a business's performance and that non-financial data should be included in any worthwhile measure.

The balanced scorecard was developed by Robert Kaplan and David Norton (and first set out in the *Harvard Business Review* in 1992) as a framework that added strategic non-financial performance measures to traditional financial ones to give managers and other stakeholders a 'balanced' view of the performance of a business. The authors described the model in the following terms:

'The balanced scorecard retains traditional financial measures. But financial measures tell the story of past events, an adequate story for industrial age companies for which investments in long-term capabilities and customer relationships were not critical for success. These financial measures are inadequate, however, for guiding and evaluating the journey that information age companies must make to create future value through investment in customers, suppliers, employees, processes, technology, and innovation.'

Kaplan and Norton suggested that managers should consider the following in developing their unique version of the balanced scorecard in addition to financial measures:

- **The customer's perspective**. How does the customer perceive the business? What steps are necessary to maintain the loyalty of customers?
- **The company's internal perspective**. What aspects of a business's internal operations may need to be improved if a business is to meet its objectives?
- **Innovation, learning and improvement**. How can the company continue to improve and to create value in the future?

The use of the balanced scorecard encourages managers to think about what needs measuring if the business is to achieve its objectives. The scorecard's measures will vary according to a business's circumstances but may include performance measures such as those set out in Table 3.6.

Area of measurement	Examples
Financial performance	• Revenues from sales • Profits and profitability such as return on capital (ROCE) • Cash flow
Customer value performance	• Customer loyalty • Delivery on time • Customer satisfaction
Internal business process performance	• Productivity • Quality • Number and effects of bottlenecks in production
Learning and growth performance	• Extent and effectiveness of training • Employee engagement and labour turnover • Effectiveness of communication systems • Innovation, percentage of revenue from new products

Table 3.6 The balanced scorecard's components

These elements within the scorecard should be quantifiable and therefore capable of measurement. They cover the organisation's activities in four categories as shown above; success in one area does not necessarily result in success in other areas.

The balanced scorecard does not just measure performance, however. Although it was originally developed as just a performance management tool, its role has developed. It is a management tool that enables firms to clarify their vision and strategy and translate them into action. The balanced scorecard can be applied to a business's strategic plan to guide managers in decision making. It helps managers to identify what should be done and to measure the extent to which these targets are achieved.

Thus, managers may use the balanced scorecard to implement strategy as well as to measure performance as shown in Figure 3.10.

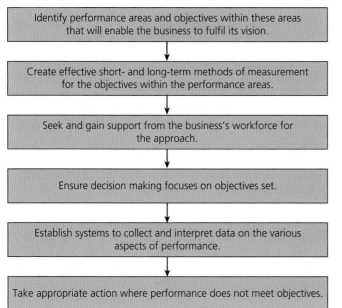

Figure 3.10 Using Kaplan and Norton's balanced scorecard

The value of the balanced scorecard

A recent global study by Bain & Company listed the balanced scorecard fifth on its top ten most widely used management tools by companies worldwide. The balanced scorecard has also been selected by the editors of *Harvard Business Review* as one of the most influential business ideas of the past 75 years.

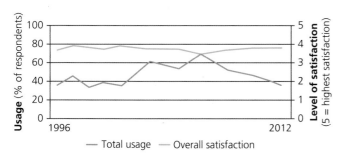

— Total usage   — Overall satisfaction

Notes to Figure 3.11: This data is based on a worldwide survey of 1,208 company executives in 2013.

Figure 3.11 The balanced scorecard – its use and level of satisfaction, 1996–2012

Source: Bain & Company, *Insights – Management Tools*, 5 June 2015

Although Figure 3.11 shows that usage of the balanced scorecard has declined in the companies surveyed in recent years, it has achieved satisfaction levels of around 70–80 per cent since it was first used. It does encourage managers to focus on factors other than finance and tends to improve performance in the areas in which goals are set.

However, at the heart of its value to managers and other stakeholders is that it is not merely a measurement tool. Much of its value to managers lies in its use as a framework within which a strategy can be implemented to attain the business's vision. That it can also be used to quantify progress towards this vision gives added value.

Elkington's triple bottom line

The term 'triple bottom line' was first used by John Elkington in 1994. It did not become a popular or widely recognised approach until the publication of his follow-up book (*Cannibals with Forks: the Triple Bottom Line of 21st Century Business*) in 1997. As its name suggests, the triple bottom line (or TBL) has three components: profit, people and planet.

Key terms

Sustainable production occurs when the supply of a product does not impose costs on future generations by, for example, depleting non-renewable resources.

Social responsibility is managing a business so as to take into account the interests of society in general and especially those groups and individuals with a direct interest in the business.

Fair trade is a social movement that exists to promote improved trading terms and living conditions for producers of products in less-developed countries.

Profit

The financial bottom line is the most familiar for managers and for students. This is the figures recorded in a business's financial statements, primarily its profits. However, when considering profit as part of a triple bottom line analysis, the idea is that profits will help sustain the broader community in which the business operates; they should be paid to the business's owners.

People

This element of the TBL measures the impact that a business's activities may have on all the people with which it is involved – that is the extent to which it is **socially responsible**. This considers the effects of the business's actions on a broad range of stakeholders including suppliers, customers, local residents as well as, of course, employees. This element of the TBL should take into account issues such as the following:

● Health and safety matters. This might include the provision of safe working environments for employees and ensuring that suppliers do the same, even if this results in higher costs.
● Financial matters. This would include offering fair rates of pay for employees and paying suppliers fair prices promptly.
● One notable element of caring for people has been the development of **fair trade**. Fair trade is a social movement that operates with the goal of assisting businesses in less-developed countries to achieve improved trading terms. The movement hopes to improve living standards in the less-developed countries and to promote sustainable methods of production.

Weblink

You can find out more about fair trade by visiting: www.fairtrade.org.uk

Planet

Businesses that are measuring their activity using TBL are likely to seek to minimise the impact of their activities on the environment. Actions to achieve this may take diverse forms such as:

● reducing carbon emissions – attractive because it is easily measurable
● reducing the quantity of waste that is disposed
● using sustainable sources of raw materials wherever possible
● reducing usage of non-renewable resources.

Businesses that take the TBL into account in decision making attempt to assess the true cost of their actions for the environment. Many businesses promote policies of this type using the term 'going green'.

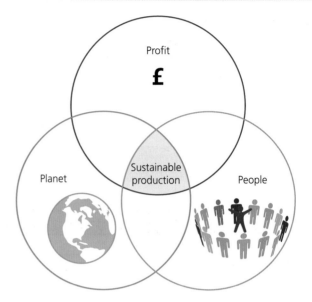

Figure 3.12 The use of Elkington's triple bottom line encourages sustainable production

What do you think?

Is a manager doing their job badly if they do not take into account the environmental consequences of their decisions?

The value of the triple bottom line

The TBL was meant by John Elkington to be a way of thinking about a business's social responsibility, not simply a method of measuring a business's performance. This emphasises its strengths and weaknesses. It is a management tool designed to make managers think about the impact of their actions on not just the business's profits (and its shareholders) but also on society and the environment, and thus other stakeholders too. In this way, it encourages corporate social responsibility and makes managers think about ways of measuring the effects of their businesses' activities in terms other than financial ones.

However, it is mainly seen as a technique of measuring or assessing business performance. In that regard it has a fundamental weakness. The three separate accounts that comprise the bottom line cannot be totalled – or compared. It is not possible to measure the planet and people elements of the TBL in monetary terms. For example, the cost resulting from disposing of toxic waste in the ocean is huge and probably impossible to put into financial terms. Similarly, the cost of using children in factories in Bangladesh to produce cheap clothing is immeasurable in terms of lost childhoods and opportunities denied. These cannot easily be added to financial costs. Equally, benefits in these areas cannot be translated into financial terms.

The TBL proved popular in the late 1990s and helped to support the development of corporate social responsibility and fair trade. At one point, the UK government considered making TBL reporting a legal requirement. More recently, businesses have focused on reducing costs, for example, by transferring production to low-cost countries such as India. However, criticisms from western consumers of such actions alongside the emerging social and environmental costs of these policies are encouraging a rethink. Perhaps the TBL will gain wider use in the future despite its shortcomings.

ASSESSMENT ACTIVITIES

(a) Knowledge check questions

1 State two examples of operations data that may be used to analyse a business's strengths and weaknesses.

2 State one reason why labour cost per unit of production might be a good measure of a business's HR performance.

3 List three items of marketing information that stakeholders may use to analyse the strengths or weaknesses of a business's marketing operations.

4 State the four areas of business operations which the UK government suggests that environmental reporting should cover.

5 Distinguish between core competencies and competitive advantage.

6 What are the three factors that can be used to judge whether an organisation's attributes are genuine core competencies?

7 List two aspects of a business's activities that may be used to judge the extent to which it is focusing on its long-term rather than its short-term performance?

8 What is meant by the term 'balanced scorecard'?

9 State the three elements of John Elkington's triple bottom line.

10 Distinguish between sustainable production and social responsibility.

(b) Short answer questions

1 Explain one circumstance in which capacity utilisation can be a vital measure of a business's performance. (4 marks)

2 Explain one reason why a law firm with high rates of employee retention may be expected to perform better than one with low rates of retention. (5 marks)

3 Explain one reason why environmental data may offer a good indication of the future performance of an oil company such as BP. (5 marks)

4 Explain why core competences are important for large multinational firms that sell a range of products in global markets. (9 marks)

(c) Data response question

Novo Nordisk

Novo Nordisk is a Danish global health care company with more than 90 years of innovation and leadership in diabetes care and 70,000 employees worldwide. Over the past 15 years, Novo Nordisk has delivered results superior to those of most other pharmaceutical companies. A key reason is that it has stuck to a highly focused long-term strategy. The company presents its results using triple bottom line (TBL) reporting – a selection of its results are shown in Table 3.7.

Novo Nordisk is a strong believer in maintaining focus on what it does best and is therefore not easily tempted to stray from its core business. As a result, its main business area today is the same as when it was founded: diabetes. Its main product then was insulin; the main product now is – insulin.

This is not to say that Novo Nordisk is not innovating: it seeks to develop new products and to benefit from patent laws which offer protection for up to 20 years. In fact, it typically spends 13–15 per cent of its revenue on researching and developing new products within its core areas. Its revenue was DKK88,806 million in 2014*, an increase from DKK83,572 million in 2013 and DKK78,026 million in 2012. (* DKK is the Danish Krone. At the time of writing the exchange rate was £1 = DKK10.24.) The company has over 4,500 employees working within its R&D organisation globally.

	2014	2013	2012	TARGET
Profit				
Net profit margin	29.8%	30.1%	27.5%	-
Social (people)				
Research and development costs (% of revenue)	15.5%	14.0%	14.0%	-
Number of diabetes patients treated with Novo Nordisk products (millions)	24.4	24.3	22.8	40 by 2020
Environmental (planet)				
Energy consumption (change from previous year)	–1%	+ 6%	+ 11%	Not to exceed + 5%
Waste (tonnes)	30 720	20 387	19 213	-

Table 3.7 A selection of Novo Nordisk performance data, 2012–14

Source: Adapted from Novo Nordisk Annual Report, 2014

Questions

1   Explain the possible reasons why Novo Nordisk spends heavily on its research and development activities.   (6 marks)

2   Use the data in the case study to analyse the strengths and weaknesses of Novo Nordisk's performance between 2012 and 2014.   (9 marks)

3   To what extent might Novo Nordisk's stakeholders have benefited from the company's use of TBL reporting?   (15 marks)

(d) Essays

1   Should all multinational companies focus on developing their core competencies? Justify your opinion.   (25 marks)

2   'The use of the balanced scorecard is more likely to allow a management team to implement its strategy successfully than triple line reporting.' To what extent do you agree with this statement?   (25 marks)

Chapter 4

Analysing the external environment: political and legal change

Introduction

This chapter examines the effects of changes in the political and legal environments in which businesses operate. It considers the ways in which these changes may impact on strategic and functional decision making within a business and the extent to which the changes may provide opportunities or pose threats.

What you need to know by the end of this chapter:

- the impact of changes in the political and legal environment, including the scope and effects of UK and EU law related to competition, the labour market and environmental legislation, on strategic and functional decision making within a business
- have an awareness of UK and EU Government policy related to enterprise, the role of regulators, infrastructure, the environment and international trade.

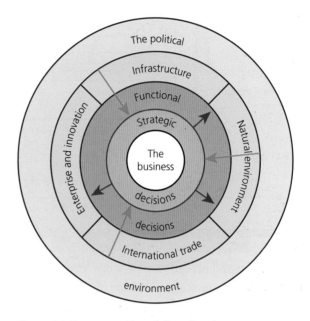

Figure 4.1 The composition of the political environment

The political environment

The political environment comprises actions taken by local, national or international authorities that affect the activities of businesses. A number of areas of government policy may be considered to shape the political environment, including:

- encouraging enterprise
- the regulation of markets
- the country's infrastructure
- issues relating to the environment
- international trade.

In this chapter we will examine each of these elements of the political environment and consider how changes in them may impact upon decision making within businesses.

> **Study tip**
>
> The economic policies of the government (for example, its monetary policy) may be considered part of the political environment, but we cover these in Chapter 5 on page 84.

Policies affecting enterprise

An enterprise-friendly business environment

The UK government seeks to establish an **enterprise-**friendly business environment, which will encourage people and organisations to develop their ideas as well as to establish and expand their businesses. This can be a risky process for those involved as entrepreneurs may give up safe, well-paid jobs and owner-managers may mortgage homes to borrow money to expand businesses. It can go wrong, but the aim of government support is to promote enterprise and to reduce the degree of risk.

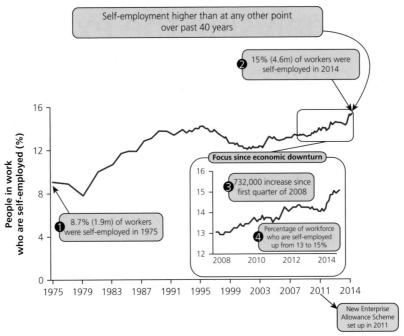

Figure 4.2 Self-employment data for the UK, 1975–2014

Source: Office for National Statistics (ONS)

Key terms

Enterprise is the skill needed to make a new idea work.
Innovation is the successful exploitation of new ideas.

One piece of evidence of whether an economy is promoting enterprise successfully can be shown by the level of self-employment – although this may also indicate a lack of employment opportunities. According to data published by the Office for National Statistics (ONS) 4.6 million people in the UK were self-employed in their main job accounting for 15 per cent of those in work in 2014. (See Figure 4.2.) This is the largest number of people ever to be self-employed in the UK and an indication that the country has a strong enterprise culture. This offers important benefits to the government and to businesses and is likely to encourage people to take the risk of starting a business.

Decisions and actions by the government and its agencies have encouraged and promoted the development of enterprise and innovation in the UK in a number of ways, both financial and non-financial, and these have changed significantly since 2010.

Financial support for enterprise

The British Business Bank manages all UK government programmes that help smaller businesses to gain access to finance. It was established in 2012 to help make sure finance markets for small and medium-sized

businesses work effectively. It does not lend directly to businesses, but will work alongside the private sector partners. It will pull in more private-sector funding to maximise its impact. In 2013, it supported £660 million of lending and investment to smaller businesses.

Weblink

To find out more about the British Business Bank visit: http://british-business-bank.co.uk/

Some of the national schemes of financial support for enterprise (specifically smaller businesses) overseen by the British Business Bank are shown below, but these are supplemented by a variety of regional and local policies.

● **Enterprise Allowance**. This is available for those who want to start their own business. It is in two parts: a grant (which doesn't have to be repaid) of up to £1,284 over six months and a loan which must be paid back within five years.
● **Funding for Lending**. In July 2012, with support from the UK government, the Bank of England launched Funding for Lending. This scheme allows banks and building societies to borrow from the Bank of England at cheaper than market rates for up to four years. It helps them to increase lending to businesses by lowering interest rates and increasing access to credit.

- **Enterprise Finance Guarantee (EFG).** EFG is a loan guarantee scheme. It allows banks and other lenders to offer small businesses, which lack security or a proven track record, a normal commercial loan. Lenders can use EFG to help businesses arrange loans and overdrafts. Loans can be guaranteed up to a value of £1.2 million. Small and medium-sized businesses with annual sales revenue below £41 million can get EFG-backed loans.

Non-financial support for enterprise

The UK government provides a range of support, advice and inspiration for entrepreneurs establishing and growing their businesses. A focal point of government support for enterprise is its website 'Business is Great'.

Weblink

To find out more about the 'Business is Great' website visit: www.greatbusiness.gov.uk

The Department for Business, Innovation and Skills (BIS) is the key UK government department concerned with developing and providing enterprise support. It works with businesses, financial institutions and other government departments, to help UK businesses start up, grow and succeed.

The government has a 'growth voucher' programme to provide strategic advice on a number of vital elements of operating a growing business. This scheme offers funding and guidance on sources of advice for:

- finance and cash flow
- recruiting and developing staff
- improving leadership and management skills
- marketing, attracting and keeping customers
- making the most of digital technology.

Other aspects of its work to provide a more 'enterprise-friendly' environment in the UK include:

- Reducing the number of regulations which constrain business activity. The government operates a policy of removing two regulations for each new one created.
- BIS is working with the tax authorities in the UK (HM Revenue and Customs) to offer support to new and small businesses by reducing the tax they pay on any profits and also the cost of employing people.
- Supporting innovation through a £4.6 billion fund and by helping researchers, developers, innovators and businesses, together with universities, to bring together the skills and technology necessary to develop new products and processes.
- The government offers a range of schemes to help entrepreneurs and businesses to develop new products and processes. These include help to develop the ideas (in terms of expertise, advice and funding) as well as support on how to protect ideas (known as Intellectual Property or IP).

Business in focus: Saffron Catering

Carla and Stacey Garey are a husband and wife team with many of the right skills to manage a catering business. Stacey used to manage a restaurant and Carla has a background in sales and marketing in the hospitality industry. Between them, they set up Saffron Catering which is growing strongly supplying a market that stretches from Manchester to Milton Keynes with great food.

Although weddings and one-off events provided much of the early business, Garey always wanted to develop Saffron as a venue caterer that would provide catering services to prestigious venues (such as hotels) and to corporate clients (currently including IKEA and Amazon) in the region. The Gareys are extending their business's involvement in this type of work.

The gaps in the couple's management knowledge were exposed when they purchased another catering company. It led to a big jump in sales but Carla had little experience of how best to develop the potential of this larger enterprise or of leadership. And that's where the Growth Voucher scheme came in. Through it they found a local business adviser and, with the help of funding from the Growth Voucher and with the adviser's support, developed a new business plan. The adviser also supported Carla in developing a new vision for the business on which its future strategy could be based.

The benefits are flowing through. At the time of writing Saffron employs 25 full and part-time staff, including operations and administrative staff, chefs and supervisors. In the past year its sales revenue has increased by 50 per cent.

Source: Business is Great website, www.greatbusiness.gov.uk/

Questions

1. Explain why the support provided by the Growth Voucher Scheme was an important element in the decision to expand Saffron Catering.

2. Do you think that non-financial help is more important than financial support to establish an enterprise-friendly business environment?

The UK government also seeks to encourage enterprise and to develop the relevant skills in young people. It:

- recruits young business owners to volunteer as enterprise champions to talk to young people about establishing and running their own enterprises
- works directly with schools and colleges to encourage the use of schemes. For example, it promotes the 'Enterprise Village', to help schools to set up businesses.

Study tip

Do be aware that, although most of these government activities and policies are intended to promote enterprise and are aimed at start-up and small businesses, they help to create a more 'business-friendly' environment for all businesses. This helps, for example, to attract large multinationals to the UK.

The European Union's enterprise policies

Creating a business-friendly environment for existing small and medium-sized enterprises as well as potential entrepreneurs is one of the EU's main objectives. The European Commission (the organisation responsible for implementing the EU's decisions) is working together with the EU countries on developing policies to support start-up, small and medium-sized businesses. It also monitors the progress of the implementation of these policies and promotes the sharing of best practices in encouraging and supporting enterprise.

The effects of enterprise policies

The impact of these policies to encourage enterprise and innovation is greatest amongst smaller organisations. It has a substantial impact on strategic decisions made by the owners of such businesses by influencing decisions on whether to start an enterprise or to expand it. However, these policies also stimulate innovation in organisations of all sizes. In many ways this could affect functional decision making significantly as managers seek to expand operations, hire additional employees to produce innovative products and plan marketing campaigns to promote them.

The role of regulators

Regulators operate in a number of capacities within the UK economy. The UK government believes that all regulators should carry out their activities in a way that supports those they regulate to comply with rules and, critically, to expand their enterprises. **Regulation**

can relate to a variety of business activities, including pricing and their impact on the environment.

There are a number of aspects of regulation that affect business activity in the UK and shape the political environment in which all firms operate. These include:

- regulation with the aim of creating free and fair competition between businesses
- regulation of certain high-profile industries such as banking and **financial services**
- regulation of **privatised monopolies** to protect consumers and other businesses
- self-regulation by businesses.

Key terms

Regulation is the enforcement of principles or rules that result from the passing of a law or series of laws.

Financial services are any products which are financial in nature and include those supplied by banks, insurance companies and financial advisers.

Privatisation is the process of transferring organisations from state ownership to that of the private sector (i.e. individuals and other businesses).

Monopoly exists when there is a single supplier within a market.

Regulation to create free and fair competition

Regulation can relate to any industry or business in the UK that is not operating in the best interests of consumers, although, as we shall see on the following page, certain industries receive particularly close scrutiny.

The focus of most regulation is to protect the consumer by ensuring that there is sufficient competition within specific industries and to eliminate any trading activities that are not in the interests of consumers. Such activities may include businesses limiting the range and variety of products available to consumers. Regulators can take a number of actions to protect the interest of consumers. These may be considered threats to businesses but may also provide opportunities.

- **Imposing 'windfall' taxes.** These are taxes on profits that are considered to be excessive and are more likely to be incurred if the business or businesses are thought to have too much market power. In 1997, the UK government levied windfall taxes on utilities that had been privatised (for example, British Gas, British Telecom and Railtrack) producing revenue estimated to be £5 billion.

- **Controlling prices**. This action by regulators frequently takes the form of limiting price rises to the current rate of inflation plus or minus some figure. For example, Ofwat, the regulator that controls the UK firms that supply households and businesses with water, announced a five-year price control plan in 2014. The proposed price controls for the 18 water supply companies will result in average water and sewage bills in 2015–20 that are 5 per cent lower compared to 2010–15. Regulators can provide firms with certainty about future prices over the medium term.
- **Restricting rates of return on capital invested by businesses**. Using measures such as return on capital employed (ROCE) can prevent businesses earning excessive profits and relates returns to the amount invested by the enterprise. Imposing this type of control helps to prevent businesses with significant market power from charging consumers excessively high prices. A significant weakness of this approach is that it removes pressure on the firms concerned to control costs, as allowing these to increase will reduce profitability. Thus, consumers may face high prices.
- **Unbundled access**. This form of regulation allows new entrants to a specific market to have access to the facilities of existing producers which may be difficult to duplicate. The aim is to encourage competition. In the UK, Royal Mail (which has dominated UK postal services for centuries and was privatised in 2013) has been forced to allow rival firms such as UK Mail to use its local delivery service.

Whilst those regulations that control prices or limit profitability are likely to be seen as threats, unbundled access offers opportunities to businesses to enter markets and could have significant implications for strategic decision making.

Study tip

We consider how the UK authorities use the law to manage and control the extent of competition within UK markets later in this chapter on page 74. You should consider this in conjunction with regulation.

Regulation of high-profile industries

Some industries in the UK are regulated particularly closely because of their potential to act against the interests of consumers or their ability to damage the economy. Banking and financial services are examples of such industries.

The UK's banks have received much criticism for their role in precipitating the financial crisis which preceded the recession of 2008–9 by allowing their investment divisions to engage in very risky banking practices that threatened the survival of some of the UK's largest banks. The UK's banks are particularly large relative to the size of the economy and, therefore, if they face problems, the impact on other businesses and the economy as a whole can be immense, as was seen in 2008. This is why they are subject to tight regulation now.

Additionally, banks have also been criticised, along with some insurance companies, for acting against the best interests of consumers by 'mis-selling' Payment Protection Insurance (PPI) to customers who did not need it.

As a consequence the banking and financial services industries are subject to regulation by a number of organisations, including those listed below. The Financial Services Act of 2012 replaced the Financial Services Authority with two new regulators:

- **The Prudential Regulation Authority (PRA)**. The PRA is controlled by the Bank of England and operates with the aim of establishing a stable financial system for the UK. It supervises approximately 1,700 banks, building societies, insurers and major investment firms in the UK. The role of the PRA is to promote the safety and soundness of these financial services businesses and, specifically for insurers, to ensure that policyholders are protected.
- **The Financial Conduct Authority (FCA)**. The FCA operates independently from the Bank of England and was given the responsibility of ensuring that financial markets operate effectively and that acceptable levels of competition exist. It also scrutinises the actions of businesses in financial markets to avoid any unacceptable behaviour.

The European Union also has some regulatory powers in relation to banking in the UK and other EU member states. The European Banking Authority subjects banks to regular tests to judge whether they would be able to cope with future financial shocks.

Regulation of privatised utilities

The UK privatised many state-owned monopolies that supplied products including water, electricity and gas during the 1980s and 1990s. This meant that these monopolies became private companies and the government established regulators (Ofwat, Ofgem and

Ofcom, for example) to ensure that the companies did not abuse their market positions. The role of these regulators is to act to ensure that consumers' interests are protected and that these natural monopolies do not charge excessive prices and make excessive profits.

Self-regulation

In some industries, the government has permitted self-regulation to operate usually through a code of conduct which all businesses within the industry agree to abide by. The government reserves the right to impose legal controls if a code of conduct is judged to be ineffective. Such self-regulation can be overseen to ensure that it operates properly and as intended.

The UK's supermarkets are large and potentially powerful. They agreed in 2002 to operate a voluntary code of conduct. However, critics argue that such self-regulation may not be tough enough. This may have prompted the UK government to appoint a Groceries Code Adjudicator to oversee the relationship between supermarkets and their suppliers. The adjudicator ensures that large supermarkets treat their direct suppliers lawfully and fairly, investigates complaints and arbitrates in disputes. This appointment may have functional implications for supermarkets and lead to operational decisions that are more favourable to suppliers.

Business in focus: Ofgem and E.ON

Ofgem is the Office of Gas and Electricity Markets and regulates suppliers of gas and electricity in the UK to protect the interests of existing and future electricity and gas consumers. Consumers in the UK rarely change electricity and gas suppliers.

In 2014 Ofgem investigated one of the UK's largest energy companies – E.ON. E.ON is a German company that operates in over 30 countries and serves over 26 million customers. Its UK subsidiary, E.ON Energy, is the UK's third largest natural gas supplier. Its UK operations are based in Coventry and employ over 16,000 people. The business has interests in electricity generation, supply and distribution, as well as gas distribution and home energy support services. Ofgem reports that in 2014 E.ON held a 17 per cent market share for electricity supply in the UK and 12 per cent of the market for gas supply. It is one of six large companies that dominate the market for electricity and gas supply in the UK. There have been suggestions that the market is not sufficiently competitive.

As a result of the Ofgem investigation, and findings that it had broken energy rules, E.ON agreed in May 2014 to

pay £12 million to vulnerable customers. E.ON has also committed to compensating any customer to whom it mis-sold.

Ofgem's investigation found that E.ON failed to properly train and monitor both its own staff and those it employed through third-party telesales agencies, leading to incorrect information being provided to customers on the doorstep and over the phone, which could have misled customers. E.ON has acknowledged its failings and made considerable changes and improvements to its processes, including ceasing to use the third-party agencies involved. Had this not been the case the penalty would have been higher.

Source: Adapted from Ofgem website
www.ofgem.gov.uk

Questions

1. Explain why E.ON has considerable power to act against the best interests of consumers in the UK.

2. Do the activities of regulators always pose a threat to businesses?

The impact of regulation on UK businesses

Regulation can be a threat to businesses in that it can control and limit their ability to charge high prices and to generate maximum profits from a market. It may also represent a threat in terms of adverse publicity if a business is fined by a regulator for unacceptable behaviour, as in the case of E.ON in the Business in focus above. Regulation in some industries is becoming stricter and this may result in businesses taking a range of functional and strategic decisions to reduce the impact of any threat. At a functional level, they may appoint specialists in relevant areas to help shape

lower risk decisions. Strategically, they may opt to avoid trading in markets that are most tightly regulated. This has been one factor influencing strategic decisions made by major UK banks, for example the Lloyds Banking Group's decision to reduce their involvement in tightly regulated investment banking.

However, regulation can also provide important opportunities, most notably in providing a stable long-term environment in which businesses can operate. A recent World Economic Forum report highlighted the successful track record of the UK regulatory system in facilitating significant levels of investment. Investment in the UK's water and sewerage industry exceeded £116 billion between 1989 and 2013. Such strategic investment decisions may not have taken place in an unregulated market where the future was less certain. Unbundling access to markets as part of the regulatory process also assists in reducing barriers to entry to particular markets and provides competitive opportunities for new entrant firms.

Infrastructure

Key term

Infrastructure refers to the physical and organisational structure required to allow both society and an economy to operate effectively, e.g. transport and communication networks.

The UK's infrastructure

The UK's infrastructure is essential for its businesses to be able to operate. Without effective systems of transport, communications and energy supply, UK businesses would not be able to engage in production and supply goods and services. Infrastructure can also help to determine the competitiveness of a country's businesses. If energy, transport and communications are provided efficiently and relatively cheaply, it can help to reduce the operating costs of businesses and sharpen their price competitiveness.

The UK's infrastructure has received considerable attention recently. The UK has not invested as heavily as some other countries in its infrastructure over the past 20 to 30 years, although investment has risen since 2009 as shown in Figure 4.3. Partly as a response to this, the government prepared its infrastructure spending plan for the period to 2033.

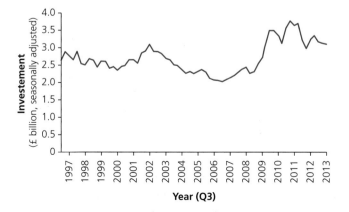

Figure 4.3 Investment in infrastructure in the UK, 1997–2013

Source: Office for National Statistics (ONS)

The National Infrastructure Plan details about £375 billion of investment in energy, transport, communications and water projects. The insurance industry also plans to spend £25 billion by 2020 using customers' payments in pension and other funds to finance this investment.

In February 2015 the Infrastructure Act became law. This Act will lead to large-scale investment into the UK economy by, for example:

- improving the funding and management of our major roads
- streamlining the planning process for major projects
- helping communities become stakeholders in renewable electricity projects
- maximising the recovery of oil and gas from UK reserves.

Examples of the UK's programme of investment in infrastructure include the Crossrail Project in London, the development of a new nuclear power station at Wylfa, North Wales and, controversially, the building of a high-speed rail line to connect London to Birmingham and, later, Manchester and Leeds. This is known as HS2.

Weblink

To find out more about the government's plans for the UK's infrastructure visit: www.gov.uk/government/organisations/infrastructure-uk

Infrastructure, opportunities and threats and decision making

Infrastructure projects create significant opportunities for businesses in the UK and overseas. There are obvious opportunities for firms in the construction industry to benefit from expenditure on building new roads, bridges and power stations. These can result in strategic decisions to expand production or to engage in joint ventures with competitors to deliver on large infrastructure projects such as Crossrail. The government's commitment to high levels of investment in the UK's infrastructure may have significant implications for senior managers in many industries, not least construction.

Other businesses in a wide range of industries are also likely to benefit from orders associated with improving the UK's infrastructure. For example, the Crossrail project has resulted in Bombardier (a Canadian multinational engineering company) receiving an order for 65 new trains for the Crossrail railway. This order will create 760 new jobs to build the trains and 80 jobs to maintain them once they are operational. Bombardier has a contract to build 60 per cent of the new trains that will be needed in the UK as it improves its infrastructure. The change in this element of the UK's political environment has enabled the company's management team to make long-term strategic decisions such as investing in new production facilities and developing new technologies for its trains.

Figure 4.4 Crossrail is Europe's largest construction project. The project will provide a new railway connection across London, has generated contracts worth over £5.5 billion for construction companies. It will create 55,000 jobs until 2018.

However, developments in infrastructure can also pose a threat to some businesses. New transport systems may result in previous ones receiving less business. The expansion of one airport (as is expected to take place at Heathrow in London) may result in fewer passengers at nearby airports. As a consequence, airlines may take decisions not to operate from these airports. The development of a new nuclear power station at Wylfa in North Wales may pose a threat for businesses engaged in transporting and supplying oil and coal to existing power stations and possibly lead to decisions about retrenchment. Finally, a significant part of the UK's infrastructure plan is to build new wind farms. These can pose threats to commercial and leisure shipping, tourism and to the local fishing industry. Research in Scotland in 2014 indicated that tourists, especially those who enjoy outdoor pursuits, are negatively affected by wind farms and are less likely to take holidays in the countryside where they are situated. This may result in a range of decisions by managers in the Scottish tourism industry, for example,

to reduce accommodation on offer in areas with a large number of wind farms.

What do you think?

Does the state of the UK's infrastructure have a major impact on strategic decisions made by foreign multinationals on whether or not to locate in this country?

The natural environment

The importance of the natural environment on the political agenda in the UK has varied since 2000. Prior to the deep recession of 2008–9, it was a significant factor influencing governmental decision making. More recently, greater priority has been given to other factors such as reducing government expenditure and promoting economic growth. As a consequence, actions and policies to protect the natural environment have become less prominent. In 2015, the government announced that simpler and smarter environment regulations will provide savings to businesses of more than £1 billion over five years. The new regulations to protect the environment are forecast to be cheaper and easier for businesses to follow. The government has reassured stakeholders that enforcement action will be targeted at companies that are not abiding by the rules.

It is easy to think of ways in which the desire of the authorities to protect the natural environment either poses threats or limits the opportunities available to businesses. For example, the opposition to fracking in many parts of the UK poses a threat to what is a new industry which could grow quickly. Hydraulic fracturing, usually shortened to fracking, is a technique designed to recover gas and oil from shale rock. Fracking is the process of drilling down into the earth before a high-pressure water mixture is directed at the rock to release the gas inside. However, there are fears about the environmental consequences of this operation and this has resulted in a temporary ban on the process in Scotland.

The activities of firms involved in the fracking industry are already tightly controlled and these controls may become stricter. The activities of many other industries are also limited by environmental considerations. Thus, house construction companies are unable to build freely in many areas such as green belt zones around London and other cities and in national parks such as the Lake District. This element of the political environment frequently increases the costs of production for businesses by making production more complex and expensive.

Environmental opportunities and decision making

The government's desire to protect the natural environment does create many opportunities for businesses. Laws designed to protect the environment, which we cover later in this chapter on pages 79–81, create work for businesses that provide expertise and advice on how to comply with them. For example, RSK plc was founded in 1989 to provide advice to other businesses on environmental matters. Since that time it has grown quickly from its UK base to employ more than 700 staff and to operate throughout Europe. The growing emphasis on the natural environment in countries across the EU has seen RSK plc expand by opening branch offices in nine European countries. The laws also provide opportunities for businesses that supply equipment to allow firms to comply with relevant legislation, for example filters to reduce air pollution.

Creating renewable sources of energy is a major growth industry throughout the EU as governments seek to meet targets for reducing emissions of carbon. The government in the UK is encouraging investment by private businesses into wind farms and the creation of lagoons in coastal locations to harness tidal power to generate electricity. Six lagoons are planned for the UK with the potential to generate 8 per cent of the UK's electricity needs. The lagoons will require an investment of £30 billion but will have enormous implications for a wide range of other businesses. The company behind the scheme has decided to create a separate public company to handle this project, possibly because of its scale and complexity.

Developing renewable energy sources will create enormous amounts of work for the firms involved, but will represent a threat to other energy suppliers, particularly businesses that generate energy by burning fossil fuels such as coal, gas and oil. The government support for the use of tidal power to generate energy is part of its policy to increase the proportion of the UK's electricity supply that is supplied from renewable sources. The government's targets are shown in Figure 4.5.

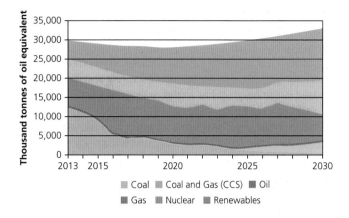

Figure 4.5 How the UK's electricity will be generated during the period 2013–30

Source: Department for Energy and Climate Change

International trade

The UK government is a keen supporter of international trade recognising that it brings many benefits to the UK, not least revenue and employment. It operates a number of initiatives to support businesses in selling goods and services in international markets. Many of these are offered through UK Trade and Investment (UKTI), a government department that works with UK businesses to help them to succeed in international markets. UKTI supports UK exporters in a variety of ways.

- It organises trade fairs overseas to promote UK exports to potential buyers.
- It is behind the 'Open to Export' initiative which brings exporting businesses together to provide mutual help and also provides relevant training.
- It provides financial support for exporters – in 2014 it provided financial support for export contracts worth over £1 billion.
- UKTI works closely with other agencies that assist business and enterprise to ensure that exporters receive integrated support from the UK government. For example, it cooperates with UK Export Finance who can provide the necessary financial support and guarantees against non-payment.

Weblink

To find out more about the UK Trade and Investment (UKTI) visit:
www.gov.uk/government/organisations/uk-trade-investment

Business in focus: Dryden Aqua Ltd

Dryden Aqua Ltd is a marine biological company specialising in innovative and sustainable water treatment technologies. Dryden Aqua's manufacturing and research is based in Edinburgh. It has a sales revenue of £5 million. Its flagship product is its Activated Filter Media (AFM), which is used in water filters as a highly effective alternative to sand. It removes harmful organisms and toxins from water.

Support from UKTI has helped Dryden Aqua to increase its exports substantially and 90 per cent of sales of AFM are now to overseas markets. Support can take a number of forms including protection against non-payment.

1. Export success in Bangladesh

Howard Dryden attended a seminar organised by UKTI in Dhaka, Bangladesh in March 2013. During his visit he was briefed by UKTI on the local business environment and opportunities in Bangladesh that were not widely known about. Dryden Aqua has since secured a £100,000 contract with Square Pharmaceuticals for water treatment of all the water entering its facility.

2. More success in the United Arab Emirates

Dryden Aqua has also worked with UKTI to build up its business in the United Arab Emirates (UAE). The company has sold:

- swimming pool systems to His Highness Sheikh Mohammed bin Rashid Al Maktoum, Vice President and Prime Minister of the UAE and Ruler of Dubai
- an AFM treatment system for the aquarium at the iconic, Burj Al Arab Jumeirah Hotel
- a water treatment system for the 5-star Atlantis hotel complex.

Howard Dryden said:

'We have been going to Dubai for around ten years, several times with UKTI's support. We have already provided our systems into high-profile locations and we're now helping to design the new zoo being built there. Around 80 per cent of the world's desalination projects are happening in the Gulf region so we see this as an area of huge potential growth for our business. We find that UKTI can open doors for us with people it would otherwise be hard to access and we shall continue to work with them as we expand in and beyond these markets.'

Source: Adapted from the UKTI website
www.gov.uk

Questions

1. Explain the possible difficulties Dryden Aqua may have encountered in exporting its products for the first time.

2. Is providing contacts with possible customers and partners overseas the best way that UKTI can help UK exporters to exploit opportunities in overseas markets?

The UK economy is very 'open' which means that it relies heavily on trade and imports and exports a high proportion of its production. For this reason, the international trade dimension of the political environment is important. This affects all businesses, whether or not they export, because foreign businesses seek to sell their products in the UK's domestic market.

Key term

Globalisation is the trend for many markets to become worldwide in scope.

The volume of trade has increased as **globalisation** has taken hold and, despite the setback caused by the recession following the global financial crisis in 2008, the volume of global trade has generally risen more quickly than the value of the world's GDP. This is illustrated in Figure 4.6 and means that international trade is steadily becoming a more important component of the political environment in which businesses operate.

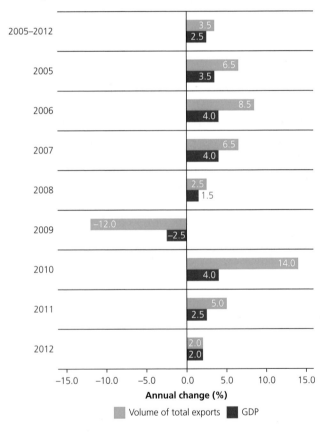

Figure 4.6 Percentage changes in the volume of global exports and value of GDP, 2005–12

Source: World Trade Organisation

The trend towards the globalisation of markets has been one factor increasing the volume of world trade. This has been encouraged by a series of decisions by governments and the UK government has played its part in these decisions. We shall now consider two key developments that have helped to shape international markets for goods and services.

Greater freedom of trade

The World Trade Organisation (WTO) was established in 1995 as a forum for trade negotiations and to resolve trade disputes. In March 2015, the WTO had 160 countries as members and it plays a prominent role in promoting international trade.

Lowering trade barriers is one of the most obvious means the WTO uses to encourage trade. The barriers concerned include customs duties (or tariffs) and measures such as import bans or quotas that restrict quantities selectively. From time to time, other barriers to trade such as bureaucracy and exchange rate policies have also been discussed at WTO meetings. The WTO focuses on lowering tariffs (customs duties) on imported goods. As a result of its efforts industrial countries' tariff rates on industrial goods have fallen steadily to less than 4 per cent.

Although the actions of the WTO have attracted much opposition from pressure groups, it has encouraged nations to take political decisions aimed at freeing trade and promoting economic growth. The current round of negotiations at Doha have lasted for more than 13 years without a clear and agreed outcome, but this should not detract from the WTO's achievements.

Weblink

To find out more about the WTO visit: www.wto.org/index.htm

The growth of the European Union

The European Union (EU) currently has 28 member states constituting a market of over 505 million people – larger than the markets of Japan and the US added together. In 2004, the EU expanded to 25 states with the entry of Cyprus, the Czech Republic, Estonia, Hungary, Latvia, Lithuania, Malta, Poland, the Slovak Republic and Slovenia. In 2007, Bulgaria and Romania joined and finally Croatia became a member in 2013. Despite recent financial difficulties in the eurozone countries, Turkey has made an application to join the EU, while some former Balkan states such as Kosovo and Serbia are engaged in discussions.

The impact of increased trade

The reduction of barriers to international trade and the enlargement of the EU offer businesses considerable opportunities. It is easier for UK businesses to sell their products in European markets than in the past. The expansion of the EU offers UK businesses unrestricted access to 105 million additional consumers as the EU population increased to 505 million. Firms expect to achieve increased sales and perhaps to benefit from economies of scale in supplying these new and extended markets. Some high-quality UK products such as luxury cars (Land Rover and Jaguar, for example), fashion clothing (Burberry) and whisky (from Scottish distilleries) have sold well in global markets. Jaguar Land Rover has responded to these and other global opportunities by making a number of strategic decisions including the following.

● Investing £240 million over a five-year period in building a factory in Itatiaia in Brazil.
● Developing its factory in Solihull to produce new Land Rover and Jaguar models for sale in global markets throughout the world. This will involve an investment of £1.7 billion and will create 1,700 jobs.

What do you think?

Jaguar Land Rover's decision to invest £1.7 billion in new production facilities at its Solihull factory was a strategic one. What types of functional decisions might it also have to make to carry through its expansion plans?

Furthermore, UK businesses have chosen to take the opportunity given by the expansion of the EU to make decisions to locate in countries such as Poland and Hungary to benefit from lower costs and, initially at least, fewer controls on business activity. The states of Eastern Europe have proved particularly attractive to manufacturers seeking to expand or transfer their European productive capacity to lower cost locations.

There are, of course, downsides to the increased freedom to trade and the expansion of the EU. Greater competition is likely to appear in some industries where the relatively undeveloped economies of eastern and southern Europe have an advantage. The French car producer Renault bought the Romanian car maker Dacia in 1999 and started producing Europe's cheapest cars. Its factory operates at 95 per cent capacity, and manufactured 512,000 vehicles in 2014. The success of this project has significant implications for businesses in the motor vehicle manufacturing industry, including those based in the UK.

The freeing of global trade has brought other threats. Highly sophisticated foreign companies, some with access to relatively cheap sources of labour are posing a real threat in domestic UK markets. UK consumers are familiar with the products supplied by Starbucks, Toyota and Samsung, but will increasingly see goods and services supplied by other companies from developing countries such as China and India. Lenovo is an example of a successful Chinese technology company; many UK retailers have taken decisions to sell its products.

The threat from overseas takes another form as well. Many UK businesses have been taken over by foreign companies seeking a foothold in the EU market or by foreign governments (such as that of China) looking for profitable investments. Cadbury, Jaguar Land Rover and Asda are among the famous UK enterprises that are owned by foreign companies. The number of foreign owned businesses in the UK decreased by 3 per cent between 2009 and 2012, but their contribution to UK GDP increased by approximately 19 per cent. This was due to a 10 per cent fall in the number of very small businesses (employing fewer than ten people), while there was an increase in the number of business with over ten employees that were foreign owned. In fact, 10 per cent of foreign-owned businesses had at least 250 people in employment compared with only 0.3 per cent for UK-owned businesses. Decision makers in large UK public companies will be aware that takeover bids are a possibility.

The legal environment

The law is a framework of rules governing the way in which our society operates. These rules apply to businesses as well as individuals. The legal framework affects businesses in a number of ways impacting on almost all areas of business activity. Marketing, production, employment, relationships with customers and competitors and even the establishment of the business itself are examples of business operations influenced by the law.

We shall consider three elements of the legal environment:

- competition
- the employment of labour
- environmental issues.

Study tip

You don't need to understand all the detail of the laws in the areas mentioned here but just require a broad understanding of the scope and effects of UK and EU law.

The law relating to competition

Competition law in the UK is intended to protect businesses and consumers from the effects of anti-competitive practices. The UK government (along with most other governments) believes that free and fair competition in markets brings many benefits. The government set out the importance of competition to the economy in 2001.

'Vigorous competition between firms is the lifeblood of strong and effective markets. Competition helps consumers get a good deal. It encourages firms to innovate by reducing slack, putting downward pressure on costs and providing incentives for the efficient organisation of production. As such, competition is a central driver for productivity growth in the economy, and hence the UK's international competitiveness.'

Source: Department of Trade and Industry

Businesses operating in the UK are subject to both UK and EU competition law. UK legislation relates to the activities of businesses in this country, whereas EU laws are designed to deal with uncompetitive business practices that have an impact across more than one member state. The major competition laws in the UK are:

- the Competition Act, 1998
- the Enterprise Act, 2002
- the Enterprise and Regulatory Reform Act, 2013.

(We look at these in a little more detail later in this section on page 76.)

Competition law in the UK operates in three main areas.

1. **Cartel activity**. Cartels involve two or more businesses working together to limit the extent of competition that exists in a market; they are considered to be a serious form of **anti-competitive practice**. Cartels are agreements between businesses not to compete with each other, for example on price, discount levels, credit terms or in respect of particular

customers or in particular areas. The outcome is that consumers will be disadvantaged, primarily because they will have to pay a higher price (agreed by the cartel) than would otherwise be the case. In addition, the economy will be damaged by a lack of competitiveness amongst its businesses.

2. Abuse of a **dominant market position**. The European Court has defined a dominant market position as: '… a position of economic strength enjoyed by an undertaking which enables it to prevent effective competition being maintained on the relevant market by affording it the power to behave to an appreciable extent independently of its competitors, customers and ultimately of its consumers.' Such markets can be national or local as well as EU-wide. Abuse of such a position can take a number of forms including:

   - imposing unfair purchase or selling prices or other unfair trading conditions
   - limiting production, markets or technical development to the prejudice of consumers
   - imposing unfair and inconsistent terms on different trading partners.

3. Other anti-competitive practices. These could include agreements with suppliers not to sell below certain prices, limiting production to drive up prices, agreeing not to sell to a competitor's customers, etc. This also includes **mergers** and **takeovers** which may be harmful to the competitive process in markets.

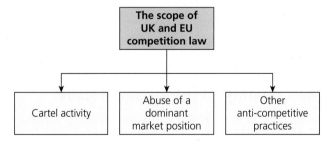

Figure 4.7 The extent of competition law

Mergers and takeovers

Takeovers and mergers have the potential to provide businesses with a high degree of market power as they create larger enterprises. They can also lead to a reduction in the degree of competition within a market. The competition authorities in the UK are required

to assess whether a merger or takeover should be prohibited on the basis of whether it can be expected to lead to 'a substantial lessening of competition'. In the UK, the primary responsibility for the regulation of mergers and takeovers lies with the Competition and Markets Authority (CMA). Mergers will be assessed by the CMA if:

- the business being taken over exceeds a given size (a sales revenue exceeding £70 million), or
- the newly merged business would control 25 per cent or more of its market.

Key UK competition laws

The legislative framework for the UK's competition policy is provided by the Competition Act 1998, the Enterprise Act 2002 and the Enterprise and Regulatory Reform Act 2013.

1. The Competition Act, 1998

This Act prohibits cartels and abuses of dominant market position. It also outlaws concerted practice, for example when businesses agree to divide up a market and not to compete in each other's 'part' of the market.

The penalties for breaching this Act can be severe. Businesses may be fined up to 10 per cent of their worldwide sales revenue if they enter into an anti-competitive agreement or abuse a dominant market position.

2. The Enterprise Act, 2002

This Act amended the Competition Act and strengthened the power of the UK authorities to deal with anti-competitive practices and market dominance. The Act had a number of important provisions:

- It placed a clear focus on the impact of the business's activities on the degree of competition. Practices were now judged as to whether they created a 'substantial lessening of competition' rather than whether they were 'in the public interest'.
- It imposed tougher penalties on those involved in cartels by criminalising their activities. Directors or other people involved may be fined or sent to prison for up to five years if involved in cartel activity. Company directors may also be disqualified from being a director for up to 15 years.
- It empowered consumer organisations to make complaints (known as 'supercomplaints') to the CMA about markets that are not working well for consumers.
- There are greater opportunities for victims of anti-competitive behaviour to gain redress. Consumer bodies will be able to make claims on behalf of individuals who have suffered. This means that businesses may be sued for damages by third parties that have been harmed by their anti-competitive actions.
- The assessment of mergers is to be less influenced by politicians and more independent.

3. Enterprise and Regulatory Reform Act, 2013

This Act was wide ranging including the creation of the Green Investment Bank, established with the aim of providing financial support for environmentally-friendly business practices. It also simplified and strengthened laws relating to equality in employment. Its main provisions relating to competition were as follows:

- It created the CMA, bringing together the Competition Commission and the competition work of the Office of Fair Trading. Thus, a single organisation became responsible for competition policy.

- It made it quicker and simpler for businesses, especially small and medium-sized enterprises, to make legal challenges to anti-competitive behaviour.
- It also made it easier for consumers and small businesses who have suffered loss due to anti-competitive behaviour to obtain redress.

Weblink

To find out more about the CMA visit:
www.gov.uk/government/organisations/competition-and-markets-authority

EU competition policy

The UK's competition policy is integrated with that operated by the EU. UK law applies if the scope of the anti-competitive behaviour is limited to the UK, and EU competition law applies if its impact extends across Europe. The scope of the law is similar for both authorities.

For example, in the case of mergers and takeovers, the EU has jurisdiction over those which have a 'Community (or EU) dimension'. The potential impact of mergers and takeovers is determined by a sales revenue test similar to that applied by the UK competition authorities. In 2009 Kraft, an American food producer, made a takeover bid for the UK chocolate manufacturer, Cadbury. The size and scope of Kraft and Cadbury's operations across the EU meant that Kraft's bid was referred to the EU authorities, rather than those in the UK. In 2010 the European Commission approved the takeover on behalf of the EU, subject to Cadbury selling off its operations in Poland and Romania.

Laws relating to the labour market

Those laws in the UK that relate to the labour market can be divided into two categories:

- those that relate to individual employees
- those that are collective and apply to groups of employees such as trade unions.

Business in focus: CMA launches inquiry into banks

The Competition and Markets Authority (CMA) is to launch a full-scale investigation into the operation of the UK's banking market which generates annual revenues estimated to be £10 billion. The inquiry will investigate whether this market is sufficiently competitive to provide an acceptable variety of products and standards of service to customers, especially to individuals and small businesses.

The inquiry will focus on the operations of the UK's four largest banks (Lloyds Banking Group, Barclays, Royal Bank of Scotland and HSBC). These four banks dominate the UK market holding around 80 per cent of the accounts of personal customers and small businesses. This dominant market position has not changed noticeably since 2000. The inquiry may result in a decision to break them up if the market is found not to be a competitive one.

Creating a larger number of smaller banks could create a more competitive market, offering customers greater variety of products and improved standards of services. The inquiry has been supported by consumer groups

such as Which? as well as those smaller banks already in the market. Paul Pester, Chief Executive Officer of TSB, believes that 'Customers have been crying out for a root and-branch investigation like this for years. The big four banks have had a stranglehold on the market for too long.'

The Chief Executive of the CMA, Alex Chisholm acknowledged that the decision to hold an inquiry had not been universally popular; although most groups consulted supported the move, it was opposed by the Institute of Directors and the UK's 'big four' banks. The investigation is expected to last for 18 months.

Source: Adapted from the *Guardian*, 6 November 2014

Questions

1. Explain why this investigation may represent both a threat and an opportunity for the UK's banks.

2. This investigation may produce a result which reduces the profits of the UK's major banks. Is this a good outcome?

Figure 4.8 UK employment legislation

Individual labour law

This aspect of employment legislation refers to the rights and obligations of individual employees. The amount and scope of individual labour law has increased in recent years, in part encouraged by the growing influence of the EU on business matters in the UK.

A number of the most important Acts relating to individuals in employment are explained as follows:

- **Working Time Regulations, 1998**. This EU legislation (hence the term 'regulation') set a limit on the hours that employees can be required to work each week to 48 hours. Employees can opt to work longer hours if they wish, but employers

cannot insist that they do so without inserting an appropriate clause in their contract of employment. The regulations also gave employees an entitlement to four weeks' paid annual leave.

- **The National Minimum Wage Act, 1998**. This highly publicised Act came into force on 1 April 1999. The key features of this legislation are:
  - a general hourly minimum wage rate – £6.50 an hour from October 2014
  - a minimum level of £5.13 for 18–21 year olds
  - all part-time and temporary workers must be paid the minimum wage.
- The penalties for employers who do not pay the minimum wage were increased substantially in 2014.

● **Employment Equality (Age) Regulations, 2006**. The main theme of this EU inspired law is that it will be unlawful to discriminate against workers under the age of 65 on the grounds of age.

  ● Making someone redundant or barring workers from training or promotion because they are too old (or too young) will be illegal.

  ● As they approach 65, workers will have to be given six months' notice that their employer wants them to give up their job and retire.

● **Equalities Act, 2010**. This act replaced a number of earlier anti-discrimination laws in the UK (such as the Disability Discrimination Act) to simplify and extend legislation in this area. The Act relates to nine protected characteristics which cannot be used as a reason to treat people differently or unlawfully. Each person in the UK is protected by this Act, as everybody has one or more of these characteristics. The protected characteristics are:

  ● age
  ● disability
  ● race
  ● gender reassignment
  ● marriage and civil partnership
  ● religion or belief
  ● pregnancy or maternity
  ● sex
  ● sexual orientation.

This Act makes unfair treatment unlawful in the workplace, in education and when supplying goods and services.

● **Enterprise and Regulatory Reform Act, 2013**. This law made a number of changes to employment law. It imposed additional charges on employees wishing to take employers to industrial tribunals in disputes over employment. It limited the maximum payment for unfair dismissal to the higher of £74,200 or one year's gross pay.

Collective labour law

This group of laws apply to the operation of industrial relations and **collective bargaining** as well as the activities of **trade unions**. Employers and employees are likely to negotiate on a variety of matters. These negotiations may include items such as working conditions and other workplace rules, basic rates of pay, overtime pay, hours of work, holidays, sick leave, retirement benefits and health-care benefits.

For many years, the law in the UK did not play a significant role in employer–employee relationships. However, this philosophy was changed when the Conservative governments of the 1980s and early 1990s passed a series of Acts intended to restrict the power of trade unions. Some examples of these laws, as well as a later one granting more powers to trade unions, are described below:

● **Employment Act, 1980**. Under this Act employers were no longer obliged to negotiate with unions – many unions were derecognised as a consequence. It also restricted picketing to employees' own place of work, thereby outlawing 'secondary picketing'. Closed shops (where only those in a specific trade union were able to be employed) were only permitted if supported by at least 80 per cent of the workforce in a secret ballot.

● **Trade Union Act, 1984**. This legislation made a secret ballot of employees a legal requirement before industrial action was lawful.

● **Trade Union Reform and Employment Rights Act, 1993**. Unions were required to give employers a minimum of seven days' notice before taking official industrial action. It also abolished wages councils and minimum pay rates.

● **Employment Relations Act, 1999**. Under this Act a trade union with a membership exceeding 50 per cent of the employees in any particular business can demand union recognition and the right to introduce collective bargaining.

Key terms

Collective bargaining is the process of negotiating the terms of employment between an employer and a group of workers.

Trade unions are organisations of workers established to protect and improve the economic position and working conditions of its members.

Unfair dismissal

Many countries have a legal definition of unfair dismissal. Unfair dismissal is the termination of a worker's contract of employment without a legal reason. In the UK, legislation relating to unfair dismissal only relates to workers once they have been in a particular job for one year or more. There are a limited number of reasons why an employee might be dismissed fairly:

- where a job no longer exists – this is redundancy
- gross misconduct – examples of this reason include theft from the employer or behaving violently at work
- failing to carry out duties in 'a satisfactory manner'
- another substantial reason, for example the ending of a temporary contract.

All other reasons for dismissal are considered unfair. Employees who think they have been unfairly dismissed can claim compensation by taking their case to an industrial tribunal.

Health and safety legislation

Health and safety legislation has been enacted to discourage dangerous practices by businesses and to protect the workforce. The legislation in the UK is designed to prevent accidents in the workplace, and has developed steadily over the last 30 years.

The main Act in the UK is the Health and Safety Act of 1974. This is an example of delegated legislation whereby parliament gives responsibility to government departments to update the scope of the legislation as necessary. This process avoids any particular aspect of legislation taking up too much of parliament's time. The Health and Safety at Work Act gives employers a legal obligation 'to ensure that they safeguard all their employees' health, safety and welfare at work'.

Environmental legislation

The media takes a great interest in business activities in relation to the environment. When firms are found to be guilty of some act of pollution adverse publicity is likely to follow. Society expects higher standards of environmental performance now than in the past.

The costs of polluting the environment

Businesses are acutely aware of their private costs, that is, the costs of production they have to pay, such as expenses for raw materials and wages. These are relatively easy to calculate and form part of the assessment of profitability. However, environmental pressure groups and others have pressed for businesses to acknowledge the costs they create for other groups in society – the external costs of production. Noise, congestion, air and water pollution all impose costs on other individuals and groups in society.

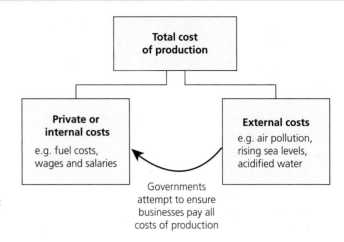

Figure 4.9 Internal and external costs of production

The total costs of production equal internal or private costs plus external costs borne by third parties as shown in Figure 4.9. By ensuring that firms pay all the costs associated with the production of a product, governments can avoid what is termed 'market failure'. Laws relating to the environment have a role to play in achieving this.

The government has passed a series of Acts of Parliament designed to protect the environment. Two acts are of particular importance:

1. **The Environmental Protection Act, 1991.** This introduced the notion of integrated pollution control recognising that to control only a single source of pollution is worthless as damage to one part of the environment means damage to it all. This Act requires businesses to minimise pollution as a whole.

2. **The Environment Act, 1995.** This Act established the Environment Agency with a brief of coordinating and overseeing environmental protection. The Act also covered the control of pollution, the conservation of the environment and made provision for restoring contaminated land and abandoned mines.

The government imposes fines on firms that breach legislation relating to the protection of the environment. These are intended to force firms to bear the full costs of their production (including external costs), although environmental pressure groups and other critics believe that the sums are not sufficient to deter major businesses with annual budgets of billions of pounds. The government also attempts to encourage 'greener' methods of production through the provision of grants.

It created the Carbon Trust, which since April 2001 has given capital grants to firms who invest in energy-saving technologies and sustainable methods of production. The intention is to slow the onset of global warming by reducing emissions of carbon dioxide. In a similar vein, the UK government has established the Green Investment Bank which is the first bank of its type in the world. It was created in 2012 and provided with an initial £3.8 billion of public funds. It uses this finance to back environmentally-friendly projects and to attract other private sector capital into developing the UK's green economy.

EU and international environmental laws

The EU issues regulations and directives related to environmental protection that must be implemented into national laws by the 28 member states. This legislation includes the following aspects which can impact on the activities of businesses:

- climate change
- air, water and land pollution
- waste management
- protection of nature, species and biodiversity
- noise pollution.

Some UK environmental laws come from international agreements. International treaties seek to regulate diverse environmental matters including climate change, access to environmental information and participation in environmental decision making. New international agreements on the environment may be negotiated as the consequences of climate change become increasingly apparent. Negotiations led by the United Nations are under way to develop a new international climate change agreement that will cover all countries. It is hoped that the new agreement will be adopted at the Paris climate conference in December 2015 and implemented from 2020.

Business in focus: Royal Dutch Shell to pay £55 million in compensation

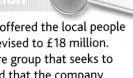

Royal Dutch Shell, the multinational oil exploration, refining and distribution company, has lost a court case concerning two major oil spillages at its operations in the delta of the Niger river in Nigeria. The oil spills occurred in 2008 and 2009 and devastated the lives of 15,600 local residents, not least by polluting waterways and land to the detriment of fishermen and farmers.

A compensation payment of £55 million has been agreed by the company's Nigerian subsidiary Shell Petroleum Development Company of Nigeria (SPDC). Each local resident will receive a payment of approximately £2,100 whilst £20 million will be paid to the community as a whole. For a community in which the minimum wage is around £60 a month and where 70 per cent of the population live below the poverty line, these payments will be life changing.

Royal Dutch Shell had originally offered the local people £4,000 as compensation, later revised to £18 million. Amnesty International, a pressure group that seeks to protect human rights, has alleged that the company intentionally underestimated the spills in an attempt to minimise compensation payments. Royal Dutch Shell has denied this.

Questions

1. Explain why forcing Royal Dutch Shell to pay £55 million is an appropriate means of combating damage to the environment.
2. Do you think that financial penalties such as this are a good way to alter the behaviour of large and powerful multinational companies such as Royal Dutch Shell?

The legal environment and decision making

Changes in the legal environment have the potential to affect both functional and strategic decision making within a business. Clearly how a business responds to a change in the law will depend upon a number of factors including:

- the type of business and its corporate objectives
- the nature of the legal change.

However, it is possible to argue that in some circumstances, the effects of legal change could impact more upon functions within the business, rather than the entire organisation. For example, the Equalities Act of 2010 prohibits businesses from discriminating against employees on the basis of nine 'protected' characteristics. It would be expected that a business's HR department would revise policies and approaches in the light of this new legislation. Thus, it would provoke decision making at a functional level. In the same way, some environmental legislation could be expected to have the most significant impact on the operations function within a business requiring it to develop new methods of production that reduce pollution, incorporate the use of renewable resources and that are sustainable.

UK and EU competition policy, on the other hand, may have more strategic implications. Recent changes in UK competition legislation have placed greater emphasis on whether or not business activities result in a 'substantial lessening of competition' and make it easier for those affected by anti-competitive practices to seek legal redress. This may require businesses to make significant long-term changes to their business models and require strategic decisions to do so. In 2014, it was announced that the American technology company Google was subject to an investigation in the USA relating to abuse of its monopoly position in some markets. If the company is found to have abused its position, it could face heavy fines and would have to make strategic decisions about its business practices.

Conclusion

Although some aspects of legal change may be most likely to result in functional responses, it may be that changes in the political and legal environments are more frequently long-term in nature. A new law, such as the Enterprise and Regulatory Reform Act of 2013, is likely to impact on the behaviour of businesses for many years until new legislation replaces it. This is most unlikely to occur until, and unless, the legislation proves to be ineffective or circumstances change requiring the law to be updated. Similarly, changes in the political environment can be expected to persist until a new government with different policies is elected – this will most probably be several years in the future. Thus, the approach of the previous coalition government to increasing private and public expenditure on the country's infrastructure will have long-term implications.

The long-term nature of changes in these environments is significant for decision making in businesses. It is more likely to provoke long-term responses from businesses and therefore impact on strategic as well as functional decisions. For example, most firms engaging in major infrastructure projects, such as the new high-speed train line from London to the north (HS2), will need to make long-term commitments that affect all functions within the business. These are strategic decisions.

ASSESSMENT ACTIVITIES

(a) Knowledge check questions

1 State two areas of government policy which might shape the political environment in which UK businesses operate.

2 What is meant by the term 'enterprise-friendly business environment'?

3 List two ways in which the UK government promotes enterprise.

4 State two actions that regulators may take to protect the interests of consumers.

5 What is meant by the term 'infrastructure'?

6 State two ways in which the UK government's policies to protect the natural environment might affect the activities of businesses.

7 List one opportunity available to UK businesses as a result of the expansion of the European Union after 2004.

8 State the benefits that stakeholders of UK businesses may receive from the government's competition policy.

9 What are the three main areas in which competition law operates?

10 What is meant by the term 'unfair dismissal'?

(b) Short answer questions

1 Explain one possible implication for UK businesses of the government's policy of creating an enterprise-friendly environment for businesses.   (4 marks)

2 Explain one reason why the UK and EU authorities have decided to regulate the activities of banks more closely.   (5 marks)

3 Explain why the UK government has implemented decisions to improve the quality and extent of the country's infrastructure.   (5 marks)

4 Analyse the possible implications of making the UK more open to international trade for a small food manufacturer that currently only sells within the UK market.   (9 marks)

(c) Data response question

UK cement market

The producers of cement have received a lot of attention from the competition authorities in the UK. This may be because the supply side is concentrated in the hands of a few businesses: five large multinational companies account for more than 90 per cent of the UK's cement market. In 2014, the Competition Commission (the Competition and Markets Authority's predecessor) produced a report following an investigation. The investigation revealed that profit margins in the industry had been stable, or in some cases had risen, despite a sharp fall in sales following the recession. As a result, one producer, Lafarge Tarmac, was ordered to sell a cement factory to allow another firm to enter the market and the industry was instructed to reduce the flow of information about prices and production between the different companies producing cement.

The UK's political and legal environments are changing in a number of ways. The UK government is committed to improving the quality and extent of the UK's infrastructure. More than 200 projects in rail, road, local transport, broadband and waste management started construction during 2014–15 and infrastructure investment will total £375 billion by 2035. Many of the projects are very complex and large, such as Crossrail (which will cost £14.8 billion) and several construction companies are working together on them. Construction companies bid competitively for the projects and may require large amounts of human and other resources for the duration of the work. For example, they may require the services of specialist companies on matters such as health and safety. Subcontracting is common on projects such as Crossrail to help to meet strict deadlines.

At the same time diverse employees are receiving greater protection in the workplace from anti-discrimination laws and the government is encouraging the recruitment of diverse workforces which offer many benefits to businesses.

Questions

1 Explain two possible effects on public companies of the UK government's anti-discrimination legislation, such as the Equalities Act.   (6 marks)

2 Analyse the possible consequences for cement producers operating in the UK of a new entrant to the market and a reduction in information flows.   (9 marks)

3 Are the improvements to the UK's infrastructure most likely to impact on functional or strategic decision making within construction companies working in the UK?   (15 marks)

(d) Essays

1 'The effects of the UK's competition laws are only significant for large businesses.' Do you agree with this statement? Justify your view.   (25 marks)

2 To what extent can globalisation be expected to be the dominant force shaping the political environment for all UK businesses over the next ten years?   (25 marks)

5 Analysing the external environment: economic change

Introduction

This chapter examines the effects of changes in the economic environment in which businesses operate. It considers the ways in which changes in a range of economic factors such as inflation, exchange rates and gross domestic product (GDP) may impact on strategic and functional decision making.

It also covers the ways in which government policies (including fiscal, monetary and trade policies) have affected decision making within businesses.

Finally, the chapter examines why globalisation is occurring and its importance, along with emerging economies such as China and India, for businesses.

What you need to know by the end of this chapter:

● the impact of changes in the UK and the global economic environment (including economic factors such as GDP, taxation, exchange rates, inflation, fiscal and monetary policy, and open trade and protectionism) on strategic and functional decision making within a business
● how to understand economic data, interpret changes in economic data for the UK, the European Union and globally, and the implications of such changes for business
● the reasons for and importance of the greater globalisation of business
● the importance of emerging economies for business.

The economic environment

A business takes strategic and functional decisions to achieve its corporate objectives. Thus, its managers may decide to enter new markets, takeover smaller competitors or to reduce the selling price of certain products in pursuit of a corporate objective of growth. These decisions will all be influenced, however, by the economic environment within which the business trades. Figure 5.1 summarises the major economic forces that might impact upon decision making. The diagram also emphasises some of the interrelationships that exist between the elements that comprise the economic environment for businesses.

Factors such as exchange rates, interest rates, inflation and government economic policies combine to shape the economic environment within which businesses operate. Thus, if an economy experiences low and possibly even negative rates of inflation (as many are at the time of writing), governments will be likely to reduce interest rates and possibly increase their own spending to offset the effects. The economic environment will be the cumulative effect of these factors.

Businesses also determine their own economic environments to some extent. The strategic decisions taken by businesses in response to opportunities and threats that appear in the economic environment also determine that environment. For example, a decision to expand production by a number of businesses because an economy's **gross domestic product (GDP)** is rising quickly may contribute to further, and possibly more rapid, rises in GDP.

Study tip

You encountered some of the elements that make up a business's economic environment when studying the external environment of business in Year 1. These were income levels (including GDP) and interest rates. It may be worth refreshing your memory on these topics by re-reading the relevant parts of Chapter 3 in *AQA A-level Business 1*.

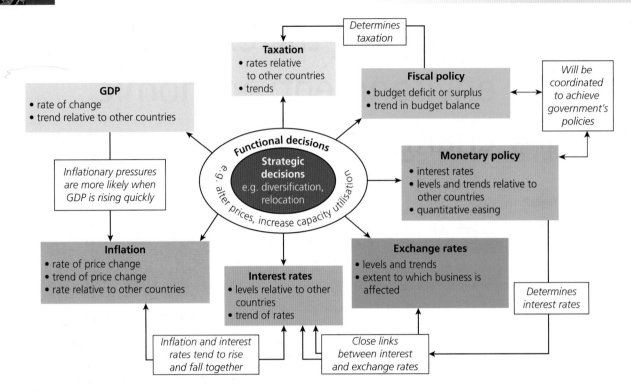

Figure 5.1 Decision making in an integrated economic environment

Gross domestic product (GDP)

All countries suffer fluctuations in the level of activity within their economies. At times, spending, production and employment all rise; during other periods the opposite is true. The value of a country's output over a period of time is measured by its GDP – this figure is determined by the level of economic activity. A rising level of economic activity will be reflected in a higher level of GDP.

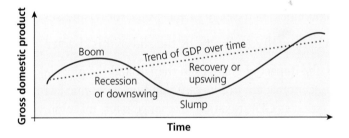

Figure 5.2 The stages of the business cycle and changing levels of GDP

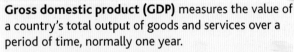

Gross domestic product (GDP) measures the value of a country's total output of goods and services over a period of time, normally one year.

A **recession** is a period of at least six months (or two quarters) during which an economy's GDP falls.

The business cycle describes the regular fluctuations in economic activity (and thus GDP) that occur over time in all economies. Figure 5.2 illustrates a typical business cycle.

Business cycles generally have four stages:

● **Recovery** or **upswing** as the economy recovers from a slump; production and employment both begin to increase. Consumers will generally spend more as they are more confident in job security. Initially, businesses may respond cautiously through functional decisions to meet rising demand by using spare capacity: businesses may utilise idle factories, offices and other assets. As business confidence increases firms may take strategic decisions to invest in new non-current assets such as factories, machinery and vehicles. Employees experience less difficulty in finding jobs and wages may begin to rise.

- A **boom** follows with high levels of production and expenditure by firms, consumers and the government. Booms are normally characterised by prosperity and confidence in the business community. Increasing numbers of firms will take strategic decisions to invest in non-current assets. However, many sectors of the economy will experience pressure during booms. Skilled workers may become scarce and firms competing for workers may offer higher wages. Simultaneously, as the economy approaches maximum production, shortages and bottlenecks will occur as insufficient raw materials and components exist to meet demand. Inevitably, this will result in their prices rising. The combination of rising wages and rising prices of raw materials and components will create inflation. It is the existence of inflation that usually leads to the end of a boom.

- A **recession** occurs when incomes and output start to fall and do so continuously for at least six months. Rising prices of labour and materials mean that businesses face increased costs of production. This will begin to reduce profits. In such circumstances the UK government has tended to reduce interest rates in an attempt to avoid GDP falling further. Falling demand from consumers and profits are likely to lead to any plans to invest in new factories and offices being delayed or abandoned. The amount of spare capacity within the economy will rise. Some businesses will fail and the level of bankruptcies is likely to increase.

- A **slump** may follow a recession. An economy may enter the upswing stage of the business cycle without moving through a slump period. Governments may take action to encourage this through fiscal and monetary policy by, for example, increasing their own spending and lowering interest rates. A slump sees production at its lowest while unemployment is high.

Figure 5.2 illustrates a smooth and regular business cycle in operation. In reality, the change in GDP is likely to be irregular as economic cycles of different duration and intensity operate simultaneously. This is illustrated in Figure 5.3. GDP is a major influence on the economic environment: as the level and rate of change of GDP alters, businesses can expect to see substantial changes in their trading conditions.

Figure 5.3 shows changes in the UK's level of GDP over a 12-year period in 'real' terms. This means that the data has been adjusted to remove the effects of inflation.

What do you think?

Is it a better idea to start a new business in a recession (when resources may be cheaper) or when GDP is rising strongly and demand for products is likely to be greater?

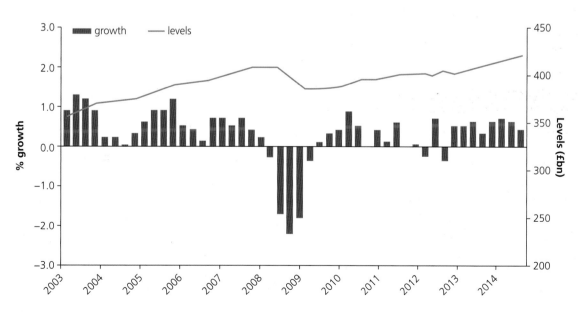

Figure 5.3 Changes in the UK's real GDP in the UK, 2003–14

Source: Office for National Statistics (ONS)

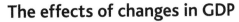

The effects of changes in GDP

Changes in the level of the UK's GDP have received a great deal of attention in recent years, mainly because of the deep recession the economy experienced in 2008–9 and its slow recovery.

The effects of changes in the level of GDP as the economy moves through the stages of the business cycle vary from industry to industry, although Table 5.1 identifies how they commonly affect decision making. Firms selling products whose demand is sensitive to changes in income (known as income elastic products), such as designer clothes and foreign holidays, may find that sales rise strongly in a boom and fall heavily during recession. Conversely, businesses selling staple products such as foodstuffs where demand is not income elastic, may be relatively unaffected by changes in the level of GDP.

It is possible to argue that changes in the level of GDP will only provoke functional decisions in many firms because its effects are relatively short-lived. Booms

Stage of the business cycle	Key features	Examples of possible decisions made by businesses
Recovery or upswing	● Increasing consumer expenditure ● Existing spare capacity used ● Production rises ● Business confidence strengthens ● Investment increases	**Strategic decisions** ● Entrepreneurs decide to start a new business ● Existing firms increase capacity **Functional decisions** ● Prices are increased ● Businesses operate nearer to (or at) full capacity
Boom	● Rate of inflation normally increases ● Bottlenecks in supply of materials and components ● Some firms unable to satisfy demand ● Profits probably high – but hit by rising costs	**Strategic decisions** ● Firms enter new geographical markets **Functional decisions** ● Firms sub-contract production to other producers ● Businesses increase prices to dampen demand
Recession	● Government reduces interest rates ● Firms reduce production as demand falls ● Spare capacity increases ● Business confidence declines and investment is cut ● Profits fall	**Strategic decisions** ● Financially weak businesses may decide to stop trading ● Firms may enter overseas markets where demand is stronger **Functional decisions** ● Businesses stockpile products ● Workers required to work short-time
Slump	● Increasing number of bankruptcies and insolvencies ● Government lowers interest rates further ● High levels of unemployment ● Low levels of business confidence and consumer spending	**Strategic decisions** ● Large-scale redundancies may be announced ● Factories, offices and stores closed to reduce capacity **Functional decisions** ● Businesses offer basic products at low prices ● Promotion focuses on price and easy payment terms

Table 5.1 The business cycle and decision making

and slumps do not last forever and businesses can take actions to see them through difficult trading periods. During periods when GDP is rising strongly managers may increase prices to restrict demand and increase profitability; they may subcontract work to other firms or seek supplies from overseas. Equally, in conditions of recession or slump, short-time working may take place. Well-managed firms will predict the onset of a boom or slump and take appropriate action in advance. Furthermore, responses at a functional level may be all that are required if governments are successful in eradicating the more extreme effects of the business cycle and, thus, fluctuations in GDP.

Exchange rates

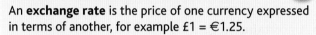

Key terms

An **exchange rate** is the price of one currency expressed in terms of another, for example £1 = €1.25.

A **currency** is the system of money in general use in a particular country, for example in the UK the currency is pounds sterling (£). The value of a currency can rise and fall against other currencies.

Price elasticity of demand measures the sensitivity or responsiveness of the quantity demanded of a product to a change in its price.

An **exchange rate** is the price of one country's **currency** when expressed in terms of another. For example, at the time of writing £1 equalled US$1.52, €1.38 or 9.5 Chinese Yuan.

London is one of the premier international centres for buying and selling foreign currencies: each day transactions total billions of pounds. Exchange rates

between most currencies vary regularly according to the balance of supply and demand for each individual currency.

Why do businesses buy foreign currencies?

The main reason why businesses purchase foreign currencies is to pay for goods and services bought from overseas. Those purchasing products from abroad are normally expected to pay using the currency of the exporting country. For example, J Sainsbury plc, one of the UK's major supermarkets purchases wine from Chile. Chilean wine producers would expect to be paid in their local currency – Chilean pesos (Ch$). Thus, traders acting on behalf of Sainsbury's would sell pounds sterling in order to buy pesos on the foreign exchange market. This process is illustrated in Figure 5.4.

Demand for foreign currencies may also arise because individuals and businesses wish to invest in enterprises overseas. Thus, a UK citizen wishing to invest in a Japanese business will require Japanese Yen to complete the transaction.

The effects of exchange rate changes

Exchange rates can change significantly over time. A rise in the value of a currency is termed appreciation; a decline in its value is called a depreciation (see Chapter 2).

In November 2014, £1 exchanged for €1.24. Just under four months later, in March 2015, the exchange rate was £1 = €1.38. This meant that the value of the pound had appreciated (increased) by just over 11 per cent in four months. Alternatively, the value of the euro had depreciated (or decreased) by the same percentage.

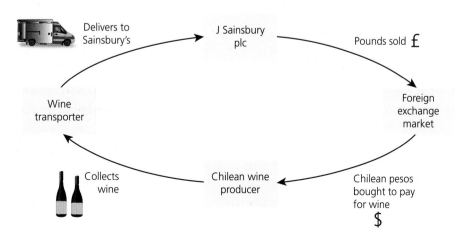

Figure 5.4 The operation of the foreign exchange market

Maths moment

$$\frac{1+b}{c}=3$$

(a) Using the exchange rate given on page 87, calculate the change in price paid by French importers between November 2014 and March 2015 of a UK export to France valued at £120.

(b) What would have been the change in the price paid by a supermarket in the UK for a bottle of champagne (valued at €30) imported from France between the same two dates?

Changes in the value of currencies affect the prices of exports and imports as shown in Table 5.2.

The exchange rate of pounds	Prices of UK exports overseas (in foreign currencies)	Prices of imported goods in the UK (in pounds)
Appreciates (rises)	Increase	Fall
Depreciates (falls)	Fall	Increase

Table 5.2 The effects of changes in the value of the pound

Using the information in Table 5.2 we can see that the rise in the value of the pound against the euro during late 2014 and early 2015 would have had the following effects:

- Prices of UK exports to countries using the euro (countries such as France and Italy, for example) would have risen by approximately 11 per cent, assuming no other changes.
- Imports into the UK from countries using the euro would have been 11 per cent less expensive, again assuming no other changes. However, the price the Europeans received in euros would not have changed. It is likely, however, that because prices were lower in the UK they would sell greater quantities of their products in the UK market, although this would depend upon **price elasticity of demand** for the imported goods and services.

Small changes in the UK's exchange rate occur all the time as demand for the currency and supplies of it alter. A series of slight rises and falls over a period of time is not necessarily a major problem for industry. Of more significance is a sustained rise or fall in the exchange rate – or a sudden and substantial change in the exchange rate. In the 18 months leading up to December 2014, the pound rose 34 per cent in value against the Japanese Yen. This resulted in UK exporters suffering a severe loss of price competitiveness when exporting to Japan, although imported products,

materials and components from Japan would have fallen in price. UK businesses trading in domestic markets with imports from Japan would have experienced more difficulty in competing in terms of price.

Exchange rate changes can create uncertainty for businesses for a number of reasons.

- **Uncertainty over revenue**. If firms agree deals priced in foreign currencies, they may receive more or less revenue from a particular transaction than expected if the exchange rate alters in the intervening period. Thus, a deal to sell whisky to America may give Scottish distillers less revenue than anticipated if the contract is agreed in terms of dollars and the pound then rises in value against the American dollar. In these circumstances the amount of dollars stated in the contract will convert into a smaller number of pounds, causing a shortfall for the exporter.
- **Uncertainty regarding quantities likely to be sold**. Changing exchange rates can affect prices and sales in overseas markets, even if the exporter avoids direct exchange risk by insisting on payment in domestic currency. For example, a London-based clothes designer may sell clothes overseas, but stipulate that they are paid in pounds sterling. A rise in the value of the pound may mean that foreign retailers are forced to increase the prices of the clothes to maintain profit margins. As a consequence, sales may be lower than expected giving the London-based design company less revenue than forecast.
- **Uncertainty regarding competitors' responses**. Competitors may take decisions to protect their firms against exchange rate changes. Foreign businesses may reduce prices to offset the effects of an exchange rate change, putting rivals under pressure to do the same or lose market share.

Price elasticity can be an important part of a discussion on the possible effects of exchange rate changes. If overseas demand for a product is price inelastic, then an increase in the exchange rate may not be too harmful. So, it might be that Americans will continue to buy Scotch whisky when the price rises. In this case demand may alter little. In contrast, if demand is price elastic, exporters might be badly affected by a rise in the exchange rate, but benefit greatly from a fall.

Business in focus: Burberry profits hit by exchange rate changes ★

The Burberry Group is a UK multinational company that sells luxury clothing, cosmetics and fashion accessories. Its brand is well known and very popular globally, especially with young consumers in developing economies such as China, where incomes are rising quickly. Its global retail business model is vulnerable to volatility in exchange rates, which can have significant effects on its financial performance.

In 2015, the Burberry Group reported that its revenue for the three months ending in December 2014 had risen by 8 per cent against forecasts of 7 per cent. The group also announced growth rates exceeding 10 per cent in markets including the Americas and Europe. Its total sales revenue for the 2013–14 year was £2,329.8 million.

The company said that the reintroduction of important products such as heritage rainwear (especially trench coats) had been successful and cashmere clothing had sold well. The star performer, however, was the runway-inspired poncho, sales of which grew very rapidly. It also expects increases in the number and size of its global retail outlets to boost sales further as its distinctive brand continues to be popular with consumers throughout the world.

However, the company's financial performance continues to be hampered by adverse movements in exchange rates. Its managers say exchange rate changes contribute to what is a challenging external environment for the company.

The company reported that revenues over the 2013–14 financial year were reduced by approximately £55 million due to the strength of the pound. As a consequence, the company's operating profit margin is expected to fall from 17.5 to 16 per cent. It forecasts that revenue

generated from licensing other firms to supply its products will be reduced over the 2014–15 financial year by about £10m due to changes in the sterling to yen exchange rate.

Figure 5.5 Burberry's brand is popular in many countries and its runway-inspired poncho proved a top-seller in 2014 and 2015.

Questions

1. Explain the exchange rate changes that have apparently weakened the Burberry Group's financial performance over recent years.
2. To what extent do you think that exchange rate changes are a major influence on the strategic decision making of companies with strong brands such as Burberry?

Study tip

Remember that most products are not sold on the basis of price alone. When considering the likely consequences of a change in exchange rates it is important to note that factors such as quality, brand image and reputation, after-sales service and meeting delivery dates are important influences on buyers' decisions too.

Decision making and exchange rates

Fluctuations in exchange rates create a great deal of uncertainty for businesses trading internationally. When exchange rates are volatile, businesses become uncertain about earnings from overseas trade. This adds to the risk businesses incur as part of their trading activities.

Firms like to operate in a relatively risk-free external environment and to reduce uncertainty whenever possible. Fluctuating exchange rates can lead businesses to take a number of functional decisions to protect their positions. The undesirable consequences of exchange rate changes can be reduced through the use of techniques such as forward foreign currency markets. This sets a guaranteed exchange rate at some future date (when transactions are completed) meaning that the amount received from overseas trading is more certain. However, fixing an exchange rate in this way does not guarantee a particular level of sales. Furthermore, the bank arranging this service may require a fee.

An alternative approach, used by Toyota, is to require suppliers to price their products in a different currency. The company, which sells cars throughout Europe, pays its UK suppliers in euros. As a result, fluctuations in the exchange rate will have less impact on the company as it pays suppliers in the same currency that it receives from European customers.

Exchange rate changes are more of a problem in markets where fierce price competition occurs. In these circumstances demand is more likely to be price elastic and businesses are under pressure to respond quickly to any change in exchange rates. These may lead to strategic decisions to minimise the effects as far as possible. For example, businesses may seek to create productive capacity in overseas markets to avoid the effects of changing currency values. A number of foreign motor manufacturers located in the UK have revealed that they are considering relocating in European countries that use the euro to avoid the difficulties imposed by fluctuations in the value of the pound against the euro.

Inflation

What are inflation and deflation?

Inflation can be defined as a persistent rise in the price level and the associated fall in the value of money. So, one can buy less with the same amount of money. For many businesses a low rate of inflation is not a problem. So long as wages are rising at about the same rate or higher, a low constant rate of price increase simply serves to help maintain demand by increasing a business's profits and helping to allow earnings to rise steadily. Inflation only becomes a major problem for businesses when it is high, rising rapidly or (worst of all) is doing both together.

A number of economies around the world, including the United States, Germany, France, Italy and Spain, have experienced deflation recently. **Deflation** is the opposite of inflation and describes a situation in which a country's prices are falling meaning that the value of money is increasing. Thus, it is a situation in which an economy suffers from negative rates of inflation. In March 2015 prices in Spain were falling at over 1 per cent per annum while in Poland the annual rate of change of prices was –1.3 per cent.

Country	Inflation rate
United States of America	–0.1%
European Union (28 member states)	–0.5%
China	0.8%
Canada	1.0%
Taiwan	–1.0%

Table 5.3 A selection of inflation rates for January or February, 2015

The world is experiencing low rates of inflation, and in some cases deflation, as illustrated in Table 5.3. Trading nations are likely to import deflation from one another as low priced exports contribute to the calculation of inflation in other countries. There have also been substantial falls in the prices of important commodities, most notably that of oil.

How is inflation measured?

In the UK the principal measure of the rate of inflation used by the government is the **Consumer Price Index (CPI)**. The CPI was introduced in 2003 and measures the average monthly change in the prices of goods and services purchased by households in the UK and the government will use this to set targets for inflation in the future. The CPI is calculated using approximately 700 separate goods and services for which price changes are measured throughout the country. Most European countries use the CPI as their official measure of inflation.

Key terms

Inflation is a persistent rise in the general price level and an associated fall in the value of money.

Deflation is the rate of decrease of the general price level and the corresponding rise in the value of money.

The **Consumer Price Index (CPI)** measures the rate of inflation based on the changes in prices of a basket of goods and services.

Decision making, inflation and deflation

Responding to inflation

Expectations can be an important part of the process of creating inflation and deflation. If managers and businesses anticipate that prices are set to rise or fall in the near future, they might take decisions which actually fuel the process of price change.

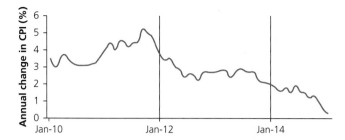

Figure 5.6 The UK's rate of inflation, 2010–15, as measured by the CPI.

Note: At the time of writing (March 2015) prices in the UK were still rising, albeit at only 0.3 per cent per annum. Forecasters anticipate that prices may begin to fall, when measured by the CPI on an annual basis, later in 2015.

Source: Office for National Statistics (ONS)

If businesses expect their suppliers to increase the prices of raw materials and components, they may raise their selling prices in anticipation of this. This avoids any possibilities of reduced profit margins if costs rise before prices can be increased. The decision also provides a windfall profit as for a while firms sell at higher prices whilst their costs have not risen.

Trade unions and other employee groups usually build in expectations of inflation into their wage demands for the coming year; they would normally seek to protect their standards of living. However, wages have risen very slowly in the UK since the financial crisis and subsequent recession as businesses' profits have been depressed.

Businesses may suffer falling sales in a period of relatively high rates of inflation. Consumers might be expected to spend more during inflationary periods as they would not wish to hold an asset (cash) that is falling in value. However, research shows that people save more (perhaps due to uncertainty) and so sales for many businesses fall. Businesses may respond by reducing production levels or by targeting other markets which may enjoy more stable prices.

It can be difficult for businesses to maintain competitiveness (and especially international competitiveness) during bouts of inflation. Rising wages and raw material costs may force firms to raise prices or accept lower profit margins. Firms operating in countries with lower rates of inflation may benefit

from improved price competitiveness and enjoy increases in market share, especially if demand for their product is price elastic.

Inflation can offer some benefits to decision makers, however. Low and stable rates of inflation may be beneficial for businesses. A steady rise in prices can create favourable expectations and encourage investment by businesses. Inflation can also encourage long-term borrowing and investment in non-current assets by businesses as the value of their repayments (in real terms) declines over time. It is for these reasons that the UK authorities have set a target rate for inflation of 2 per cent per annum.

The impact of deflation

If the UK succumbs to deflation, this will be a new experience for management teams and other decision makers within businesses operating here. Prices measured using the government's preferred measure of inflation last fell in the UK over 55 years ago, in March 1960.

There are mixed views about the likely implications of deflation for businesses in the UK. If prices fall for a short time only, it may provide a temporary boost to spending by consumers and increase the sales of many businesses, especially those who sell products other than necessities. Deflation could allow managers to maintain prices while their costs are falling, effectively increasing profit margins.

If deflation persists in the UK, especially if prices begin to fall sharply, it can pose a significant threat to businesses and require some difficult decisions. Firstly, businesses may experience declining sales as consumers postpone purchases to wait until prices are even lower. Secondly, managers may have to reduce the wages and salaries of employees and this may be difficult to achieve without damaging levels of motivation and engagement.

Finally, and arguably most significantly, deflation increases the burden of debt for consumers and businesses. Because prices are falling it is likely that consumers' incomes and business profits will fall too. Thus, repaying debt in the form of mortgages or business loans will take an increasing proportion of income and therefore increase the burden it imposes.

Consumers will have less disposable income to purchase goods and services and this will further reduce sales. Businesses may be reluctant to invest in new non-current assets because the falling level of sales may not justify it and because any debts incurred as part of the investment will increase in value in real terms over time.

Business in focus: Retailers and deflation

High-street price cuts deepened in February 2015 as fresh food costs dropped at the fastest rate for over eight years, according to industry figures. This will reinforce expectations the UK is headed for a brief period of deflation.

The British Retail Consortium (BRC) reported deflation in overall shop prices for the 22nd consecutive month, as prices in February fell 1.7 per cent on the same month in 2014. That followed deflation of 1.3 per cent in January.

Non-food products again drove the overall drop, helped by clothes discounts and special offers on furniture and DIY items, the BRC explained. Non-food items were down 2.5 per cent on the year, the biggest drop for eight months. Online prices are also showing similar trends to those in the high street.

Food prices also fell in February, signalling a change of trend after they had risen throughout much of 2014. In February, they were down 0.4 per cent partly due to falling commodity prices, such as sugar and corn, and also because of the price war between UK supermarkets continues.

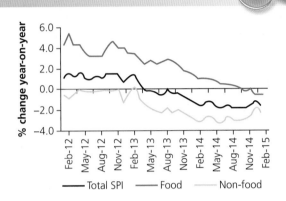

Figure 5.7 The UK's index of shop prices, 2012–15

Source: Adapted from the *Guardian*, 4 March 2015

Questions

1. Explain the actions that UK retailers might take to maintain their market share during a period of deflation.
2. Are multinational companies protected from the effects of deflation in the UK?

Taxation

Almost every business and consumer in the UK pays taxes in one form or another. Taxes are financial levies or payments imposed on a variety of business activities.

The UK'S main business-related taxes

Income tax

This is the most important tax to the UK government in terms of tax yield and it is paid by all UK taxpayers earning over a certain amount annually. In 2014–15 income tax is forecast to yield £167 billion, over 25 per cent of the government's receipts from **taxation**. It is paid by employees on their wages and salaries and by sole traders or partners on the profits made from their businesses.

Key term

Taxation is a payment that has to be made to the government or other authority by households, firms or other organisations.

Value added tax (VAT)

This is a tax levied on spending. Most goods and services sold in the UK have VAT at a rate of 20 per cent added to their price. Some items such as car seats for children have a 5 per cent rate while other products, including most foods, are zero-rated so purchasers do not have to pay VAT on these products. VAT is a tax that is imposed in all member states of the EU, although rates vary. In January 2011 the UK government increased VAT from 17.5 to 20 per cent.

National insurance payments

National insurance payments are contributions made towards the cost of certain state benefits such as pensions. In the 2014–15 financial year both employers and employees will pay national insurance contributions on earnings over £153 per week. Employees pay 12 per cent of their salary up to earnings of £805 a week and employers pay 13.8 per cent of the employee's salary over the same range of income.

Corporation tax

Corporation tax is paid by companies in the UK on their profits. The UK government is committed to creating a very competitive tax regime for corporation tax in the expectation of attracting international businesses to the UK. The rate of corporation tax in the UK has been cut from 28 per cent in 2010 to 20 per cent in 2015 – this is the joint lowest in the G20 group of major economies as shown in Figure 5.6.

Customs and excise duties

Customs duties are paid on some imported products. Excise duty is a tax on the production of certain products in the UK including tobacco, petrol, alcohol and gambling. Demand for these products is often price inelastic.

The taxation policies of governments are subject to a number of influences. They are designed to raise sufficient revenue, as far as possible, to cover government expenditure. They may also be used to encourage consumers and businesses to increase consumption of some products, such as renewable sources of energy, and discourage consumption of others, such as fossil fuels or tobacco products. They will also be influenced by the government's fiscal policy which we shall cover in the following section.

Changes in taxation and business decision making

Most businesses operate with the intention of making a profit and some aim to make the maximum possible profit. If a business is able to minimise its liability for taxes, it is possible to generate higher profits and to use this to reward shareholders or to invest in activities intended to promote growth. It is common for businesses to use specialist taxation lawyers to help to devise ways of minimising tax liabilities while remaining within the law, although this is currently a controversial topic.

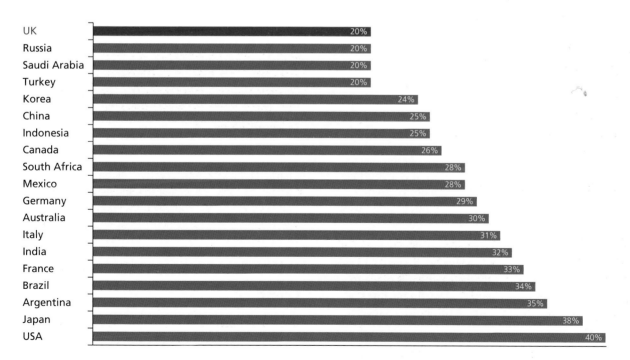

Figure 5.8 Corporation tax rates for the G20 group of 20 major economies, 2015

Source: HM Treasury, *A Guide to UK Taxation*

Taxation rates can have significant effects on businesses and may influence strategic decisions, for example relocation. The Republic of Ireland has a tax rate on company profits of 12.5 per cent – its equivalent of corporation tax. This is very low by international standards, as can be seen from Figure 5.8, and has helped it to attract many leading companies to relocate there. Nine of the world's ten largest pharmaceutical businesses have operations in Ireland as well as prominent American technology companies including Twitter, Google and Facebook. Rates of corporation tax will also have an impact on investment decisions by businesses. Reducing rates of corporation tax (as is happening in the UK currently) can help to improve the rates of return on capital investment. For businesses seeking higher returns, such tax cuts may help to create a case in favour of business investment.

Taxation can also impact on functional decisions within businesses. In April 2014 the UK government reduced the amount of national insurance payable by employers by up to £2,000 per year for small businesses. In effect, this is reducing a tax on employment. The intention was to increase employment and tax cuts of this type may result in businesses taking decisions to increase employment or not to take decisions to introduce capital intensive methods of production.

Changes in some taxes impact on businesses indirectly as well as directly. In 2011 the UK government increased the rate of value added tax (VAT) in the UK from 17.5 to 20 per cent. This had two negative effects on businesses.

1. It increased the costs faced by many businesses as they paid a higher amount of tax on many inputs used in production. In theory, they can pass this on in the final price paid by consumers or other businesses. However, this is not always possible in a competitive market.

2. Consumers faced paying higher prices for many products which reduced their overall demand for goods and services. The Centre for Retail Research estimated that the rise in VAT reduced production in the UK by between 0.5 and 0.8 per cent.

Business in focus: Amazon and taxation

Politicians and pressure groups have called on consumers in the UK to repeat the successful action taken last year against Starbucks, a boycott which successfully persuaded the coffee chain to resume paying tax in the UK, and stop buying products from the online retailer Amazon until it too starts to pay a 'fair' amount of tax here. In the past financial year Amazon achieved sales in the UK valued at £4.3 billion but paid just £4.2 million in tax – less than 0.1 per cent of its revenue. The chair of Parliament's public accounts committee, Margaret Hodge, has been one of Amazon's most outspoken critics. 'It is an outrage and Amazon should pay their fair share of tax,'said Hodge. 'They are making money out of not paying taxes. I no longer use Amazon. We should shop elsewhere.'

Amazon uses a subsidiary based outside the UK to avoid paying more taxes here. When a shopper in the UK makes a purchase from the company the payment is made to this subsidiary based in Luxembourg where the rates of corporate taxes are much lower. A UK shopper's receipt will show payment was made to Amazon EU S.à.r.l. rather than to Amazon.co.uk because Amazon has arranged its operations so that its UK operations only supply services, such as storage and delivery, to the business in Luxembourg. As a result its tax liability within the UK is much reduced. Over a four year period Amazon's sales revenue in the UK amounted to £23 billion, while it has only paid £10 million in corporation tax over a decade.

Amazon employs approximately 7,000 people full time in the UK in roles in its warehouses as well as in designing and maintaining its websites. The company has growth objectives in a number of markets including entertainment.

Charlie Elphicke, a Conservative MP has also criticised the company. 'People will look at this and feel it's incredibly unfair, that they work hard and pay their taxes while big American multinationals engage in industrial-scale tax avoidance. This is why international tax reform is badly needed.'

Source: Adapted from an article in the *Guardian*, 9 March 2015

Questions
1. Explain the benefits to Amazon of arranging its tax affairs in this way.
2. Do you think that the drawbacks to Amazon from reducing its tax liability in this way might exceed the benefits in the long term?

This may result in businesses taking decisions to reduce production temporarily or possibly to cut prices and increase promotion to maintain sales as far as possible. Some businesses used the fact that they would not pass on the rise in VAT to their customers as part of their promotional activities. Presumably they calculated that the reduction in profit margins might be compensated for by higher sales.

Fiscal and monetary policies

We have looked at a number of factors that shape the economic environment in which businesses trade. One important one is the policies pursued by the UK government to try and achieve its macroeconomic objectives. The government pursues a number of macroeconomic objectives of which the following are the most important:

- Steady annual increases in real GDP of around 2–3 per cent each year.
- Inflation at an annual rate of 2 per cent.
- A low and stable rate of unemployment.
- A balanced balance of payments on current account (a financial record of the UK's trading and some financial transactions with the rest of the world).

To these should be added the desire to correct the economy's **budget balance** (that is, the balance between government expenditure and receipts from taxation and other sources). Since the financial crisis and subsequent recession of 2008–9 the UK's public finances have been in a weak state. This is illustrated in Figure 5.9.

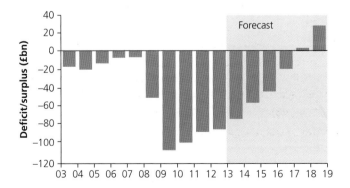

Figure 5.9 The UK's actual and forecast budget deficit/surplus, 2003–19

Source: Office for National Statistics (ONS) / Office for Budget Responsibility (OBR)

The government has three main policies it can use to manage the economy in pursuit of its macroeconomic policies. These are:

1. **fiscal policy**
2. **monetary policy**
3. supply-side policies.

Key terms

The **budget balance** is the difference between government spending and revenue over the financial year.

Fiscal policy is the use of taxation and public expenditure to manage the level of economic activity.

Monetary policy is controlling the amount of money and/or interest rates within the economy in order to achieve the desired level of economic activity.

Fiscal policy

Fiscal policy is the use of government expenditure and taxation as a means of controlling the level of activity within the economy. The central element of fiscal policy is the relationship between the level of government expenditure and the amount raised in taxation in any given year. The balance between taxation and government expenditure is determined annually when the Chancellor of the Exchequer announces the annual budget, usually in March.

The difference between government spending and revenue over the fiscal year is called its budget balance. The UK government often runs a budget deficit, when its revenue (mainly from taxation) is less than its expenditure. If the government's revenue exceeds its expenditure over a fiscal year, the result is a budget surplus. Recent and forecast budget balances for the UK government are shown in Figure 5.9.

The government can operate two broad types of fiscal policy:

1. **Expansionary fiscal policy**. This entails cutting taxation and/or increasing government expenditure on items such as health, education, social services, defence and transport. The effect will be to increase the amount the public sector borrows to fund its expenditure for the year, or possibly to reduce the size of any surplus. The amount by which the

public sector's revenues fall short of its expenditure is known as the public sector net cash requirement (or PSNCR).

2. **Contractionary fiscal policy**. This is brought about by reducing government expenditure or increasing taxation, or by both policies simultaneously. The effect is to reduce the government's budget deficit or to increase the surplus on its budget for the fiscal year.

Figure 5.10 summarises the operation of fiscal policy. Fiscal policy can help to stabilise the economy (avoiding the worst effects of fluctuations in the level of GDP) through the operation of the 'automatic stabilisers'. For example, lower unemployment when the level of economic activity is high means temporarily lower welfare spending, higher income tax receipts and higher National Insurance contributions. Higher company profits generate higher corporation tax receipts, and higher spending by consumers yields higher VAT receipts and excise duties. These factors together will have a contractionary effect, as tax revenues rise and government expenditure falls. Thus, a contractionary fiscal policy operates automatically to stabilise the economy when GDP is growing quickly in an economic boom. The reverse will happen in a slump as government expenditure rises, tax receipts

fall and an expansionary fiscal policy is implemented automatically.

The effects of the government's taxation and expenditure policies

Tax and expenditure policies can have immediate effects on the level of economic activity, although the precise effects will depend upon the types of tax and the nature of government expenditure.

Taxation

1. **Direct taxes**. These are taxes on income and profits and include income tax and corporation tax (levied on company profits). Direct taxes take a larger amount from individuals earning high salaries and companies announcing handsome profits. The government can forecast with some accuracy the effects arising from an increase (or reduction) in income tax. Although the overall effect may be predicted, the implications for individual businesses will vary according to the type of product supplied. Firms supplying luxury goods (long-haul foreign holidays, for example) might be significantly affected by a change in income tax rates, especially for those earning higher incomes, whilst those selling basic foodstuffs may be relatively unaffected.

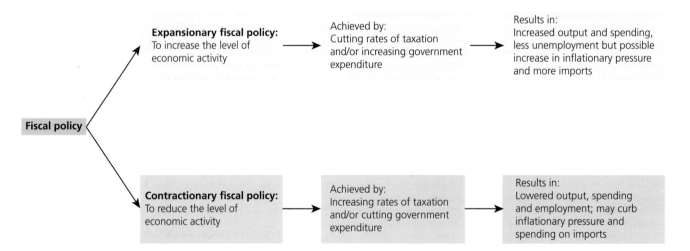

Figure 5.10 The operation of fiscal policy

2. **Indirect taxes**. VAT and other taxes on spending are classified as indirect. Changes in this type of taxation can have a rapid effect on the level of economic activity, although its effects are difficult to predict. An increase in VAT will cut consumer spending, reducing demand for goods and services and eventually lower the level of economic activity. However, the extent of the fall in demand will depend upon the price elasticity of demand for the goods in question, as well as consumer confidence. Consumers will continue to purchase essentials such as fuel and food, although demand for products associated with DIY, for example, may decline. An important side-effect of increasing indirect taxes is that it is inflationary.

Government expenditure

Government expenditure is the other half of fiscal policy. Governments may adjust spending in a range of areas. The major elements of government expenditure are shown in Figure 5.11. The 'remainder' category includes a broad range of government expenditure including that on defence, the environment and law and order. It also includes expenditure on the economy's infrastructure (see Chapter 4, pages 69–70).

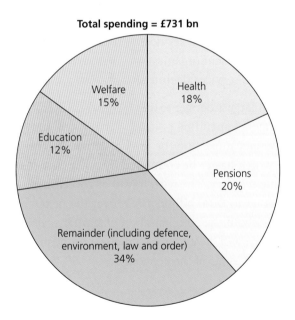

Total spending = £731 bn

Figure 5.11 The major elements of UK government expenditure, 2015

Source: UK Public Spending website,
www.ukpublicspending.co.uk/government_expenditure.html

The UK's budget deficit – managing a crisis

Fiscal policy has been dominated in recent years by the desire of the UK government to reduce its budget deficit. As can be seen from Figure 5.9, this soared to an annual figure of over £100 billion in the wake of the financial crisis and recession. This resulted in a level of borrowing by the government that was not sustainable in anything but the short term.

As a consequence, all political parties in the UK have made a commitment to reducing the size of the budget deficit. Some would focus mainly on cutting government expenditure to achieve this, whilst others prefer a combination of tax rises and reductions in expenditure. Using fiscal policy to manage the level of activity in the economy has become secondary to reducing the government's budget deficit. As a consequence, the UK government has become dependent upon monetary and supply-side policies to manage the economy. These policies are covered later in this section on pages 98–102.

The previous coalition government in the UK relied primarily on restraining government expenditure to reduce the size of the budget deficit over the period 2010–15, although it did increase VAT from 17.5 to 20 per cent in January 2011. This tight control may initially appear ineffective when considering the actual level of public expenditure, as it has remained above £700 billion since the financial crisis in 2008–9. However, a better measure of government expenditure is as a percentage of GDP for which actual data and forecasts are shown in Figure 5.12. Using this measure public expenditure has fallen substantially in the UK and will continue to do so. In 2014–15 it will be 40.7 per cent of GDP compared with 44.8 per cent in 2010–11. The Conservative government elected in May 2015 plans to continue the tight control of public expenditure until the 2019–20 financial year. This would take public spending as a percentage of GDP down to approximately 36 per cent – its lowest percentage for over 50 years.

The government's commitment to reducing its expenditure significantly as a percentage of GDP has many implications for businesses in the UK and provides opportunities and threats for businesses. Opportunities exist for businesses that seek to supply services which may have been provided previously by central or local government. The government has encouraged charities to become involved in the provision of local services in its place. In other industries the government has reduced

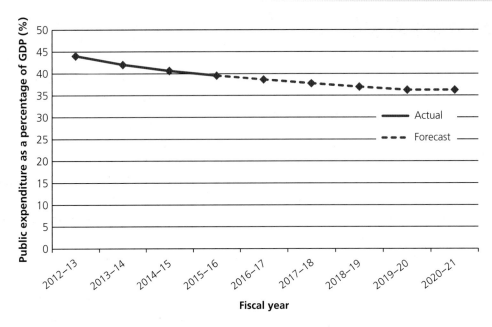

Figure 5.12 Public spending as a percentage of GDP

Source: Office for Budget Responsibility (OBR), Economic and Fiscal Outlook, July 2015

its expenditure by using private sector businesses to supply services. Examples of this have occurred within the NHS and also in the State Forensic Service, which conducts forensic examinations for criminal trials in the UK. The UK's forensics market is estimated to generate sales between £60–80 million annually. The government has said that public services do not have to be delivered by public sector businesses. More opportunities may occur in the future for private firms to deliver public services as the government seeks to tightly control its expenditure. Government contracts are usually awarded as the result of a bidding process and management teams for large public companies such as Capita and Serco make strategic decisions on whether or not to make a bid.

The government's spending decisions have also had considerable implications for the UK's labour markets and thus for all businesses. It is estimated by the Office for Budget Responsibility (OBR) that 1.1 million jobs in the public sector in the UK will be lost between 2010–11 and 2018–19. This is one reason why wage rates in the UK have not risen much as the number of employees entering the labour market has been high.

The reduction in government spending as a percentage of GDP over time may pose a threat to the large number of businesses that supply local and central businesses with goods and services. Examples include businesses operating care homes for elderly customers who have seen the number of customers referred by local councils falling. Cable & Wireless, which provides communication services to local government and other government organisations, has seen public spending on its services decline sharply.

Probably the largest danger to all UK businesses from the government's spending policies is that it will have a contractionary impact on the level of activity in the economy, which has to be countered by other elements of government policy. The withdrawal of government spending of up to £100 billion a year over the next few years, without the compensation of similar scale tax reductions, will have a profound effect on business activity in most areas of the economy.

Monetary policy

Weblink

To find out more about the OBR visit: http://budgetresponsibility.org.uk/

Study tip

This material on interest rates builds on that covered in Year 1 of the specification. You may wish to review the pages on interest rates in Chapter 3 of *AQA A-level Business 1*.

Key term

Interest rates are the price of borrowed money.

This type of economic policy involves adjusting the amount of money in circulation and hence the level of spending and economic activity. Monetary policy can make use of one or more of the following:

- altering **interest rates**
- controlling the money supply
- manipulating the exchange rate
- the use of quantitative easing and forward guidance.

At times, all the techniques have been used. Over the period 1997–2009 the UK authorities tended to use interest rates as a major means of managing the economy. Since 1997 the Monetary Policy Committee of the Bank of England has had responsibility for setting interest rates. The Monetary Policy Committee sets interest rates monthly with the aim of achieving the government's target for inflation whilst attaining long-term growth in the economy.

Interest rates

Table 5.4 sets out the aims that may lie behind the authorities altering interest rates and, importantly, the possible implications for decision making by businesses. Broadly speaking, rises in interest rates depress the level of economic activity and reductions promote an expansion of economic activity.

Although the Bank of England sets the base rate, many other interest rates operate in the UK. The precise rate of interest charged on a loan depends on several factors, including the time period of the loan and the degree of risk attached to it.

In the UK, expenditure by consumers on products supplied by businesses is sensitive to changes in interest rates. One major reason for this is mortgage interest payments. Millions of UK consumers have mortgages. A rise in interest rates increases the payments made on mortgages, leaving less money available for other types of expenditure. Similarly, a cut in rates reduces mortgage payments freeing money for other forms of expenditure.

Interest rates have become more difficult to use as a means of managing the economy since 2009 as they have been at an historic low of 0.5 per cent, leaving the Bank of England with little room for manoeuvre. This has resulted in the use of other forms of monetary policy which we consider later in this section on pages 100–1.

Effects of changes in interest rates

The impact of rising interest rates will depend upon the size of the change as well as the initial rate. A small increase at a relatively high level of rates will have little impact, while a larger increase from a low base rate will have a significant impact.

	Rising interest rates	Falling interest rates
Likely objectives	<ul><li>Reducing the level of consumer spending in the economy.</li><li>Limiting inflationary pressure in the economy.</li><li>Slowing the level of economic growth (as measured by GDP).</li><li>Avoiding increasing imports creating a deficit on the balance of payments.</li></ul>(In general, higher interest rates will assist in dampening down an economic boom.)	<ul><li>Reducing levels of unemployment.</li><li>Stimulating the level of production and thus GDP in the economy.</li><li>Promoting export sales by reducing the exchange rate of the pound.</li><li>Increasing rates of economic growth in the economy.</li></ul>(Reducing interest rates can assist an economy in recovering from a slump.)
Possible consequences for business	<ul><li>Many businesses may experience falling sales as consumers increase savings and businesses decide to reduce production.</li><li>Businesses may decide to cancel or defer investment plans.</li><li>Firms may seek to lower costs by reducing borrowing.</li><li>The pound sterling may rise in value (pushing up export prices) dissuading businesses from entering or expanding in overseas markets.</li></ul>	<ul><li>Demand and sales are likely to increase, especially for products bought on credit, prompting managers to expand production, possibly by using capacity more intensively.</li><li>Export sales of products in price elastic demand may rise as the exchange rate of the pound declines whilst imports become less competitive.</li><li>Businesses may undertake increased investment promoting growth in industries such as construction.</li></ul>

Table 5.4 Changes in interest rates – objectives and consequences

Not all businesses are affected equally. We can identify several categories of businesses that are particularly susceptible to changes in interest rates:

● Small firms are often affected greatly by changes in interest rates as they have smaller financial reserves and a relatively greater need for borrowing. Significant rises in interest rates can lead to substantial increases in bankruptcies among small firms.

● Even larger firms with high levels of borrowing (and therefore high levels of gearing) can be affected by alterations in interest rates. For example, a rise in rates can lead to a hefty increase in interest payments forcing firms to reduce costs elsewhere or to pass on the extra expenses in the form of higher prices – if this is possible. Alternatively, a cut in interest rates offers a substantial reduction in expenses to such firms improving their competitiveness.

● The decisions of firms trading overseas are affected by alterations in interest rates. Rising interest rates tend to lead to an increase in the exchange rates as individuals and businesses overseas purchase sterling to invest in UK financial institutions to benefit from higher rates. A fall in interest rates would have the opposite effect. Rising interest rates may result in managers accepting changes in profit margins to protect market share or focusing on quality and other non-price factors when promoting products in foreign markets.

However, it is not only the direct effects of altering interest rates that affect businesses. The use of interest rate policy by the authorities can have a profound impact upon the general economic environment in which businesses operate. The Bank of England's Monetary Policy Committee changes interest rates to assist the government in achieving its economic objectives. This means that altering rates affects the level of unemployment, inflation and growth in the economy. They also change managers' expectations of these key economic variables affecting their day-to-day and strategic decisions.

Table 5.5 illustrates the relationship that exists between the level of interest rates and key economic variables such as economic growth and inflation.

Other economic variables	Rising interest rates	Falling interest rates
Inflation	Falling demand and output reduces inflationary pressure	Increasing output and spending causes prices to rise fuelling inflation
Economic growth	Will slow as businesses cut output and investment	Is stimulated by cheaper loans and rising business investment
Exchange rates	The value of the pound is likely to rise	Exchange rate of the pound generally falls
Unemployment	Unemployment increases as levels of production decline	Unemployment declines as the level of economic activity rises

Table 5.5 Interest rates and other economic variables

Quantitative easing and forward guidance

Since March 2009 interest rates in the UK have been held at 0.5 per cent by the Bank of England, the lowest figure ever. This has effectively removed the possibility of lowering interest rates further to expand production and to help the economy achieve higher rates of economic growth and so recover from the 2008–9 recession. Some foreign governments have opted for negative interest rates: they are –0.10 per cent in Sweden and –0.75 per cent in Switzerland at the time of writing. Negative interest rates effectively require consumers and businesses to pay financial institutions to hold money in their accounts: the aim is to discourage saving and encourage consumption spending and investment. Thus far the Bank of England has opted to hold interest rates at 0.5 per cent and use other techniques of monetary policy. The favoured policies have been quantitative easing (QE) and forward guidance.

The way the central bank implements QE is by buying assets – usually financial assets such as government and corporate bonds – using money it has simply created. The institutions selling those assets (either commercial banks or other financial businesses such as insurance companies) will then have 'new' money in their accounts, which in turn boosts the money supply. The hope is that this money is subsequently used to purchase goods and services and to boost output and growth. The UK government has injected £375 billion into the UK economy through QE since March 2009.

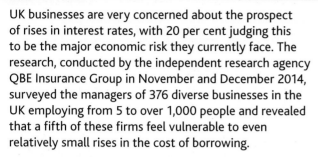

Business in focus: UK businesses fear rises in interest rates

UK businesses are very concerned about the prospect of rises in interest rates, with 20 per cent judging this to be the major economic risk they currently face. The research, conducted by the independent research agency QBE Insurance Group in November and December 2014, surveyed the managers of 376 diverse businesses in the UK employing from 5 to over 1,000 people and revealed that a fifth of these firms feel vulnerable to even relatively small rises in the cost of borrowing.

Nearly 25 per cent of respondents admitted that even a small rise of half of 1 per cent in interest rates would have an impact on their businesses. Nearly half (47 per cent) of the businesses surveyed feared that a more substantial rise of up to 1.5 per cent in interest rates would lead to financial pressures. Such a scenario would result in many businesses reviewing expenditure budgets and monitoring their cash flows and working capital even more closely. Over a third of managers (36 per cent) also expressed

fears about the risks involved in granting trade credit to their own customers if UK interest rates rose.

Trevor Williams, Head of Credit and Surety Europe at QBE, believes that the economic difficulties faced by the eurozone, a major trading partner for the UK, together with doubts about the UK's future economic performance have created a lot of uncertainty in the minds of managers. 'Margins continue to be squeezed and payment terms extended, leaving businesses susceptible to being starved of cash,' said Mr Williams.

Source: Adapted from *Commercial Risk Europe*, 22 January 2015

Questions

1. Explain why the UK's small businesses might be concerned at the prospect of a rise in interest rates.

2. Are large businesses protected to some extent against the effects of changes in UK interest rates?

Since August 2013 the Bank of England has been instructed by the government to issue 'forward guidance' on its monetary policy (that is to communicate its own forecasts and expectations of future levels of interest rates) in order to influence business and consumer confidence and decision making. The expectation is that guidance from the Bank of England on the length of time over which the Bank Rate will remain low will help to hold down longer term interest rates in the economy boosting levels of consumption and investment. It also helps households and firms to plan spending and investment with greater levels of confidence.

Supply-side policies

Supply-side policies are a range of measures intended to improve the operation of free markets and the amount that is produced by the economy; they have gained in importance in recent years because the government is unable to use fiscal policy as a means of managing the economy. Supply-side policies can take a number of forms, including those set out below.

Labour market measures

In recent years, UK governments have implemented a range of measures intended to allow labour markets to operate more effectively. The unemployed have been encouraged back into the labour force through the provision of training programmes designed to equip

them with employable skills, by limiting the availability of unemployment benefit to those in genuine need and the cutting of income tax rates on low earners to make it worth people's while to work.

Privatisation

This is the process of transferring organisations from the state to the ownership and control of individuals and other businesses. In recent years, governments have tended to move away from the policy of full privatisation, principally because there are few state-owned enterprises remaining to be sold. They prefer to see the public and private sectors cooperate on a range of projects. Two systems have been used:

- **Public–Private Partnerships (PPP).** This is collaboration on relatively small-scale projects using private and public sector money. In Birmingham a PPP agreement was reached to provide care for patients with mental health problems from 2015 onwards.

- **Private Finance Initiatives (PFI).** These rely entirely on funding from the private sector. This approach is used for major capital projects such as building schools and hospitals. The Midland Metropolitan Hospital is to be built in Smethwick as part of a £353 million PFI deal in 2015. This policy has been called into question as many analysts consider it to be an expensive way of providing public services.

Business in focus: Global economic data

	Real GDP growth			Interest rates			Inflation		
	2013	2014	2015	2013	2014	2015	2013	2014	2015
UK	1.6%	2.6%	2.7%	0.50%	0.50%	0.50%	2.7%	1.9%	0.3%
USA	1.9%	2.9%	2.4%	0.25%	0.25%	0.25%	1.6%	1.6%	−0.1%
Germany	−1.8%	1.0%	1.6%	0.75%	0.25%	0.15%	1.6%	1.4%	−0.4%
China	7.6%	7.5%	7.3%	6.00%	5.60%	5.35%	2.0%	2.5%	0.8%
India	7.0%	6.5%	7.5%	7.75%	8.00%	7.50%	10.8%	9.1%	5.1%
Russia	0.8%	2.0%	0.7%	5.50%	5.50%	16.00%	7.4%	6.8%	15.0%

Table 5.6 A selection of economic data from 2013–15
Source: Trading Economics

Questions

1. Explain the implications for the strategic decisions made by businesses based in Russia of the data in Table 5.6.

2. Has the economy of India provided a better economic environment for businesses than the other economies included in Table 5.6?

Study tip

The specification requires you to be able to understand and interpret economic data. Practising reading data such as that displayed in Table 5.6 and considering the likely consequences for decision making in businesses will help you to develop important skills.

What do you think?

Is economic data such as that presented in Table 5.6 of limited use to managers as it is historical?

Trade and protectionism

We considered international trade in some detail as part of the political environment in Chapter 4 on pages 71–4. Most governments in the world today are in favour of free trade. The development of international trade has gone hand-in-hand with globalisation as governments have been persuaded of the benefits of being an integral part of a global economy. The movement towards free trade has been driven by global institutions such as the World Trade Organisation (WTO) and the creation and enlargement of trading blocs such as the EU. As we saw in Chapter 4 on page 73, greater freedom of trade can impact heavily on strategic and functional decision making by creating opportunities and threats

for all businesses in economies such as the UK which are open to trade.

Protectionism

Although there are strong global forces promoting greater international trade, this does not mean that all countries are wholly committed to it. Disputes over trade do occur between different countries and these can lead to **protectionism** where governments seek to implement measures designed to limit the number of imports entering a country and to 'protect' domestic industries and employment.

Key term

Protectionism is a government policy which favours the use of measures intended to prevent the free entry of imports into a country.

A government may use a range of measures to protect its businesses from the full force of international competition:

● **Tariffs**. A tariff is a tax on imports. The imposition of tariffs increases the price of imported products. This can help to protect a relatively inefficient domestic industry, and can be effective when demand for a product is price elastic, though it will not encourage the development of more efficient methods of production by domestic suppliers. It may also provoke retaliation by other governments.

- **Import quotas**. These are physical limits set on the number of units of a products that can be imported into a country over a given time period. Governments usually issue licences to importers and control the number of products for which they grant licences.
- **Subsidies**. Governments can use subsidies (a payment to a domestic producer for each unit of output produced) to help high-cost home suppliers charge artificially low prices.
- **Soft loans**. A government may support a weak or failing business by providing a generous loan on much softer terms than could be negotiated with private sector lenders. This helps to reduce the costs of businesses competing with foreign firms.
- **Technical barriers to trade**. These include stringent demands in relation to factors such as design or safety standards. The intention is to increase the costs of production of overseas producers thereby reducing their competitiveness.
- **State procurement policies**. The use of this type of barrier to trade occurs when a government favours domestic suppliers when agreeing contracts for government spending such as that on military equipment.

Governments continue to implement protectionist policies, despite many economists arguing powerfully in support of free trade. In 2014 a number of countries complained about China's non-tariff protection measures as the country imposed barriers including delays on customs clearance and quality restrictions to curb raw material imports. China initiated 89 food safety and animal and plant health measures in 2013, compared with 25 in 2012, according to the WTO. In October 2014 the Chinese government put a 3–6 per cent tariff on imports of coal. This is likely to have huge consequences for Australian mining companies for whom China is a vital export market.

Fears that protectionism is rising within the global economy were reflected in a report published by the WTO in November 2014. The report says that of the 1,244 restrictive measures recorded amongst the G20 group of major economies since 2008, only 282 have been removed. The number of restrictive measures in place increased by 12 per cent between 2013 and 2014.

Figure 5.13 Large-scale production in Australia's mines results in competitively-priced supplies of coal being available in global markets.

Protectionism can provoke a range of strategic decisions:

- Businesses may be forced to use more expensive domestic suppliers if trade barriers prevent or restrict imports. For example, Chinese manufacturers are using domestic coal supplies rather than imports from Australasia or Indonesia.
- Businesses with sufficient resources may establish production facilities within countries that impose import restrictions to avoid any such barriers.
- Others may lobby governments and international bodies to persuade countries to remove barriers to trade.

Globalisation

What is globalisation?

The world's economies have developed ever-closer links since 1950, in trade, investment and production. This process has resulted in globalisation (see Chapter 4, page 72) and its pace and scope have accelerated in recent years, to include more industries and more countries.

At its simplest, globalisation refers to the trend for many markets to become worldwide in scope. Because of globalisation many businesses trade throughout the world, whereas in the past they may have focused on one country, or possibly a single continent such as Europe.

Globalisation has been associated with an increase in world trade as is shown in Figure 5.14. However, it can be seen that the rate of increase in trade in merchandise (goods and not services) has slowed since 2010, although trade continues to grow more quickly than GDP.

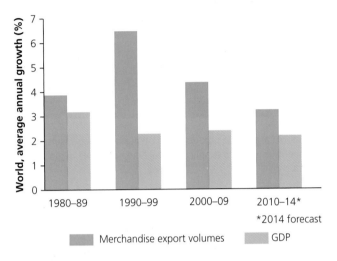

Figure 5.14 Merchandise exports and GDP, 1980–2014

Source: *The Economist*, 13 December 2014; World Trade Organisation data

Reasons for the greater globalisation of business

Globalisation has its opponents, many of whom fear loss of traditional jobs and also of distinct cultures in particular countries and regions. However, there are a number of powerful forces behind globalisation.

The support of many governments and major businesses

An important reason why globalisation has occurred is that many governments and businesses believe that increased and freer trade between nations will offer prosperity and growth for all. Globalisation, they argue, has already brought many benefits: global food production has risen steadily over the last 20 years and malnutrition rates have fallen accordingly. Citizens in less-developed countries have access to health care, often supplied by foreign businesses.

For its supporters globalisation offers an opportunity rather than posing a threat. The leaders of the world's major economies and big businesses are committed to protecting and promoting global commerce and trade and emphasise the benefits it can bring.

The falling cost of international transport and communications

Improved transport and communication links have made the practical processes of producing and selling products in global markets easier and more cost effective. Two trends in transport are particularly important. The fall in the cost of air travel in real terms has made it feasible to transport some products such as fruit and vegetables by air enabling growers in Chile, for example, to sell products to wealthy consumers in North America and Europe. Simultaneously, the development of containerisation and much larger ships has brought down costs of sending products across the world by sea. When containers were first introduced they cost just $0.16 per tonne to load, compared with $5.83 per tonne for loose cargo. This reduction in costs has underpinned China's rise as the world's premier manufacturing economy.

Developments in technology have also made it quicker, simpler and less costly to send information around the world and to provide services. This has, for example, made it possible for many UK businesses to establish customer service facilities in countries such as India where wage costs are significantly lower.

The growth of global trading blocs and the reduction of barriers to trade

We saw in Chapter 4 on page 73 that the EU, one of the world's largest free trading blocs has expanded to 28 countries with a total population of over 505 million. This allows many businesses to sell internationally without hindrance. International trading blocs have also been established and expanded including the North American Free Trade Association (NAFTA) and the Association of Southeast Asian Nations (ASEAN) with similar consequences for trade. At the same time, despite some setbacks, the WTO has successfully reduced barriers to global trade.

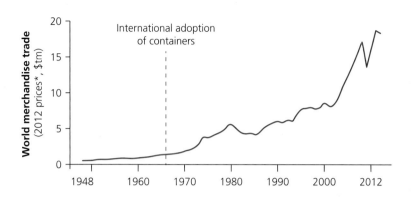

Ports worldwide	1965	1970
Port labour productivity, tonnes per hour	1.7	30.0
Average ship size, tonnes	8.4	19.7
Number of loading ports in Europe	11	3
Insurance costs**, £ per tonne	0.24	0.04
Value of goods in transit***, £ per tonne	2	1

* Deflated by US consumer prices
** Australia to Europe
*** Hamburg to Sydney

Figure 5.15 World trade, containerisation and other trade data

Source: *The Economist*, 16 May 2013; World Trade Organisation and US Bureau of Labour Statistics data

The growth of multinational companies

The growth of multinational companies such as Nissan, Apple and Lenovo can be seen as a cause of globalisation as well as a consequence of it. A driving force of globalisation has been multinational companies, which since the 1970s have constantly, and often successfully, lobbied governments to make it easier for them to put their skills and capital to work in a previously protected national market.

This has resulted in the rapid growth of some major well-known companies who sell high proportions of their production overseas. Many such companies are Asian as shown in Figure 5.16.

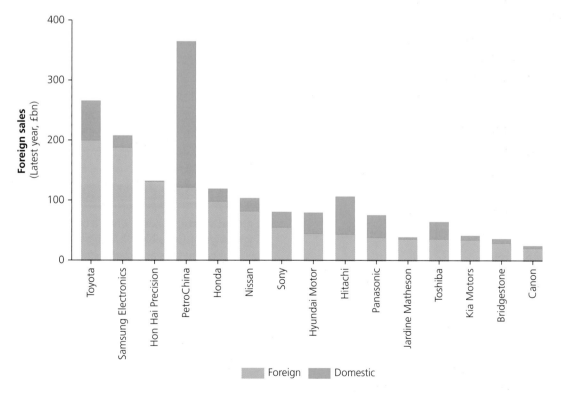

Figure 5.16 Some of Asia's prominent multinational companies and their export sales

Source: *The Economist*, 31 May 2014

Increasing global incomes and growing demand for goods and services

Many millions of consumers across the world are enjoying rising incomes as a result of economic development. For example, average incomes in China increased by approximately 500 per cent between 2000 and 2014. This gives Chinese consumers, as well as those in many other countries, the ability to buy many products produced elsewhere in the world and, thus, fuels trade. As an example, Jaguar Land Rover (JLR) sells an increasing proportion of its cars overseas as consumers' incomes rise and enable them to afford such products. This is shown in Table 5.7. Globalisation is also allowing JLR to take a strategic decision to produce its products in other countries. It already operates a factory in China and is in the process of building one in Brazil.

Country or region	Sales 2013–14	Sales 2012–13	Percentage change
UK	76,721	72,270	6%
North America	75,671	62,959	20%
Europe	82,854	80,994	2%
China	103,077	77,075	34%
Asia Pacific	22,795	17,849	28%
All other markets	73,193	63,489	15%
TOTAL	**434,311**	**374,636**	**16%**

Table 5.7 Jaguar Land Rover's sales have become more global as incomes have risen.

Source: Jaguar Land Rover Annual Report, 2014

Maths moment

$$\frac{1+b}{c}=3$$

Use the data in Table 5.7 to calculate the percentage of the increase in Jaguar Land Rover's total rise in total sales between the two years that was achieved in China.

The importance of globalisation for businesses

Globalisation offers a number of opportunities to businesses from any country and not just the UK:

- **Increased sales, revenues and profits**. Being able to trade freely in international markets offers the chance to increase sales substantially and to enjoy higher revenues and profits – if the business is sufficiently competitive. It has become possible to sell similar products to billions of global consumers and this has offered unrivalled opportunities for growth. Companies such as McDonald's and Coca-Cola have derived enormous benefits from this increased access in terms of rising revenues.

- **Cheaper resources**. Increased volumes of trade also make more resources available to businesses and allow them to source raw materials and labour significantly more cheaply than in the past. For example, many UK manufacturers including the train-maker Hornby and cosmetic manufacturer Avon have moved production facilities to China and Poland respectively to take advantage of cheaper labour. This has only been possible as a result of reduced costs of transportation and political and economic changes that have made it possible for UK businesses to locate in these countries.

- **Economies of scale**. The increased scale of production gives greater potential to benefit from economies of scale. This is especially true if it is possible to implement a **global strategy** whereby a similar product can be sold to consumers across the world. This means that fixed costs such as R&D can be spread across larger volumes of production lowering unit costs. At the same time, the company is likely to benefit from marketing and purchasing economies.

- **Developing different products for different markets**. The increased scale of production and access to large overseas markets such as China and India means that foreign companies can produce cars that meet the needs of local consumers. Thus, for example, increasing awareness of environmental issues and limited incomes mean that most Asian car consumers will wish to purchase small cars. The product that will be required will be different from those purchased in North America.

Key terms

A **global strategy** exists when a business produces a single product (possibly with slight variants) to meet the needs of consumers across the global market.

But globalisation brings drawbacks for all businesses too:

- **Downward pressure on prices**. All businesses have access to cheaper sources of raw materials and labour enabling them to reduce costs and selling prices. This has led to a sharpening of price competition. Prices of clothing, footwear and electronic products have fallen in the UK over recent years once inflation is taken into account. This means that for businesses to remain competitive in markets such as these it is imperative that they are able to reduce prices to match the general market trend. Some businesses have, however, recognised that they cannot compete in terms of price with producers based in countries with lower costs. As a result, they have adopted strategies to differentiate their products by, for example, developing a unique selling point (USP) based on quality or advanced technology.

- **New producers**. Established businesses in markets in Europe and North America have found themselves facing new competition from businesses in developing countries. For example, Petro China is China's largest company and was only founded in 1999. However, by 2014 it had generated annual revenues of more than £350 billion. Clearly, this company has become a fierce global competitor drilling and refining oil. Established producers have found that many markets have been subject to increased levels of imports from producers in countries such as Indonesia and India.
- **Increased need for investment**. Globalisation, by sharpening competitive pressures, has increased the pressure for businesses to invest to compete with firms from around the globe. Investment is required to produce new products which are differentiated from those currently available or to increase the skills and productivity of the businesses' workforces. These competitive strategies require investment in R&D and in training employees.
- **The threat of takeover**. Globalisation has seen the development of larger businesses more able to face the full force of global competition. Many businesses have taken over smaller competitors to give them greater economies of scale and, in some cases, a brand name that is familiar in other parts of the world. Smaller successful businesses might be particularly vulnerable to takeover because of the globalisation of markets.

Strategic decisions in response to globalisation

Globalisation is likely to remain an important issue for businesses for the foreseeable future. Some consumers from developed and developing countries can be expected to continue to voice their opposition to the actions of businesses that damage their local cultures

and their local environments. Multinationals need to achieve a tricky balance in their strategic planning between achieving their ambitions to operate in a global market whilst ensuring they do not alienate large numbers of the consumers who make up that market.

Some multinationals may opt for strategic alliances with businesses from other parts of the world to respond to the changes in the world economy that have been created by globalisation. This has been apparent in the car manufacturing and supermarket industries. For example, in 2015 Mahindra, an Indian vehicle manufacturer based in Mumbai, and Peugeot Citroën announced they were in talks to establish a strategic alliance. This would involve collaboration on technology, mutual sharing of production capacity in France and India as well as a major programme of investment.

Global strategies

Many products are sold in global markets nowadays. Examples include soft drinks sold by Pepsi-Cola and Coca-Cola, sport clothing produced by companies such as Nike and Adidas, and computers manufactured by Sony or Acer. Businesses may adopt global strategies when worldwide patterns of demand are similar and a single product or range of products, possibly with slight variants, is likely to meet the needs of the global consumer. Coca-Cola is a good example of a company that pursues a global strategy. This approach offers enormous scope for benefiting from economies of scale and the development of a global brand.

Multi-domestic strategies

Others businesses will take decisions to establish production capacity through the world and to sell differentiated products targeted to meet the needs of consumers in local markets. Toyota has adopted this strategy, producing different cars for the American and Asian markets. Businesses operating this type of multi-domestic strategy produce different products for different countries and markets. Decisions are taken at a local level wherever possible to allow the business to meet the needs of different customers. This strategy can encourage an entrepreneurial spirit at relatively junior levels in the organisation and high levels of innovation. Activities such as R&D may be conducted in local markets and supplies may be sourced locally.

The importance of emerging economies for business

Key terms

An **emerging market** (or economy) describes a country with low incomes per head but one which is enjoying high rates of economic growth.

Economic growth is the rate of increase in the size of an economy over time.

The **BRIC countries** are Brazil, Russia, India and China and are often referred to as prime examples of emerging markets.

A **multinational business** is one that has production capacity in more than one country.

The rise of **emerging markets** is inextricably tied up with globalisation. Globalisation is the result of the freeing up of trade by reducing political and legal barriers to it and by improving international communications and transport links. These developments have allowed economies such as China, India and Mexico to thrive. Freer trade and political systems have allowed businesses to succeed in emerging markets and have encouraged established producers to locate in these countries. At the same time domestic businesses in these emerging markets have grown rapidly. These changes, in total, have helped some emerging economies to achieve very high rates of **economic growth**.

China is probably the most immediately recognised of the so-called emerging markets or emerging economies. It has received much attention in the media for its spectacular rates of economic growth. Although these are beginning to slow, its economy still grew by 7.3 per cent in 2014. In 1980 the Chinese economy was about 25 per cent of the size of the UK's; by 2014 it was more than twice as large.

There are a number of other emerging economies, some of which are already very large. The economies of India and Brazil possess enormous potential. India's population exceeds 1.1 billion people and the country has specialised in providing services. Brazil has a smaller population (just over 200 million people in 2014) but huge natural resources, not least land and minerals. Both are already major economic powers. Russia, despite facing some economic difficulties at the time of writing, is also well endowed with natural resources in the form of oil and gas. Together, these four emerging economies are often referred to as the **BRIC countries**.

Other emerging economies include Turkey, Mexico, Poland, Indonesia, Saudi Arabia, Taiwan, Vietnam, Iran, Argentina and Thailand.

The growth rates achieved by the emerging economies such as India and China are much higher than that achieved by developed economies such as the UK and the USA. The UK's rate of economic growth has averaged 2.25–2.5 per cent over the period 1991–2014, whilst the more spectacular rates achieved by India and China are shown in Figure 5.17.

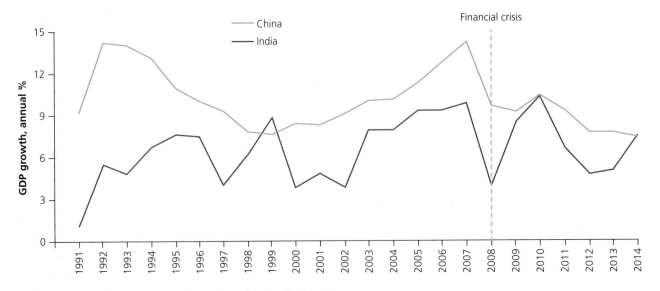

Figure 5.17 Rates of economic growth in India and China, 1991–2014

Source: World Bank national accounts data and OECD national accounts data files

Business in focus: Volkswagen invests in its Mexican factory

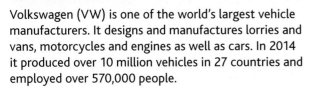

Volkswagen (VW) is one of the world's largest vehicle manufacturers. It designs and manufactures lorries and vans, motorcycles and engines as well as cars. In 2014 it produced over 10 million vehicles in 27 countries and employed over 570,000 people.

In March 2015 the company announced that it intended to invest $1 billion into its existing factory in Puebla in Mexico. VW opened the factory in 1964 and it currently manufactures 500,000 cars there each year, including the best-selling VW Golf. The proposed expansion will enable it to build a new version of the Tiguan, a four-wheel drive car, many of which will be built to customers' individual orders. The latest version of the car is larger to meet the needs of American consumers. The company plans to build 500 of the cars each day, many of which will be exported to other countries in North and South America.

'Localization has become key to safeguarding our competitive position on the global market and manufacturing the Tiguan in Mexico will bring production closer to the US market,' said Michael Horn, president and CEO of Volkswagen Group of America.

Mexico is the seventh largest manufacturer of cars in the world, although 80 per cent of vehicle production is exported. The Mexican Automotive Industry Association reported that in January 2015 over 266,000 vehicles were manufactured in the country, a rise of 6.8 per cent from January 2014.

Questions

1. Explain the possible reasons behind VW's decision to expand its factory in Mexico.
2. Can VW gain any competitive advantage from a decision to increase production in a country where many of its rivals also manufacture cars?

The importance of emerging economies for businesses

Emerging economies have numerous strengths and are hugely important to many businesses, not just as markets in which to sell goods and services, but also as attractive low-cost locations for production facilities. As such, they can be an essential part of a business's response to the process of globalisation and important for a number of reasons.

Enormous labour resources

China and India are the world's two most populous nations with 1.3 billion and 1.1 billion inhabitants respectively, while Indonesia's population exceeds 250 million. This helps wages to remain very low and has permitted the production of manufactured goods at very low costs, although wages have risen as the economies have grown. India's workforce is large and many Indians speak fluent English. An increasing proportion is highly educated allowing the country to provide large numbers of employees for the global IT industry. The immense pools of relatively cheap labour have attracted many global businesses to establish facilities in emerging economies. Others use companies based in emerging economies as suppliers. The Foxconn Technology Group is an electronics contract manufacturing company which employs 1.2 million people. It operates 13 factories in China and manufactures products for Amazon, Apple, BlackBerry and Sony.

Large markets

The large number of people in emerging economies also means that Brazil, Mexico, China, Indonesia and India are important markets for many companies because of the number of consumers and the fact that their incomes are generally rising rapidly. Companies such as McDonald's and Coca-Cola have targeted increasing sales in these countries as their inhabitants' incomes have increased. For some companies, such as those supplying tobacco, these markets can be exceptionally attractive as levels of health education are lower than in developed economies.

Rapid growth rates

Although their growth has slowed over recent years, many of the emerging markets are still expanding at impressive rates. Both China and India are achieving annual growth rates of over 7 per cent. In 2014 Indonesia's economy grew at 5 per cent, Malaysia's at 5.8 per cent and Vietnam's at 6.9 per cent. This growth means that many consumers have rising levels of disposable income to spend on consumer goods such as cars, clothes and electrical goods. Emerging economies are increasingly attractive markets for many **multinational businesses** because of the number of consumers and their rising incomes.

Natural resources

Some of the emerging economies, notably Brazil, Russia and Argentina benefit from having extensive natural resources. Brazil has huge amounts of timber, agricultural land and mineral resources. This is one factor influencing global manufacturers to develop production facilities in these countries.

The risks of emerging economies

Businesses that make decisions to establish production facilities in emerging economies are taking risks as a consequence. The benefits are attractive, but it can go wrong to a greater or lesser degree.

Economic risks

Inflation is a pressing problem for several of the emerging economies. In spring 2015 India was experiencing inflation of over 5 per cent and Indonesia's rate of price increase exceeded 6 per cent. We saw earlier that in Russia prices were rising at 15 per cent. High growth rates are not guaranteed. Economic growth in Brazil slowed alarmingly in 2014 and by early 2015 the economy was in recession.

It can be difficult to export to countries such as India, China and Russia. The governments there may impose taxes or other restrictions on imports or limit the ability of foreign businesses to operate there. Some emerging economies are very dependent on one or two products and are vulnerable to falling demand or prices for these products. The Russian economy has been hit hard by dramatic falls in global prices for oil and gas, for example.

Political risks

Not all emerging markets have stable political systems. The Russian economy is performing very poorly at the time of writing because many western economies have opposed its actions in Ukraine and have imposed economic sanctions. Similarly, Iran is subject to sanctions over developments in its nuclear industry. Unstable governments can take political decisions which can be very damaging to the business activities of multinational enterprises.

Risks to brand or corporate image

Benefiting from producing overseas in emerging or other economies can result in damage to a business's reputation. Low costs may be achieved at the cost of exploiting local employees or damaging the environment.

Apple has received a great deal of adverse publicity from its use of Foxconn as a manufacturer for its iPhones and other products. In December 2014, an investigation by the BBC revealed poor working conditions in one of Foxconn's factories in China where iPhones are manufactured. Even a brand as revered as Apple's is not immune to such criticism.

Study tip

The emerging economies are very different and businesses become involved with them for different reasons. Some produce there, others buy resources from emerging economies, whilst a third group of companies sell their products in emerging markets. You should consider these differences when writing about this area.

ASSESSMENT ACTIVITIES

(a) Knowledge check questions

1 Define the term 'gross domestic product' or 'GDP'.

2 Distinguish between a recession and a boom in an economy.

3 State what happens to the prices of exports and imports when a currency appreciates.

4 What is the difference between 'inflation' and 'deflation'?

5 State three main taxes that are paid by businesses in the UK.

6 List the macroeconomic objectives that are pursued by the UK government when operating its fiscal and monetary policies.

7 State two techniques of monetary policy that are available to the UK government.

8 State three methods of protectionism that a government might use to reduce imports of goods and services.

9 List three factors that have led to greater globalisation of businesses.

10 State two reasons why emerging economies or markets are important to many businesses.

(b) Short answer questions

1 Explain one possible benefit to UK businesses from the government decision to balance its budget as soon as possible. (4 marks)

2 Explain one possible drawback to a start-up business of the UK suffering from a period of deflation. (5 marks)

3 Explain why businesses may be disadvantaged in the long term if their governments implement measures intended to protect against imports. (5 marks)

4 Analyse the possible implications of a substantial fall in the pound's exchange rate for large UK businesses manufacturing chocolate, such as Cadbury. (9 marks)

(c) Data response question

Japan Tobacco International

Almost 160 years of cigarette manufacturing in Northern Ireland is ending after Japan Tobacco International (JTI), the maker of Silk Cut and Benson & Hedges, announced plans to close the UK's last remaining tobacco factory with the possible loss of 900 jobs.

JTI is restructuring its manufacturing facilities, which will see production moved from Northern Ireland, Belgium and Germany, to Eastern Europe, probably to two emerging economies: Poland and Romania. The company can see benefits from globalisation and sales of tobacco products are higher and more stable in some emerging markets.

JTI blamed new European rules which will prohibit tobacco companies from selling cigarettes in smaller packs than 20 while Menthol cigarettes will also be banned altogether. Cigarette production at its Ballymena factory would have fallen by almost a third in 2016 and 2017 due to these changes. Tobacco consumption in the UK has fallen steadily (as it has in most developed countries) since 1974. The UK government imposes heavy taxes on tobacco products totalling more than £12 billion in 2013–14. The company also said that taxation in the UK had influenced its decision.

'This restructuring proposal will allow JTI to optimise its operations, strengthen its competitive position and achieve its financial commitments in a challenging operating environment. Its implementation is to be phased, recognising the needs of each country, with factory closures completed between 2016 and 2018,' the company said in a statement.

Source: Adapted from an article in the *Daily Telegraph*, 8 October 2014

Questions

1 Explain how taxation in the UK might affect JTI's decision about relocating its factory.   (6 marks)

2 JTI is expected to make a decision to transfer cigarette production to Poland and Romania. Analyse why there might be relatively few risks in moving production to these emerging economies.   (9 marks)

3 'JTI is likely to benefit from continuing globalisation.' Do you agree with this statement? Justify your decision.   (15 marks)

(d) Essays

1 'Globalisation offers benefits to large businesses in the UK and imposes many costs on smaller ones.' To what extent do you agree with this statement? Justify your view.   (25 marks)

2 To what extent are changes in the level of a country's GDP the most important element of the economic environment influencing strategic decisions by its businesses?   (25 marks)

Chapter 6

Analysing the external environment: social and technological change

Introduction

This chapter considers the threats to, and opportunities for, businesses that are created by changes in their social, technological and competitive environments. Social changes will include those that are taking place in relation to migration and the lifestyles and buying behaviour of consumers, including the use of online businesses. This section also looks at the importance of Corporate Social Responsibility and contrasts the stakeholder and shareholder concepts. We also examine the pressure that business faces to behave in a socially responsible manner. We consider the profound changes that are taking place in the technological environment, not least the power of the smartphone to communicate with customers and how businesses may respond to this through functional and strategic decision making.

What you need to know by the end of this chapter:

- the impact of changes in the social and technological environment, including demographic changes, population movements and technological advances, on strategic and functional decision making within a business
- the reasons for and against corporate social responsibility (CSR), the differences between stakeholder and shareholder concepts and Carroll's CSR pyramid
- the pressure on businesses to behave in a socially responsible way.

Social changes

Businesses can be affected by social changes in two major ways. Social changes may lead to different goods and services being demanded. For example, the average age of the UK's population is rising, prompting increased sales of products associated with the later stages of life. Simultaneously, social changes can impact on the way that businesses produce goods and services. Thus, the increased use of tablets and smartphones to purchase products has led to many retailers increasing their online operations, sometimes at the expense of traditional shops.

Study tip

We looked at demographic factors as a component of the external environment of businesses in Chapter 3 of *AQA A-level Business 1*. You may wish to review the relevant pages of that chapter to refresh your memory before continuing with this chapter.

Demographic change and population movements

Key term

Demography is the study of human populations including their size, growth rates and movements.

Demographic change

We saw in Unit 1 of *AQA A-level Business 1* that the size and make-up of a population in terms of age can have important implications for businesses. Businesses draw on populations for their workforces and they also represent their consumers. Thus, **demographic** change can impact upon a business's costs of production as well as the level of demand for its products.

The population of the UK is demonstrating two major trends.

1. **It is growing quickly**. Since 1964 the population of the UK has grown by over 10 million people or 18.7 per cent. Partly this is due to people living longer and partly because of a rise in the birth rate. Approximately 50 per cent of this rise in the UK's population has taken place since 2001. Figure 6.1 shows that the rate of growth has been significantly higher since 2006.

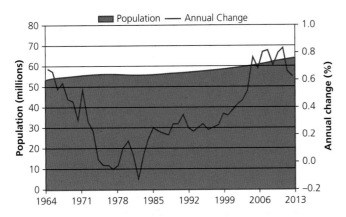

Figure 6.1 The UK's population size and rate of annual change, 1964–2013

Source: Office for National Statistics (ONS)

2. **It is ageing**. By 2045 there will be more than 10 million people over 75 years in the UK, twice as many as in 2015.

The combination of these two trends is that the UK's population will have more older and more younger people for the foreseeable future. These trends will change the shape of the family from a horizontal one to a vertical one: that is, to a family with more layers – grandparents and great grandparents – but fewer people in each generation as the numbers in the middle-age ranges will be lower.

These are important changes and will continue to have great implications for businesses. A larger population will lead to a rising demand for goods and services, and one with higher proportions of young and old people will demand different types of products. At the same time, businesses are likely to have ageing workforces and the proportion of people in the economy who are not working may rise. This could, for example, increase demand for leisure products.

In Chapter 5 we studied the importance of the process of globalisation. Globalisation means that for many UK businesses it is not just the changes in the UK population that matter, but changes in the global population.

The UK's membership of the EU grants the right of free movement to citizens of 27 other European countries providing an enormous potential workforce and market. At the same time, many employers in the UK are hiring employees from countries outside the EU if they have the skills that are required. We consider the impact of migration later in this chapter on pages 115–16.

The global population is expected to rise steadily throughout the 21st century, although the precise growth rate is a matter of some debate. Figure 6.2 shows a range of scenarios, influenced heavily by the birth rate with data indicating 80 and 95 per cent confidence intervals – that is, forecasts which statisticians are 80 and 95 per cent certain will prove correct.

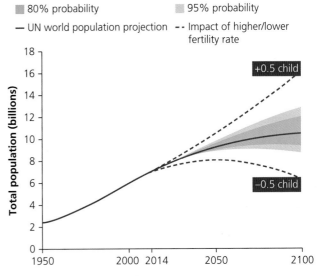

Figure 6.2 Global population forecasts for the remainder of the 21st century

Source: The *Guardian*, 18 September 2014

The growth in population will not be spread evenly across the globe. Much of the growth will occur in Africa. Sub-Saharan Africa is forecast to be the fastest growing region: its population is expected to rise from approximately 1 billion in 2014 to between 3.5 and 5 billion by 2100. In contrast, the population of Europe will grow much more slowly and will age. The population of Europe is currently 12 per cent of the world's population; by 2050 that figure is expected to

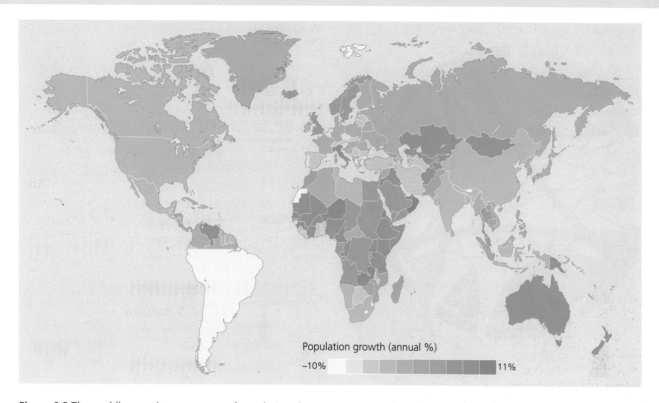

Figure 6.3 The world's annual average rates of population change

Source: World Bank data, http://web.worldbank.org/WBSITE/EXTERNAL/0, contentMDK:22547097~pagePK:50016803~piPK:50016805~theSitePK:13,00.html

fall to 7 per cent. Figure 6.3 illustrates the differences in population growth rates for most countries in the world and highlights the rapid changes in Africa and parts of Asia.

The effect of ageing populations is high on the agenda for governments in Europe and Japan currently. However, this problem will impact on countries that currently have young populations over time as their population growth slows. For example, in 2014 Brazil had 8.6 people of working age for every person over 65, but this ratio is expected to decline to 1.5 by 2100. China and India will face similar issues over time.

Population movements

Key terms

Migration is the movement of people between countries or regions.

Urbanisation is the movement of people from the countryside to live in cities.

Research into **migration** by the International Organisation for Migration has produced some startling statistics:

- In 2014, approximately one person in every seven is a migrant: 232 million people are international migrants, or 3.2 per cent of the world population, and 740 million are internal migrants.
- Since 1990, the number of international migrants increased by 65 per cent (53 million) in the Northern hemisphere and by 34 per cent (24 million) in the southern hemisphere.
- The share of international migrants in the total population varies widely across countries: it is high in the UAE (84 per cent), Qatar (74 per cent) and Kuwait (60 per cent) and is relatively high in traditional destination countries like Australia (28 per cent) and Canada (21 per cent).
- In Spain, Germany, the UK, France and Italy, migrants account for between 10 and 12 per cent of the population, but in Sweden the figure is 16 per cent.

Weblink

To find out more about the International Organisation for Migration visit:
www.iom.int/cms/en/sites/iom/home.html

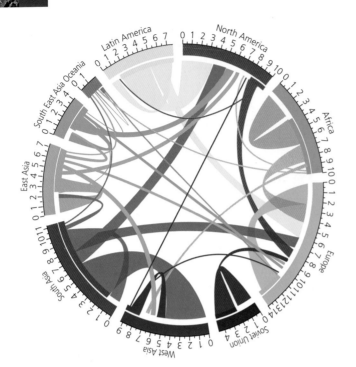

Figure 6.4 Flow of migrants between the world's countries and regions, 2005–10

Source: Guy Abel, https://gjabel.wordpress.com/

Figure 6.4 gives some indication of the size, sources and destinations of flows of international migrants. Many migrants move from countries with relatively low incomes to those with higher average incomes.

In addition, there are large-scale population movements taking place within countries. One of the most prominent of these is the movement of people from rural areas to towns and cities. This is a process called **urbanisation**. It has taken place on a large scale in developing countries where workers move from the countryside to seek better paid employment in the increasing number of factories that are operating in urban areas. *The Economist* estimates that China's urban population rose by 500 million between 1984 and 2014. It forecasts that the country's cities will be home to approximately 1 billion people – about 70 per cent of the country's population.

But urbanisation is not limited to emerging economies such as that of China. Most countries in the world have experienced this phenomenon. In 2013, for example, 82 per cent of people in the UK lived in urban areas. Table 6.1 shows the rates of urbanisation for a selection of countries as well as the increases between 2000 and 2013.

Figure 6.5 Some consequences of the rapid urbanisation that has taken place globally

Source: PWC Megatrends, www.pwc.co.uk/

Country	Percentage living in urban areas	
	2000	2013
Japan	79	92
Argentina	89	91
Netherlands	77	89
UK	79	82
Portugal	54	62
China	36	53
Indonesia	42	52

Table 6.1: Urbanisation rates for a selection of countries, 2000 and 2013

Source: World Bank data set,
http://data.worldbank.org/indicator/SP.URB.TOTL.IN.ZS?page=2

Maths moment

In 2000 the population of Japan was 127 million and by 2013 it had risen slightly to 127.4 million. Use the data in Table 6.1 to calculate how many additional Japanese people were living in urban areas in 2013 compared with 2000.

The implications of demographic change and population movements for businesses

The implications of demographic change and population movements are potentially immense but also difficult to predict as population forecasts can vary widely, as seen in Figure 6.2 on page 114. The picture is further complicated by a lack of certainty about likely income levels in some countries which experience rapid population growth. Demand for a wide range of goods and services could increase rapidly along with the size of the population over the long term, even if the more modest demographic forecasts are correct.

However, if income per head remains low, or even declines, the impact on demand may diminish considerably. The population of Nigeria is expected to increase from 200 million currently to 900 million by 2100: if incomes rise, this would be a highly attractive market for many businesses as it will have a larger population than the USA. It would also comprise many younger consumers who might buy the products of fashion clothing and technology companies at a time when demand in some countries with declining and ageing populations may be stalling. Businesses may need to make strategic decisions about entering new markets to take advantage of these opportunities. These may be profitable in the longer term but could involve a high degree of risk. Other firms will find these opportunities attractive and they could prove highly competitive.

Business in focus: Demographic change and the leisure industry

In 2013 Visit England commissioned Trajectory, a leading insight and futures consultancy, to report on forecast changes in the external environment for businesses in the leisure and tourism industry. The information below is part of its report.

Type of demographic change	Possible implications
Ageing society	As life expectancy increases, there will be increasing numbers of older people in society
Vertical family	Driven by both rising life expectancy and lower fertility rates, the shape of the family is changing
Baby boom	Over the past 15 years a sustained rise in the birth rate has caused a mini baby boom
Untraditional families	New types of family are emerging – including step families, gay parents and older parents
Changing ethnic profile	A rising number of both BME and foreign born people, whose tourism habits need to be understood
Squeezed middle generation	Amid rises in the number of younger and older people, the number aged 35–49 is falling
Multispeed demography	For different regions and local authorities, the speed and nature of these changes will vary

Table 6.2 A summary of population and social change trends

Key implications for the leisure industry

- Families are changing in size, shape and composition, and are far removed from the traditional 'nuclear' family – tourism businesses need to be flexible and responsive.
- A baby boom and an ageing population will see an emphasis on the intergenerational family holiday.
- Grandparents will be 'younger' than ever before, and retiring baby boomers will prioritise their leisure time.
- A sharp rise in the number of over-80s will see a generation keen to go on holiday but potentially reluctant (or unable) to travel far.
- The 'squeezed middle generation' (those aged 35–49 in 2020) will be time poor and willing to treat themselves.
- Black and minority ethnic (BME) and immigrant populations' tourism habits are currently poorly understood – but are an increasingly large part of the market.

Questions

1. Explain the possible decisions that a UK hotel chain might take in response to the opportunities provided by the forecast demographic changes for the UK.
2. Do forecast global demographic changes offer more opportunities than threats for UK businesses?

The ageing populations of Europe and Japan will provide increasing opportunities for a range of businesses supplying products such as health care and leisure products. However, the scale of these opportunities can be difficult to predict over the longer term. The Office for Budget Responsibility (OBR) has predicted that health care spending in the UK could range from 7.8 to 16.6 per cent of GDP in 2061, compared with 6.8 per cent in 2016–17. At the same time, the UK will have a larger number of young people due to a rise in its birth rate since the 1990s. We have explored some of the effects that may result from changes in the size and composition of the UK's population in the Business in focus feature on page 117. Businesses, and not just those in the leisure and tourism industries, will have opportunities in the form of the development of new markets (for some ethnic groups), as well as the expansion of existing ones such as those for the young and very elderly. The latter may prove attractive as it may involve functional and less risky decisions as businesses seek to increase sales in growing markets in which they already operate.

Opportunities will also exist for HR managers to harness the innovative potential of diverse workforces towards achieving businesses' goals. Recent research has identified a strong correlation between those businesses that employ diverse workforces and the level of the businesses' performance. Drawing on the changing composition of populations, as is occurring in the UK, can enhance a business's competitiveness. The most innovative companies are already using increasingly diverse workforces in terms of gender, ethnicity, age and values.

For many other businesses opportunities and threats will coexist. Changes in the structure and location of population caused by age changes, urbanisation and migration will create new or expand existing market segments or niches. Agile and proactive enterprises may be able to exploit new markets, especially with the use of appropriate technology. The threats of competitors growing at their expense will be greater for businesses that do not recognise that this element of their external environment is changing rapidly.

What do you think?

Are businesses in the fashion and technology industries most likely to be affected by the forecast changes in population?

Urbanisation throws up a range of different opportunities and threats for businesses. Opportunities exist in providing many different goods and services to markets that are growing quickly. The consumers of these goods may be individuals, other businesses and governments. For example, Figure 6.5 illustrates the likely scale of investment in just four cities over a ten-year period. This high level of investment is likely to be replicated in urban areas across the world as governments seek to provide transport and communication facilities to allow cities to flourish. Companies that can provide technological solutions to problems such as providing large amounts of cost-efficient renewable energy, high-technology low-carbon transport and how to fund such developments will benefit from the process of urbanisation. Urbanisation can also provide opportunities for new businesses to establish themselves to supply the needs of migrants to the cities which may not be well catered for by existing businesses. It is, of course, easier to gain a customer base in a market that is growing.

Figure 6.6 Masdar City will incorporate the latest technology in construction, energy supply and transportation. It will be completed by 2025 and will be home to 50,000 people and 1,500 clean technology businesses.

The threats to businesses of demographic change and population movements can take the form of increased competition, possibly from overseas businesses, attracted by the growing market. Competition may force up the price of resources such as land and property, pushing up the operating costs of businesses in urban areas. Rents for offices in major cities are rising quickly: rents for office space in New York are approximately four times those in rural areas in the USA. Businesses in urban areas may face squeezed profit margins as a consequence unless they can take decisions to locate in less costly areas.

Changes in consumer lifestyle and buying behaviour

Key term

Ethical behaviour is that which is regarded as being morally correct, such as using sustainable sources of supply for resources used in production.

Lifestyles and consumer buying behaviour are closely related. When a consumer experiences a significant change in lifestyle, such as becoming unemployed or getting married, their buying behaviour is likely to change. It is possible to identify a number of contemporary influences on consumer lifestyles and to consider how these might impact on the spending behaviour of consumers.

The impact of technology on lifestyles and buying behaviour

Technology is having a significant impact on lifestyles. Consumers are embracing developments that synchronise their home appliances with tablets and smartphones and can control domestic appliances from outside the home. They are also increasingly willing to wear technology that monitors factors such as blood pressure and distance walked. Over 21 million wearable devices were sold worldwide in 2014. These types of technology allow consumers to focus on issues of importance such as health, controlling expenditure and convenience. Some of these products encourage consumers to record lots of data about themselves for personal use, and perhaps to share with companies. As a result, consumers are increasingly willing to invest in this technology and companies may have access to large amounts of data about consumers and their behaviour.

Research by Mintel in 2015 showed that:

- over 20 per cent of adults in the UK use a wearable device or a mobile app to monitor their health and 40 per cent are interested in doing so
- in the USA 59 per cent of consumers expressed an interest in using an app to control household appliances in their homes.

Such developments not only increase consumer expenditure on smartphones, tablets and wearable gadgetry, but also on sophisticated devices that can engage with them such as the latest TVs and digital controls for air-conditioning or heating systems.

Technology can also affect consumer buying behaviour directly by providing more information and thereby shaping purchasing decisions. For example, technology can provide consumers with details about a business's operations. Research suggests that a majority of UK consumers are influenced in buying decisions by the ethical or environmental behaviour of businesses. Technology helps them to identify businesses that behave in undesirable ways. Social media provide a vast amount of information about the activities of businesses and apps are being developed to provide data to help consumers rate firms and products according to their ethical and environmental performance. Specialist websites also provide consumers with a great deal of information about businesses and their actions that have damaged the environment, resulted in perceived underpayment of taxes or have behaved unethically. Whether or not a business is perceived as exhibiting ethical behaviour (or not) can greatly affect customers' buying decisions. Ethical Consumer is an example of this type of specialist website that provides such information.

Weblink

Find the Ethical Consumer website at: www.ethicalconsumer.org/

Health and well-being

Personal health and well-being are increasingly important to many consumers in the UK who are concerned about adopting or maintaining a healthy lifestyle for themselves and their families. This may take the form of seeking an improved work-life balance, a nutritious diet, weight loss or more exercise.

Consumers are increasing expenditure on a range of foods and other products with the intention of promoting their health and well-being. Figure 6.7 shows that the effects of this change in consumer lifestyle is not limited to the UK, but is a global trend. Consumers in emerging markets such as India and Brazil are spending increasing amounts on products related to their health and well-being. Global expenditure is expected to reach $1,000 billion by 2017 according to Euromonitor International.

This change in consumer lifestyle has prompted increased expenditure on services and consumer durable products, as well foodstuffs as illustrated in Figure 6.7. Companies are selling increased volumes of sports clothing, sports equipment such as exercise bicycles, juicers and gym memberships.

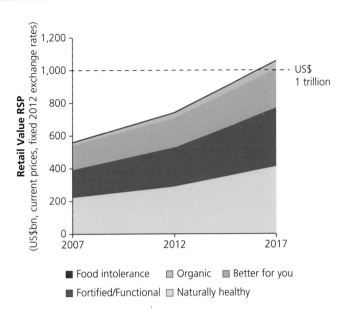

Figure 6.7 Global spending on foods intended to promote health and well-being, 2007–17

Source: Euromonitor International

Consumer confidence

In 2008, the UK and many other countries suffered a financial crisis which threatened the survival of a number of very large banks. As a consequence, their lending activities were severely curtailed and this reduced consumer expenditure and the level of business activity. In turn, this resulted in the UK suffering a deep recession and one in which consumers'

incomes, in real terms, were only restored to their 2007 levels in 2015. Employment in the UK appears to have recovered with more people in work than at any other time – nearly 31 million in January 2015. However, this is misleading to some extent. Many jobs are part-time or 'zero hours' contracts where workers are not guaranteed regular hours. In 2014, approximately 3 million employees in the UK said they would like more hours.

The effects of the recession, lack of hours, slow increases in real pay rates and diminished consumer confidence have all combined to have a significant effect on consumers' buying behaviour. Consumers have been reluctant to spend freely on non-essential products, have focused on repaying debts and even spending on basics such as food has been muted.

Figure 6.8 shows that consumers in the UK only experienced a recovery in their spending power in late 2014. Average household discretionary income was 8.9 per cent higher in December 2014 than in December 2103. This rise in spending power has been accompanied by a welcome fall in the price of many essential products including energy. Despite this evidence of recovery in consumer confidence, the uncertain nature of some employment continues to have an impact on spending patterns and levels, and some economists believe the recovery in consumer confidence and spending is still very fragile.

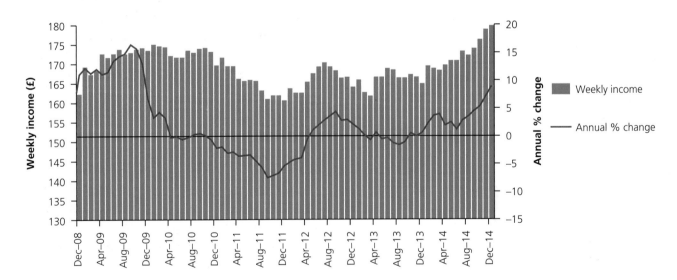

Figure 6.8 Average weekly discretionary incomes and annual changes in discretionary income for the UK, 2008–14

Source: Centre for Economics & Business Research

Business in focus: Wearable health and fitness products

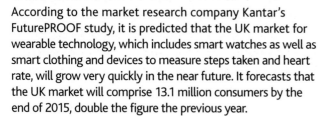

According to the market research company Kantar's FuturePROOF study, it is predicted that the UK market for wearable technology, which includes smart watches as well as smart clothing and devices to measure steps taken and heart rate, will grow very quickly in the near future. It forecasts that the UK market will comprise 13.1 million consumers by the end of 2015, double the figure the previous year.

In 2014, when the research was conducted, 6.7 million people in the UK owned wearable technology and UK consumers had spent somewhere between £225 million and £375 million in this market so far. Of those surveyed, 90 per cent used a free app, while as many as 50 per cent only used software that was available without charge. The company's research revealed other data of interest to businesses operating (or planning to enter) this market:

- nearly 90 per cent of respondents said they would consider paying for a health app
- over 20 per cent of those surveyed were interested in purchasing smart clothing and approximately 30 per cent would buy smart jewellery

- of those who pay for software, 79 per cent owned wearable technology to enable them to track data.

Rioch Brewer, one of Kantar's statisticians said: 'The health and fitness wearables market is still in its infancy, and brands targeting younger audiences as well as those in the sport and leisure categories are leading the way. These figures are set to increase as brands innovate in this space as a means of attempting to engage with consumers and extend the overall brand experience. It is also interesting to see that consumers are happy to pay for apps and devices, which opens up additional opportunities for manufacturers and developers.'

Source: Adapted from an article in *The Drum*, 16 October 2014

Questions
1. Explain the possible implications of this trend for businesses other than those that manufacture wearable technology.
2. Is manufacturing wearable technologies a risky market for firms to enter?

The implications of changes in consumer lifestyles for businesses

Well-managed businesses monitor changes in consumer lifestyles and respond to the opportunities. For example, Nike has made a major decision to engage in a joint project with Apple to produce wearable technology. This strategic decision will help to promote the Nike brand and enable the company to link the new technology to Apple's existing products.

Businesses also have to respond to the threats that result from changes in consumer lifestyles. Low levels of consumer confidence resulted in dramatic shifts in consumer spending in the UK groceries market. In November 2014, UK consumer spending on groceries fell (by 0.2 per cent) for the first time in 20 years. This decline and the increased popularity of shopping in small local stores has led supermarkets such as Tesco, Sainsbury's and Morrisons to take a number of decisions:

- to close some larger and loss-making stores
- to focus on smaller, local convenience stores
- to cut prices to attract customers away from rivals
- to establish new alliances – for example Sainsbury's has formed a partnership with the low-price supermarket Netto to support Netto's re-entry to the UK market.

The increased amount of information consumers want and have access to has led to businesses developing new products to meet these needs. Many new health monitoring products are available for consumers to buy and supporting services such as free blood pressure checks are available from instore pharmacies.

Advances in technology alongside changes in consumer behaviour mean that businesses have to be increasingly aware of protecting their image and reputation and prepared to respond rapidly to adverse comments on social media by apologising, compensating, explaining or correcting unsatisfactory behaviour as appropriate. Functional decisions to establish and expand social media teams to carry out these duties are essential for businesses.

The growth of online businesses

Online businesses are predicted to grow rapidly over the next few years in all countries and their expansion is supported by changes in consumer lifestyle, particularly the increasing use of smartphones, tablets and other internet-linked devices.

The growth of online businesses has already had a huge impact on the retail industry in the UK and elsewhere. The Centre for Retail Research in the UK forecasts further growth in online retail sales. It says that online is the fastest growing part of the retail market in Europe. Sales in the UK, Germany, France, Sweden, the Netherlands, Italy, Poland and Spain are expected to grow by 18.4 per cent from £132.05 billion in 2014 to £156.67 billion in 2015, reaching £185.44 billion in 2016. The proportion of the retail market that is conducted online varies enormous across Europe. It offers considerable potential for growth in online sales in high income countries such as Italy and Spain (as shown in Figure 6.9) at a time when online retailing is in its infancy.

Figure 6.9 The share of the retail market held by online businesses in selected European countries in 2014 and 2015

Source: Centre for Retail Research

Weblink

To find out more about the work of the Centre for Retail Research visit:
www.retailresearch.org

However, it is not just the retail industry that is in the process of being transformed by developing its online presence. Increasingly, transport companies are selling their products online. For example, low-cost airline easyJet sells 90 per cent of its flights online and its sales volume can reach 100,000 customers a day. The online model also allows the company to adjust its prices to reflect peaks and troughs in demand. This helps it to maximise its revenue from sales.

Many other online markets are developing, offering a range of opportunities to innovative businesses. One example is the growth of online broadcasting. Some TV and radio stations are online only, allowing them to reach a global audience. Other companies have established websites to allow consumers access to TV and radio stations from around the globe. Streema.com is a small business that offers its consumers access to radio and TV stations from countries across the world. Other industries, such as gambling and companies that operate websites providing product reviews and comparisons, have thriving operations on the internet.

The implications of the growth of online businesses

The Centre for Retail Research forecasts that the retail industry in the UK will change profoundly by 2018, and a major driver of change is the rise of online retailing. The Centre's forecasts are as follows.

● Total store numbers will fall by 22 per cent, from 281,930 in 2014 to 220,000 in 2018 and result in an estimated 316,000 job losses.
● The share of online retail sales will rise from 13.5 per cent in 2014 to 21.5 per cent by 2018 or the end of the decade.
● There will be a further 164 major or medium-sized retailers facing financial difficulties by 2018. Many of these companies will survive but only through closing 22,600 stores and reducing employment by 140,000 employees.

Managers of retail businesses will have to take a range of strategic and functional decisions in response to this changing environment. Online developments pose a threat and will reduce the sales of many established retailers. For example, Tesco has already announced store closures and the reduction in its retailing capacity. The growth of online retailing offers a huge threat to many retailers, especially small ones whose products can easily be sold online. The number of bookshops in the UK has declined sharply, for example, due to the rising online sales of books, especially by Amazon, the world's largest retailer. The owners of small bookshops have responded by providing a wider range of in-store facilities such as cafés and crèches with mixed results. The number of shops in the UK has declined steadily since 1950 as shown in Figure 6.10, but this decline is accelerating again due principally to online retailing.

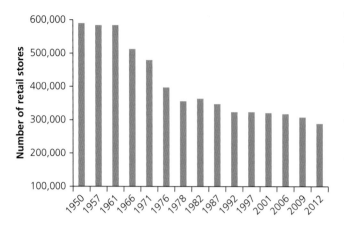

Figure 6.10 The number of retail stores in the UK, 1950–2012

Source: Centre for Retail Research

However, these changes also offer opportunities for retailers of all sizes. Retailers with large stores are dividing the floor space and renting some to other retailers. Online developments are also encouraging businesses to cooperate in other ways. Amazon offers local pick-up points for the products it sells for those who do not want postal deliveries. Customers may, for example, pick up their Amazon delivery from a local newsagent.

The increasing use of the internet by people in the UK and elsewhere offers opportunities for entrepreneurs to start up or expand small businesses, as well as to multinationals such as Amazon. Crowdfunding is a comparatively new industry that has developed using the power of the internet. Companies such as Funding Circle invite individuals with spare savings to lend money to other individuals or businesses through their websites in a process called crowdfunding. The internet allows crowdfunding companies to link lenders and borrowers in an effective low-cost model.

Online trading has supported other businesses in developing their business models and increasing sales. Market research companies use online surveys in addition to other methods of collecting data. Many newspapers and magazines are experiencing falling sales of 'hard copy' but rising viewing figures of online versions suitable for reading on tablets and smartphones as well as laptops, although their articles are also viewed through other websites. Some industries now operate almost exclusively online, for example dating agencies.

Trading online offers businesses the potential for substantial benefits.

- There is the prospect of lower costs if a business needs less property, especially if it is needed in expensive city locations.
- It may also be able to operate with fewer employees reducing labour costs.
- Another major benefit relates to marketing. Possessing an effective website offers even the smallest businesses the chance to reach a large market. Small businesses can sell to global markets in a way that would not have been possible 20 years ago.
- Finally, the internet provides entrepreneurs with a means of developing start-up enterprises quickly and cheaply. Snapchat, a business providing a photo messaging application, was established by three Stanford University students in 2011. By 2014, the app's users were sending 700 million photos and videos each day and the business was valued at $10 billion.

Corporate social responsibility

Corporate social responsibility (CSR) is a business philosophy that emphasises that firms should behave as good citizens – this is sometimes simply termed 'social responsibility'. They should not merely operate within the law, but should consider the effects of their activities on society as a whole. Thus, a socially responsible business attempts to fulfil the duties that it has towards its employees, customers and other interested parties. Collectively, these individuals and groups are termed a business's **stakeholders**.

Key terms

Corporate social responsibilities (CSR) are the duties a business has towards employees, customers, society and the environment.

Stakeholders are individuals or groups within society who have an interest in an organisation's operation and performance.

A **pressure group** is a group of people with common interests who organise to influence public opinion and the decisions of businesses and governments.

Ethics are moral principles that can shape the way a business behaves.

Stakeholder group	Possible nature of stakeholder's interest
Shareholders	● Regular dividends ● Rising share prices ● Preferential treatment as customers – for example, lower prices
Employees	● Steady and regular income ● Healthy and safe working conditions ● Job security ● Promotion and higher incomes
Customers	● Certain and reliable supply of goods ● Stable prices ● Safe products ● After-sales service and technical support
Suppliers	● Frequent and regular orders ● A sole supplier agreement ● Fair prices
Creditors	● Repayment of money owed at agreed date ● High returns on investments ● Minimal risk of failure to repay money owed
The local community	● Steady employment ● Minimal pollution and noise ● Provision of facilities (for example, scholarships, art centres or reclaimed areas) for the local community

Table 6.3 Stakeholders' interests

Over recent years businesses have become increasingly aware of the expectations of stakeholder groups. In the past, managers often operated businesses largely in the interest of the shareholders. A growing awareness of business activities by consumers and other stakeholder groups, driven by recent developments such as the widespread use of social media, has complicated the task of management teams. Businesses are also subject to the attention of **pressure groups** pursuing a particular interest. For example, Greenpeace and Friends of the Earth campaign to protect the environment and their activities have significant implications for businesses. This means that managers have to attempt to meet the demands of a number of stakeholder groups which are likely to conflict at times.

Meeting social responsibilities has many implications for businesses including:

● taking into account the impact of their activities on the local community – protecting employment and minimising noise pollution, for instance
● producing in a way that minimises pollution or the reckless use of finite resources
● treating employees fairly and not simply meeting the demands of employment legislation
● considering the likely sources of supplies (and whether they are sustainable) and the ways in which suppliers meet their social responsibilities.

Study tip

When writing about stakeholders it is important to develop answers fully. This is impossible if you attempt to cover too many stakeholder groups – just concentrate on two or three.

Some businesses willingly accept these responsibilities partly because their managers want to do so and partly because they fear a negative public image. It may be argued that socially responsible behaviour can pay off for businesses in the long term, but may entail additional short-term expenditure.

Archie Carroll developed his CSR pyramid in 1996 as a way of setting out the ways in which an organisation could meet its social responsibilities. Carroll stated that: 'corporate social responsibility involves the conduct of a business so that it is economically profitable, law abiding, ethical and socially supportive. To be socially responsible then means that profitability and obedience to the law are foremost conditions when discussing the firm's **ethics** and the extent to which it supports the society in which it exists…' By creating different layers in the pyramid as a hierarchy as in Figure 6.11, it can assist managers in understanding the different types of obligations that a business has towards society.

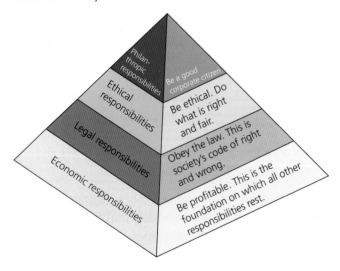

Figure 6.11 Carroll's CSR pyramid

Carroll's pyramid sets out a hierarchy of four types of responsibility that a business should meet to be socially responsible:

1. **Economic (or financial) responsibilities**. This is the responsibility to be profitable. Without this the organisation would be unlikely to survive in

the long term and thus not able to fulfil its other responsibilities to society.

2. **Legal responsibilities**. Businesses should obey the laws of the countries in which they are operating. Meeting these responsibilities will help to ensure the business acts in the best interest of society by, for example, paying minimum wages and avoiding activities that cause pollution.

3. **Ethical responsibilities**. This is a step beyond meeting legal responsibilities and entails behaving in a morally correct way to meet ethical responsibilities. Thus, for a business in the UK, this might entail paying the living wage (a recommended wage to enable employees to pay the basic costs of living) rather than the legally-enforceable minimum wage. At the time of writing, the living wage is £9.15 an hour in London and £7.85 an hour in the rest of the UK, while the national minimum wage is £6.70 an hour for adults aged 21 and over.

4. **Philanthropic responsibilities**. These responsibilities relate to discretionary behaviour by businesses to improve the lives of others in society. Examples include making charitable donations, providing recreational facilities for communities or sponsoring sports events.

Carroll argued that CSR requires businesses to satisfy all four levels of the pyramid consecutively. Using this as his basis, Carroll defined CSR as encompassing 'the economic, legal, ethical and philanthropic expectations placed on organisations by society at a given point in time'.

Business in focus: 'Tax shaming'

In the UK, a number of multinational companies, including Amazon, Starbucks and Google, have received public criticism for paying small amounts of tax or, in some cases, no tax at all here. This adverse publicity, dubbed 'tax shaming', has led to threats of customer boycotts and resulted in Starbucks making a voluntary tax payment of £20 million to HMRC during 2013 and 2014.

A similar trend has emerged in the USA where the government is thought to have missed out on billions of dollars of tax revenue due to tax avoidance. Pressure groups have been established there, calling for companies to behave fairly rather than taking advantage of loopholes in the country's laws to reduce their tax liabilities. Many people have expressed concern at the extent of the underpayment of business taxes in the USA. The proportion of the American government's total tax yield which comes from businesses has steadily fallen:

- In 1952 businesses paid 32 percent of federal taxes, individuals contributed another 42 percent and payroll taxes were 10 percent.
- By 2011 the proportion of federal tax revenue paid by individuals remained at 42 per cent, payroll taxes had risen to 40 per cent and taxes on businesses was just 9 per cent.

Two pressure groups (Citizens for Tax Justice and US PIRG) commissioned a report on the issue entitled 'Offshore Shell Games' which summarised the extent of the problem:

'Only 55 Fortune 500 companies disclose what they would expect to pay in US taxes if these profits were not officially booked offshore. All told, these 55 companies would collectively owe $147.5 billion in additional federal taxes. To put this enormous sum in context, it represents more than the entire state budgets of California, Virginia and Indiana combined.'

The companies involved reduce their tax payments by registering their businesses in tax havens outside the USA such as the Cayman Islands and Bermuda. (There are currently more than 18,000 American companies registered in the Cayman Islands alone.) The report showed that the revenues of the subsidiaries of American companies in these two countries amounted to $145 billion, whilst the total GDP of Bermuda and the Cayman Islands jointly was only $9 billion. These figures clearly do not compute.

Source: Adapted from an article in the *Guardian*, 22 July 2014

Questions

1. Explain how Carroll's CSR pyramid could be used to assess the behaviour of many large businesses in the USA.

2. Is tax shaming a better way to encourage businesses to accept their social responsibilities than passing new laws?

Shareholder and stakeholder concepts

The shareholder concept

A school of thought exists that supports what is known as 'the shareholder concept'. This view, originally developed by the economist Milton Friedman, argues that management teams should only aim to meet their responsibilities to shareholders and that this is best done by maximising the business's profits. They argue this should result in increasing share prices and higher dividend payments which will satisfy shareholders. The needs of other stakeholders are regarded as of secondary importance. Using the shareholder approach has some risks. It tends to encourage short-termism in decision making and also the increased taking of risks to generate maximum profits. In extreme cases, pressure on management teams to improve profitability has led to the falsification of financial statements as in the case of Enron.

The stakeholder concept

Some management teams operate with the expectation that the business will take into account the obligations it may have to society in general in all its decision making. This is known as 'the stakeholder concept' whereby a business considers the needs of its stakeholders, and not just its shareholders. The stakeholder concept or theory was first set out by Edward Freeman in his book *Strategic Management: A Stakeholder Approach* in 1984, and it has influenced the behaviour of many businesses since. It can be an important component of corporate social reporting, which we consider below.

An alternative way – enlightened shareholder value

Enlightened shareholder value (ESV) is the idea that companies should pursue shareholder wealth with a long-term orientation that seeks sustainable growth and profits based on responsible attention to all relevant stakeholder interests. Essentially, it is a middle way that focuses on generating shareholder value, whilst having regard to the long-term external impacts on stakeholders.

The ESV approach was taken up by the UK government and is now a legal requirement on businesses as part of the Companies Act, 2006. The emergence of ESV constitutes an important development in corporate governance, particularly in determining what directors must consider when managing the affairs of their companies and a clear move away from the shareholder concept.

Corporate social reports

Key term

Corporate social reports are documents setting out a business's targets for meeting its social obligations and the extent to which previous social targets have been achieved.

One way in which businesses can demonstrate their commitment to meeting their social responsibilities (and not just the needs of shareholders) is by producing **corporate social reports**. Corporate social reports are documents that set out a business's targets for meeting its social obligations and document the extent to which

previous social targets have been achieved. Corporate social reports are increasingly important as businesses are held responsible for the consequences of their actions. Over 8,000 businesses around the world have signed the UN Global Compact pledging to demonstrate good global citizenship in the areas of human rights, labour standards and environmental protection.

A growing proportion of businesses are engaging in social responsibility reporting. This form of reporting entails setting out the costs to the business of acting in a socially responsible manner (making charitable donations, for example) and the benefits received, which are usually difficult to quantify in monetary terms. A few businesses include their social reports within their annual reports. Under a corporate social report a 'successful' business might not be the most profitable, but the one of most value to all sections of the community in which it operates.

Corporate social reports frequently have several elements, although they vary between businesses. Firstly, firms tend to draw up and implement policies stating the ways in which they will conduct the aspects of their business which impact upon society generally. This may include issues such as the following:

- using sustainable sources of raw materials
- ensuring suppliers trade responsibly avoiding, for example, the use of child labour
- operating an extensive health and safety policy above the legal requirements, thereby protecting the well-being of employees
- engaging in a continuous process of environmental management and monitoring the effects of production on the environment
- trading ethically and taking account of the moral dimension in decision making.

Figure 6.12 illustrates the approach to corporate social reporting taken by the multinational fast-food retailer McDonald's. Its corporate social report is based upon five 'pillars' which encompass its commitments to its stakeholders.

It is common for an independent body to monitor the effectiveness of CSR policies and the effects on society generally. This helps to persuade stakeholders that the results published are genuine. Once the corporate social report is complete, firms review their social and environmental policies in the light of the information from the auditors.

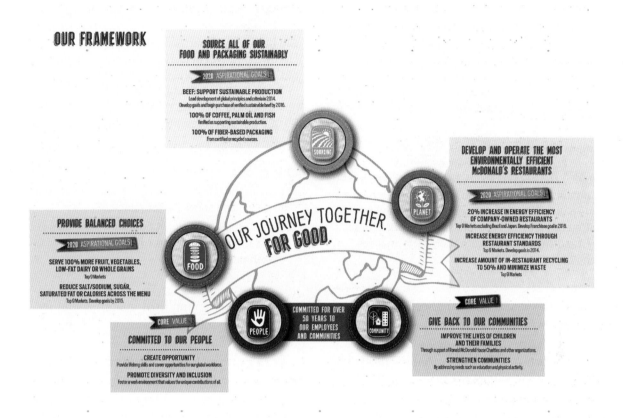

Figure 6.12 The framework for McDonald's corporate social reporting

Source: McDonald's Corporate Social Responsibility & Sustainability Report
www.aboutmcdonalds.com/

Corporate social reporting can be a valuable exercise for firms to conduct. For example, it may identify anti-social behaviour before problems arise. They also help to promote the corporate image of the business as a caring and responsible organisation. However, conducting an audit of this kind is not a guarantee that a firm is socially responsible. Managers must ensure that social policies are carried out effectively at all levels within the organisation and that employees are committed to them. Sufficient resources must be devoted to ensuring that the business remains socially responsible and problems identified in social audits should be resolved speedily. The danger of a less active approach is that social audits publicise weaknesses and firms are seen not to respond with damaging consequences for their corporate image.

The trend to social and environmental reports continues with many large firms producing some form of report. The quality of many of the reports is improving, though some do not cover all the relevant issues. Also, many companies still do not have their corporate social reports independently audited to confirm their accuracy.

A further criticism is that some firms do not analyse their supply chains. This means that suppliers could engage in practices such as employing children without it being revealed in the corporate social report. It is possible that the effects of slow rates of economic growth in many countries might reduce the numbers of businesses prepared to devote resources to producing a corporate social report, or to improving its quality and extent.

The pressures for socially responsible behaviour

We have already seen that consumers in the UK and elsewhere are better informed about the activities of businesses with respect to the environment and their stakeholders. Developments in technology and notably the rising use of social media to report behaviour by firms that is deemed unacceptable has had a significant impact on corporate decision making. Bad news about a company can be tweeted and re-tweeted thousands of times reaching many potential consumers. Companies have to be aware of this and aim to avoid being the subject of bad news.

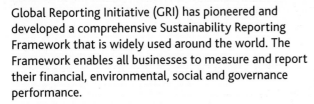

Business in focus: Global Reporting Initiative

Global Reporting Initiative (GRI) has pioneered and developed a comprehensive Sustainability Reporting Framework that is widely used around the world. The Framework enables all businesses to measure and report their financial, environmental, social and governance performance.

The Framework enables businesses to be more transparent about their performance and this transparency and accountability builds stakeholders' trust in organisations, which can lead to many other benefits. Thousands of businesses of all sizes and in many different industries use GRI's Framework in order to understand and communicate their performances to stakeholders.

GRI has its headquarters in Amsterdam in the Netherlands. This acts as a hub, coordinating the activity of GRI's many network partners. GRI has regional offices in Australia, Brazil, China, India and the USA. Its global network includes more than 600 supporters as well as 30,000 people representing different businesses and industries.

Questions

1. Explain the difference between an oil company's financial and social performance.
2. Do you think that all UK businesses should use GRI's standard format to report their performance to stakeholders?

Businesses have to care about being socially responsible because their customers do. A number of studies have shown that a business's CSR policies increasingly influence consumers' spending decisions. For example, a survey by Landor Associates, the branding company, found that 77 per cent of consumers say it is important for companies to be socially responsible.

Being judged to be a socially responsible business can help organisations to attract the best employees and to build a strong employer brand. In a global workforce study by Towers Perrin, the professional services firm, CSR was identified as the third most important influence on employee engagement. And it is likely to become more important: a survey by the accountancy firm Deloitte revealed that amongst employees aged 18 to 26 a business's degree of social responsibility is an important influence on their decision to work there.

Acting in a socially responsible manner can also help businesses to access new markets and this can be very attractive at a time when globalisation is increasing competitive pressures. C.K. Prahalad made a case for the fastest growing new markets and entrepreneurial opportunities being found among the billions of poor people 'at the bottom of the [financial] pyramid'. Thus, companies that can incorporate socially responsible behaviour within their strategic decision making may be able to gain access to these markets and benefit over time from their growth.

Visa, the American multinational financial services company known for its credit and debit cards, has built partnerships with local governments and non-profit enterprises around the world with the aim of increasing the degree of financial inclusion of the world's poorest people. Visa's integration of CSR into its strategic decision making is offering the poor in developing countries new means to pay and receive money, as well as save. It is also increasing the company's revenues.

The technological environment

In the UK in the 18th century news of technological developments spread at the rate of about one mile per year. In the opening years of the 21st century people and businesses throughout the world learn quickly of technological changes. New technological products are often obsolete within a few years. The internet has probably been the biggest single technological factor leading to change in business behaviour, but it is the interaction between the internet and other devices, especially the smartphone, that is expected to have a huge impact over coming years.

Figure 6.13 shows the rapid growth in the global shipment of smartphones between 2009 and 2019. This data reflects an astonishing rate of growth annually in the actual and forecast worldwide sales of these products. It is the astonishing growth rate of the latter that is most remarkable. Andreessen Horowitz, a venture capital firm, estimates that 2 billion people currently use smartphones and that this figure will reach 4 billion by 2020 – 80 per cent of the world's adult population. This growth has the greatest potential to alter the way in which businesses research markets, produce products and hire and use staff to meet customers' needs.

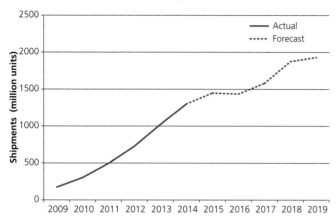

Figure 6.13 Numbers of smartphones shipped by manufactures, 2009-19

Source: Drawn from Statista.com data

Global smartwatch shipments (millions)	2015 (Forecast)	2014 (Actual)
Apple Watch	15.4	0.0
Others	12.7	4.6
Total	**28.1**	**4.6**

Table 6.4 Forecast sales of global smartwatches, 2014 and 2015

Source: Strategy Analytics

Technology and marketing opportunities

Technological advances have not only created new markets for new products but also new ways to sell these products.

Technology and new products

New technology can create new and highly valuable markets for businesses and generate streams of future revenue. Some new technology-based products may have short product life cycles, although it is common for businesses to produce a succession of products based on one technological advance.

In April 2015 technology company Apple launched its Apple Watch. This small device is the result of technological developments by Apple's employees. It contains a tiny but powerful processor and a screen that responds differently to being touched and tapped. The Apple Watch connects with the owner's iPhone and allows users to respond to phone calls, use a variety of apps and to control devices and appliances in their homes, as well as to track fitness levels. Sales forecasts for this product are positive as demonstrated in Table 6.4.

Using technology in the products themselves, rather than in the production process, also offers great advantages to businesses. Firms possessing a technological lead over rival producers are frequently able to charge a high price for their products – at least until the competition catches up. This technique of price skimming is likely to boost profits, which can be invested in further R&D to help to maintain a technological (and competitive) advantage. Possessing a technological edge may attract new customers to a business as well as maintaining the loyalty of existing customers. BMW's i8 hybrid sports car represents a substantial advance in technology. It is a very stylish petrol/electric sports car that can use a combination of electric and petrol engines to achieve impressive acceleration and speeds, or use the plug-in electric engine to cut emissions. In 2015, UK customers had to wait a year for an order for this car to be fulfilled, despite it being priced at nearly £100,000.

The scale of the benefits to a business from introducing new, high technology products can be immense. In 2015, Boeing, the American aircraft manufacturer, reported that it had implemented technological advances that dramatically improved its products' fuel efficiency. As a consequence, the company announced it had increased revenues by approximately 35 per cent since 2011 and secured a backlog of customer orders valued at nearly half a trillion dollars.

Technology and promoting and selling products

Advances in technology have made it easier for businesses to communicate with customers for marketing purposes. The American technology company Cisco has forecast that by 2020 there will be seven times as many devices in the world connected to the internet as there will be people. In the UK in 2014, the average person spent more than one hour and ten minutes a day on devices linked to the internet. Such developments will increase the opportunities for businesses to use technology for promotional purposes.

Some businesses rely entirely on technology to distribute their products. Apple is famous for producing innovative technological products such as the iPhone and Apple Watch, but the company also uses technology to distribute its products. Its iTunes store allows purchasers to download music, TV programmes, apps, games and audio books. It is also used to download applications for the company's devices such as the iPhone.

Using technology in this way offers substantial cost advantages. Apple does not have to pay to distribute its online products, nor does it have to pay retailers commission on each sale. This increases the company's profit margin and increases its flexibility in pricing decisions. The company also receives marketing benefits in that it can easily collect large amounts of data about its customers and their preferences, enabling it to target its future marketing effectively.

Technology and operations management

Technological advances also affect the ways in which businesses operate and create opportunities for new types of operations. This is where the most profound and far-reaching changes are occurring. New businesses such as Funding Circle (a crowdfunding enterprise) and Uber, whom we consider later on page 131, are being created and growing remarkably quickly on the back of developments in technology.

Technology and communications

Communications within businesses have been transformed by technology. Businesses can communicate simply, cheaply and quickly across the globe. Developments in **cloud computing** have provided great improvements in communication. Information, such as databases, can be stored using cloud computing services and encrypted to restrict access. However, authorised users can access this and read and update it as necessary from any location. For example, market research companies may hold research findings in this way enabling them to be updated and accessed regularly by the business's employees as necessary.

Developments in multimedia communications have made it simpler and quicker for businesses to exchange information with groups, including employees using a flexible range of methods of communication. Businesses such as Redwood Technologies have developed communications modules which allow information to be automatically converted from one format to another, for example email to voice or SMS. This enables businesses to automatically adapt how they communicate to match recipients' preferences.

Weblink

To find out more about Redwood Technologies' work, visit: www.redwoodtech.com/

Technology and production

Perhaps the major advantage of technology to businesses is that it allows the development of new methods of production resulting in lower costs. This permits the firm to enjoy higher profits on each sale. However, in an increasingly competitive global market firms seek to improve their market position by offering high quality and sophisticated products at lower prices to increase consumer value. Using ever-more sophisticated technology in planning, designing and producing products is one way of achieving lower costs. The potential for technology to reduce costs exists from the design stage through to distribution.

The use of **computer-aided design (CAD)** by businesses is relatively commonplace nowadays. For many years manufactures have used computer programmes to design new products. However, this technology is moving forward quickly. Developments in 3D computing are creating software and devices that will allow designers and others to project virtual objects into the real world. Microsoft has developed 3D software and high technology goggles to provide a user interface for this software. The company says that its goggles (called HoloLens, see Figure 6.14) could be used by architects to visualise new designs, by NASA scientists to explore the surface of Mars, and by business executives for video conferencing in which virtual objects could be incorporated. Probably the most immediate use of this technology, which is being developed by a number of companies, is in designing products. Teams of designers can work on the same virtual product simultaneously, using this technology.

Figure 6.14 Microsoft's 3D glasses called 'HoloLens'

The process of manufacturing in many industries has been transformed by automation whereby machines do jobs previously carried out by people. The most dramatic aspect of this has been the use of computer-controlled technology on the production line. The use of computer-controlled technology is termed **computer-aided manufacture (CAM)** and is an integral part of lean production. Its use allows businesses to control the production line to supply variants on a standard product to meet the precise demands of consumers. Thus, Vauxhall's car factory at Ellesmere Port uses computer-aided manufacturing systems to produce different colours and styles of cars in succession in response to customers' orders. This is part of the company's JIT (or 'pull') manufacturing system.

The use of technology in the form of CAD and CAM has assisted in improving productivity levels in many manufacturing industries, helping to keep costs down and enhance productivity. Because of this its use has spread to many industries including food processing and the manufacture of pottery.

Developments in technology have prompted huge changes across entire industries. The widespread and increasing use of smartphones is behind some of the most revolutionary changes. Some people are using their smartphones to allow them to become freelance delivery drivers for businesses. Having registered, they can take on work as and when suitable – if they are in a convenient location, for example. Similarly, Uber's app is causing dramatic and controversial changes in the taxi industry in many cities throughout the world, as shown in the Business in focus feature below. This use of technology provides opportunities for some businesses while creating significant threats for others.

Key terms

Cloud computing involves the centralised storage of data in remote servers (the 'cloud') and online access by users worldwide on internet-connected devices.

Computer-aided design (CAD) is a combination of hardware and software that allows businesses to create, modify and adapt plans for new products.

Computer-aided manufacturing (CAM) is the use of machines controlled by computers as part of a production process.

Business in focus: Uber

Uber is a simple idea that has created an enormously successful business, which was valued at $41 billion in 2015 with a forecast revenue of $10 billion for the same year. Uber is an app that can be downloaded without charge and connects a smartphone user with any nearby cars registered with Uber using GPS and Wi-Fi to identify locations and provide communications. The cars may be taxis or private vehicles. Uber's app allows a user to request a particular car for a journey. The fare is calculated based on distance travelled and time taken for the journey. The cost is deducted from the passenger's account through their smartphone. Prices tend to reflect the balance between demand for and supply of taxis. Uber was criticised for its 'surge' in price on New Year's Eve when demand for taxis rises sharply.

The idea for Uber was dreamed up by two Americans, Travis Kalanick and Garrett Camp, in 2009 and in March 2015 it operated in 53 countries and 200 cities across the world. Despite its popularity with drivers and passengers, it has proved unpopular with established taxi companies and drivers. London taxi drivers have protested that vehicles registered with Uber are really taxis and should be subject to the same tight regulations as the famous black cabs. However, cars operating through Uber are classified as minicabs and subject to fewer regulations, helping them to operate with lower costs. Drivers of vehicles registered with Uber can overcome their lack of geographical knowledge of London by using satellite navigation systems.

Questions

1. Explain the possible implications for the taxi industry's stakeholders of the growth of Uber.
2. Do you think that Uber should be more tightly regulated by governments?

Technology is not only used in production processes in the manufacturing sector. It is also widely used by businesses that supply services. For example, companies such as Aviva supply insurance products using the internet. Policyholders enter their requirements onto the company's website and complete their personal details.

Avivia's technology computes the price and deducts the appropriate sum from the customer's credit card before downloading the policy to the customer's computer. The whole production process is based on technology.

Technology and human relations

Humans within businesses are always affected by technological change. This is particularly true when new technology is introduced onto the production line. Such change may lead to some minor changes in the duties of employees. On the other hand, technological developments can result in enormous changes for a business's workforce. For some it may be redundancy: replaced by technology as part of the process of automation. Many high-street banks have made workers redundant owing to advances in technology. Other employees may be required to undertake duties dramatically different from those with which they are familiar as a result of the increasing use of technology in the banking sector. Between 2008 and 2015 Lloyds Banking Group reduced its workforce by over 50,000 people and closed many bank branches. Many of these jobs were lost as the Bank responded to increasing numbers of its customers using online banking services and therefore a smaller branch network was required.

Employees' reactions to technological change can be equally diverse. For some employees it may represent an opportunity. They may have a chance to acquire new skills, to make their jobs more secure and enjoy higher wages or salaries. The new working practices may offer great benefits. Technology can allow employees greater control over their working lives leading to increased responsibility and possibility of achievement. This can result in greater motivation.

Others may fear technological change as it increases job insecurity. This is likely to be true of those with few skills who carry out tasks that may be easily automated. Fear of unemployment may lead to industrial action as workers seek to protect their jobs. In such circumstances the introduction of new technology may be awkward and expensive. Redundancy payments may be expensive and corporate images may suffer.

New technology-based products create jobs and unemployment at the same time. For example, the increasing popularity of reading newspapers online has led to falls in circulation of hard copies for many publications. Between 2011 and 2014, circulation figures

for daily newspapers in the UK fell by about 6 per cent per year on average. This resulted in a loss of jobs for printers and those involved in distributing newspapers and magazines. Simultaneously, employment has been created in industries creating and maintaining the websites of newspapers and other online publications.

The reaction of employees to technological change may depend upon the culture of the business. Businesses operating traditional culture, placing great emphasis on bureaucracy and convention, may experience difficulties in adapting to technological change. The existence of a task culture may make the process less difficult. It may be most appropriate if the managers of businesses that are affected by technological change develop a culture that is responsive to change and one where employees' attitudes are to embrace change rather than to resist it.

The implications of technological change for businesses' strategies

Key term

Data analytics is the process of investigating raw data with the intention of drawing conclusions from the information.

The price of new technologies continues to fall dramatically meaning that such technologies are no longer solely the privilege of businesses in developed economies. Simultaneously, the time it takes to go from breakthrough to the mass market is falling. In the USA it took 76 years for the telephone to reach half of the population, the smartphone did it in less than 10 years. This means that technology is becoming increasingly relevant for more businesses.

The potential for technology to transform businesses over the next 10 or 15 years is immense. Businesses will have to adapt their strategies to fit this new environment if they are to repel threats and take advantage of the opportunities that will become available. New strategies may need to be based on four key elements of digital technology:

- **Social media**. This may involve, for example, using its power to communicate with consumers and to shape their views.
- **Mobile technology**. The most obvious application here is the smartphone with its enormous potential to change the ways that business operates.

- **Data analytics**. Advances in data handling and analysis have allowed businesses to identify trends and draw other important conclusions from huge amounts of raw data (often called 'big data').
- **Cloud computing**. Using the capacity of massive remote servers to store and analyse information.

The use of a combination of these aspects of technological development will allow new business strategies to be established and new markets to be created or old ones to be developed in different ways. Some analysts believe that the first stage of a digital economy is drawing to a close. This is sometimes called the 'first digital wave'. It was based around e-commerce as providing another way in which businesses could communicate with customers and sell them goods and services. Many, if not most, businesses have adapted to this change.

The next stage of technological change will see businesses explore other ways to take advantage of the opportunities available. We saw earlier that many media companies increasingly use the internet to get their readers to go to their websites, although it has been difficult to make this a profitable business as people are reluctant to pay for online news and information. However, consumers are increasingly sourcing information they want to read through social media websites or through messaging services. Snapchat, a website that allows pictures to be sent that fade away after a few seconds, has launched a new service, called Discover, that offers articles and videos from news organisations which disappear after 24 hours. The initial take-up is immense, reporting millions of views per day, per publisher. This is an example of what some analysts believe to be the 'second digital wave' in which information is shared though connected devices and different channels.

Business in focus: Technology, labour costs and strategy

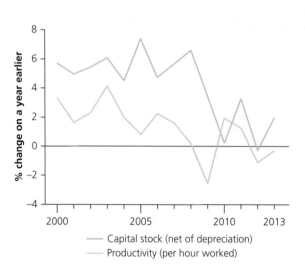

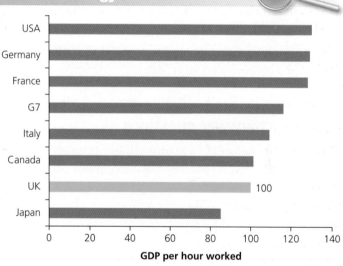

Figure 6.15 Data relating to the size of the UK's capital stock and its trend in labour productivity

Source: Office for National Statistics (ONS)

There is concern that some UK businesses are not taking up technological opportunities and basing strategies on technology to the extent that is occurring in other economies. Part of the problem arises because labour in the UK is relatively cheap: in 2015 only Greece and Portugal have lower hourly wage rates. Free immigration within the EU has also ensured that there is a large supply of cheap workers. The result has been a low level of investment in technology (reflected in small rises in the UK's capital stock of capital equipment used in production). It has also led to low levels of productivity as illustrated by the tiny increases in capital stock and the resulting poor performance in terms of productivity shown in Figures 6.15 and 6.16.

Figure 6.16 A comparison of UK labour productivity rates with selected countries, 2013

Source: House of Commons Library Briefing Paper Number 06492, *Productivity in the UK*, 3 July 2015

One conclusion that can be drawn from this is that some UK businesses are opting to develop strategies based around the low cost of labour rather than taking full advantage of the latest developments in technology.

Source: Adapted from an article in *The Economist*, 14 March 2015

Questions

1. Explain why using technology in production is likely to increase labour productivity.

2. Does it matter if many UK businesses base their strategies on low-cost labour rather than the latest technology?

Technological change can be expected to have a profound impact on the strategies of many businesses. It will affect the ways in which businesses communicate information and interact with stakeholders. It may result in greater use of alliances and joint ventures between enterprises, as well as changing the ways in which businesses design and produce products for their customers. It may be, however, that it is the products themselves which are the most obvious manifestation of the impact of technology on business activity.

ASSESSMENT ACTIVITIES

(a) Knowledge check questions

1 Identify the two major changes currently taking place in the UK's population.

2 Distinguish between migration and urbanisation.

3 State two possible ways in which advances in technology may affect consumer buying behaviour.

4 List two possible implications of the continued growth of online businesses.

5 Distinguish between corporate social responsibility and a corporate social report.

6 State two possible examples of the implications for businesses of meeting social responsibilities.

7 List the four types of responsibility set out in Carroll's CSR pyramid.

8 State two ways in which advances in technology have affected production processes within businesses.

9 What are the four key elements of digital technology that will influence business models in the future?

10 Distinguish between CAD and CAM.

(b) Short answer questions

1 Explain one benefit a manufacturer operating in a price competitive market may receive as a result of population movements.   (4 marks)

2 Explain one implication of the increase in online purchases for retailers.   (5 marks)

3 Explain why the management team of an oil company, such as BP, might decide to operate the business according to the stakeholder concept.
(5 marks)

4 Analyse the possible reasons why multinational manufacturers of sports clothing are under considerable pressure to be socially responsible.
(9 marks)

(c) Data response question

UK house builders

The population of London is growing rapidly as a result of growing birth rates and an inflow of migrants as urbanisation continues. A recent report by the mayor of London has suggested that its population will rise from just over 8 million in 2015 to 11 million by 2050. This would require 50,000 additional homes a year in the capital. Housing supply has not matched demand in London, meaning property prices soared to an average price of £514,000.

David Ritchie, the CEO of house builder Bovis Homes, warned in early 2015 that a shortage of bricklayers and other workers is holding back the construction of much-needed new housing in the UK. Some bricklayers in the UK have been paid up to £1,000 a week. Despite this, the company has enjoyed a successful year. Profits increased by 69 per cent to over £133 million and the company built 3,635 homes in 2014, a 29 per cent increase from 2013, and plans to build as many as 5,000–6,000 a year in the near future.

Bovis Homes issues a corporate social report each year, as do most of the UK's major house builders. The company seeks to meet its social responsibilities in several ways. It designs and builds sustainable homes reducing carbon emissions and conserving water and energy, and engages with the company's stakeholders. It seeks to operate as efficiently as possible and to minimise the amount of resources it uses to build homes, although this can conflict with sustainability. The company's corporate social report for 2013 records its achievements in these areas, though not its targets.

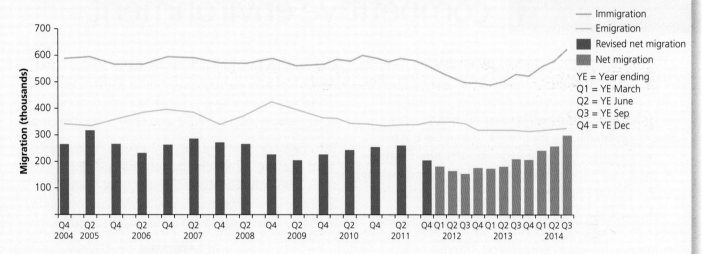

Figure 6.17 UK migration, 2004–14

Source: Office for National Statistics (ONS)

Questions

1. Explain two possible implications of urbanisation for UK house builders. (6 marks)

2. Analyse the possible benefits of recent trends in migration for house builders in the UK. (9 marks)

3. Do the benefits of Bovis Homes issuing a corporate social report outweigh the drawbacks? Justify your view. (15 marks)

(d) Essays

1. 'Responding to changes in the technological environment will be more important for businesses than responding to changes in the social environment.' To what extent do you agree with this statement? Justify your view. (25 marks)

2. 'It is a waste of time and resources for retailers in the UK to produce corporate social reports.' Do you agree with this statement? Justify your view. (25 marks)

Chapter 7

Analysing the external environment: the competitive environment

Introduction

This chapter discusses the competitive environment for businesses using Michael Porter's five forces model as a framework. It looks at the five forces identified by Porter and considers how changes in these may have implications for the decision making and profits of a business.

What you need to know by the end of this chapter:

- Porter's five forces: entry threat, buyer power, supplier power, rivalry and substitute threat
- how and why these forces may change
- the implications of these forces for strategic and functional decision making within a business
- the implications of these forces on a business's profits.

Changes in the competitive environment

A business's competitive environment is made up of a number of factors. It includes the power of rivals and the potential rivals that the business faces in a battle to win customers and market share, but it also includes its customers and its suppliers and the influence that they wield. It is possible to argue that the process of globalisation has increased the degree of competition to which new businesses are exposed.

One way of assessing a business's competitive position is through the use of Michael Porter's five forces model as illustrated in Figure 7.1.

Porter's five forces model

Michael Porter's famous five forces of competitive position model provides a simple framework for assessing and analysing the competitive strength and position of a corporation or business. Porter's five forces model can be used to good analytical effect alongside other models such as SWOT and PEST-C analysis tools.

Porter's model provides suggested points under each main heading, by which managers can develop a broad and sophisticated analysis of competitive position, as might be used when creating strategy plans or making investment decisions about a business or organisation.

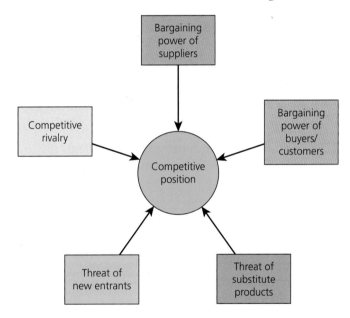

Figure 7.1 Porter's five forces

Five forces analysis looks at five key areas, namely:

1. the power of suppliers
2. the power of buyers
3. the threat of substitutes
4. the threat of new entrants
5. competitive rivalry.

If firms faced the same competitive pressures in all markets, then profitability (for example, ROCE) would be very similar in them all. This, however, is not the case. Some industries have high profits while others have low profits and, to some extent, this can be explained through analysis of the different competitive environments.

High profit industries	Low profit industries
These are likely to show: ● mild competition between businesses ● suppliers with little power ● customers having little power ● little threat of substitute products being developed ● no real prospect of a new entrant to the industry.	These are likely to show: ● intense rivalry between businesses ● very powerful suppliers ● customers with considerable power ● imminent threat of the development of substitute goods or services ● a high likelihood of new entrants to the market.

Table 7.1 Competitive factors influencing the profitability of industries

The power of suppliers

Suppliers are a vital element of an effective organisation. Raw materials are needed to complete the finished product of the organisation. Suppliers can be very powerful and this power arises from a variety of sources.

- The number of suppliers that are operating – fewer suppliers normally means more powerful suppliers.
- The cost involved in changing suppliers – if it is difficult or expensive, suppliers have greater power.
- The availability of substitutes – if there is no other substitute for their product or if the items they supply are scarce the supplier has greater power.
- The customer's size relative to the size of the supplier – if the supplier is much smaller they have less power over the bigger customer.
- Whether or not other uses exist for the products sold by the supplier.
- To what extent the supplier poses a creditable threat to integrate forwards and enter its customer's market as a rival, or to takeover the business itself.

Some small businesses in the UK have complained about the power of suppliers in the energy industry. They claim that the market for supplying gas and electricity, which is dominated by six large companies, charges prices that are too high and that the suppliers are often slow to respond to problems.

What do you think?

Why are many of the suppliers of gas and electricity in the UK so powerful?

Some businesses find that a major influence on the competitive environment in which they trade is the power of their suppliers. Powerful suppliers who hold a dominant position in a market have control over prices and this power is increased if the product they sell has few or no substitutes. The implications for businesses can be severe, especially if the supplier provides a large percentage of the resources used by the business. In this event, a policy of increasing prices as the supplier's market power increases can squeeze the business's profit margins.

The power of buyers

Buyers or customers can exert influence and control over an industry in certain circumstances. This happens when:

- The products sold by businesses are similar and it is therefore easy for buyers to find substitutes.
- Products have a high price elasticity of demand, that is the demand from customers is sensitive to price.
- Switching to another supplier's product is cheap and straightforward and there are many other businesses offering supplies.
- Customers buy a large quantity of products and place these orders regularly.

One factor that might limit the power of buyers is if the producer represents a significant threat to take over the buyer's business, or that of a rival and operate in competition. In such circumstances a buyer may not use the power it has for fear of invoking the action, such as a takeover, that is possible.

There have been a number of allegations of supermarkets in the UK abusing their power as buyers and imposing unfavourable terms on businesses that supply them. The next Business in focus feature explores this further.

Business in focus: Tesco faces investigation

The grocery industry regulator is launching an investigation into Tesco's treatment of its suppliers, posing a major problem for the UK's largest retailer. Christine Tacon, the groceries code adjudicator, said she had a reasonable suspicion that Tesco had breached the code, which governs how the major supermarkets deal with their direct suppliers.

Urging suppliers to come forward if they had evidence of breaches by supermarkets, Tacon said she could widen her inquiry if she had reasonable grounds for suspicion that others had also breached the code.

Tacon said the possible violations by Tesco, involving many suppliers and large sums of money, included:

- penalties imposed when Tesco claimed items were missing from deliveries

- charging suppliers more than an item cost if a customer returned it to Tesco
- delays in refunding suppliers when there were errors over invoices
- charges for in-store promotions that were either incorrect or not agreed.

Source: Adapted from an article in the *Guardian*, 5 February 2015

Questions
1. Explain the possible reasons why Tesco has considerable buyer power.
2. Would reducing Tesco's power be in the best interests of all the company's stakeholders?

An increase in the power of a single large buyer can pose difficulties for a business, particularly if it is relatively small and the dominant customer purchases a large proportion of its output, such as Tesco in the case above. In such circumstances a change in the competitive environment that gives buyers additional power could have a range of adverse consequences for suppliers.

The buyer will have increased bargaining power and may be able to negotiate substantial reductions in the price at which products are supplied. They may use the threat of transferring to another supplier to achieve its ambitions. Being forced to sell at lower prices could reduce or, in extreme cases, eliminate the supplier's profit margins.

Buyers may request changes in the specifications of products to be supplied or may impose tough conditions in terms of delivery dates or the quality or appearance of products. Such outcomes are likely to put the supplier under pressure and to increase costs of production. Once again the ultimate effect could be to reduce profits.

A dominant buyer may ask for generous trade credit terms, for example a 60-day trade credit period. This can cause liquidity problems for suppliers, not least because the size of the order will mean that the sums involved are substantial. In such circumstances the supplier may have to negotiate expensive overdrafts with its bank.

The threat of substitutes

A substitute is an alternative product that offers purchasers similar or the same features and benefits. The threat of substitute is high when:

- the price of that substitute product falls, making it more attractive to customers
- it is easy for customers to switch from one substitute product to another
- customers are willing and able to substitute the supplier's products for those of another supplier.

In Porter's model substitute products come from other industries. For example, low-cost airlines have taken many customers from the cross-Channel ferries between England and France. This was one factor contributing to the insolvency of the French ferry company, Sea France, in 2013. The threat of substitute products most usually manifests itself by keeping prices in an industry low, thereby depressing profits. Thus, the existence of cans as a substitute to bottles for holding liquids helps to prevent bottle manufacturers raising prices too high to increase their profit margins.

The threat of new entrants

Key term

Barriers to entry are those factors, such as high advertising costs, that make it difficult for a business to sell products in a market for the first time.

The threat of a new business entering the industry is high when it is easy for an organisation to enter the industry, that is **barriers to entry** are low. An organisation will look at a range of factors to assess the extent of a threat of new businesses entering a market. These will include the following:

- The degree of customer loyalty to existing businesses and products.
- How quickly and easily a new entrant to an industry might be able to benefit from economies of scale.
- Whether the new entrant would have access to suppliers.
- The extent to which government legislation prevents or encourages new entrants to the industry.

The size and financial power of any potential entrant is, of course, an important factor in assessing the extent of the threat of new entrants to an industry. BT Sport was launched in August 2013 as a direct competitor to established sports TV broadcasters such as Sky, ITV and the BBC. The company is owned by BT plc, a large and financially powerful telecommunications company. The extent of its threat to existing sports broadcasters was shown by its ability to bid successfully for expensive rights to broadcast live premiership rugby and football matches.

Competitive rivalry

Competitive rivalry is a major force affecting a business's competitive position. Generally, competitive rivalry will be greater if:

- entry to an industry is straightforward – if a market becomes attractive, new competitors will flood in
- it is easy for customers to move to substitute products, for example oil to gas as a fuel
- there is little differentiation between the products sold between customers
- competitors are approximately the same size as each other
- the competitors all have similar corporate strategies
- it is costly to leave the industry and so businesses do not do so
- the market is not growing, meaning that to win a customer requires taking one from a rival.

If there is great rivalry between businesses in an industry, it can be expected that the firms involved will respond to this environment in one of a number of ways.

- By engaging in competitive pricing in an attempt to win customers from rivals. This is more likely to be used, and to be effective, when demand is price elastic. At the time of writing, the UK's major supermarkets are engaged in intense price competition brought about, in part, by the entry of discount supermarkets such as Aldi and Lidl to the market and their subsequent success.
- The use of promotional offers and special deals. These may be used to attract customers and may be more effective when products are purchased infrequently, such as foreign holidays. Technology may soon enable firms to increase competitiveness by tailoring special offers to individual customers. Apple's iBeacon technology is set to allow retailers and app publishers to identify customers in stores from their smartphones. Relevant special offers will be made available via their smartphone.
- Innovation. Developing and launching new products, especially if done regularly, can be an effective competitive strategy and one which maintains customer loyalty as well as attracting new customers. Car manufacturers rely heavily on innovation to remain competitive.

Dominant businesses

A dominant business is able to have a substantial influence over market prices and, in some cases, may determine them with other, less powerful firms, following its lead. A dominant firm is likely to be the largest in an industry and to hold the greatest market share. As a consequence, it will probably be highly profitable, though it may not be highly efficient and innovative, especially if its supremacy is not immediately challenged.

Dominant businesses may emerge through internal or organic growth as in the case of Microsoft. Other firms may achieve dominant positions in their markets as a result of a strategy of takeovers and mergers. It is this approach that Vodafone has used to create much of its market power, although it is not a dominant business in the UK.

A notable example of a dominant business is Google. Google has an estimated search engine global market share of 88.1 per cent in January 2015 (see Figure 3.7 on page 53). The company also holds powerful positions in other markets including operating systems for mobile devices with its android product and its Google Play store for apps.

If a business is becoming more dominant in a market, this represents a threat for its competitors. The growing power of a single business may lead to its rivals losing sales and market share and a decline in profitability. The dominant business's competitors may have to invest in new products, new marketing campaigns and cut prices to protect their market positions. This may become increasingly difficult to do if the dominant business uses its market power ruthlessly to maintain its position within the market.

The impact of changes in the competitive environment

The ways in which businesses may respond to changes in their competitive environment may be diverse and will clearly depend upon the nature of the change. The entry of a new competitor to a market or the emergence of a dominant business may provoke a number of strategic reactions. Affected businesses may take strategic decisions to seek new markets or develop new product ranges. Alternatively, they may seek alliances or mergers with other businesses in the same industry to increase their own market power in response to these changes in the competitive environment.

Changes in the competitive environment which manifest themselves as increasing power of suppliers can create major difficulties for businesses, especially if no alternative suppliers exist. In this situation managers may take functional decisions, for example, to consider its production process and ways in which it might adapt to reduce its reliance on the products sold by the supplier in question. Other decisions in this situation could include taking over the supplier (in what may be a hostile action) or negotiating favourable deals with smaller rival suppliers in the hope of fostering greater competition.

Increasing power of buyers could lead to businesses making functional decisions such as reducing prices or offering enhanced credit terms and accepting the adverse consequences in terms of profit margins or working capital. However, these could prompt managers to implement more strategic decisions such as selling in new markets to less powerful customers.

The threat of substitute products may require managers to take decisions to increase (or emphasise) the degree of differentiation between their products and those of potential rivals. This may entail heavy investment in R&D to allow innovation to take place or perhaps investment in training to produce unrivalled levels of customer service.

The managers of a business must endeavour to understand and predict changes to their competitive environment and to analyse the business's competitive position in order to respond effectively with appropriate strategic and functional decisions.

ASSESSMENT ACTIVITIES

(a) Knowledge check questions

1 List two factors which make up a business's competitive environment.

2 Define the term 'barriers to entry'.

3 List the five forces that comprise the model Michael Porter developed to assess a business's competitive position.

4 Name one other model of business analysis that could be used alongside Porter's five forces model.

5 State two competitive characteristics that are associated with high profit industries.

6 State two possible sources of a supplier's power.

7 State two circumstances in which buyers or customers can exert influence and control over an industry.

8 Define the term 'substitute'.

9 State two circumstances in which competitive rivalry is likely to be high.

10 Define the term 'dominant firm'.

(b) Short answer questions

1 Explain one competitive factor which makes the painting and decorating industry a low profit one in the UK. (4 marks)

2 Explain one reason why customers in the European market for low-cost flights have considerable power. (5 marks)

3 Explain why the new entrant threat to the motor vehicle manufacturing industry is relatively low. (5 marks)

4 Analyse the ways in which producers in the UK grocery market, such as Tesco and Asda, might respond to the high level of rivalry that exists within the industry. (9 marks)

(c) Data response question

Research In Motion

The number of people using BlackBerry smartphones in the UK has fallen steadily, and Windows phone has overtaken the BlackBerry-branded products made by the Canadian manufacturer Research In Motion (RIM) in terms of sales and market share. The UK had previously been a stronghold for RIM in Europe, but the company's competitiveness has deteriorated.

RIM is a relatively small business in comparison to many of its rivals – the smartphone market has a small number of large-scale producers such as Apple and Samsung. However, the market has seen several new producers emerge. The Windows phone was launched in the UK in 2011 and Google also entered the market with its Nexus phone based on its popular Android operating system.

RIM's managers dismissed the threat from the iPhone in 2008 believing that consumers would not be happy using a touchscreen. RIM launched the technically sophisticated BlackBerry 10 in 2013, far too late to win significant market share from rivals such as Apple and Samsung. The company has also seen its sales suffer as consumers have preferred to purchase products such as tablets rather than updating their mobile phones. RIM's senior managers believed tablet sales would decline quickly. The company eventually produced the Playbook, but it lacked the technical sophistication of the tablets sold by its rivals. In 2013, Thorsten Heins, RIM's CEO blamed the company's poor performance on the unwillingness of mobile phone network suppliers in the USA to support and promote the company's products.

In 2015, however, it was reported that the company was working with Samsung and IBM to produce a new high-specification tablet as part of its latest competitive strategy. RIM and Samsung have announced a strategic partnership and many analysts believe a merger will occur in due course.

Many of RIM's BlackBerry products are manufactured in China and other low-cost locations to keep costs as low as possible. Rivals such as Apple use major suppliers such as Foxconn to produce millions of smartphones each month.

Questions

1 Explain two possible reasons why RIM has become less competitive. (6 marks)

2 Analyse the possible factors that influence the degree of competition that exists within the smartphone manufacturing industry. (9 marks)

3 Discuss the extent to which Porter's five forces model might assist RIM in developing a new strategy to strengthen its competitive position. (15 marks)

(d) Essay

'The UK banking industry is often regarded as being uncompetitive. The major cause of this is the barriers to entry that exist.' To what extent do you agree with this statement? (25 marks)

Chapter 8

Analysing strategic options: investment appraisal

Introduction

This chapter looks at some of the financial methods that managers can use to assess possible investments when analysing options as part of the strategic decision-making process. We consider how to assess investments using the payback, average rate of return and net present value methods. The chapter also investigates the factors that influence investment decisions made by managers including investment criteria, risk and uncertainty. Finally, we consider the value of using sensitivity analysis as part of investment appraisal.

What you need to know by the end of this chapter:

- the financial methods of assessing an investment including the calculation and interpretation of payback, average rate of return and net present value
- the factors influencing investment decisions including investment criteria, non-financial factors, risk and uncertainty
- the value of sensitivity analysis.

Investment is an important activity for businesses and often entails managers taking strategic decisions. Investment can mean a decision to purchase part or all of another business, perhaps as a result of a takeover bid. However, it is perhaps more common to use the term in relation to the purchase of non-current assets or some other major expenditure. What is common to all forms of investment is that it involves a degree of risk. This must be judged against the likely returns. The final decision will depend upon managers' assessment of these two factors: risk and returns.

Businesses take decisions regarding investment in a variety of circumstances:

- **When contemplating introducing new products.** A business may assess the likely costs and returns from investing in one or more new products.
- **Expansion.** This may entail evaluating whether or not to invest in new fixed assets as part of a planned programme of growth. Tottenham Hotspur Football Club is set to invest an estimated £400 million in developing a new stadium, built in part on its existing ground – White Hart Lane. The Club hopes to increase its sales revenue by attracting larger crowds into the new stadium which will have a capacity of 56,000 spectators and open in 2018.
- **Investing in new technology.** This is often undertaken to reduce costs and improve productivity. For example, in 2015 Virgin Media announced it is to invest £3 billion in improving its fibre optic broadband network, increasing the network's reach from 13 million to 17 million homes.
- **Investing in infrastructure.** We saw in Chapter 4 on page 69 that the UK government has drawn up a National Infrastructure plan which details planned spending of about £375 billion by 2033. This will include major investments such as that in HS2 which will require extensive **investment appraisal**.
- **In other decisions.** Businesses may also use techniques of investment appraisal before spending heavily on promotional campaigns, developing new brands or products or retraining the workforce.

In each circumstance, however, the business must adopt an appropriate appraisal technique to decide whether the returns received from an investment are sufficient to justify the initial capital expenditure.

Key term

Investment appraisal is a series of techniques designed to assist businesses in judging the desirability of investing in particular projects.

The data provided from investment appraisal is frequently an important element of the quantitative data used by managers when taking strategic decisions such as whether or not to enter a new market, takeover another company or extend significantly the use of technology within the business.

Financial methods of assessing an investment

A number of techniques are available to managers to assist them in taking decisions on whether to go ahead with investments, or to help in making a judgement between two or more possible investment opportunities. This section looks at three of the most important investment appraisal techniques:

- Payback.
- The average rate of return (ARR).
- Net present value (NPV).

These financial techniques are valuable but do depend upon a number of assumptions:

- All costs and revenues can be easily and accurately forecast for some years into the future.
- Key variables (for example interest rates) will not change.
- The business in question is seeking maximum profits.

There are two major considerations for managers when deciding whether or not to invest in a non-current asset or another business:

1. The total profits earned by the investment over the foreseeable future.
2. How quickly the investment will recover its cost. This occurs when the earnings from the investment exceed the cost of the investment.

The process of assessing these factors is called investment appraisal and refers to the evaluation of one or more potential investments. Forecasting future costs and revenues can be a very difficult and, at times, expensive exercise to undertake. Forecasts about future revenues can prove to be inaccurate for a number of reasons:

- Competitors may introduce new products or reduce their prices, reducing forecast sales and revenues. The new Apple Watch is expected to take a high proportion of the sales in the smartwatch market with huge implications for the sales figures of rivals such as the Pebble Technology Corporation.
- Tastes and fashions may change resulting in an unexpected slump, or rise, in demand. McDonald's, the multinational fast-food retailer, suffered a 2.2 per cent fall in global sales in 2014 and a heavier 4.4 per cent fall in the USA.

- The economy may move into recession or slump (or alternatively into an upswing) unexpectedly, resulting in radically different sales figures from those forecast.
- Costs can be equally tricky to forecast. Unexpected periods of inflation, or rising import prices, might result in inaccurate forecasts of expenditures. This can lead to a significant reduction in actual profits when compared with forecasts.

Companies that operate in a stable economic environment are much more easily able to forecast into the future as they have confidence that their predictions on the rate of inflation, likely rate of interest, level of unemployment and hence demand are as accurate as they can make them. A stable economic environment should lead to more accurate forecasts of both costs and revenues associated with investment projects.

What do you think?

Should only managers whose companies operate in stable economic environments use techniques of investment appraisal?

Payback

Payback is a simple technique that measures the time period required for the earnings from an investment to recoup its original cost. Quite simply it finds out the number of years (or months) it takes to recover the cost of an investment from its net inflows of cash. In spite of the obvious simplicity of the payback technique, it remains the most common method of investment appraisal in the UK.

An example of payback:

Year	Cash outflow (£)	Cash inflow (£)
1	500,000	100,000
2		200,000
3		200,000
4		150,000

In this case the calculation is simple: payback is achieved at the end of Year 3 when the initial investment of £500,000 is recovered from net inflows of cash (revenue minus costs) – £100,000 in Year 1 plus £200,000 in each of Year 2 and Year 3.

Calculations can be a little more complex, however, as shown in the following example:

Year	Cash outflow (£)	Cash inflow (£)
1	500,000	100,000
2		100,000
3		200,000
4		300,000

In this case, payback is achieved during the fourth year. The formula used to calculate the point during Year 4 at which payback is achieved is as follows: Number of full years + (amount of investment not recovered/revenue generated in next year).

In the second example the investment has recovered £400,000 after three years. Therefore, £100,000 remains to be recovered in Year 4 before payback point is reached. During Year 4 the investment will generate £300,000.

Thus, payback is $\frac{3 \text{ years} + £100,000}{£300,000} = 3\frac{1}{3}$ years or three years and four months. Figure 8.1 illustrates the concept of payback in the form of a graph.

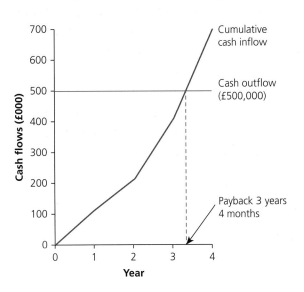

Figure 8.1 Payback on a graph

Payback has the advantage of being quick and simple to calculate and this probably explains its popularity, especially with small businesses. However, it does have disadvantages. It ignores the level of profits that may be generated ultimately by the investment. For profit maximising businesses this may represent an important omission. Furthermore, payback ignores the timing of any receipts. The following example highlights this weakness.

Two investment projects (A and B) each require an investment of £1 million. Their expected earnings are as follows:

Year	Project A cash inflow (£)	Project B cash inflow (£)
1	500,000	100,000
2	300,000	200,000
3	200,000	300,000
4	100,000	500,000

Both investment projects achieve payback at the end of Year 4. However, Project A is more attractive because it yields greater returns in the early years. Payback does not take into account the timing of any income received and this is a significant drawback of the technique.

Business in focus: Payback on MBAs

Taking a Master's degree in Business Administration (an MBA) is expensive – tuition fees alone at top schools can come to over £70,000. Then there's the cost of living and the opportunity cost of not working. Is it worth the investment? If so, which schools offer best value for money?

The research firm QS believes that it has the answer. By analysing the costs associated with the programmes at European business schools and then weighing them against average salary increases post-MBA (assuming employment after three months of graduation) and bonus payments, it believes that it has calculated the average payback for business schools in Europe.

University	Payback in months
University of Bath	16
University of Strathclyde	17
University of Edinburgh	17
Durham University	20
Bradford University	25
University of Warwick Business School	26

Table 8.1 The payback period for students taking MBAs at a selection of UK universities

The results are, perhaps, surprising. MBAs get their money back quickest at schools that don't usually top the rankings. There's no London Business School in this list, for example. Instead, the University of Bath School of Management, the University of Strathclyde and the University of Edinburgh Business School provide the fastest payback periods. However, those who have aspirations to work in finance, may wish to look elsewhere – other rankings of MBAs based on the proportion of graduates securing jobs in top investment banks provide very different results.

This list may have more to do with the relative cheapness of these schools, rather than their career enhancing credentials. It costs 'just' £28,000 to study at Bath and £27,100 at Edinburgh. The fees at the London Business School, meanwhile, are over £67,000.

Source: Adapted from e-financial careers website, http://news.efinancialcareers.com/

Questions

1. Explain the advantages and disadvantages of using the technique of payback for the purpose of evaluating MBAs offered by different universities.

2. Are methods of investment appraisal appropriate to help with most decisions taken in a business?

Average rate of return

The average rate of return (ARR) is a more complex and meaningful method of investment appraisal. This technique calculates the annual percentage rate of return on each possible investment. The resulting percentage figure allows a simple comparison with other investment opportunities, including investing into savings products offered by banks and building societies. It is important to remember, however, that a commercial investment (such as purchasing CAD/CAM equipment for a production line) involves a degree of risk; the returns may not be as forecast. Therefore, it is essential that such an investment earns significantly more than the rate of interest available from zero risk investments such as savings accounts with financial institutions. If the percentage return on purchasing

the CAD/CAM equipment was identical to that on a high-interest account with a bank, the latter would represent the better investment, as it carries little risk.

The formula for calculating ARR is:

$$ARR = \frac{\text{average annual profit} \times 100\%}{\text{asset's initial cost}}$$

$$\text{Average annual profit} = \frac{\text{total net profit before tax over asset's lifetime}}{\text{useful life of asset in years}}$$

Key term

Cash flow is the movement of cash into and out of a business over a period of time.

The average rate of return is considered to be more useful than the payback method because it considers the level of profits earned from an investment rather than simply the time taken to recover the amount invested. It also offers easier comparison with returns on other investments, investments in financial institutions such as banks as well as in other industries. Research in 2014 revealed that investments by oil companies in the Norwegian sector of the North Sea produced an ARR of 18 per cent; this is simple to compare with other possible investments.

However, this technique also fails to differentiate between investments that generate high returns in the early years and those that offer greater rewards later on and this can have significant implications for a business's **cash flow** position.

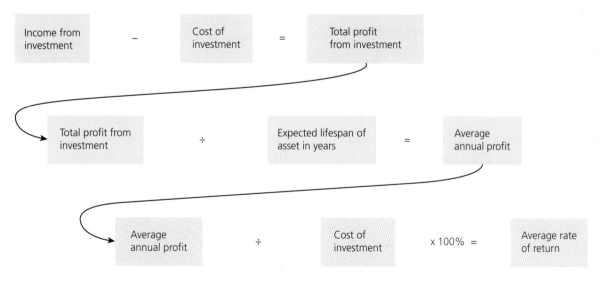

Figure 8.2 How to calculate ARR

An example of calculating the ARR:

Purchasing two new delivery vans for G. Layton Ltd will cost £120,000 and a net inflow of cash of £220,000 over five years is anticipated.

The total profit from using the new vehicles over 5 years = £220,000 − £120,000 = £100,000

This means that average annual profit $= \dfrac{£100,000}{5} = £20,000$

$\text{ARR} = \dfrac{£20,000}{£120,000} \times 100\% = 16.67\%$

The managers at G. Layton Ltd may consider this to be an attractive investment as a rate of 20 per cent is considerably higher than that available on any interest-bearing account at a bank or building society, even allowing a premium for risk. However, the business may have an alternative investment offering a higher rate of return.

Maths moment

Use the information in the example of ARR above to calculate the rate of return G. Layton Ltd would have received if the cost of the vehicles was £140,000 and all the other data was unchanged.

Net present value

Key terms

Discounting is the process of reducing the value of future income to reflect the opportunity cost of an investment.

Opportunity cost is the best alternative foregone as a result of a decision.

Present value is the value of a future stream of income from an investment, converted into its current worth.

More sophisticated methods of investment appraisal take into account how the value of returns from an investment depends on when they are received. Net present value (NPV) is one technique that recognises this and incorporates a technique called **discounting**.

Discounted cash flow

The technique of discounted cash flow takes into account what is termed the 'time value' of money. The time value of money is based on the principle that

money at the present time is worth more than money at some point in the future. Thus, according to this principle £1,000 today is of greater value than £1,000 in one or two years' time. There are two major reasons why this time-value principle exists:

1. **Risk**. Having £1,000 now is a certainty; receiving the same amount at some point in the future may not occur. The full £1,000 payment may not be received; indeed no payment at all may be made. An investment project may fail to provide the expected returns because of a competitor's actions, because of a change in tastes and fashions or as a result of the consequence of technological change.

2. **Opportunity cost**. This is the best foregone alternative. Even if no risk existed, the time value of money would still exist. This is because the money could be placed into an interest-bearing account generating a return. Thus, if we assume that a rate of 5 per cent is available on an interest-bearing account, £1,000 in one year's time is worth the same as £953 today. The reason for this is that by investing £953 at an interest rate of 5 per cent, an investor would have £1,000 after one year.

This time-value principle means that the longer the delay before money is received, the lower its value in present-day terms. This is called **present value**.

Year	Investment Project A Net cash inflows (£ million)	Investment Project B Net cash inflows (£ million)
0 (Now)	(500)	(500)
1	400	100
2	100	100
3	100	100
4	100	400

Table 8.2 Two similar investment projects with different patterns for cash inflows

Table 8.2 shows two investments requiring identical outlays. Both projects also receive the same cash inflow over a four-year period and would generate the same ARR (10 per cent). However, the majority of the cash inflow for Project A occurs in Year 1, while in Project B this is delayed until Year 3. The time-value principle would suggest that Project A is preferable to Project B. To show the effect of the time principle we need to calculate the present value of cash inflows and outflows through the use of discounting.

Discounting

Discounting is the process of adjusting the value of money received at some future date to its present value, that is its worth today. Discounting is, in effect, the reverse of adding interest. Discounting tables are available to illustrate the effect of converting future streams of income to their present values, though these are obsolete nowadays as software exists to conduct the necessary calculations and comparisons.

The rate of interest plays a central role in discounting – in the same way as it does in predicting the future value of savings. Table 8.3 shows the discounting figures and the value in present-day terms of £100 million over a period of five years into the future. If the business anticipates relatively high interest rates over the period of the investment, then future earnings are discounted heavily to provide lower present values for the investment. Lower rates result in discounting having a lesser effect in converting future earnings into present values.

The basic calculation is that the appropriate discounting factor is multiplied by the amount of money to be received in the future to convert it to its present value. Thus, at a rate of interest of 10 per cent the present value of £100 million in two years' time is £82.6 million (£100 million × 0.826). The present value of £100 million received in four years' time is £68.3 million using the same process with the relevant discounting factor. This figure is lower because the time interval is greater and the effect of the time-value principle is more pronounced.

From these examples we can see that the rate of interest has a significant effect on the present value of future earnings. The higher the rate of interest, the greater the discount. Thus, the present value of £100 million in three years' time is £75.1 million if the rate of interest is assumed to be 10 per cent. However, if the rate of interest is estimated to be 5 per cent the present value is greater: £86.3 million.

The choice of interest rate to be used as the basis for discounting is an important decision by a business undertaking investment appraisal. The discounting rate selected normally reflects the interest rates that are expected for the duration of the project. However, this can be difficult to forecast as rates may change in unpredictable ways during the lifetime of a major investment.

Using the NPV technique

Discounting expected future cash flows is the basis of calculating returns from investments using the NPV method. This method of investment appraisal forecasts expected outflows and inflows of cash and discounts the inflows and outflows. To calculate NPV we need to know:

- the initial cost of the investment
- the chosen rate of discount
- any expected inflows and outflows of cash
- the duration of the investment project
- any remaining or residual value of the project at the end of the investment. (If the investment is to purchase production equipment, this may have scrap value once it is obsolete, for example.)

The outflows of cash are subtracted from the discounted inflows. This entails totalling the figures recorded in the 'present value' column, at least one of which will be negative, making the calculation a little more complex. The resulting figure is the NPV. This figure is important for two reasons.

1. If the NPV figure is negative, the investment is not worth undertaking. This is because the present value of the stream of earnings is less than the cost of the investment. A more profitable approach would be to invest the capital in an interest-bearing account with a financial institution.

Year	Discounting factor used to convert to present value (Assuming 10% rate of interest)	Present value of £100 million at a discount rate of 10% (£m)	Discounting factor used to convert to present value (Assuming 5% rate of interest)	Present value of £100 million at a discount rate of 5% (£m)
0 (Now)	1	£100.0	1	£100.0
1	0.909	£90.9	0.952	£95.2
2	0.826	£82.6	0.907	£90.7
3	0.751	£75.1	0.864	£86.4
4	0.683	£68.3	0.822	£82.2

Table 8.3 The process of discounting

2. When an enterprise is considering a number of possible investment projects it can use the present value figure to rank them. The project generating the highest NPV figure is the most worthwhile in financial terms. In these circumstances a business may select the project (or projects) with the highest NPVs.

An example of calculating NPV

Reston Technology plc manufactures components for satellites and other high technology communications equipment. The company's directors are about to make a major investment decision. The rising cost of domestic gas and electricity has prompted the company to investigate installing its own energy supplies. The directors are considering two options. They can install solar photovoltaic panels on the roofs of the company's factories or build an anaerobic digester onsite to generate electricity from waste products supplied by other businesses. Installing solar photovoltaic panels is the cheaper option for the company, although it will generate lower returns. Both investments will produce positive cash flows after the initial cost as the electricity generated will be valuable whether used by Reston Technology itself or sold to the company that owns the grid.

The cash flows associated with these proposals over a five-year period are set out in Table 8.4. These show the cost of installing the two alternative sources of energy and the expected revenues less operating costs for the site each year. Reston Technology plc's finance director estimates that a 10 per cent discount rate would reflect likely market rates of interest, as he anticipates that

the Bank of England will raise interest rates in the near future.

Reston Technology would opt for building an anaerobic digester on the basis of this financial information shown in Table 8.4, as the NPV for the more expensive proposal is higher than that for installing solar panels. The net present values for both investment projects are positive, indicating that each is a worthwhile and viable investment, but the digester offers better returns. However, non-financial information may affect this investment decision: for example, operating a digester would entail lorries delivering waste products daily which may prove unpopular with people who live nearby.

A comparison of investment appraisal methods

The method of investment appraisal chosen will depend upon the type of firm, the market in which it is trading and its corporate objectives. A small firm may be more likely to use payback because managers may be unfamiliar with more complex methods of investment appraisal. Small businesses also often focus on survival and an important aspect of any investment will be how long it takes to cover the cost of the investment from additional revenues. Payback is therefore valuable for firms who wish to minimise risk.

Larger firms having access to more sophisticated financial techniques may use the ARR or discounted cash flow methods. These methods highlight the overall profitability of investment projects and may be more appropriate for businesses where profit maximisation is important.

| Year | Install solar photovoltaic panels | | | Build an anaerobic digester | | |
	Annual cash flows (£m)	Discounting factors at 10%	Present value (£m)	Annual cash flows (£m)	Discounting factors at 10%	Present value (£m)
0	£(6.85)	1	£(6.85)	£(8.20)	1	£(5.2)
1	£1.90	0.909	£1.73	£2.46	0.909	£2.24
2	£1.95	0.826	£1.61	£2.55	0.826	£2.11
3	£2.14	0.751	£1.61	£2.67	0.751	£2.01
4	£2.25	0.683	£1.54	£2.72	0.683	£1.86
5	£2.31	0.621	£1.43	£2.91	0.621	£1.81
NPV			1.07	NPV		4.83

Table 8.4 Comparing Reston Technology plc's choice of investment projects using NPV

Method of investment appraisal	Advantages	Disadvantages
Payback	● Easy to calculate ● Simple to understand ● Relevant to firms with limited funds who want a quick return	● Ignores the timing of payments ● Excludes income received after payback ● Does not calculate profit
ARR	● Measures the profit achieved on projects ● Allows easy comparison with returns on financial investments (bank accounts, for example)	● Ignores the timing of payments ● Calculates average profits – they may fluctuate wildly during the project
Discounted cash flow	● Makes an allowance for the opportunity cost of investing ● Takes into account cash inflows and outflows for the duration of the investment	● Choosing the discount rate is difficult – especially for long-term projects ● A complex method to calculate and easily misunderstood

Table 8.5 A comparison of investment appraisal techniques

Business in focus: Investment decisions and the price of oil

Investment in the UK's oil and gas industry slumped in the final three months of 2014, following a dramatic collapse in the price of oil. Business investment fell by £600 million in the final quarter of 2014, down 1.4 per cent on the previous three months (the third quarter from July to September 2014), the Office for National Statistics (ONS) reported. The unexpected drop marked a second quarterly fall in investment. The Bank of England had forecast that investment would grow by 2.5 per cent for the period.

The price of a barrel of oil slumped from $115 in June 2013 to around $45 in January 2015. Oil prices subsequently recovered somewhat, but at just over $60 a barrel in March 2015 oil values remain too low to justify some investment projects.

'Falling investment by the oil and gas extraction industry is a large component of this decrease,' the ONS said. It continued: 'Given the recent steep fall in oil prices, it might be expected that investment by the oil extraction industry might also fall, as oil production becomes less profitable.'

In 2014 as a whole, business investment rose by 6.8 per cent, its fastest annual growth rate in seven years.

Source: Adapted from the *Telegraph*, 26 February 2015

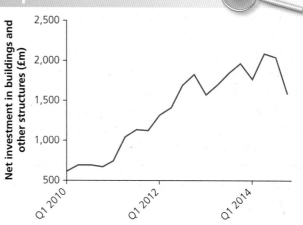

Figure 8.3 Investment by the UK's oil and gas industry, 2010–14

Questions

1. Explain why the dramatic fall in the price of oil would make investment less attractive for UK oil and gas firms, no matter what method of investment appraisal they used.

2. Does the sudden drop in the price of oil and its huge impact on business investment in the UK indicate that all techniques of investment appraisal are of little value?

Maths moment

Use the information in the first paragraph of Business in focus above to calculate the total level of business investment in the UK in the third quarter of 2014 (July to September).

Factors influencing investment decisions

There are a number of factors that a business might take into account when making an investment decision alongside the results of investment appraisal methods such as NPV.

Investment criteria

Once the investment appraisal process has produced an answer this needs to be compared with something in order to make a decision. There are a number of criteria that a business may use to make an investment decision.

(a) The rate of interest

ARR and NPV methods produce figures that can be compared with the rate of interest. Any interest rate chosen for this process will be based on the interest rate set by the Monetary Policy Committee at the Bank of England. In essence, the managers of the business will seek a return that will either be greater than the current and forecast interest rates if the ARR is used or, in the event of using NPV, the interest rate that is current should produce a positive NPV.

Using the interest rate as a criterion does involve a number of problems, however. Firstly, many investment projects are long term and expenditure and returns may take place over many years. It is highly unlikely that interest rates will remain unchanged for this period of time; many forecasters believe that the bank rate of interest set by the Monetary Policy Committee will rise slowly during the period 2016–2018. Therefore, managers have to decide on a rate or range of rates to use in their calculations.

Secondly, investments involve risks – we consider this more fully in the section below. When choosing a minimum rate of return the management team have to build in an allowance for risk.

Key term

Return on Capital Employed (ROCE) is the net profits of a business expressed as a percentage of the value of the capital employed in the business.

(b) The level of profit

When we looked at company accounts and ratio analysis in Chapter 2, we saw that a series of ratios can be used to assess the profitability of a business. One of these, **Return on Capital Employed (ROCE)**, provides a figure which measures profits generated against the value of resources available to the business. It is not unusual for a business to set itself targets in terms of ROCE. Barratt Developments plc, a leading UK house builder, has set itself a challenging ROCE figure of 25 per cent for the financial year that ends in 2017

and says it is on target to achieve it. Managers may insist that any new investment project should generate returns which will at least match (and hopefully exceed) the business's overall target for ROCE.

(c) Alternative investments

It would be unusual for a business to only consider a single investment project. Most managers contemplating a major investment will have other options. These could be very different investments or simple variants on the first proposal. The business may simply select the project or projects which perform the best subject to some minimum criteria in terms of profits or percentage returns. In such circumstances opportunity cost is an important concept for managers to bear in mind.

Study tip

Investment criteria can be useful to you when responding to questions on investment appraisal. When judging whether or not a business should go ahead with a particular investment, it is important to think what criteria the business would expect the investment to meet. The information you are given may directly state these or they may be implied. In either case, by relating your answer to the criterion or criteria you have a basis for making a judgement that you are able to justify.

Non-financial factors

The financial aspects of any proposed investment will clearly have an important influence upon whether a business goes ahead with the plan. However, a number of other issues may affect the decision.

(a) Corporate image

A firm may reject a potentially profitable investment project, or choose a less profitable alternative, because to do otherwise might reflect badly on the business. Having a positive corporate image is important in terms of long-term sales and profits and may be considered more important than gaining short-term advantage from profitable investments. In 2014, Johnson & Johnson, an American multinational consumer goods company, decided to invest approximately $25 million in an advertising campaign designed to improve the company's corporate image. The company's directors would have had to take a range of qualitative factors into account when judging the worth of such an investment against alternatives available.

(b) Corporate aims and objectives

Most businesses will only undertake an investment if they consider that it will assist in the achievement of corporate objectives. For example, Rolls Royce, a UK engineering company that publicly states its aim to produce high-quality products, may invest heavily in training for its staff and in R&D. This will assist in the manufacture of world-class aero engines and vehicles.

(c) Environmental and ethical issues

These can be important influences on investment decisions. Some firms have a genuine commitment to trading ethically and to inflicting minimal damage on the environment. This is a core part of the business philosophy of some firms. As a consequence, they would not exploit cheap labour in developing economies or use non-sustainable resources. In 2014, the Church of England received a great deal of criticism for investing in Wonga, a company that provides payday loans at high rates of interest. Other firms may have a less deep commitment to ethical and environmental trading but may avoid some investments for fear of incurring damaging publicity.

(d) Industrial relations

Some potentially profitable investments may be turned down because they would result in a substantial loss of jobs. Taking decisions that lead to large-scale redundancies can be costly in terms of decreased morale, redundancy payments and harm to the business's corporate image.

> ### Study tip
>
> It is essential to think about quantitative and qualitative factors when making decisions on investment projects. Most case studies will include some qualitative issues for you to weigh up and you will need to take these into account as well as any quantitative information.

Business in focus: Dyson's investment

Innovative solid-state batteries could hold twice as much electricity as current batteries for longer lasting smartphones, tablets and electric cars. Entrepreneur James Dyson is investing $15 million (about £10 million) in a new type of battery that promises to double smartphone battery life and allow electric cars to drive over 600 miles per charge.

The owner of the UK company that is famed for its vacuum cleaners was alerted to the University of Michigan development called Sakti3. The University has developed next generation solid-state technology that can store twice as much energy as traditional rechargeable batteries. As part of the investment, Dyson has entered into a joint development agreement to commercialise Sakti3's solid-state battery technology. The new batteries promise to store twice as much energy as today's liquid-based lithium batteries that are used in everything from smartphones and tablets to cars, robots, and renewable energy sources such as solar panels and wind turbines.

'Sakti3 has achieved leaps in performance, which current battery technology simply can't,' said James Dyson, who is one of the UK's richest people. 'It's these fundamental technologies – batteries, motors – that allow machines to work properly.'

Battery technology is one of the major limiting factors of portable or cordless electronic products today. While surrounding computer technologies have progressed at a staggering rate, batteries haven't kept up, leading to user frustration and limits on what can be done. Mobile electronics companies have been forced to choose: either be heavier and thicker, or else suffer from poor battery life, which is one of the reasons products like the iPhone rarely last longer than a day on a single charge.

Source: Adapted from an article in the *Guardian*, 16 March 2015

Questions

1. Explain why techniques of investment appraisal may only be of limited use in these circumstances.
2. Do you think this was a good decision by James Dyson?

Risk and uncertainty

It is not a simple matter to assess the degree of **risk** involved in an investment decision. Risk is the chance of something adverse or bad happening. Risk should be distinguished from uncertainty. Uncertainty is not measurable and cannot be included in numerical techniques of investment appraisal. An investment project which appears to have a high degree of uncertainty attached to it may not be undertaken because the firm in question may be unable to assess its likely costs and benefits.

In the context of investment decisions there are two broad ways in which risk may manifest itself: costs may be higher than forecast or sales lower than expected.

Forecasting future sales can be a very difficult, and often expensive, exercise. Market research can be used but it is costly and not always reliable. The difficulties in forecasting sales arise from a number of factors.

- **Timescales**. It is much harder to forecasts sales accurately many years into the future. Over a longer timescale it is more likely that tastes and fashions may change or that new competitors or new products may enter the market.
- **New markets**. If an investment project is based on a business entering a new market (either in geographical or product terms), then the business has less experience and no financial records to use as a guide in forecasting sales. In 2007, Tesco entered the US market for groceries setting up a series of small supermarkets throughout California. This was not a successful enterprise and sales were below expectations. Tesco withdrew from the American market in 2013 having incurred losses reported to be around £1 billion. Apparently, even one of Britain's largest companies does not find it easy to forecast its sales accurately.
- **Competitors' reactions**. Deciding on a particular programme of investment may bring a business into competition with rivals in news ways. Entering a new market (as in the case of Tesco above), producing new products or developing new methods of production may all provoke a response from competitors. This may take the form of increased advertising, cutting prices or bringing out new rival products. Each of these actions will impact on the sales associated with the investment project. However, not knowing the type or extent of reaction in advance makes it very difficult to estimate its effect on future sales.

Equally, costs may rise above the forecast level, reducing the returns from the investment. Alternatively, they may fall – meaning an alternative investment may have been much more profitable.

The prices of commodities on global markets have been very volatile over the period 2014–15. Apart from the large drop in the price of oil, cotton prices have fallen by nearly 50 per cent in the period June 2014 to February 2015 while between March 2014 and March 2015 the price of zinc rose from $1,900 to $2,400 a tonne on global markets before falling back to $1,990 a tonne again. The volatility of prices for such fundamentally important products highlights the difficulties that firms face when attempting to forecast future costs of production.

Managing risk

Managers may seek to identify and manage the risk in an investment decision by taking a range of actions including the following:

1. **Purchasing raw materials on forward markets**. This means that the firm concerned negotiates a price at the present time for a product to be delivered at some agreed date in the future. For example, many airlines have agreed future prices for the delivery of aviation fuel and therefore know for certain this element of their future costs. Although it removes the risk of a sudden increase in costs, it may be judged a mistake if prices fall between agreeing the deal and the delivery of the product. Unfortunately for the UK low-cost airline Flybe, this has been the case. The firm signed an agreement to buy oil at $129 a barrel for 97 per cent of its fuel intake until March 2016, whereas at the time of writing the price of a barrel of oil is around $55.

2. **Building in allowances for fluctuations in sales revenue and costs**. Prudent managers may opt to forecast a range of sales figures and costs of production which are based on their market research, but allow for the market to change in some way that may be either adverse or favourable. Building in this flexibility in forecasting and thinking about how wide the ranges for sales revenue and costs should be, will help managers to judge the degree of risk as well as the value of an investment project. We look at this aspect of investment decisions more fully in the following section, 'The value of sensitivity analysis'.

3. **Ensuring the business has sufficient financial assets available**. If a business is trading in a volatile or rapidly changing market, it would be

sensible to make certain the business has sufficient resources to deal with any adverse circumstances. Tesco was fortunate to have sufficient finance to support its unsuccessful business in California whilst it was operational and to cover its losses when it withdrew from the market.

The value of sensitivity analysis

Key term

Sensitivity analysis is a technique that uses variations in forecasts to allow for a range of outcomes.

We saw on the previous page preparing accurate forecasts for revenues and costs when conducting investment appraisal can be a difficult task, especially for firms that operate in markets where costs, prices and demand can be volatile. In such circumstances, managers can benefit when making investment decisions from building in variations to key figures in their forecasts such as sales volumes or unit costs of production to see what impact these have on the outcomes of the investment appraisal techniques. Sensitivity analysis, or what-if analysis as it is sometimes called, allows for managers to alter independent variables such as costs and sales volumes in investment appraisal techniques and to see the outcomes. This helps to judge the degree of risk involved in making a specific investment.

For example, a manager might allow for a rise in variable costs of 5 per cent per unit and, as an alternative, for a fall of 5 per cent in variable costs per unit. The extent of the change in the outcome of the investment decision will show how sensitive the investment is to a change in key variables such as costs or revenues.

An example of the use of sensitivity analysis in an investment decision

The scenario

A management team is presented with the information in Table 8.6 about a possible investment in a new machine that is available for lease for a three-year period and can be used to produce components used in aircraft manufacture.

Cost of three-year lease for the machine	£800,000
Forecast annual sales	200
Selling price per unit	£12,500
Variable cost per unit of production	£9,250
Annual fixed costs of operating the machine	£220,000

Table 8.6 Selected data associated with an investment

The management team has chosen to use the NPV method and a discount rate of 10 per cent to appraise this investment. It calculates that the value of annual sales in each of the three years would be £2.5 million (200 × £12,500) and that annual total costs would be £2.07 million ([200 × £9,250] + £220,000). They have produced the summary data shown in Table 8.7 below.

Year	Net cash flow (£)	Discounting factor	Present value (£)
0	(800,000)	1	(800,000)
1	430,000	0.909	390,870
2	430,000	0.826	355,180
3	430,000	0.751	322,930
NPV			**268,980**

Table 8.7 The NPV calculation for the new machine

The outcome of the NPV calculation looks promising from the management team's point of view. There is a comparatively large, positive NPV. This looks like a worthwhile investment. However, in this investment, as in most others, there are risks. The most obvious area for risk is the sales forecast of 200 components per year for the next three years. A range of factors could cause this to be proved incorrect. Competitors might reduce prices, airline manufacturers might suffer a fall in the sales of their planes or new technology may appear making this component less attractive. Thus, actual sales may be above or below the forecast figure of 200.

Using sensitivity analysis

The management team might allow for a 20 per cent variation in sales. Thus, they can conduct the NPV calculation on the basis that they might achieve:

- high sales (20 per cent above their forecast) so 240 a year
- low sales (20 per cent below their forecast), thus 160 a year.

This enables them to produce the following results:

Outcome	Annual sales	NPV
High sales	240	£592,160
Low sales	160	(£54,200)

Table 8.8 The effects of differing sales volumes on the investment's NPV

The sensitivity of the NPV of this investment project to variations in sales can be shown on a graph as in Figure 8.4.

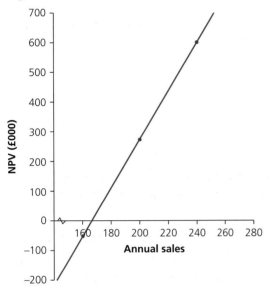

Figure 8.4 The sensitivity of NPV of the investment project to sales of the component

Interpreting the result

The managers of the project may not be too reassured by the results of this sensitivity analysis. It suggests that the NPV of this project is sensitive to variations in sales volumes because the line in Figure 8.4 is steep. This means that a relatively small change in sales produces quite a large change in the NPV figure. However, if the team's forecast of 200 unit sales a year is correct, the investment will generate a positive NPV. Furthermore, so long as annual sales exceed approximately 167 units on average over the three years, the investment will generate a positive NPV.

However, this sensitivity analysis has only considered possible changes in the volume of sales. Other changes may take place, such as changes in the market price or in either fixed or variable costs. Any of these changes, or two or more in combination, could impact on the NPV generated by the project. Further sensitivity analysis would be required to assess this project more fully.

How useful is sensitivity analysis?

Sensitivity analysis can assist managers in considering the degree of risk involved in an investment decision by helping them to measure how sensitive outcomes (in the form of payback times, ARR or NPV figures) are to changes in other variables in the calculation, such as selling prices or volumes. If there is a high degree of sensitivity, then the risk involved in the investment is greater. If there is a high degree of sensitivity and the investment is taking place in a market which is volatile and therefore likely to see changes in variables, the risk of making the investment may be judged to be too great.

Sensitivity analysis is, like many similar techniques, only as good as the data on which it is based. Our example above showed an investment that was sensitive to changes in the volume of sales. However, it appeared that the business had a substantial margin for error, in that its forecast sales were considerably above the level at which NPVs became negative. However, if the sales forecast was inaccurate, then the value of the analysis was much reduced.

A further weakness of sensitivity analysis is that it considers changes in one variable at a time. Where there are too many changes its value can be reduced. If, in our example above, the components were exported (and possibly materials imported), this could introduce another variable into the analysis – exchange rate changes. Too many variables can produce a very wide range of results, but also indicate that a higher degree of risk exists.

Although we have discussed sensitivity analysis in relation to investment decision making, it is a more general technique that can be used in a wide range of business decisions, and is used extensively by organisations such as the European Commission and the American government. It has some similarities to the technique of decision trees, which we considered in Year 1, but does not attach probabilities to each of the possible outcomes.

ASSESSMENT ACTIVITIES

(a) Knowledge check questions

1 State three business decisions that may require the application of investment appraisal techniques.

2 List the two major considerations for managers when deciding whether or not to make an investment.

3 State one reason why forecasts of sales revenues arising from an investment may prove to be inaccurate.

4 AB Ltd is considering an investment that is forecast to cost £150,000. The expected net cash flow arising from the investment is £40,000 per annum. Which of the following is the payback period of AB Ltd's investment?

   (a) 4 years

   (b) 3 years and 3 months

   (c) 3 years and 9 months

   (d) 3 years

LM plc is considering the purchase of a non-current asset. It will require an investment of £900,000 and would cost £100,000 each year to operate. Over its ten-year life the asset would generate £280,000 in revenue each year.

5 Which of the following is the average annual profit associated with LM plc's investment?

   (a) £1.8 million

   (b) £180,000

   (c) £900,000

   (d) £90,000

6 Which of the following is the average rate of return (ARR) from LM plc's investment?

   (a) 10%

   (b) 100%

   (c) 20%

   (d) 64%

7 Define the term 'discounting'.

8 State two items of information that a manager will require to calculate the net present value (NPV) of an investment.

9 State two criteria that a business may use as part of making an investment decision.

10 State two examples of variables that could be altered as part of a sensitivity analysis into a proposed investment in building a new factory.

(b) Short answer questions

1 Explain the possible reasons why a start-up business might use payback as a method of investment appraisal. **(4 marks)**

2 Explain two qualitative factors that an oil company may consider as part of the appraisal of a proposed investment to extract oil from the seabed under the English Channel. **(5 marks)**

3 A rapidly-growing company is considering buying a similar-sized competitor in a South American country. Explain one reason why this investment decision might carry a high degree of risk. **(5 marks)**

4 Saxon Markey plc is considering a first major investment in a market in which demand is price elastic. Explain why the company may benefit from the use of sensitivity analysis in these circumstances. **(9 marks)**

(c) Data response question

Tidal Lagoon Power

Tidal power is a major energy creation opportunity for the UK. A UK company, Tidal Lagoon Power Ltd (TLP Ltd), has proposed a six-mile sea wall (or lagoon) scheme in Swansea Bay. This has an estimated cost of £1,000 million and would generate enough electricity to supply 120,000 homes. TLP Ltd has received encouragement from the UK government, which agreed to talks on subsidies, as part of its budget announced in March 2015. The Prudential insurance company has agreed to be a major investor in the project.

The scheme, which could be operational from 2026, is expected to have a lifespan of 120 years and will help to protect the UK's energy supplies in the future when energy prices may be difficult to forecast accurately, although they are expected to rise. It is the first of a number of possible tidal lagoon schemes being considered by TLP Ltd which could give a major boost to the UK's ability to meet demanding international climate change targets.

Ed Davey, the UK government minister who was responsible for both climate and energy, said 'Britain has some of the best tidal resources in the world – tidal lagoons could provide 8 per cent of our electricity needs, replacing foreign fossil fuels with clean, reliable, home-grown electricity and creating fantastic economic opportunities.'

Greenpeace welcomed the move but said the UK's renewable industry, of which tidal power could form a major element, needed a long-term strategy to be agreed.

One business analyst has forecast the costs and revenues for the first five years of the lagoon's operations if a decision is made to go ahead with the investment, but before any financial support from the government in the form of subsidies (which could amount to between £40 million and £50 million a year is made). The data is shown in Table 8.9.

Year	Forecast revenue (£m)	Forecast operating costs (£m)
2026	110.40	60.65
2027	113.72	62.41
2028	117.14	64.91
2029	120.66	66.86
2030	124.28	68.87

Table 8.9 A forecast for the Swansea Bay Project

Questions

1 Use the data in table 8.9 to calculate the forecast ARR for the first five years of this project's life.   (6 marks)

2 Analyse the case for and against using the ARR as a method of investment appraisal in these circumstances.   (9 marks)

3 Do you think that TLP should make the decision to proceed with this investment? Justify your decision.   (15 marks)

(d) Essays

1 Discuss whether the existence of uncertainty means that techniques of investment appraisal are a waste of time for businesses supplying goods and services with short product life cycles when considering strategic options.   (25 marks)

2 'In a world in which the effects of climate change are becoming more worrying, qualitative factors are more important in investment decisions than financial factors for all businesses.' To what extent do you agree with this statement? Justify your view.   (25 marks)

Case study: Unit 7 Analysing the strategic position of a business

Marks & Spencer plc targets international expansion

Marks & Spencer plc (affectionately known as M&S) is one of Britain's best-known retailers with a positive corporate image. The business was established as a single market stall in 1884 and has since grown into a large international retailer. M&S has nearly 86,000 employees, has stores in 54 countries and sells clothing, home products including furniture and food. Its key objective is growth to transform M&S from a traditional shop-based British retailer to an international, multi-channel retailer.

Plan A and the UK market

M&S introduced its Plan A in 2007. The plan set out 100 commitments to achieve within five years including becoming carbon neutral, stopping sending waste to landfill and helping to improve the lives of those employed in its supply chain. Recently, the company has updated its plan with the aim of becoming 'the world's most sustainable major retailer' by 2020.

M&S's sales in Britain remain subdued, especially for clothing sales which have fallen steadily for over three years despite the company spending heavily on promotion. Annual profits for M&S were recently overtaken for the first time by Next, a clothing retailer, and some analysts have questioned whether M&S has too many stores in Britain. The company's dividend payment per share has not risen since 2011.

International expansion

In 2014, M&S's sales from its international businesses rose by 6.2 per cent as it opened 55 new international stores. It achieved high rates of growth in its 'priority' markets including Russia and China and has opened stores in other emerging markets such as India and Vietnam. The company is pursuing a strategy of international expansion with the intention of opening 250 stores outside the UK by 2017. The company's managers are confident of success in international markets with one commenting that: 'Britishness is as saleable as ever in any part of the world.'

The retailer's international expansion plan has been described as 'capital-light' in that it will require relatively little financing from the company. This 'capital-light' strategy will be achieved:

- by offering franchise agreements whenever possible
- through partnerships with suitable overseas retailers (that reflect M&S's values)
- use of websites (such as M&S's website on TMall by China).

Many other retailers have failed with their international expansion plans; for example, Tesco has sold its businesses in the USA and a part of its Chinese operations.

Item	2014 (£m)	2013 (£m)
Revenue	10,309.7	10,026.8
Operating profit	694.5	753.0
Profit for the year	506.0	444.8
Current assets	1,368.5	1,267.9
Current liabilities	2,349.3	2,238.3
Non-current liabilities	2,847.0	2,852.9
Total equity	2,706.7	2,519.5
Earnings per share	32.2 (pence)	28.2 (pence)

Table 1 Selected financial data for M&S, 2013–14

Source: Marks and Spencer's annual reports

UK data	Revenue from food – £5.1bn Revenue from clothing & home products – £4.1bn	798 stores
International data	Revenue from all sales – £31.2bn	455 stores
Multi-channel revenue (i.e. from online sales, not shops)	£800.1m	

Table 2 Some key facts about M&S, 2014

Source: Marks and Spencer's annual reports

Questions

1 Analyse why non-financial factors may form an important element of any investment appraisal conducted by M&S as part of its international expansion. (10 marks)

2 Analyse the possible reasons why M&S plc chose to implement a strategy of international expansion. (10 marks)

3 Discuss whether or not it is possible for M&S's stakeholders to assess the company's performance fully without the use of techniques such as Elkington's triple bottom line. (16 marks)

4 Do you think that the financial position of M&S plc was the major reason for it choosing a 'capital-light' method of international expansion? (20 marks)

5 To what extent is it essential for all British retailers to operate globally to be successful? (24 marks)

Unit 8

Choosing strategic direction

Strategic direction: choosing which markets to compete in and what products to offer

Introduction

In this chapter we consider what is meant by the strategic direction of a business. This means we examine how managers make strategic decisions about the long-term direction in which the business is headed. This involves decisions about which markets to compete in and what products to offer. Get these decisions wrong and the whole business is in trouble. In particular we compare and contrast four types of strategy using a model called the Ansoff matrix and consider why a business might choose a particular strategy.

What you need to know by the end of this chapter:

● the factors that influence which markets to compete in and which products to offer
● how to analyse the strategic direction of a business using the Ansoff matrix
● how to assess the value of market penetration, market development, new product development and diversification as business strategies
● how to analyse and evaluate the reasons for choosing and value of different options for strategic direction.

Strategic direction

Strategic choices involve deciding the direction in which a business should move and the methods by which it should pursue its plan. In this section we consider the possibilities for the strategic direction of a business. In the following sections we consider how these strategies are pursued and then how a given strategy is implemented.

The strategic direction of a business refers to the decisions made regarding the markets it competes in and the products it offers. With continuous internal and external change, managers must regularly review where their business is at any moment and where it should be headed. This means the strategic direction of the business will change.

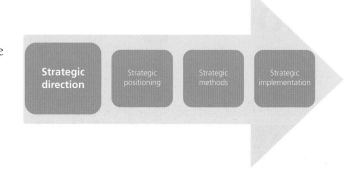

Figure 9.1 Strategic direction

Imagine you are the captain of a ship. You will be continually checking coordinates to make sure you are where you are supposed to be and are pointing in the right direction, and to ensure that you are moving at the right speed. Changes in weather conditions may force you to adjust your plan and, in some cases, may require you to change your overall direction. In the same way, a chief executive will keep monitoring key measures of performance from the business to ensure all is on target and keep reviewing the plan to ensure it remains relevant to the business environment in which it operates. Changes in the business environment may require a change in strategic direction. In some cases, this can completely change the shape of the company over time.

Did you know that Nokia began as a paper producer? Or that Nintendo started by producing playing cards? The carpet maker Desso has now moved into playing surfaces such as those used by Manchester City and Liverpool football clubs. The strategic direction of these businesses has changed as opportunities have emerged in new markets, with new products and as threats have developed in their existing markets. You may have a view of how your life will unfold, but you may find it turns out differently because of opportunities and threats along the way. Similarly, the development of a business will follow various twists and turns as it grows and gets older.

Key terms

Strategic choices involve deciding the direction in which a business should move and the methods by which it should pursue this plan.

The **strategic direction** sets out which markets a business will compete in and what products it will offer.

Ansoff matrix

One way in which the strategic direction of a business can be analysed is using the Ansoff matrix; this is a model developed by Igor Ansoff. This matrix considers a firm's strategy in terms of the products it offers and the markets in which it operates.

	Existing products	New products
Existing markets	Market penetration	New product development
New markets	Market development	Diversification

Figure 9.2 Ansoff matrix

Figure 9.2 highlights the four main strategic directions that a business might choose.

- **Market penetration**. This involves developing strategies to boost sales of existing products in existing markets. The business is aiming to boost its market share. For example, an organisation might invest more in promotional activity or change its pricing approach in order to sell more. This strategy involves relatively little risk in terms of decision making because the products and markets are familiar to the managers. However, if the existing market has little growth potential – for example, because it is a mature market – a business would probably not want to focus solely on market penetration.
- **Market development**. This approach involves offering existing products but targeting new market segments with them. This could be a new segment in terms of:
  - geographical area; for example, offering a product in a new part of the country or the world
  - demographic features; for example, a business might target a younger or different socioeconomic customer group.

Although the business knows this type of product already, it needs to ensure that what it has been offering matches the needs of the new target market. It will need to understand the conditions of the new market including the existing competitors, the distribution systems and the key factors that influence customers' buying decisions. Entering a new market segment can be dangerous – for example, existing business may respond by protecting their sales and may try to force a new entrant to the market out.

- **New product development**. This involves developing new products for existing customers. The business may be responding to changes in customer requirements or anticipating future change. Investment in new product development can take time – researching, testing and launching new products properly can take months, even years. It is also high risk as many new product ideas fail to succeed even after they have been launched. In 2015, for example, Google Glass was withdrawn from the market for further development. However businesses may want to invest in new product development to broaden their portfolio and if the sales of existing products are in decline. W. L. Gore, for example, is constantly developing new products in areas such as electronics, fabrics, industrial and medical products. The company which developed Gortex has annual sales of over $3 billion and has a culture and tradition of innovation.

Weblink

To find out more about W. L. Gore's approach to innovation, visit: www.gore.com

- **Diversification**. This strategy involves offering new products to new customer groups. There is quite a high level of risk here since the products and target customers are both unfamiliar. There is likely to be high levels of uncertainty as a result. However, in other ways this strategy may be reducing risk because by moving into new markets and developing new products, the business may be less vulnerable to changes in one of its market segments. If you are totally reliant on one range of products in one market, for example, then you are vulnerable to change.

Business in focus: New product development – Cadbury

Figure 9.3 A range of Cadbury products

The Cadbury chocolate company, which began in 1824 and is now owned by Kraft Foods, is constantly researching, improving and developing new products. It is monitoring market conditions, customers' tastes and competitors' products to ensure it meets its consumer tastes and wants. In 2012, the company opened its Global Centre of Excellence for Chocolate Research and Development in Bournville. This £17 million centre included innovation labs, a pilot plant and a kitchen for experimentation.

Questions

1. What factors do you think Cadbury considers before launching a new chocolate bar?
2. What factors do you think determine the success of a new chocolate bar launched by Cadbury?

Business in focus: Product failures

Product failures can occur for many reasons. The product may not be developed properly and, therefore, fail to impress or there may simply not be a need for it. Two high-profile examples of product failures are:

1. The Ford Edsel

The Edsel was a new model of car released by Ford in 1957. The car was named after Edsel B. Ford, the company's former president and Henry Ford's only son, who had died in 1943. The development of the Edsel cost over $350 million (equal to around $3 billion in today's terms). The car was heavily promoted, but new features such as electronic controls proved to be unreliable. The price also proved to be too high in an economic downturn. The car was taken off the market after just four years.

2. The Newton Message Pad

Even successful companies such as Apple have had product failures. Apple's Newton Message Pad was one of the first products to offer basic computing functions in a handheld device. At the time, this technology was revolutionary. One of the key selling points was its handwriting feature, but this failed to work effectively at first and meant customers did not feel the product justified its high price.

Questions

1. Why do you think that even successful businesses can have product failures?
2. What do you think businesses can do to reduce the likelihood of a new product failing?

The Ansoff matrix provides a simple framework to analyse different strategic options facing a business. In its most basic form, it categorises strategic options in terms of 'existing' or 'new' products and markets. In reality, there are many different versions of these strategies. For example, a 'new' product may mean an existing product that is slightly modified, one that is simply new to the business but not the market, or something that is highly innovative and has not been produced by anyone before. There are, therefore, degrees of 'newness'. Similarly, a 'new' market may mean expanding into a region a few miles away from where you operate already, or may mean expanding globally and dealing with very different market conditions. It is possible, therefore, to have a scale on the axes to show just how new the products and markets are rather than simply categorising them as 'existing' or 'new'.

It is also important to appreciate that there may be several strategies being pursued by a business at the same time. A business may be trying to boost its sales of its existing products in its existing markets, whilst also developing new offerings and pursuing overseas expansion. Apple, for example, has tried to get more of the smartphone market (market penetration), launched new products and offered products in new markets such as China (market development). Coca Cola modifies its existing products (e.g. by having different packaging for Coca Cola) whilst developing new products such as Coca Cola Life and moving into new markets with its venture with Monster energy drinks.

Maths moment

1. A business is pursuing a market penetration strategy. At present, it has a 5 per cent share of a market that has total sales of £2,400,000. It hopes to increase this to a 7 per cent share. How much would its sales need to increase by in order to achieve this?
2. The price elasticity of demand for a product is estimated to be −2.5. A company hopes to increase its sales by 12.5 per cent by cutting its price. How much does it need to cut its price by (in percentages) to achieve this target?

Figure 9.4 Ansoff matrix with scale

Business in focus: The Arcadia Group

The Arcadia Group is a leading high-street retailer made up of many well-known brands. It is a private company owned by Philip Green and includes:

- Dorothy Perkins
- BHS
- TopShop
- TopMan
- Evans
- Miss Selfridge
- Outfit

The Arcadia Group has physical outlets in Europe, the Far East and the Middle East. It employs over 45,000 people. It is constantly looking to developing its portfolio of brands, the regions in which it operates and the products it sells in its stores.

Figure 9.5 Arcadia Group businesses

Questions

1. How would you describe the strategic direction pursued by Arcadia?
2. Why do you think it follows this direction?

Selecting a strategy

When considering which strategy or strategies to choose a business will consider many different factors:

- **The expected costs**. For example, what investment is required? Last year, GlaxoSmithKline spent £2.5 billion in searching for new pharmaceutical medicines.
- **The expected returns**. For example, what are the likely profits relative to the initial investment?
- **The opportunity costs**. What are the alternatives if this project is not pursued?
- **The risk**. What would the downside be if the strategy fails? This is a very important aspect of a strategic decision. Managers will want to assess the damage that might be done if the strategy was unsuccessful. For example, what is the financial risk and what is the risk to the brand?
- **The fit with the resources and strengths of the business**. For example, is the project affordable? Does the business have the competences (for example the expertise and experience) to perform well? Does the business have the capacity required?
- **The impact on other stakeholders**. For example, are they likely to support the plan or resist it? What objections might they have?
- **The ethical issues involved**. For example, are the managers and owners happy to be associated with the project or could it be criticised for being unethical?

As well as considering where to compete in terms of products and market, a business will also consider how to compete, for example, how to position itself relative to its competitors. This is known as strategic positioning.

Maths moment $\frac{1+b}{c}=3$

	Probability	Expected outcome
Strategy A: Market penetration	Success = 80%	£2m
	Failure = 20%	(£1m)
Strategy B: Diversification	Success = 30%	£20m
	Failure = 70%	(£6m)

Table 9.1 Probability of success and failure and expected outcomes for market penetration and diversification strategies

Which of the above strategies would you choose? Why?

Business in focus: The tobacco industry

The tobacco industry is one which faces a great deal of external pressure and, therefore, tobacco companies have to review their markets and products and plan for the future.

Features of the tobacco market include the following:

- Over 6 trillion cigarettes a year are sold around the world.
- The global market is dominated by four companies – British American Tobacco (BAT), Imperial Tobacco, Japan Tobacco and Phillip Morris. These four companies have a combined market share of over 40 per cent.
- The Chinese tobacco market is the biggest in the world with over 350 million smokers.
- Over 10 per cent of tobacco products that are sold are the result of illegal trafficking.

In the future there:

- are likely to be fewer people smoking and those who continue to smoke will smoke less. However, there is likely to be continued growth in consumption in emerging markets as populations and incomes grow
- is likely to be greater regulation of the industry leading to plain packaging, restrictions on where it is possible to smoke and how tobacco products can be displayed
- will be product innovation with new technology leading to nicotine inhalation products, aerosol nicotine and electronic cigarettes.

Questions

1. How might this analysis of the tobacco market affect BAT's strategic direction?
2. Do you think the tobacco market is a good one to be in?

Why does strategic direction matter?

Strategic decisions are long-term, high-risk decisions that are full of uncertainty and determine the survival and ongoing success of a business. These decisions are made by senior managers and getting the strategic direction right is essential. If a business ends up offering the wrong products or competing in the wrong markets then, however hard and however well it fights, it is going to be difficult to be successful. Imagine that 20 years ago a business had continued producing typewriters. Or, more recently, imagine a business relied totally on export sales to Russia at a time when political sanctions were imposed against this country and its currency fell in value substantially – this, again, would make success more difficult. A great manager understands and anticipates where markets are going and makes sure the business offers the right products in the right markets. Getting the strategic direction right is essential for business success. The difficulties of Tesco in recent years highlight the problems a business encounters if the strategic direction is wrong. Tesco was building more hypermarkets at a time when customers were shopping more online and wanted local stores for top-up shopping.

The strategic direction of a business needs to be clear to everyone within the organisation because it provides a focus for all the parts of the business and all the elements within it. All employees should know what the business is trying to achieve, why it is trying to achieve this and how it intends to do so. This helps them to decide what to do when and what matters most. This can clarify for employees their role in the organisation, how best to do their job and what their priorities are.

The strategic direction of a business should influence decisions and targets throughout the organisation. When managers at every level and in every part of the business are set targets these functional objectives should link to the overall corporate strategy; the targets for each individual should help to ensure that everyone within the organisation is working towards the same end goal.

What do you think?

Do you think all businesses need to diversify at some stage?

Business in focus: 'Angry Birds'

Figure 9.6 'Angry Birds'

In 2015, the profits of Rovio Entertainment, the business that created 'Angry Birds', fell by over 70 per cent. The popularity of the game fell and this in turn reduced sales of merchandise such as toys, mugs and t-shirts. The game was released originally in 2009 as an iPhone app and has been downloaded 2 billion times. However, after a number of years of growth, mobile gamers now seem to be moving on to new titles. This creates problems for Rovio Entertainment which has built a theme park in Finland and has made a film based on the game. Analysts argue that the company needs to move forward with new products quickly.

Questions

1. Why do you think Rovio Entertainment has not successfully developed new products to add to its portfolio?

2. Do you think app businesses inevitably have a short life?

ASSESSMENT ACTIVITIES

(a) Knowledge check questions

1 Explain what is meant by 'a strategic decision'.

2 What is meant by 'the strategic direction of a business'?

3 State what is on the axes of the Ansoff matrix.

4 According to Ansoff, what is the name of a strategy that offers new products in a new market?

5 According to Ansoff, what is the name of a strategy that offers new products in an existing market?

6 Explain one way a business might pursue a market penetration strategy.

7 Explain why the strategic direction of a business matters.

8 Explain one reason why a business might choose a diversification strategy.

9 Explain one risk of choosing a new product development strategy.

10 Explain one possible influence on the strategic direction of a business.

(b) Short answer questions

1 Explain one way in which a clothes retailer that mainly targets 30–45-year-old women might attempt to penetrate more of the market. (5 marks)

2 Explain one reason why a tobacco business might choose a diversification strategy. (5 marks)

3 Explain one reason why a games app business might choose a new product development strategy. (5 marks)

4 Explain one risk involved in a fast-food business choosing a market development strategy of targeting new countries. (5 marks)

5 Explain the possible risks involved for a family that has owned and run a working farm for generations using their farm as a holiday campsite. (5 marks)

(c) Data response question

King Digital Entertainment

King Digital Entertainment is the $5 billion computer games company that produced 'Candy Crush Saga'. This product is now its cash cow. 'Candy Crush' was only launched in 2012 and was a tremendous success following on from the success of King Digital's previous main product 'Bubble Witch Saga', which became the second most played game on Facebook. The company is truly global – it was founded in Sweden, is based in London, has a head office in the Republic of Ireland, is listed on the Stock Exchange in New York and is managed by an Italian.

In 2011, the company had 110 employees. It now employs over 1,200 and has 356 million users a month. The company's growth has been so great that it moved from its cramped Soho offices to take over Facebook's Convent Garden offices. From there, it developed 'Farm Heroes Saga' which was launched in 2014. Unlike many of its rivals, King Digital is actually profitable. In 2014 revenue increased to $2.2 billion up from $1.8 billion the year before and just

$164 million in 2012. Pre-tax profit reached $768 million last year compared with $714 million in 2013 and $11 million in 2012. The company's rate of growth has been so fast that its annual report actually highlighted that it might struggle to manage the growth effectively.

The managers of King Digital claim their games are more like crosswords than, say, 'Call of Duty'. The games are only intended to be played for a few minutes and this has proved especially popular with women. (About 70 per cent of its users are female.)

'Candy Crush' games are played 957 million times a day mainly by a core of 91 million users. However, the company gains most of its profits from small numbers who buy extra lives, tips and levels in the game. This number is falling – it was 8.3 million in the final quarter of 2014 compared to 13 million in the third quarter. However, managers point to the fact that it has other products ('Candy Crush' accounts for less than half of its revenue) such as the success of 'Candy Crush Soda', which is a franchise from the original game. Nevertheless, the company faces great competition. For example, this year's major hit has been 'Minecraft', which was developed by Markus Persson, an ex-King Digital employee.

Questions

1 Explain the key features of King Digital's strategy to date. (6 marks)

2 Analyse the factors that you think should influence the strategic direction King Digital should take in the future. (9 marks)

3 To what extent do you think it is likely that King Digital will still be in business in 15 years' time? (15 marks)

(d) Essays

1 Do you think market penetration is a better strategy than market development for a business wanting to grow fast? Justify your answer. (25 marks)

2 To what extent do you think a strategy of diversification is too risky for a market leader to choose? Justify your answer. (25 marks)

Chapter 10

Strategic positioning: choosing how to compete

Introduction

In the last chapter we considered how a business choses which markets to compete in and which products to offer. We now consider how a business competes in its chosen market. Does it try to offer more benefits than its rivals at a similar price? Does it offer similar benefits at a lower price? There are many ways a business can compete successfully (it may be a premium or a discount brand, for example). In this chapter we consider the different strategic positioning options open to a business and the factors that influence why a business might choose one rather than another. We also discuss the problems associated with remaining competitive over time.

What you need to know by the end of this chapter:

● how businesses compete in terms of benefits and price
● what is meant by strategic positioning, including Porter's low-cost, differentiation and focus strategies
● how to analyse strategic positioning using Bowman's strategic clock
● how to analyse and assess influences on the choice of a positioning strategy
● how to evaluate the value of different strategic positioning strategies
● the benefits of having a competitive advantage
● the difficulties of maintaining a competitive advantage.

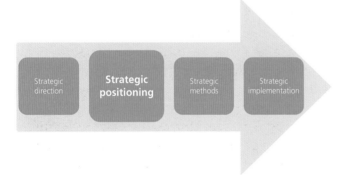

Figure 10.1 Strategic positioning

Strategic positioning

Once the strategic direction of the business is decided (that is, what markets the business is competing in and what products it is offering) managers must decide where to position the business relative to its competitors. How will it compete relative to others in the segments that are being targeted? For example, how does Sports Direct want to be thought of by customers relative to Decathlon? For example, how does Next differ from River Island? Mercedes to Lexus? The **strategic positioning** of a business refers to how it is perceived relative to other businesses in the industry. Managers will decide where in the market they want the business to compete compared to its rivals. For example, Premier Inn is more of a budget hotel chain than Hilton; Nintendo is more of a family games console than Xbox. Of course, where a business would like to position itself and where it actually sits in customers' minds may be very different things.

Strategic positioning can be analysed using Porter's strategies and Bowman's strategic clock.

Porter's strategies

According to the famous business consultant and writer, Michael Porter, a competitive business strategy is about being different. It involves deliberately choosing a different set of activities to be able to deliver a unique mix of value relative to competitors. The value a business offers depends on the combination of benefits relative to the price paid. Porter identified two possible positioning approaches for a business:

● Cost-leadership strategy.
● Differentiation strategy.

Key terms

A **cost leadership strategy** involves achieving lower costs than rivals in the same industry

A **differentiation strategy** involves offering more benefits than rivals in the same industry

Cost-leadership strategy

A **cost-leadership strategy** involves becoming the lowest-cost organisation in the industry in which the business is competing. This may be achieved through:

- **Lower input costs**: A business may find a way of reducing the cost of its inputs. This may be by owning some of its suppliers and thereby avoiding the profit margins of its suppliers. Morrisons, for example, owns many of the farms that supply its products; Zara also owns its suppliers; and IKEA designs and develops all its own products. Alternatively, a business could be located nearer supplies than competitors reducing transportation costs.

Business in focus: Poundland

Figure 10.2 One of Poundland's 500 stores

The Poundland company was set up in 1990 and is now the UK's largest single price value retailer. It offers thousands of products, all priced at £1, in over 500 stores. It has set a target of operating over 1,000 stores.

Last year, Poundland sold:

- over 5 million boxes of Maltesers and over 5 million bars of Toblerone
- over 2 million umbrellas
- around a quarter of a million garden gnomes.

Questions

1. How do you think Poundland manages to offer products at such a low price?
2. Do you think Poundland will ever sell items for more than £1?

- **Economies of scale**: The business may have cost advantages by being bigger than its rivals. For example, it may be able to spread fixed costs over more units if it is big enough, thereby reducing unit costs.
- **Experience**: The managers and employees may be more experienced than rivals enabling them to source cheaper materials and make more efficient decisions.
- **Product/process design**: The design of the product or the process used to produce it may be more cost efficient than competitors. For example, budget airlines use local regional airports where it is cheaper to take off and land than it is at the major airports such as Heathrow and Gatwick; they provide a basic service without pre-booking seats and without food and newspapers provided.

By being a cost leader a business can charge similar prices to its competitors and earn higher returns or, if needed, it can reduce prices lower their competitors can and still make the same profit margin as they do.

Differentiation strategy

A **differentiation strategy** occurs when a business provides some degree of uniqueness relative to its competitors that is sufficiently valued by customers to allow a price premium to be charged. For example, a business may offer more features or provide a higher level of customer service than its rivals. If the higher price charged by the business exceeds the extra costs of providing these benefits, a business can earn higher returns than its rivals.

The differences between Porter's strategies

Figure 10.3 on page 170 presents the following differences visually:

- Cost leadership with parity involves charging the same price as rivals but because costs are lower the profit margin is higher.
- Cost leadership with proximity involves having a lower price than rivals but because costs are lower it is possible to still make the same or higher profit margins than them.
- A differentiator can charge a higher price and still make a high profit margin if the additional charge for the added benefits is more than the cost of providing them.

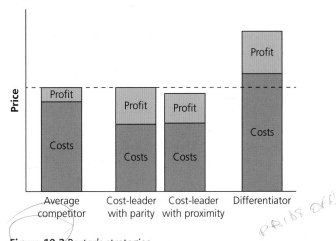

Figure 10.3 Porter's strategies

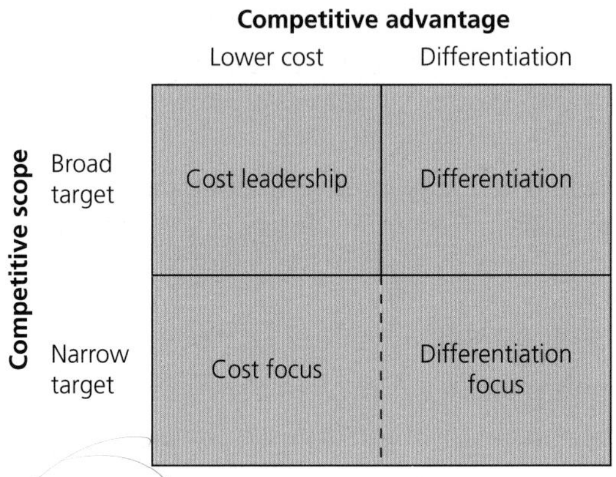

Figure 10.4 Porter's low-cost and differentiation strategies

Porter highlighted that a low-cost or differentiation strategy could be aimed at the market as a whole or at a small part of the market (called a 'focus' strategy). He described the amount of the market targeted as the competitive scope of the business – a broad scope targets the market as a whole, whereas a narrow scope focuses on a niche.

According to Porter, a business should decide which of the generic strategies to choose (that is cost-leadership or differentiation) and whether to target the mass market or a niche; it should then pursue this strategy rigorously and aggressively. A business should avoid being 'stuck in the middle' where it is not clear internally or to customers what the business's strategy actually is. Porter argued that a business has to be low cost or differentiated; it cannot combine the two – it has to be clear in terms of what it wants to be and how it wants to be positioned in the market. However, some analysts disagree with this view and argue that it is possible to keep costs low and still try to differentiate.

Business in focus: GlaxoSmithKline

GlazoSmithKline is a leading, global pharmaceutical business. The company has several aims:

- **Being a leader in its chosen markets** – By innovating and continuing to improve its customer service it aims to generate growth opportunities.

- **Building on its strong global presence** – The company is an international business but it is continuing to develop its geographical reach.

- **Differentiating itself through technology** – GlaxoSmithKline develops innovative technology to maintain its competitiveness. It is responding to emerging customer requirements.

- **Developing operational excellence** – The company has a culture of operational excellence and, through continuous improvement processes, aims to deliver exceptional quality and customer service.

- **Achieving above market growth** – The company believes that sustainable, managed growth is essential to its success.

Questions
With reference to the above information:
1. Analyse the strategic direction(s) being pursued by GlaxoSmithKline.
2. Analyse the strategic positioning pursued by GlaxoSmithKline.

Study tip

Remember that choosing a strategic position does not in itself guarantee success. If a business decides to focus on cost leadership, it has to have ways of ensuring its costs are lower than its competitors. Similarly, a business cannot simply decide to differentiate – it has to be able to offer something that customers value more than their competitors and be able to protect this.

Bowman's strategic clock

Another approach to strategic positioning was developed by Bowman and is known as the strategy clock.

Bowman's model plots the options open to a business on a 'clock'. From this, it is possible to analyse the strategic positioning a business has now and where it may want to be in the future. The 'clock' highlights that there are many options open to a business that enable it to be competitive. For example, a restaurant may:

- offer a fairly basic menu, self-service and limited customer service. Provided the price is low enough, this may be regarded as good value for money and the business may be competitive
- offer a four star menu that is highly rated by food critics in a luxury hotel environment with superb customer service from the waiters. The price may be high but if the food and service merit this, it, again, may be seen as good value for money.

However, some combinations will not be competitive or realistic. For example:

- offering a basic service at a relatively high price is uncompetitive; customers will switch to rivals
- offering a luxury service at a low price would be very attractive to customers, but is unlikely to be financially viable. The business will not be able to cover the costs of the high level of benefits provided.

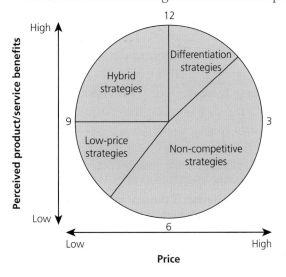

Figure 10.5 Bowman's strategic clock

Different strategic positions highlighted by the clock include:

- differentiating without a price premium (12 o'clock) – this may be used to increase market share
- differentiating with a price premium (1 o'clock) – this may be used to increase profit margins
- focused differentiation (2 o'clock) – this may be used for customers who demand the very highest quality and will pay a big premium. For example, Philippe Patek watches.

- a low-price strategy (8 to 9 o'clock) – this seeks to achieve higher benefits and lower prices relative to those of competitors
- a 'no frills' strategy (7 o'clock) – this approach focuses on price sensitive market segments. For example, this is the strategy of low-cost airlines such as South West Airlines and Ryanair.
- hybrid strategies (9 to 12 o'clock) – these occur where there are relatively high benefits but relatively low prices can be used to enter markets and build position quickly, as an aggressive attempt to win market share or to build volume sales and gain from mass production. A classic example of a hybrid strategy is IKEA, which offers high-quality design at a low price.

Business in focus: IKEA

IKEA aims to provide well-designed products for the home that are affordable to many households. It aims for good quality at a low price. To achieve this:

- it designs its own products
- it uses low-cost materials
- it buys resources in large quantities to get a lower price
- it develops products that can be flat packed, making it cheaper to transport and store them
- it designs products that customers can build themselves, again reducing costs.

Questions

1. Draw Bowman's strategy clock and plot on it where you think IKEA is trying to position itself.
2. What do you think could cause IKEA to reposition itself?

Unlike Porter, the strategic clock model by Bowman:

- focuses on the prices to customers rather than the costs to the organisation
- highlights the full range of options open to a business, whereas Porter's model provides relatively few distinct choices in terms of strategic positioning.

What do you think?

Do you think it is getting more difficult for a business to protect itself from competitors?

NETFLIX

Figure 10.6 Netflix, Inc. is an American provider of on-demand internet streaming media available to riewers in North America, Australia, New Zealand, South America and parts of Europe, including the UK.

Netflix is a global internet TV business. It offers films and TV series. It does not have any commercials and charges a monthly fee for which customers have unlimited viewing (rather than charging per programme). It sets out to be focused in what it does rather than offer a whole range of different forms of entertainment. For example, it does not offer news, music or reality TV shows.

In 2015, the company spent over $600 million in marketing to attract people around the world to try it. At the moment it is available in about 50 countries, but very soon aims to be accessible in every country.

The markets Netflix entered first were Canada, Latin America, the UK, Ireland, the Nordic countries and the Netherlands.

Questions

1. What do you think determined the markets that Netflix targeted first?
2. What do you think determined how Netflix has chosen to position itself?

Influences on a positioning strategy

The factors influencing a positioning strategy include the following:

- **Where the competitors are positioned**. When deciding where it wants to fit within a market a business will naturally assess where its competitors are. In some cases, if the market segment is big enough and a business feels strong enough, it may want to compete with its competitors head on. In other cases, it will deliberately position itself elsewhere in the market to avoid direct conflict.
- **The external environment**. External changes will influence market conditions and where businesses need to position themselves. For example, many businesses have had to become more environmentally conscious in their activities because that's what customers are demanding. When economic conditions are poor this might put pressure on businesses to move towards offering lower prices.
- **The strengths and competences of the business**. The right positioning for a business will depend on what it is able to deliver. There is no point aspiring to a differentiation strategy if the business cannot consistently deliver higher benefits than its rivals. Similarly, to be a low-cost leader a business must have a way of getting and keeping costs lower than rivals. Managers must assess where their competitive advantage may lie and then pursue this positioning fully.

Positioning strategy over time

The strategy chosen by the business is not fixed and may well change over time. In recent years, for example, easyJet has increased the benefits it provides as it has tried to target business customers to a greater extent. Seeing the success of this repositioning, Ryanair has recently followed suit. Meanwhile, the supermarket Morrisons announced in 2014 that it was slashing product prices to compete with the discounters such as Aldi and Lidl, and so was trying to reposition itself in terms of its price benefit positioning.

Study tip

Remember that a strategy is the product of its internal and external environment. As these factors change the strategy will need to adapt. The right strategy and strategic positioning will help the business build on its strengths, protect its weaknesses, defend against threats and exploit opportunities.

What do you think?

Do you think businesses have to change their strategies more often now than they did in the past?

Business in focus: Iceland

Figure 10.7 Iceland – a market leader in frozen foods

Iceland is a UK supermarket specialising in frozen foods. The company is proud of its record of innovation. For example, it became the first supermarket to remove artificial colours, flavourings and non-essential preservatives from its own-brand products in 1986. In the same year, it became the first UK supermarket to remove monosodium glutamate (MSG) from its own-brand products. In 1998, Iceland became the first national food retailer anywhere in the world to ban genetically-

modified ingredients from all of its own-brand products. In these areas and others the company led the way; its decisions have been followed by many other stores.

The company argues that freezing food is a natural process that does not usually require the use of any preservatives. It also seals in freshness, ensuring the retention of vitamins and minerals that may otherwise be lost during the harvesting, transport and storage of fresh products.

The test for any product Iceland sells is that it must offer better quality than any other major UK supermarket at the same or lower price, or comparable quality at a significantly lower price. The company has an independent benchmarking team to regularly assess products according to a range of criteria to ensure that its standards are being maintained.

Iceland places a high degree of importance on innovation. It works closely with suppliers to develop new products that are assessed in its own test kitchens.

Questions
1. Using Bowman's model, analyse the strategic positioning being pursued by Iceland.
2. What factors may have determined the positioning Iceland has chosen?

Why does strategic positioning matter?

Choosing the right arena in which to compete is obviously important. If a business has the wrong products and is in the wrong market, it will find it difficult to do well. However, a business also needs to consider where it fits in the market relative to others. Does it want to be Swatch or Tag Heuer? Apple or ASUS? Sky or BT Sport? It is important to have a clear position in the eyes of consumers so they can place the business relative to others in the market and know where it 'fits'.

The problems of Tesco in 2014, when its profits were lower than expected and it had to change its Chief Executive, highlighted the importance of clear positioning – the company had lost its way and customers no longer understood where it fitted in the market, whereas rivals had much clearer positioning so everyone knew what to expect. It is also important to have the right positioning for market conditions. If a business is moving upmarket and offering more premium products when customers want more basic items, for example, this would be poor strategic positioning.

This means that over time, businesses may want to reposition themselves as internal and external conditions change. Repositioning can take some time; for example,

Skoda has been trying hard for many years to reposition itself away from the perception of it as being a cheap but very basic brand. Waitrose in recent years has been trying to convince customers it is not as expensive as they think it is.

Sustainable competitive advantage

Competitive advantage occurs when a business creates value for its customers that is both greater than the costs of supplying the benefits it offers and is superior to that of other businesses. For example, a competitive advantage may be due to offering similar benefits to rivals at lower prices (a low-cost strategy) or higher benefits at a similar price (a differentiation strategy). However, if one business has an advantage over others, these rivals will naturally want to copy it, thereby removing the advantage. A business will, therefore, want to develop a sustainable competitive advantage, that is one that it can protect over time.

Key term

Competitive advantage occurs when a business offers superior value compared to its rivals, either via lower prices or by providing greater benefits that justify higher prices.

Business in focus: Supermarket wars

The strategic positioning of a business may change over time to reflect different circumstances. For example, a major shift in retailing has occurred in recent years with the success of the discount stores such as Aldi and Lidl. This has forced the established businesses to rethink their strategic positioning and consider whether or not they need to move towards lower prices.

In July 2014, for example, Morrisons announced major price cuts and accepted that profit margins were going to have to be much lower in future because of the dramatic change in market conditions. At the end of 2014, Asda's Chief Executive, Andy Clarke, announced that 2015 was likely to be challenging with further threats posed by the discounters. In 2014, Aldi and Lidl reached a record combined market share of 8.6 per cent of all shopping done at major UK grocery chains. Their sales have increased at the expense of the 'Big Four' supermarkets, namely Tesco, Asda, Sainsbury's and Morrisons.

The discounters are predicted to gain even higher market shares in the future as more businesses adopt this approach. For example, Netto, the Danish discounter, is returning to the UK after 14 years away. It is doing so in partnership with Sainsbury's, which sees this as a way into the discount segment. Netto stores will stock over 2,000 products especially created for UK customers, as well as best-selling branded goods such as Heinz beans. They will also have a Danish feel to them, offering some of the country's well-known products, such as Lego, as well as Danish pastries from in-house bakeries.

The marketing director of Morrisons says that whereas the number one factor affecting store choice used to be convenience, it is now price. The fierce competition between the stores has led to lower prices in the market. In 2014 food prices actually fell by 1.7 per cent. However, the discount stores do not suit every shopper; for example, they typically carry only around 10 per cent of the product range of more established retailers. Interestingly, the higher end, higher priced retailers such as Waitrose have not been affected much by the discounters.

Questions

1. What does the text above suggest about the strategic positioning that supermarkets may have to adopt to be successful in the future?
2. What do you think might account for the success of the discounters' strategy in recent years in the UK?

The ways in which a business might protect its competitive advantage include the following:

- Legal protection such as laws by the government that protect a business or industry from foreign competition, or patents which give legal protection to new inventions for a given number of years.
- Control over resources, perhaps through ownership of different stages of the supply chain; if a business controls some resources, it may be able to prevent others accessing them. For example, de Beers controls a significant proportion of the supply of diamonds in the world.
- A particular culture. The culture of a business refers to the values and attitudes of its employees – the way they think and how they behave. Culture is difficult to suddenly copy because it relies on what people actually believe and is influenced by a whole host of factors, including the experience of its members and the history of the business. Unlike a new piece of equipment, culture cannot simply be bought and installed; it has to grow over time and be incorporated into the way people think and operate. For example, when one business buys another creative business such as an app design company, an advertising agency or a management consultancy it is paying for the culture and the skills and talents of the staff – it is the abilities of the employees, the way they think and the way they work together that create a competitive advantage for the company.

Weblink

To find out more about legal protection for ideas or inventions, visit:
www.gov.uk/government/organisations/intellectual-property-office

According to the writer John Kay there are three main sources of sustainable competitive advantage:

1. **Innovation**. Although in reality much innovation can be imitated, in some cases a business can protect its developments with a patent, or the process may be so secret that it can protect it from others.
2. **Architecture**. Kay uses this term to describe the relationships with suppliers and customers. These relationships may have been built up over time and it may not be easy for others to replicate them. Good architecture provides good information and a good understanding of suppliers and customers and their needs.

3. **Reputation**. In one sense this is part of architecture, but Kay thinks it is so important that he says it should be listed separately. Reputation takes time to build and cannot easily be copied, so if it is looked after and protected it can be a sustainable advantage. A good reputation opens doors, makes customers willing to listen and try your products and adds value to the product or service.

Business in focus: Halford's strategy

The strategy of Halford plc is aimed at maximising its returns for its shareholders.

The company has been associated with travel for over 110 years. It now says that its vision is to ensure that 'We help and inspire our customers with their life on the move.'

Halford's is now the UK's biggest retailer of automotive and leisure products, and the leading independent operator in garage servicing and auto repair.

The company's strategy has three main elements. These are to:

1. support drivers of every car
2. inspire cyclists of every age
3. equip families for their leisure time.

To deliver growth in these areas, the company has a programme that includes:

- a service revolution – this involves a significant improvement in service levels
- Stores Fit to Shop – this involves investing in Halfords' stores
- developing 21st-century infrastructure – that is developing systems and infrastructure to support service and sales
- Click with the Digital Future – this is creating an attractive digital online offering.

Halfords' positioning strategy is to create a good, better and best selection of products (so you can buy a brand or model that is good or one that is better or one that is the best), facilitating up-selling (that is enabling customers to trade up) and customer choice (because it will stock something that fits everyone's budget and requirements).

The company has over 460 stores and over 300 auto centres in the UK, which means it is within 20 minutes' drive for 90 per cent of the country's population. Its multichannel offer, which makes up over 11 per cent of retail sales, means that the company is never more than a 'click' away.

Source: Halford's website, www.halfordscompany.com/strategy/

Figure 10.8 Halfords is a household name across the UK.

Questions

1. Discuss the factors that might have made Halfords compete in the three markets identified in the text.
2. Discuss the ways in which Halfords might maintain a competitive advantage in these markets.

Study tip

It is important to assess a strategy in terms of its sustainability. How can a business protect its strategy from competition? What does it have that is not easy to imitate?

ASSESSMENT ACTIVITIES

(a) Knowledge check questions

1   What is meant by 'strategic positioning'?

2   Explain what is meant by Porter's 'low-cost strategy'.

3   Explain one factor that might enable a business to pursue a low-cost strategy effectively.

4   Explain what is meant by Porter's 'differentiation strategy'.

5   Explain one way in which a business might pursue a differentiation strategy effectively.

6   Is a differentiation strategy likely to involve a high or low price? Explain your answer.

7   What is meant by a 'sustainable competitive advantage'?

8   State what is on the axes of Bowman's strategy clock.

9   Is offering low benefits at a high price likely to be a competitive strategy? Explain your answer.

10 Explain one way a business might try to ensure its competitive advantage is sustainable.

(b) Short answer questions

1   Explain how a hotel chain might pursue a differentiation strategy.   (5 marks)

2   Explain how a budget airline such as Ryanair has pursued a low-cost strategy.   (5 marks)

3   Explain how having a clear strategic direction can be important for a business operating in many different countries.   (5 marks)

4   Explain the factors that might influence the strategic positioning of a new web design business.   (5 marks)

5   Explain why the strategic positioning of a health and fitness chain may need to be reviewed and changed.   (5 marks)

(c) Data response question

Morrisons

Figure 10.9 A Morrisons local store

In 2014, the supermarket Morrisons announced dramatic price cuts to try and revive its fortunes. The company's Chief Executive, Dalton Phillips, announced that the business would be restructured and streamlined to reduce costs by £1 billion. Restructuring involved many job losses and the removal of layers of management.

These cost cuts would be spent over three years on lower prices, developing a loyalty scheme and improving its own-brand goods. On average, its price would be 17 per cent lower. These were permanent price cuts not price promotions. The strategy was to re-establish the company as a 'value-led grocer with a passion for food'. Mr Phillips compares the shift in the UK grocery market to the changes seen in the airline industry, when new disruptive players – the budget airlines – arrived. According to Phillips, the changes in the groceries industry were permanent and would not be reversed, this was a new price norm. On its website, Morrisons is also introducing a new feature so customers can compare prices easily.

Morrisons' profit performance has been poor in recent years. It has been very slow to provide a loyalty card and to go online. Morrisons only started deliveries through online grocer Ocado in January 2015, having signed a £200 million 25-year deal last year. This service covers only 20 per cent of UK households. The company has also been slow to recognise the move by customers from big out-of-town stores to local convenience stores. It opened 90 last year and plans 100 new ones in 2015. (By comparison, Tesco has around 1,700 convenience stores in the UK.)

Several commentators felt that Phillips' plan was too late and flawed – for example, with convenience stores having been opened in the wrong locations. Ken Morrison, the previous owner and Chief Executive, compared Phillips' strategy to the manure produced by his cattle!

By January 2015, the company results had still not improved – in fact Morrisons had a very disappointing Christmas period and Dalton Phillips announced he was standing down. He was replaced by former Tesco director David Potts. Morrison's chairman said it was important to return the company to growth and this needed a new perspective. Defenders of Phillips say the company has managed to reposition itself effectively on price.

Questions

1 Explain the factors that might have influenced the price paid to Ocado to deliver Morrisons products online. (6 marks)

2 Analyse the factors influencing Morrisons' decision to cut prices so significantly. (9 marks)

3 To what extent do you think clear positioning is the key to success in the UK supermarket industry? (15 marks)

(d) Essays

1 To what extent is differentiation the best strategic position for a start-up business to adopt? Justify your answer. (25 marks)

2 To what extent is a low-cost strategic position a better one for a food retailer to adopt than differentiation? Justify your answer. (25 marks)

Case study: Unit 8 Choosing strategic direction

Aston Martin

Figure 1 Will this Aston Martin appeal to Charlotte?

In 2014, Andy Palmer was appointed as Chief Executive of the luxury car company, Aston Martin. Within six months he had announced a new strategy for the business. Although Aston Martin is one of the most famous car brands in the world, it has been making a loss for many years and its sales have been falling. Since it was established over 100 years ago the company has only sold 70,000 cars, so annual sales have never been high. Recently they have been even lower than usual with annual sales of around 4,000 cars, down from 7,300 10 years earlier. The company has been losing sales to rivals such as Bentley, Ferrari and Porsche who have invested far more heavily in new product development and brought out new models that have appealed to the market. Andy Palmer has been brought in to turn this situation around; before he was appointed the company did not actually have a chief executive for 18 months. Interestingly, Palmer had previously worked for Nissan, the Japanese motor manufacturer which had previously looked at buying Aston Martin, so he had prior knowledge of the company before he joined.

Palmer has decided to broaden Aston Martin's portfolio and has raised £500 million of investment to help him do it. One of his new target market segments is young wealthy female buyers – a group that previously had shown little interest in this luxury brand. Palmer has created an imaginary customer called Charlotte who represents the type of customer he wants to target with new models and designs. The Aston Martin, made famous in James Bond movies, has typically appealed to males – less than 4,000 cars have been sold to women in the entire history of the company. Palmer wants to change this.

Palmer also wants Aston Martin to target markets in the emerging economies such as Brazil, Russia, India and China (BRIC economies). Amazingly only 2,500 Astons Martins have been sold directly to customers in BRIC economies. These countries have high populations and incomes are growing fast so they are an appealing market for such an iconic brand. However, entering them successfully will not necessarily be easy given the lack of a well-developed infrastructure and supply chain. The markets are also very different from the UK market culturally and so Aston Martin is opening offices in China and Thailand to try and get closer to their new target customers.

Aston Martin will also continue to build niche products such as the Vulcan, a £1.8 million supercar designed for the race track, so only 24 are being made.

Previously Aston Martin had sales staff but no one focused on marketing. The challenges now facing the business mean it needs to think much more about its potential customers, its positioning in the market, its rivals and future opportunities. This means it needs to be more market focused. For this reason and to move the company forward, staff are being appointed specifically to focus on the brand and on identifying new market opportunities.

Source: Adapted from an article on the BBC News website, 5 March 2015

Questions

1. Analyse the possible reasons why Aston Martin might have been losing sales. **(10 marks)**

2. Analyse the likely reaction from employees to the arrival of Andy Palmer as the new Chief Executive at Aston Martin. **(10 marks)**

3. To what extent do you think design costs are likely to be the biggest problem facing Aston Martin when repositioning the business to target women? **(16 marks)**

4. Do you think Aston Martin should be targeting emerging economies such as the BRIC economies? Justify your answer. **(20 marks)**

5. To what extent do you think the success of a new strategy depends on having an effective marketing team? **(24 marks)**

13A Wednesday 30 Nov Pt. /25 test 2nd Dec

Unit 9

Strategic methods: how to pursue strategies

Assessing a change in scale

Introduction

In the last chapter we considered how a business chooses its strategic positioning within a market. In this chapter we begin to examine the strategic methods a business may use to achieve its objectives; we focus on changing scale (that is growing or shrinking). We look at why a business might want to grow or shrink and the benefits and problems this can cause. We also discuss the different ways in which businesses can grow, such as by taking over a competitor or franchising its business, and we examine the cases for and against these growth methods.

What you need to know by the end of this chapter:

- how to analyse the reasons why businesses might grow or retrench
- the different types of growth including organic and external growth
- how to manage and overcome the problems of growth or retrenchment and how to analyse the issues with growth including: economies of scale, economies of scope, diseconomies of scale, the experience curve, synergy and overtrading
- how to analyse the issues with managing growth, including Greiner's model of growth
- that methods of growth include mergers, takeovers, ventures and franchising
- types of growth, including vertical (backward and forward), horizontal and conglomerate integration
- how to analyse the impact of growth or retrenchment on the functional areas of a business
- how to assess methods and types of growth.

Key term

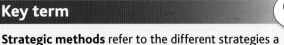

Strategic methods refer to the different strategies a business might pursue to achieve its objectives.

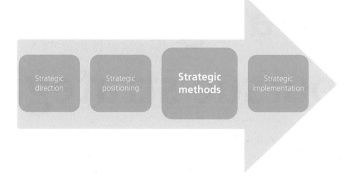

Figure 11.1 Strategic methods

Strategic methods

Strategic methods refer to the different strategies a business might pursue to achieve its objectives. Having chosen which products to offer and which markets to operate in, the business must consider options such as whether or not to:

- grow and, if so, how
- go international and, if so, where
- innovate
- go digital.

In this section we focus on changing scale as a strategic method.

Changing scale

A business may change its scale by growing – this is a common business objective. It shows that the managers are moving the business forward and that it is being more successful in terms of sales. Over the next three years, for example, Whitbread aims to increase the size of Premier Inn by 45 per cent to around 75,000 rooms and double the sales of Costa to around £2 billion.

Growth can be seen as important because it:

- shows progress; this can be good for managers in terms of their own careers and in terms of showing shareholders why they are valuable. It can also provide a sense of achievement (Maslow's self-actualisation needs).

- can create financial benefits such as higher revenues and lower unit costs
- creates momentum which can be important – for example, it means there are new opportunities

for employees which can help keep them focused and engaged. People feel part of something that 'works' and that is growing rather than shrinking. This can help staff retention rates and attract the best employees.

Business in focus: It's all about the long term

In 1997, the Chief Executive of Amazon wrote to its shareholders setting out its vision of the future. It continues to send a copy of this letter to investors in every annual report to show it remains true to its core values. In the letter the managers state that they are committed to creating shareholder value over the long term. To do this they believe it is essential to have market leadership. Dominating a market means, they say, higher revenues, higher profits and stronger returns on capital. The most important measure of success at Amazon, therefore, is the extent to which there is revenue and customer growth. Everything else is thought to flow from this.

To achieve this growth the company invests heavily to build its customer base, its brand and its infrastructure. It says that because it focuses on the long term, it may make different decisions to other companies.

Questions

1. Why do you think growth is seen as so important to Amazon?
2. How do you think focusing on the long term influences the decisions that are made at Amazon?

Forms of growth

If a business does decide to expand then this growth may be:

- **Organic**. This occurs when a business grows through expanding its own operations; for example, it sells more of its existing products or launches new products for its customers.
- **External**. This involves growth by joining with other businesses; for example, one business may gain a controlling share of another organisation. This is called a takeover (see Chapter 4, pages 74–5). The owners of company A gain ownership of the majority of the shares of company B and now control it. They may do this by buying the shares with money (this is called a cash offer) or by offering shares in their own business in return for the shares in the target business (this is called a 'paper offer'). Alternatively, one business may join with another, which is called a merger (see Chapter 4, page 75). In a merger the owners of company A and company B become joint owners of a new organisation. Many of the big companies continue to grow by adding on new businesses through mergers and takeovers. General Electric, Google and Intel have between them bought more than 500 firms in the past five years.

External growth leads to an immediate jump in the scale of a business; once the deal is completed the old business has a new business as part of it and is immediately bigger – this means a sudden increase in its size. Organic growth will tend to be slower as a business gradually increases the scale of its operations. There are examples of businesses that do grow organically very quickly – for example, in the technology world where one idea can rapidly gain sales (think Facebook and Google which are still relatively young). However, organic growth does not usually involve the same overnight change in scale. External growth, in particular, will bring the problems of coping with a quick increase in the number of employees and the scale of operations, although rapid growth of any form brings with it management challenges.

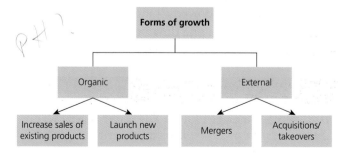

Figure 11.2 Forms of growth

Business in focus: Netflix

Netflix has been growing very fast in recent years. However, it recognises that growth often brings challenges and is determined to overcome these in a positive and innovative manner. Many businesses when growing fast introduce all kinds of rules and systems to maintain control over what happens. The result can be that independent thinking and initiative is quashed. Netflix aims to increase people's freedom rather than restrict it when growth happens. It believes this will help the business to stay ahead of its competitors and help attract the best employees. For example, the company has no policy on holidays and expenses. You take the holidays you need and that you think are sensible at times that work for the business rather than being allocated a set number of days of holiday a year.

Similarly, it has no expenses policy – employees are told to spend the company's money as if it was their own. Netflix argues that people are able to take decisions for themselves in their own lives and, therefore, should be able to do the same in their working lives. The company expects high performers and will not accept poor performance, but as the business grows it aims to give employees more space to make decisions not less.

Questions

1. Why do you think businesses tend to introduce more controls as they grow?
2. Do you think the Netflix approach would work for all organisations?

External growth will also encounter problems of bringing together organisations that may have their own ways of doing things and their own priorities. This can bring benefits in that decisions may be approached in new ways, but it can also lead to clashes because of different styles and priorities and different ways of doing things. This is known as a culture clash and has led to poor performance in a number of mergers or takeovers such as Aol Time Warner, Daimler Chrysler and News Corporation and My Space. Different styles of management, different priorities, different ways of rewarding and motivating staff can all lead to disagreements that prevent the organisation from functioning effectively. In the case of News Corporation and My Space, for example, a big corporate business with strategic plans, budgets, committees and clear financial targets (News Corporation) met an organisation that was less formal, more interested in creativity than the financials and younger in outlook and approach (My Space). With Chrysler the focus was on volume, whereas Daimler wanted quality and so disagreements followed! Imagine putting your school together with one down the road; think what might happen…

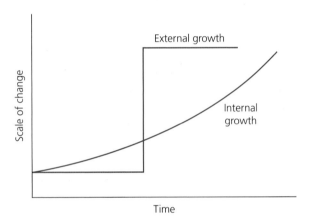

Figure 11.3 Speed of growth

Business in focus: Twitter

Twitter, the social networking business, was created in March 2006 by Jack Dorsey, Evan Williams, Biz Stone and Noah Glass. It was launched in July 2006 when Jack Dorsey sent the first tweet. Twitter says that its mission is 'to give everyone the power to create and share ideas and information instantly without barriers'. By 2015, Twitter had 288 million active users and 500 million tweets were sent per day. 77 per cent of Twitter accounts are outside of the US. It employs 3,600 staff, 50 per cent of whom are engineers. Twitter has grown mainly organically, although it did take over Vine in 2012.

Questions

1. Why do you think Twitter has been able to grow so quickly?
2. Do you think it will continue to grow so quickly? Justify your answer.

Internal growth	External growth
Tends to be slower	Sudden change in scale
May be easier to manage	There may be clashes in the way organisations operate

Table 11.1 A comparison of internal and external growth

Economies of scale

If a business is pursuing growth, this may be because of **economies of scale**. Economies of scale occur when the unit costs fall as the scale of operations increases. These economies can occur due to:

- **Purchasing economies**. As a business gets bigger it will purchase more supplies. This gives it more bargaining power over suppliers. Suppliers become dependent on the business and may be willing to reduce their prices to keep the orders. In recent years, for example, the big supermarkets have been accused of pushing the price they pay to farmers for milk below the actual cost of producing it.

- **Technological economies**. These occur when a large scale of operations enables particular technologies to be used efficiently. For example, imagine a small farm has to have various pieces of equipment, such as a tractor and harvesting equipment. Given the size of the business this expensive equipment may not be used very often and, therefore, it is inefficient. If the farm expands, then, up to a point, it can continue with only one of each piece of equipment which can then be used more fully. The costs of the tractor, for example, can now be spread over several crops and this becomes more efficient, reducing the unit cost. Similarly, think of a production line for an industry such as car manufacturing. If only one car was produced, this would be incredibly expensive, but if the production line costs can be spread over many thousands of cars the unit cost falls. This is why car companies are so eager to ensure demand is high. The same is true of bottling plants, telecommunications companies, energy businesses, all of which have very high fixed costs.

Figure 11.4 A bottling plant will produce thousands of bottles per day.

- **Financial economies**. As a business gets bigger it has more assets and this may mean a bank is willing to lend to it at lower interest rates as the risk is lower. (If the company fails to repay, the bank can seize the assets.) This reduces interest costs.

- **Managerial economies**. As a business expands it may bring in specialists to focus on parts of the business. For example, an expanding business may create a specialist HR department which is probably not cost effective in a small business. This expertise may enable better decision making in the larger company, which can increase efficiency and reduce unit costs.

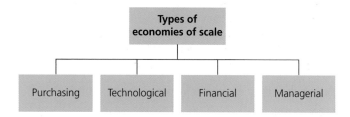

Figure 11.5 Types of economies of scale

Key term

Economies of scale occur when unit costs fall as a business expands; these economies relate to the volume of output.

Business in focus: Travelodge

Travelodge was the first budget hotel brand to launch in the UK in 1985. Since then, Travelodge has opened over 500 hotels and now has over 37,000 rooms. It has gone from being a roadside hotel chain to one of the UK's biggest and fastest growing budget hotel brands. Last year, for example, over 16.5 million people stayed with Travelodge. What is amazing is that, despite the growth in its scale, its prices have changed little – in fact, they have often fallen! In 1985, rooms were available from £24.50, rooms in their first hotel are now available from £19. If the room price had kept pace with inflation, it would now be over £60.

The company continues to invest to enable growth. This investment includes a brand-new room design that includes:

- an upgraded new luxury king size bed (The Travelodge Dreamer), a quilted mattress topper and a new design of covering
- a selection of colours in the room to help induce sleep, vertical stripes on the curtains to make the room look taller and a dark blue stain- and water-resistant carpet
- a stylish white contemporary en-suite bathroom with a power shower
- a larger desk area, new reading lights and a phone charging socket built into the bed frame.

Questions

1. Using Bowman's strategic clock model (see Chapter 10, pages 170–1), how would you describe Travelodge's strategy?

2. Why do you think Travelodge wants to grow?

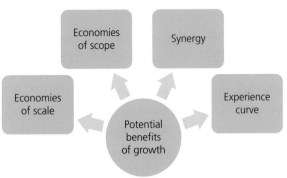

Figure 11.6 The benefits of growth

Businesses may also benefit when they expand in scale from:

- **Economies of scope**. Whereas economies of scale refers to unit costs falling when more of one product is produced, economies of scope are cost savings from operating in several markets or providing several products. For example, when the brand Cadbury is promoted the cost of advertising can be spread over several different products such as Dairy Milk, Crunchie, Star Bar and Double Decker, whereas a small producer may have to absorb all the costs within one brand, thereby increasing its unit cost. Similarly, the management costs of a company such as Procter & Gamble, which produces many different products, can be divided between these different products as can other head office costs such as the legal department and the HR department. When Procter & Gamble distributes many different products to supermarkets the transportation costs can be spread over a range of its brands such as Head & Shoulders, Duracell and Gillette; again, as

the scope of the firm's operations have increased this can reduce some unit costs. Economies of scope, therefore, relate to cost savings from increasing the scope of the activities (that is the number of products offered) rather than just the scale.

- **The experience curve**. As businesses grow employees gain experience. Their managers become more familiar with what needs doing when, who to ask to do what, where to get supplies from, how to fix problems and how to deal with particular issues. This makes decision making faster and better. Any business starting up and operating on a smaller scale may lack this experience and, therefore, make more mistakes and be less efficient. The advantage of experience held by established firms is a major barrier to entry – it makes it difficult for new firms to enter markets because their initial unit costs will be so much higher. This is one reason why external growth is appealing – it enables a business to enter a market segment buying the expertise and experience of a business that already exists without having to take the time and energy to recreate it. According to the Boston Consulting Group (BCG) (who developed the Boston Matrix), the **experience effect** is a very significant influence on unit costs.

Key terms

Economies of scope occur when a business gains cost advantages by sharing costs between different products and divisions; these economies relate to the scope of the activities of the business.

The **experience effect** is the cost advantages that occur having been in an industry for some time and, therefore, being able to make better decisions

Figure 11.7 Procter & Gamble products

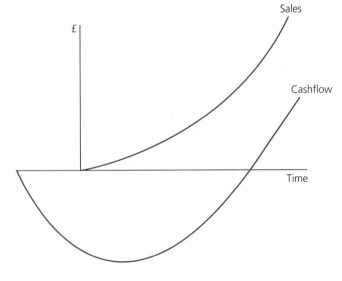

Figure 11.8 The experience curve

- **Synergy**. Synergy occurs when you put two businesses together and as a combined unit they perform better than they did as individual parts. Sometimes synergy is described as 2 + 2 = 5. For example, imagine you put together a company that has a strong design team with another business that has generated high levels of funds from its existing products but is struggling to find new areas to invest it; together, they work better than they did individually.

Business in focus: Mothercare

In recent years, the Mothercare business has expanded rapidly joining with another business and entering overseas markets. The company aims to be the world's leading specialist retailer of parenting and children's products. A key part of this strategy involved the takeover of the Early Learning Centre in June 2007.

Mothercare aims to:

- develop innovative and exciting own-brand products
- ensure its staff are experts in their areas
- achieve growth.

To achieve growth, Mothercare intends to:

- maximise the synergies that are available from joining with the Early Learning Centre
- restructure the combined Mothercare and Early Learning Centre property portfolio

- build the online business
- expand overseas.

The synergies with Mothercare come from:

- sourcing products together
- putting new Early Learning Centres into Mothercare stores and, where there is one of each brand near each other geographically, bringing them together.

Questions

1. Analyse the synergies gained by Mothercare with the acquisition of the Early Learning Centre.

2. Do you think these synergies would have occurred if another business had acquired the Early Learning Centre?

Business in focus: Royal Dutch Shell

In 2015 the energy business Royal Dutch Shell announced that it will buy the oil and gas company BG Group. The deal places a value on BG Group of £47 billion. This was 50 per cent higher than the market value given BG's share price. The combined company would have a market capitalisation of over £200 billion.

BG Group is the third largest energy company in the UK and employs over 5,000 employees in 24 countries. BG was created in 1997 when British Gas demerged (split) into two different companies: BG and Centrica. BG runs the exploration and production of energy, whilst Centrica runs the retail business. Shell hopes the combined company will make annual savings of well over £1 billion a year. The deal would increase Shell's oil and gas reserves by 25 per cent and increase its production capacity by around 20 per cent.

The deal is regarded as a defensive move by Shell, given the huge fall in the price of oil in recent months. In the six months before the deal was announced, oil prices fell about 50 per cent. This has reduced the value of many energy companies' assets and led to a decline in investments because they are now not profitable.

Shell had recently announced that it would be cutting its spending by nearly £10 billion over the next three years. Once the deal has gone through it is expected to sell assets worth over £20 billion. Job cuts are also likely.

Questions

1. Why might Shell be making this takeover deal?

2. Why would Shell be willing to pay a 50 per cent premium to buy BG Group?

What do you think?

Do you think the desired growth of a business is likely to be driven by managers' own desire to achieve something for themselves?

Figure 11.9 Potential problems of growth

Problems of growth

Whilst there are potential benefits from operating on a larger scale, a business may be concerned about expanding too much because of **diseconomies of scale**. Diseconomies of scale occur when the cost per unit increases as the business increases its size.

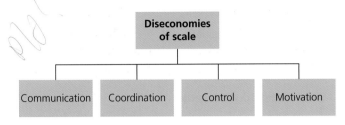

Figure 11.10 Diseconomies of scale

Diseconomies of scale can occur due to:

- **Communication problems**. As a business grows it is likely to start operating in a range of markets, possibly all over the world, and it may have several divisions within the overall business. This means communication can become more complex. Growth can, therefore, lead to inefficiency through slower decision making and poor decisions being made.
- **Control and coordination problems**. With more employees, more products, more decisions being made and more communication flows, controlling who does what and monitoring the quality of the work can become more difficult. Equally, coordinating activities so that people feel informed and understand how they are doing and what they need to do when can become more challenging. There is a greater chance that mistakes are made and problems occur, thereby increasing unit costs.
- **Motivation issues**. As a business grows it may be that employees lose contact with the senior managers and the overall vision of the business. They may feel they are not very significant to the success of the business as a whole and this may lead to demotivation. In terms of Maslow's hierarchy of needs theory, employees may not feel noticed so their ego needs are not met. Poorly motivated staff may reduce productivity and lead to more mistakes and higher costs.

Of course, the extent to which diseconomies of scale might occur depend on the extent and speed of growth. It also depends on how well managed the business is and what systems are in place to maintain control and communication. For example, the use of budgets, appraisals, target setting and a clear mission statement and set of values can potentially help to avoid some of the problems of diseconomies of scale.

Another problem of growth can be cash flow problems during the growth phase. This is caused by **overtrading**. Imagine a coffee shop business has set itself the target of rapid growth and, as a result, is opening new stores regularly. For example, imagine it opens one store in the first month, two in the second month, three in the third, and so on. The business is growing ever faster but this requires ever increasing spending to buy the land, train the staff, get the equipment, promote the new store, and so on. The number of stores is growing exponentially but so is the flow of cash out of the business. There is a danger, therefore, of a liquidity crisis as the business runs out of cash. The answer is to manage the growth effectively and ensure that expansion is not too rapid; this will involve effective budgeting and cash flow management. For example, if the business opened a few stores then waited for these to establish themselves and payback before expanding further, then the financial position could remain healthy. However, sometimes there is a pressure to build quickly on success and expand rapidly perhaps to establish the brand or enter markets before competitors.

Key terms

Diseconomies of scale occur when unit costs increase as a business expands.

Overtrading occurs when there are liquidity problems linked to the financing of rapid growth.

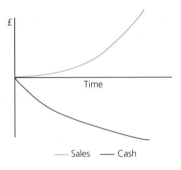

Figure 11.11 Overtrading

Study tip

When a business is growing you should consider whether it is doing this in the best way – are there systems in place to manage the process? Growth brings many potential benefits but also many challenges, so don't assume it is the right strategy for all businesses.

Managing growth

A growing business will bring with it many organisational issues relating to management, such as coordination and communication. These are highlighted in Greiner's model of growth in Figure 11.11. The model considers the challenges a business is likely to encounter as it gets bigger and older. On the horizontal axis is the age of the business and on the vertical axis is the size. As we move along the line the business is increasing in size and age.

In Phase 1 of Greiner's model of growth, 'growth through creativity', the business is just starting out. This means there are likely to be relatively few employees involved and the approach is likely to be fairly informal. There may not be many clear rules and procedures. Job descriptions may be fairly broad and people will tend to help out as and when needed.

At some point, if the business grows, this approach may cause problems – there may be overlap as individuals end up duplicating the tasks they do; other jobs may not be undertaken as it is assumed someone else is doing them. At this point, there may be a 'leadership crisis' and a need for clearer direction. The business may benefit from bringing in professional managers and from defining jobs, roles and the organisational structure more formally. This can provide 'growth through direction' (Phase 2).

This new approach can lead the business forward as it continues to grow and get older. However, at some point, with more products, more employees and with the business operating in more markets, there may be pressure from some managers of the various divisions for more independence. There may be a need to respond to local market conditions and, therefore, for more decentralisation. There is a desire for more autonomy (independence); there may be an 'autonomy crisis'.

In this situation managers may create more self-running units; for example, they may create separate profit centres that are more self-governing and take more control for their own operations and performance. Again, this may aid and help growth for a period as the business gets older and bigger. This would be 'growth through delegation' (Phase 3).

If growth continues, the next crisis point is likely to be one of control. There may come a point when senior managers at the top of the organisation feel they do not control these semi-independent units sufficiently, and that perhaps the business as a whole is losing shape and direction. There may be a 'crisis of control'.

At this stage, the senior managers may decide they need to ensure there is overall control by establishing systems such as budgets to provide targets and monitor the processes in place. This is Phase 4, 'growth through coordination'. This can enable further growth and balance the need for autonomy with the need for control as well. However, the danger is that with continued growth the centralised system put in place to keep control may become burdensome and bureaucratic – it can lead to time-consuming paperwork and slow up effective decision making because key decisions have to be approved by head office. This can cause a 'crisis of red tape' (red tape refers to too much paperwork and form filling).

After this, with further growth, the business will try to develop processes that encourage collaboration between the different parts of the business without too much central regulation (Phase 5). For example, senior managers may move around the business, individuals may experience centralised training to instil core values but then be given high levels of independence. Reward systems may focus more on collaboration, sharing and teamwork, with the sharing of information between senior managers in all parts of the organisation being encouraged.

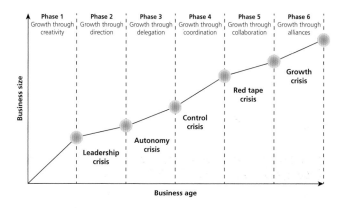

Figure 11.12 Greiner's model of growth

However, continued growth may lead to a growth crisis which means that it is difficult to grow further internally and maintain appropriate levels of control. To avoid the difficulties of internal growth, the business may decide at this stage to pursue external growth through alliances or takeovers and mergers (Phase 6). Greiner called this an 'extra organisational solution' to the difficulties of internal growth, although alliances, venture and takeovers all bring new problems with them.

What Greiner's model highlights is the ongoing push and pull of different forces as organisations grow. There is a desire that different parts of the business have the freedom to act independently and respond to local conditions. At the same time there is pressure to unify and standardise. Businesses are continually shifting backwards and forwards with different systems and structure to balance these forces and find the right approach given the size and maturity of the organisation. The solution to a given problem may, however, generate problems of its own. Of course, a business may move at different speeds through the stages, may skip some stages and may revisit some stages, but the model still has value as it highlights some key issues in organisational growth.

Business in focus: Spotify

Spotify enables people to find the music they want, when they want it and where they want it. They can listen on their phone, on their tablet and on their computer. There are millions of music tracks on Spotify. The business has been growing extraordinarily fast. The company was set up in 2006 by Daniel Ek, a serial entrepreneur and technologist who started his first company in 1997 at the age of 14, together with Martin Lorentzon.

By early 2015 the key data for Spotify showed it had:

- over 15 million paying subscribers
- over 6 million active users
- over 20 per cent ratio of paying subscribers to active free users
- paid $2 billion in revenue to rights holders since its launch
- over 30 million songs
- added over 20,000 new songs per day
- created over 1.5 billion playlists so far
- become available in 58 countries.

Questions

1. Why do you think Spotify has been able to grow so fast?
2. What challenges might have faced Spotify as it grew?

Methods and types of growth

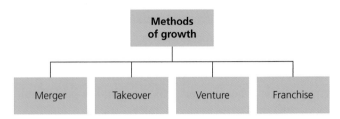

Figure 11.13 Methods of growth

There are several different methods of growth that a business can adopt. We will look at mergers, takeovers, joint ventures and franchising in turn.

Merger

As we have seen, a merger occurs when the owners of two or more businesses become owners of a new shared organisation. Companies such as GlaxoSmithKline are actually made up of many pharmaceutical businesses that have joined over time to create one overall business. Mergers are agreed deals and so all parties involved should be relatively open about their assets and strengths. By joining together, they are able to share their resources and strengths. Perhaps one business has a stronger distribution system in Asia and another has a strong brand presence in Europe. Bringing them together enables them to use each other's resources and benefit from one another's strengths.

Takeover

A takeover differs from a merger in that one business gains control of the other and gains ownership of it. This deal can be voluntary, where both sides agree it is in their interest – this might be because of the benefits of shared resources. Alternatively, it may be a hostile takeover. This occurs when one company wants to buy control of the other but the directors of the target company do not advise the shareholders to sell. In this situation the buyer has to convince the owners of the target company to sell their shares against the guidance of their own directors. Hence the term 'hostile'. In this case, the price offered may have to increase in order to get the shareholders to sell; if the deal does go ahead, this will increase the pressure to make high returns to pay for the high price paid. Also, because the bid is hostile, the potential buyers will not have access to all the information they might want about the company they are bidding for; this makes it a riskier deal because not all information will be openly shared. As with a merger, a takeover involves bringing two different businesses together and they may disagree about priorities, values and ways of doing things. This can cause friction due to cultural clashes.

Business in focus: International Airlines Group

In December 2014 International Airlines Group (IAG), the company that owns British Airways, made a takeover bid for Aer Lingus that was rejected. The deal would have given IAG access to valuable landing slots at Heathrow where Aer Lingus is the third biggest airline landing and taking off. Aer Lingus operates a fleet of 47 Airbus aircraft and carries more than 10.6 million passengers a year.

- A takeover of Aer Lingus would involve the backing of both Ryanair and the Irish government who are both shareholders. Ryanair owns 29.9 per cent of Aer Lingus. It would also need to meet the needs of the

competition regulators by showing that it did not harm competition on certain routes or give IAG unfair advantages by having the additional landing slots.
- The initial bid for Aer Lingus was worth €2.30 per share. When this was rejected, IAG increased the offer to €2.40 per share.

Questions
1. Why might British Airways have wanted to take over Aer Lingus?
2. Why might Aer Lingus have rejected the offer?

Business in focus: Poundland

In 2015 the budget retailer Poundland announced that it wanted to buy the 99p Stores for £55 million. This deal was subject to the competition authorities (the Competition and Market Authority) which wanted to ensure that customers would not be worse off. The sale involved the purchase of 251 shops. Over time, the 99p Stores will be rebranded as Poundland shops. The Chief Executive of Poundland said that the company would bring its experience and range of products to the 99p Stores. Poundland has opened almost 600 shops in the UK, Ireland and Spain since 1990. It plans to open 16 new shops per year for the next two years.

The deal will help ease Poundland's expansion into the south of England.

Questions
1. Analyse the reasons why Poundland wants to take over the 99p Stores.
2. What problems do you think Poundland might face after the takeover?

(Joint) venture

One way in which organisations can gain some of the benefits of collaboration without the problems of complete integration is by forming a venture (also called a joint venture). This involves businesses sharing information and resources on some projects, but each retaining their own identity. For example, businesses may combine their expertise and finance to undertake shared R&D in one specific area – this may well build on different skills – and share the results. A venture has the benefits of collaboration but does not require a full union, possibly avoiding some of the issues of culture clashes.

Franchise

A business may decide to grow by selling the right to use its name and sell its products to other organisations. The business selling the **franchise** is known as the

franchisor. The business buying the franchise is known as the **franchisee**. The franchisee pays an initial fee for the franchise as well as ongoing fees, such as a percentage of the franchise's revenue once it is up and running. The terms and conditions of the relationship between a franchisor and franchisee will be defined in a contract. This will set out exactly what the franchisee provides, for example in terms of equipment, materials and training, what control the franchisor has over the use of the brand, the fees paid by the franchisee and what rights the franchisee has (for example, whether it has the exclusive right to a geographical area).

Key terms

A **franchise** occurs when one business sells the right to another business to use its name and sell its goods or services in return for a fee.

A **franchisor** sells the franchise to a **franchisee**.

Figure 11.14 Papa John's is a restaurant and takeaway franchise founded in the USA in 1983.

The advantages of selling a franchise as a means of growth are as follows:

- It is a relatively quick way of growing, as some, if not all, of the injection of funds to open a new franchise is provided by the franchisee. Therefore, the original business does not need to finance all the growth itself.
- Franchisees may be relatively highly motivated as they have ownership of the franchise and it is, in many ways, their business. They, therefore, may have the incentive to provide a good quality service generating more funds both for themselves and for the franchisor.
- From a management perspective, the original business is managing the franchisees who are then responsible for managing their own franchises. This means there is less management work for the franchisor than if they were managing the business as a whole and directly running each individual franchise unit. The franchisor can take more of a supervisory role and can worry less about the day-to-day operations.

Advantages of selling a franchise	Disadvantages of selling a franchise
Quick growth as funds are provided by franchisee	Lose complete control over what franchises do
Franchisees may be very motivated as they own part of the business	Do not gain all the profits from the operations

Table 11.2 Advantages and disadvantages of selling a franchise

Advantages of buying a franchise	Disadvantages of buying a franchise
As buying an established product, no need to think of own idea	Do not have complete independence to decide what to do
Data should exist on the success of the business and also on important issues such as buyer behaviour and costs	Do not gain all the profits from the operations; have to pay money to the franchisor
May be provided with training, experience and support and ideas of other franchisees	

Table 11.3 Advantages and disadvantages of buying a franchise

Maths moment

A franchisee is asked to invest £0.6 million to buy the franchise and set up the business. Expected sales for the first five years are £0.5 million, £1 million, £1.5 million, £2 million and £3 million. The average profit margin is 10 per cent. The annual fee to the franchisor is 2 per cent of turnover.

Calculate the average rate of return (ARR) for the first five years of this franchise.

Study tip

When evaluating the method of growth chosen by a business consider the risk involved, the costs, the speed of growth and the impact on control. Franchising, for example, may be cheaper and faster than organic growth, but involves giving up some control over day-to-day decisions.

What do you think?

Do you think franchising is a good way to grow?

Types of integration

Integration occurs when businesses join together. This can be via a merger, a takeover or a joint venture. There are different types of integration: vertical, horizontal and conglomerate.

Key terms

Vertical integration occurs when one business joins together with another business at a different stage of the same production process.

Horizontal integration occurs when one business joins together with another business at the same stage of the same production process.

Conglomerate integration occurs when one business joins together with another business in a different production process.

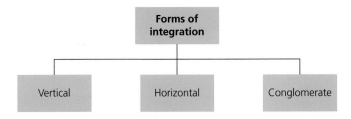

Figure 11.15 Forms of integration

Vertical integration

Vertical integration occurs when a business joins with another business at a different stage of the same production process. For example, if one business joins with a business that supplies it, this is called backward vertical integration. The benefits of backward vertical integration are that the business will be able to gain control of supplies at a better price than it would have to pay buying them in from an external supplier. Alternatively, a business can join together with an organisation closer to the final customer. This is called forward vertical integration. For example, a manufacturer may join with a retailer. This can guarantee access for its products to reach markets. By controlling the retail outlet, for example, a manufacturer can determine the way the product is promoted and is priced.

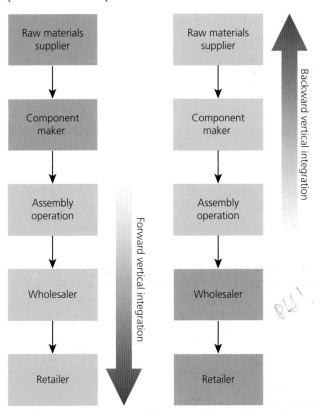

Figure 11.16 Backward and forward vertical integration

Horizontal integration

Horizontal integration occurs when a business integrates with another business at the same stage of the same production process. This enables the businesses to share facilities and resources. For example, Nippon Glass has a strong presence and distribution system in Asia, whilst Pilkington Glass has a well-established presence in Europe; by joining together they were able to make use of each other's market presence and distribution system. Equally, the portfolio of products of the combined business may complement each other, providing a better range of services to customers.

Conglomerate integration

Conglomerate integration occurs when one business joins with another business that operates in a different industry. For example, a computer games business joins with a sportswear business. Google has been investing in recent years in wind energy and health-care businesses; this is conglomerate integration. The advantage of this form of growth is that it may spread the risk of a business of being affected by change in one market.

Business in focus: Tata

The Tata group is a conglomerate business, it has businesses in many different markets. Tata's core purpose is to improve the quality of life of the communities it serves globally by creating long-term stakeholder value and demonstrating leadership based on trust.

Tata was founded by Jamsetji Tata in 1868. Its headquarters are in India, and the company is now made up of over 100 operating companies. It operates in more than 100 countries across six continents and exports products and services to over 150 countries. Tata companies employ over 581,470 people worldwide.

A key part of Tata's approach is good corporate citizenship. Many of the shares of the group are owned by trusts that were created to do good acts and improve society.

Each Tata company operates independently and has its own board of directors and shareholders. There are 32 publicly-listed Tata enterprises with a shareholder base of 3.9 million. Tata companies include Tata Steel, Tata Motors, Tata Consultancy Services, Tata Power, Tata Chemicals, Tata Global Beverages, Tata Teleservices, Titan, Tata Communications and Indian Hotels.

Questions

1. What benefits do you think Tata gains from its scale?
2. Why do you think Tata wants to be a conglomerate business?

Reducing scale: retrenchment

Although organisations may often seek growth, there may be occasions when it is necessary to reduce the scale of operations. This is known as **retrenchment**. This may happen because the business has been experiencing diseconomies of scale and wants to refocus its operations. However, it may also be because of changes in market conditions and the fact that there is now a lack of demand for the products of the business. The world car industry, for example, has significant excess capacity at present and this means most producers have been reducing their production by shutting down car plants.

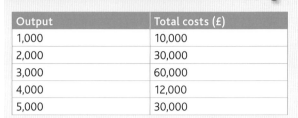
The impact of growth or retrenchment on the functional areas of the business

Growing a business will have an impact on all the functional areas. For example:

- **finance.** Capital may be needed to finance the growth. This may come from external sources such as investors or internally from retained profits. During the growth phases managers need to be particularly aware of cashflow. Cash can flow out to pay for expansion and it may take time to come back in whilst operations are being set up. Without careful budgeting this can lead to cashflow problems.
- **human resources.** Growth can be quite positive for employees in that it can provide opportunities for new responsibilities and for promotion. However, in the short term it may mean extra duties and place a greater a burden on staff unless recruitment is undertaken at the appropriate times. Growth will usually require additional staff and may also necessitate training if new skills are required, perhaps because the organisation is moving into new areas.
- **operations.** In the short term growth may improve capacity utilisation but this can place additional burdens on the business if resources are working to their absolute maximum for a period of time. We can all work very hard to get an important piece of homework completed but may not be able to sustain this level of effort 24 hours a day, every day. Over time therefore, organisations may need to invest in new capacity, which is where the raising of funds and the careful management of expenditure comes in.
- **marketing.** Increased marketing efforts may be required to generate the demand for growth. This may be in existing or new markets. In some cases it

will require more investment (again requiring more finance) but in other instances it will require better use of funds, for example, a more effective and targeted marketing approach.

As ever the functions are all interrelated. A business cannot grow successfully if the demand is not there, if the business cannot secure the funds and staff and if it cannot deliver the quantities required at the appropriate level of quality.

Retrenchment involves a reduction in the scale of a business's activities. This strategic move will have implications for the different functions. The precise effect will depend on the nature of the retrenchment but may include:

- **finance**. Scaling down the operations is likely to cost money in the short term as redundancy payments have to be paid. The exact amount paid will depend on the contracts of the individuals concerned, but by law employees will receive some payment linked to the number of years they have worked for the business. However, finances may be improved if the business is able to raise funds from selling off assets or particular divisions of the whole organisation. Over time, there may also be lower costs perhaps due to delayering.

- **human resources**. With retrenchment there are likely to be redundancies and managers may have to negotiate who is made redundant. For example, are redundancies made on the basis of 'last in first out'? In some cases, the organisation may help employees find alternative employment. There may also be other job opportunities within the organisation – for example, if the business is pulling out of some markets but growing in others. In which case, it may be possible to redeploy staff.

- **operations**. The scale of operations will be reduced by retrenchment. This may be more efficient – in many cases the business will be scaling back because of diseconomies of scale. Retrenchment may, therefore, reduce unit costs.

- **marketing**. Marketing activities are likely to be more focused on a smaller core business. This may enable better integration and more consistency in approach.

ASSESSMENT ACTIVITIES

(a) Knowledge check questions

1 If unit costs fall as a business expands, this is known as _____ of scale.

2 'Diseconomies of scale occur when total costs rise with less output.' Is this statement true or false?

3 State three types of economy of scale.

4 What is meant by 'economies of scope'?

5 If a business takes over one of its suppliers, this is known as _____ integration.

6 If a business takes over another business at the same stage of the same process, then this is known as _____ integration.

7 Explain the difference between a merger and a takeover.

8 Explain the difference between a franchisor and a franchisee.

9 What is meant by 'synergy'?

10 State what is on the axes of Greiner's model of growth.

(b) Short answer questions

1 Explain the possible benefits of two airlines joining together. (5 marks)

2 Explain the possible disadvantages of a business that has established a number of stores selling homemade frozen foods selling franchises of its stores across the UK. (5 marks)

3 Jamie McAllen set up his business on his own producing cheeses. It was his first business venture after having lost his job in marketing for a theatre company. The business has proved extremely successful and has grown very rapidly. Explain one problem Jamie might face whilst his business grows. (5 marks)

4 Explain how backward vertical integration may benefit a supermarket. (5 marks)

5 Explain how conglomerate integration may benefit an interior design business. (5 marks)

(c) Data response question

Kingfisher

In March 2015, Kingfisher plc, the owner of the UK DIY chains B&Q and Screwfix, announced that it would close around 60 B&Q stores in the UK and Ireland over the next two years. This will lead to around 3,000 positions being made redundant although the company hopes to redeploy about half of these members of staff elsewhere, for example in its Screwfix business.

These changes were part of a new strategy for Kingfisher lead by the recently appointed Chief Executive Véronique Laury. After a strategic review, Laury felt it was essential for the business to increase its efficiency so that it could pass on these costs savings to its customers in the form of lower prices. Store closures is one step in this plan.

The closures of B&Q stores follow earlier attempts to make the stores more profitable by leasing out parts of outlets to other retailers such as Asda. This tactic did not prove especially successful, and therefore lead to Laury's decision to develop a new cost-saving plan. The B&Q closures follow competitor Homebase's similar decision five months earlier to shut down around 70 of its stores; Homebase argued that Do It Yourself was decreasing in popularity in the UK, therefore reducing demand for its products. Consumers seem to have moved towards spending their disposable income on buying clothes and going out rather than on decorating and doing up their houses. This trend can also be seen in the change in our TV viewing habits, with the decline in popularity of television shows such as 'Changing Rooms' and 'Ground Force' which used to be primetime TV in the nineties and noughties.

Even though market conditions are clearly difficult Laury believes that there is still potential in the market. For example, the average house in the UK is 60 years old and so will need to be improved and updated in the near future. In order to tap into this market, she intends to reposition B&Q by offering more original and innovative DIY products and appealing to younger people with fewer skills in renovating property.

As with many established businesses with physical outlets, B&Q faces a serious threat from online businesses, for example online DIY specialists such as Toolstation and Victoria Plumb, which have significantly reduced overheads. To counteract this, Laury sees benefits in improving IT across the Kingfisher Group and in greater coordination of the different parts of the Kingfisher business. At the moment Kingfisher businesses, which include Screwfix, B&Q, Castorama and Brico Depot, stock around 400,000 different products. Laury's aim is to reduce these items by half. For example, the group sells 1,000 different types of glove; this number could be reduced considerably, cutting ordering and stockholding costs and yet have very little effect on sales – the expected impact is just –2%.

The changes come at a time when B&Q's profits are falling. In 2014 pre-tax profits fell by more than 15% to £644 million. The closure of the 60 stores will involve a one-off cost of £350 million. Laury said that unfortunately a number of 'sharp decisions' needed to be made given the position and ambitions of the business.

Source: Adapted from an article in the *Guardian*, 31 March 2015

Questions

1 Explain one external factor that influences demand for DIY products.   (6 marks)

2 Analyse why Kingfisher has decided to reduce the number of B&Q stores.   (9 marks)

3 To what extent is this retrenchment by Kingfisher bound to face opposition from stakeholders?   (15 marks)

(d) Essays

1 To what extent do you think it is better for a business seeking to boost profits to be bigger rather than smaller? Justify your answer.   (25 marks)

2 To what extent do the problems of growing as shown by Greiner's model of growth, mean that it is not worth a cinema chain expanding? Justify your answer.   (25 marks)

Chapter 12

Assessing innovation

Introduction

In this chapter we consider innovation as another way in which a business might pursue its objectives. Innovation involves developing new products and processes. It can help a business provide more benefits for its customers (think of living in a world before social media and the internet existed!) and also help a business become more efficient (there once was a time without bar codes and scanning). We will examine how a business might try to ensure it is innovative and is moving forwards in terms of its competitiveness rather than getting left behind. We will also discuss how a business might protect its innovation to prevent rivals copying it and also assess the impact of innovation on the different functions of the business.

What you need to know by the end of this chapter:

- the meaning of, and the pressures for, innovation
- the different types of innovation, that is product and process innovation
- the value of innovation
- the ways of becoming an innovative organisation including Kaizen, R&D, intrapreneurship and benchmarking
- how a business protects its innovation and intellectual property, including patents and copyrights
- the impact of an innovation strategy on the functional areas of the business.

The meaning of innovation

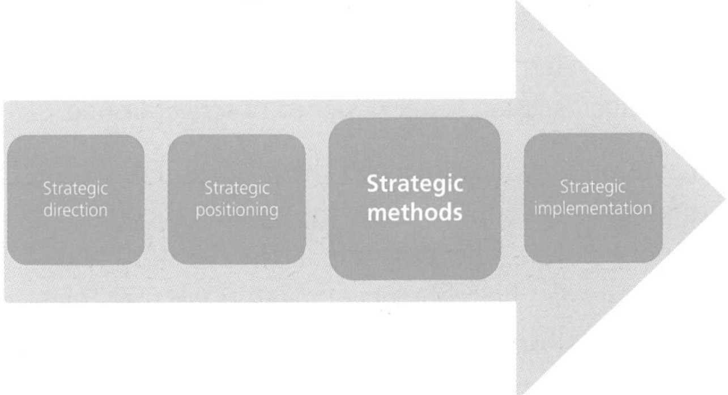

Figure 12.1 Strategic methods

Innovation (see Chapter 4, page 65) occurs when a new idea is brought to fruition and turned into a good or service that can be used and/or sold. Having ideas is interesting, but the key is to turn them into something that is actually produced and adds value; this is what is meant by innovation.

As markets become more open with greater globalisation, and as accessing markets and customers becomes easier with better transportation and communication, this makes it all the more important for businesses to get better at what they do. Standing still is not an option for businesses that want to remain competitive – they have to innovate to develop what they offer and how they provide it. If they don't, their competitors will.

Aspects of the external environment are constantly changing and businesses must either anticipate or respond to this. The needs and wants of customers and how businesses compete with each other are constantly evolving and businesses must ensure they continue to be competitive. Uber is one of the world's biggest taxi companies and yet does not own a taxi. eBay is one of the world's biggest retailers and yet does not own any products. Airbnb is one of the world's biggest accommodation businesses and yet owns no properties to rent out. Just think how much the world has changed and the changes in how businesses operate from 100 years ago! Car manufacturers now produce to order not in advance of orders, we can stream whatever music we want wherever we want, and we have access to suppliers of almost anything we want online ready to be delivered direct to our homes, often within 24 hours.

The world we live in is shocking and surprising to anyone comparing it with the world just 20 years ago, let alone 100 years ago, and this is due to ongoing innovation. The world keeps turning and arguably it is turning ever faster thanks to the innovation that is occurring. Just think about how our lives are much more fully interconnected than ever before, where your printer measures its ink levels and automatically reorders, your washing machine reads the chips in your clothes to know how long to wash them for, where cows are linked to the internet so farmers can monitor their health and milk output and diagnose change in diets if needed and where your car reports the need for a check-up to its garage.

Innovation changes what we do with our time (computer gaming vs TV), what we consume and use in our daily lives (microwave meals vs homemade food), how we communicate (mobile phones vs landlines). It also affects the work we do. Many of the jobs that you will go on to do in your careers do not even exist yet – technology is changing so fast that new industries and new jobs are being created all the time. Who would have thought of a career in social media or knowledge management 20 years ago? In innovative companies such as Google, Entertainment Arts, Dreamworks and Snapchat work is much more collaborative, much more creative, much more knowledge based and data driven than in the past.

In terms of changing industries and what businesses do, the importance of innovation can be highlighted by Formula 1 motor racing. It is said that if there were no changes to the car that won the first race of the racing season it would come last by the end of the season because of all the improvements being made to the other cars. This highlights the rate of change in many industries and the dangers of not innovating.

Pressures for innovation

The pressures for innovation come both externally and internally. Externally, there are changes in the PEST-C environment that create opportunities for innovation and require a business to prepare and respond. For example:

- political change may open up new geographical markets through trade deals requiring a new approach or changes to the product
- economic change may create pressure for a lower cost solution to a problem
- social change may put pressure on businesses for new environmentally-friendly approaches
- technological developments may create opportunities for new ways of doing business. Just think of the pressure these days to have an online presence
- competitive pressure from rivals may require businesses to respond or they will lose market share.

Internally, some employees may be eager to experiment and try out new ideas. Employees will, hopefully, be curious and pushing at existing ways of doing things and challenging existing thinking to improve it. This leads to pressure to innovate.

The pressures for innovation have always been there but these pressures are growing as there is more competition – the need to offer more benefits or lower costs is growing as customers have access to more alternatives, so a business is more likely to lose them if it does not innovate.

Business in focus: Moore's Law

In the technology industry there is a law known as Moore's Law, named after Gordon Moore one of the co-founders of Intel. The law states that 'The number of transistors incorporated in a chip will approximately double every 24 months'. This law still dominates everything Intel does. Through investment in technology and manufacturing Intel has made Moore's Law a reality. To double the number of transistors every two years leads to exponential growth over time and, therefore, puts enormous pressure on the business to keep innovating and increasing the power of its products.

Questions

1. Why does Intel want to make Moore's Law a reality?
2. What do you think Intel will need to achieve this target over a period of time?

Product and process innovation

Some innovation will be aimed at developing new products. This may be the result of pure technological development in which technology moves forward and then the organisation tries to work out a use for it. Or it may be the result of research commissioned specifically to meet a customer need that has been identified. Examples of innovation in recent years include the smartphone, electric cars and 3D printing.

Product innovation provides extra benefits to the consumer in terms of what they are buying – for example, the product is faster, better designed or longer lasting.

Innovation may also focus on the process. For example, it may aim to make the operations of a business more efficient or faster – the use of digital technology can help organisations to track resources, monitor workflows and measure quality at all stages, therefore improving the overall process. Process innovation may affect how the customer finds out about the product, how they purchase it or how it is produced and delivered. Online check-in for airlines, online ordering and click and collect are all examples of process innovation. Process innovation improves the transformation process and the customer experience – for example, it is easier or quicker to produce or to order.

Process innovation will also affect how we work. More and more people now communicate with colleagues globally online via programmes such as Skype. It is not unusual these days to have teams made up of people all over the globe. It is also far more common to work from home – with improvements in communications there is far less need to be based in an office all day. It may be far more efficient to work from home and use a workstation at the main office on certain days when it is useful to meet colleagues face to face.

Study tip

Make sure you appreciate that innovation can affect all aspects of the business – such as how it communicates with suppliers, how employees work and how customers are targeted. It is not just about new products so keep your thinking broad.

The value of innovation

Innovation of some form is almost certainly necessary to remain competitive and to maintain the profitability of a business. Depending on the form of innovation, it will enable a business to offer better quality, lower costs, faster delivery or more reliability. All of these developments can help a business to be more competitive. Cliché though it is, if you are not moving forwards these days by innovating, you are probably moving backwards! With rising rates of competition and competition coming from new and, in some cases, unexpected areas, a business needs to tap into the ideas of employees, suppliers and other partners to find ways of creating more value for its customers.

However, it must be recognised that innovation can be risky. Many new ideas fail to come to market and,

if they do, many still fail. Similarly, many ways of improving the process do not come to fruition or prove less successful than hoped. Managers must consider the resources involved, the likely returns (which can be difficult to estimate) and the risks involved when deciding whether or not to invest in innovations.

What do you think?

Do you think it is a good idea to try and be the most innovative business in your industry?

Business in focus: Post-it notes

Figure 12.2 Post-it notes

Whilst businesses are often eager to innovate and work hard at making it happen, innovation sometimes happens by accident or by mistake. One of the most famous examples of this is Post-it notes. In 1968 a DuPont scientist, Spencer Silver, developed paper that could be stuck on and then peeled off when he was actually trying to make a very strong adhesive. Once Silver developed this new peel-off paper he had no idea what it could actually be used for. It took some time for the company to work out why this innovation might be useful! If innovations are difficult to plan for, this can affect managers' approaches to how employees are expected to use their time. It might also mean some aspects of budgets are kept vague to enable employees to pursue their own ideas.

Questions

1. If many innovations happen by accident, how do you think managers can help these 'accidents' to happen?
2. Why do you think it might be difficult to budget for innovation?

The ways of becoming an innovative organisation

To develop an innovative organisation managers need to create an environment where:

- it is acceptable to fail. Some new ideas will inevitably fail and take up time and money developing them before it is realised that they will not work. Managers must accept this and allow people to feel they can take risks. If failure is punished, it is likely that people will not try to do anything new.
- there is funding available for experimentation and for trying new things. If all of a budget is allocated to existing projects, then innovation is unlikely to take place. Some organisations deliberately leave a certain percentage of a budget for undefined activities to allow the budget holder to try out new things. In some businesses these unplanned, undefined activities are called 'skunkworks'.
- it is good to share. Innovation often comes when individuals from different departments or sections sharing ideas. This means people need to be encouraged to see themselves as part of

the whole and be willing to talk and work with whoever can help them from anywhere in the business. Organisations must avoid what is known as the 'silo effect', whereby people only think of themselves as part of a department (or silo) and only talk to those in their area. The key is to create cross-functional teams and encourage the open sharing of information. This means there must be the opportunities for individuals from across the business to meet, talk, share and work in teams. Teamwork enables employees to:

- bounce ideas off each other
- challenge each other
- share different skills, experiences and perspectives.

However, managers need to think carefully about the teams they build to ensure they function effectively. It is important to balance the team to ensure there is the right mix of skills. To build effective teams from internal staff means the business must have the right skills in the first place, which highlights the importance of recruitment and training. Innovative organisations need to attract and retain talented people.

Business in focus: Team roles

Meredith Belbin is well-known for her studies of teams and what makes up an effective team. Belbin argues that individuals play different roles within teams. These roles complement each other. An individual employee may play more than one role. An effective team includes the following roles:

- The **Plant** provides the ideas and creative input into the team. 'Plants' are highly creative and good at solving problems in unusual ways.
- The **Monitor evaluator** provides a logical input into the group. This role assesses ideas and judges them in a logical and dispassionate manner.
- The **Coordinator** focuses on the team's objectives and helps to get team members to work together.
- The **Resource investigator** is good at finding out what other teams and businesses outside of this team are doing and feeding back this information to the group.
- The **Implementer** is practical and focuses on the detail to make a plan work.
- The **Completer finisher** is good at ensuring the project is on schedule and meeting the required quality standards.
- The **Teamworker** helps to keep the members engaged and motivated and feeling part of a team.
- The **Shapers** provide momentum by challenging and

ensuring the team does not lose momentum.

- The **Specialist** has detailed specialised knowledge of a key area of the project.

Figure 12.3 Team roles

Questions

1. Why do you think teams help creativity?
2. What problems do you think there might be in getting teams to function effectively?

Leadership

Ultimately what happens in an organisation should come down to leadership. What do the leaders want to happen, what do they value, what do they encourage, what do they reward? This influences the culture of the business and how employees behave and what they prioritise. Find an innovative organisation and you will have leaders at the top with an innovative vision. To show that innovation matters, resources must be made available for it and it needs to be clearly stated in terms of the targets set. For example, managers may set a target of a certain percentage of revenue being generated from new products or products launched within the last few years. Innovation must be on the agenda, must be seen as important, must be resourced, must be rewarded and must be assessed.

Listening

It's important to listen. Whether it be listening to customers, partners, employees or to anyone you work with, it is important to listen to learn what is working, what is not working and what can be improved. Where there is a complaint there is the opportunity to innovate and develop a solution. Innovation is basically a new way of solving a problem.

To allow innovation managers may encourage R&D. R&D involves technical or scientific research activities to develop new products and processes. It involves laboratories, experiments, prototypes and testing. Whereas marketing research identifies possible needs and wants of customers, R&D is aiming to turn an idea for a product or process into a reality. R&D aims to produce improved or new products and services through the use of scientific methods. High levels of spending in R&D are common in industries such as pharmaceuticals, computers, aerospace and the automobile sectors. In 2014, the biggest spenders on R&D were Volkswagen (a total R&D investment of €11.7 billion) followed by Samsung (South Korea) and Microsoft (US). R&D leads to technological innovations – for example at the BBC R&D led to noise-cancelling microphones in the 1930s, the first transatlantic TV transmission in the 1950s, digital radio in the 1990s and HDTV in the 2000s. R&D keeps moving industries forward. However, it does require investment and often the expected financial outcomes can be difficult to estimate accurately. Many projects suffer setbacks at some time and many do not lead to the successful launch of products.

Business in focus: Dyson

Figure 12.4 James Dyson's passion for innovation can be seen in Dyson products

Dyson, a UK manufacturing business, puts research at the heart of its operations. It is well-known for its innovative design and the new technology it brings to industries such as vacuum cleaners, hand dryers and fans. It is now looking to invest over £250 million to expand its R&D base in the UK. The new facility should increase the number of engineers to around 5,000. The centre will have the latest biometric scanners for security to protect its designs.

The founder, James Dyson, says that his company is founded on new technology and that the business needs to 'relentlessly invent'. The company is constantly striving to make things work better. To help develop the skills it needs, Dyson has helped to fund university research projects in the UK. The company aims to invest a third of its profits in research into new products.

Questions

1. What factors do you think should determine how much a business invests in R&D?

2. Dyson manufactures abroad in Malaysia but keeps its research in the UK. Why do you think this is?

Business in focus: R&D investment

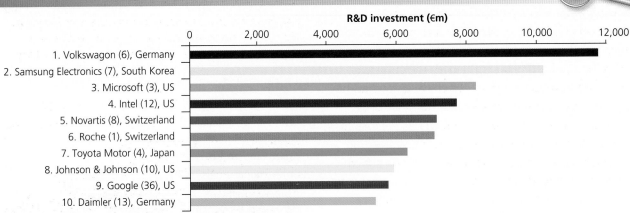

R&D investment (€m)

1. Volkswagon (6), Germany	
2. Samsung Electronics (7), South Korea	
3. Microsoft (3), US	
4. Intel (12), US	
5. Novartis (8), Switzerland	
6. Roche (1), Switzerland	
7. Toyota Motor (4), Japan	
8. Johnson & Johnson (10), US	
9. Google (36), US	
10. Daimler (13), Germany	

Figure 12.5 Some of the world's top 50 companies by their total R&D investment (€m) in the 2014 Scoreboard

Source: European Commission fact sheet, World trends in R&D private investment – Facts and figures, Brussels, 4 December 2014, http://europa.eu/rapid/press-release_MEMO-14-2347_en.htm

Questions

1. What do you think determines how much a business spends on R&D?
2. What do you think determines the success of a firm's R&D?

Maths moment

$$\frac{1+b}{c}=3$$

A business is considering investing £20 million in R&D. Its R&D team has produced the following estimates:

		Expected outcome
Likelihood of success	0.3	+ £100m
Likelihood of failure	0.7	− £40m

Table 12.1

On the basis of the data in Table 12.1, would you go ahead with this investment?

Study tip

Remember that all businesses will want to improve. The issue is how highly is innovation regarded within the business – how much of a priority is it? How many resources are devoted to it? How much is it measured?

Business in focus: GlaxoSmithKline

The pharmaceutical industry is clearly one where innovation is critically important. Businesses in this industry depend on their breakthrough drugs and being able to protect these. Their products can range from everyday health-care products to life-saving medicines and vaccines.

One of the world's leading pharmaceutical companies is GlaxoSmithKline. It has over 13,000 employees working in its R&D facilities. To develop a new medicine requires heavy investment in R&D and can take many years – it is often 15 years from the initial idea to having the drug approved by the various regulatory authorities. Many ideas fail along the way. The process might begin by investigating 5,000 different chemicals to end up with just one that can finally be tested on humans. Then development involves numerous clinical trials to ensure the product is safe; these are carefully regulated and investigated at each stage.

When developing medicines GSK looks for ones that:

- can selectively target diseases
- are safe
- remain in the system long enough to have an impact
- can be manufactured effectively
- have relatively few side-effects.

Questions

1. What problems do pharmaceutical companies face when developing new products?
2. Why might it be difficult for a new business to enter the pharmaceutical industry?

Kaizen groups

The word 'kaizen' is Japanese for 'continuous improvement'. A kaizen approach appreciates that regular, small improvements can lead to major improvements in performance over time. To bring about such improvements businesses often introduce kaizen groups. These are small voluntary meetings of employees who gather to focus on how to improve what is happening in their specific work area. Kaizen groups are encouraged to come up with ideas, however small, on how to improve their area of work; they are expected to do this on an ongoing basis. For kaizen groups to work effectively employees must feel valued and want to contribute; they must feel appreciated and well treated by managers. They must also feel that something will improve as a result of these groups and that their managers will act on their ideas. However, some employees may resist membership of a kaizen group. They may feel they are doing well enough already and may not be interested in helping the business do better.

Intrapreneurship

Entrepreneurs are individuals who have their own business ideas and are willing to take the risk to develop them. Entrepreneurship occurs when people start up their own businesses. In big organisations, what matters is that this same entrepreneurial spirit is captured and applied within the business – this is called **intrapreneurship**. Intrapreneurship occurs when individuals come up with ideas within their

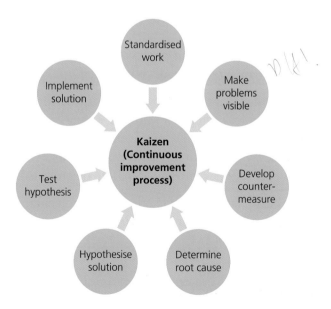

Figure 12.7 The kaizen approach

Business in focus: British cycling

Figure 12.6 Sir David Brailsford, CBE is now General Manager at Team Sky. The team had a hugely successful Tour de France in 2015, with their team leader, Chris Froome, claiming his second tour victory.

When Dave Brailsford was Performance Director of British Cycling he made a number of small but very significant changes that had a huge effect on how the team performed. He believed in kaizen or what he called 'marginal gains'. Every aspect of racing was broken down into its component parts and then Brailsford sought ways of improving it in some way. For example, riders were given heated shorts so that their muscles didn't get cold between races as this meant it took longer for them to get up to speed in the next race. He also had the tyres sprayed with oil to prevent dirt sticking to them and slowing up the riders. Riders had their own pillows which they took with them to every hotel to ensure they slept properly. They were also trained to wash their hands properly to reduce the danger of infection. The combination of many different improvements paid off with eight gold medals in cycling for the Great Britain team at the 2012 Olympics.

Questions

1. In what ways can Brailsford's approach to cycling be called a kaizen approach?
2. How could you apply the marginal gains approach to your studies?

division, department, team or business unit and follow them through. This requires a culture which supports such efforts and encourages and rewards initiative. At Google, for example, employees are encouraged to compete against each other with their ideas and to pitch them directly to senior executives. Similarly, at LinkedIn, all employees can come up with a new idea, put a team together and present this to senior managers at events held once every three months. If their idea is approved, they can spend another three months developing it. At Facebook, employees take part in hackathons to thrash out new ideas. The highly successful 'Like' button on Facebook was the result of a hackathon. Efforts to encourage intrapreneurship help to retain the best staff as it provides them with a way to develop and enhance their careers.

Benchmarking

Benchmarking occurs when managers identify the best in their field for a particular aspect of their work and then try to learn from them. For example, when it comes to managing large numbers of visitors a business might set Disney as the best in its field and then set out to learn from Disney how it does things. The aim of benchmarking is to adopt the best practices from the best in the world and therefore improve your own performance. The best in the world provide the standard (the benchmark) you want to match. However, for it to work you need to able to learn enough about the processes used by the best in the world and also be able to adopt and implement these processes effectively within your own organisation. This may not be easy. The business being asked to give data on how it operates is more likely to do so if it is not in the same industry and, therefore, not a direct rival; even so, there may be some reluctance to share information. Also, to adopt the process may require more resources than you have or the culture within your business may not welcome a new approach. It may also be difficult, at least in the short term, if there is not enough experience and skill within the organisation.

However, a business that benchmarks is clearly focusing on improvement and learning from the best and this suggests that it will bring about change internally if it can.

What do you think?

What problems can you imagine you might face in trying to build a more innovative organisation?

Protecting innovation and intellectual property

To maintain its competitiveness a business must be able to protect its advantage to prevent rivals from copying what it does. One way in which this can be done is by protecting its intellectual property. This means it gets legal protection for its ideas, inventions or trademarks to prevent others imitating them. If there is an infringement of these intellectual property rights, a business can take the guilty party to court and seek damages. Intellectual property is something unique that a business physically creates – it is not just having an idea. For example, if you write a book, then the words can be protected not the idea of the book.

It is possible to get intellectual property protection for:

- the names of your products or brands
- inventions
- the design or look of your products
- things that are written, made or produced.

In some cases a business or individual has the rights automatically – for example, if you write a song or book, these are automatically protected. However, in most cases, you need to register the intellectual property (such as a new invention) for it to be protected.

It is possible to have more than one type of protection for a single product, for example a business might:

- register the name and logo of the product as a trademark
- protect a product's unique shape as a registered design
- patent a completely new working part
- use copyright to protect drawings of the product.

Intellectual property	Protects	How to gain protection
Copyright	Literary works (including writing), art, photography, films, TV, music, web content, sound recordings	Automatic right
Trademarks	Product names, logos, jingles	Need to be registered
Patents	Inventions and products, e.g. machines and machine parts, tools, medicines	Need to be registered
Design rights	Shapes of objects	Automatic right
Registered design	Appearance of a product including shape, packaging, patterns, colours, decoration	Need to be registered

Table 12.2 Types of intellectual property and protection

Source: Intellectual Property Office, www.ipo.gov.uk

Being able to protect intellectual property is important for innovation. If businesses felt that their inventions were going to be copied immediately by rivals, this would be a major disincentive to invest in developing new ideas. On the other hand, if businesses feel that they can protect their inventions, this means they are more likely to be able to gain a good return on their investment; this should encourage more innovation. To protect their intellectual property businesses will have to take any person or organisation that steals this property to court. This provides protection, although it can be slow and expensive to sue others. For global businesses, they need to protect their intellectual property in different regions by registering it around the world and, in some areas, the protection is limited and difficult to enforce.

Study tip

Make sure you understand the difference between the different forms of intellectual property as these often get confused.

Business in focus: Patents

In 2015, Apple lost a case regarding patent infringement of some of the technology used in iTunes. The company had to pay £44 million to Smartflash for unauthorised use of technology within its products for which Smartflash owns the patent. Smartflash, which is based in the British Virgin Islands, owns and licenses tech-related patents but does not make products itself. Smartflash originally sought $852 million in damages for Apple's unauthorised use of the patents, basing its calculation on the number of Mac computers, iPhones and iPads that had been sold.

This defeat is one of many in recent years to companies referred to as non-practising entities (NPEs), and which are called 'patent trolls' by their critics.

A few months before the Apple decision, Samsung had to pay Rembrandt IP $15.7 million for infringing two Bluetooth-related patents, and the security firm Symantec had to pay Intellectual Ventures $17 million for using two anti-malware inventions it owned.

Some commentators criticise patent trolls for suing big companies for technology they have not actually produced. Others say that they play an important role in creating a market for inventions developed outside the laboratories of the big firms.

Questions

1. Do you think patent trolls play a useful role?
2. What is the value of the patent system?

Business in focus: Toyota

In 2015, the car producer Toyota announced that it was going to share nearly 6,000 patents that covered hydrogen fuel cell technology. This is to try and get the development of this technology to happen faster and to be more widespread across the industry. Without this sharing of information, interest in the technology might not develop and therefore the work Toyota has already done could be wasted. The range of patents that will be made available cover areas such as fuel cells, hydrogen tanks, software systems and the various processes involved in generating and supplying the gas. Toyota's view is that to develop this technology over the next five years requires a high level of collaboration between supposed 'competitors' to share the costs and

breakthroughs. Whilst the network of power points for electric vehicles is gradually being built up, refuelling stations for hydrogen cars are much harder to find. Toyota hopes to build momentum in the industry which would lead to more investment in this area.

Toyota's move follows that of Tesla Motors, which shared its patent portfolio in 2014 for similar reasons.

Questions

1. Do you think it is a good idea for a business to share its patented technology?
2. What factors do you think will determine whether hydrogen fuel cell technology is likely to be successful?

Business in focus: UK patents

	2012	2013
Number of patent applications in the UK	15,370	14,971
Number of patents granted in the UK	2,974	2,464

Note: a patent is only granted if the invention is genuinely new technology and is capable of manufacture so some applications are rejected.

Table 12.3 Patents applied for and those granted, 2012 and 2013

Source: Intellectual Property Office

Organisation	Patent granted
International Business Machines Corporation	134
Broadcom Corporation	103
Baker Hughes Incorporated	87
Dyson Technology Limited	87
Schlumberger Holdings Limited	64
GM Global Technology Operations, Inc.	56
Hewlett-Packard Development Company, L.P.	52
General Electric Company	51
Canon	49
Rolls-Royce plc	47
Top 10 total	**730**

Table 12.4 Patents granted to top 10 companies, 2013

Source: Intellectual Property Office

Questions

1. Calculate the percentage of patents applied that were actually granted in 2012 and 2013 in the UK.
2. Calculate the number of patents granted to the top ten organisations gaining patents in 2013 as a percentage of the total granted for the UK.
3. What do you think determines the number of patents applied for by a business?
4. What might be the consequence in the number of patents applied for reducing between 2012 and 2013?

What do you think?

Do you think it is a good idea to share new technology with your rivals?

How much innovation?

Whilst improving products and processes is important, businesses will differ in terms of how much emphasis they put on innovation. In some cases, a business will make new product development an essential part of its strategy – think of Dyson and W. L. Gore. In other cases, businesses will focus more on following others. Zara, for example, tends to follow the fashion design of others. Trying to be innovative does not guarantee success. It uses up time, money and other useful resources and may not lead to commercial rewards. Being innovative is therefore a risky strategy and some businesses may prefer to follow the innovation of others rather than try and lead from the front. The danger of following others is that the original innovator gains a first mover advantage; this means it establishes a clear lead in the market and develops such brand loyalty that it is difficult for followers to take away customers if they enter the market later. The innovator may also protect its ideas through patents and trademarks making it even more difficult for those entering later to make much impact. On the other hand, it is possible that by entering the market later a business may be able to learn from the mistakes and difficulties of the first mover.

Disruptive innovation

The term 'disruptive innovation' was developed by Clayton Christensen of Harvard Business School. It describes innovations that create new markets by discovering new groups of consumers. This can be achieved by using new technologies, developing new ways of doing business or even using old technology but in a new way. Think about Skype, iTunes, Google, eBay, Uber and Twitter and how they have created new markets and replaced old technologies in many cases. Christensen argues that, whereas innovation often simply improves existing products, disruptive innovation brings about very significant change both for those innovating and for the established businesses that find themselves about to be replaced. When disruptive innovation occurs the key question for businesses is whether to abandon what they do already or hold on to the old approach. As the new PC market emerged, IBM held on to its mainframe computers for companies but set up a division to focus on personal PCs. By comparison, when online streaming became possible Netflix acted much more radically and abandoned its business of posting DVDs to customers.

The pace of change continues and the likelihood of disruptive technology increases. Google are threatening to change the car industry with self-driving cars. Amazon is looking to develop drone delivery and 3D printing may have a major impact on manufacturing. There will also be major innovations in the health industry, with companies helping us monitor our own health more effectively. Intel has recently launched earphones that you can wear whilst exercising that will monitor your heart rate, and there are already many self-diagnosis products on the market with more to follow.

Business in focus: Graphene

Figure 12.8 Graphene

In 2004, Andre Geim and Konstantin Novoselov, two Russian-born scientists at the University of Manchester, developed the material graphene. They were later awarded the Nobel Prize for Physics for this invention.

Graphene is a material that is:

- 200 times stronger than steel
- 1 million times thinner than a human hair

- the world's most conductive material
- transparent, flexible, stretchable and impermeable.

The potential for graphene is incredible. For example, it may be used:

- in the aircraft industry to make lighter, more fuel-efficient aircraft
- to make clothing for the defence industry (such as bullet-proof vests)
- to create sensors that can detect minute traces of gases or dangerous chemicals
- to develop flexible and bendable mobile phones, cameras and wearable technology
- to develop more energy-efficient light bulbs as the material is so conductive.

The UK government has invested £38 million in the National Graphene Institute at the University of Manchester and more than 35 companies have partnered with the university to develop projects.

Questions

1. Explain why the patent system is important to the developers of graphene.
2. Why do you think the UK government has invested in the National Graphene Institute?

The impact of innovation on functional areas

Building an innovative organisation will have implications for the different functions of a business. For example:

- **HR**. The way in which employees are managed and rewarded must encourage them to bring ideas forward and share them. Management must reward initiative and thinking of how to develop, even if it is only through praise. A culture of trial and experimentation needs to be developed. In terms of organisational structure, employees must not draw clear lines between jobs and must be willing or able to ask for advice and ideas from other departments. Creating project teams and encouraging collaboration will be important.
- **Finance**. Money will need to be made available for R&D. This may require raising finance externally. In some cases, this may require the long-term commitment of funds and will involve a high level of risk given how many product ideas fail to come

to commercial fruition. Innovation projects will need to be evaluated financially just like any other project, and so managers will be assessing measures such as the payback period and the return on investment. This is not necessarily straightforward as the outcomes in terms of what is developed and how successful it is may be difficult to estimate. It is likely, therefore, that investment appraisal techniques will be undertaken for a range of possible outcomes.

- **Marketing**. The initial stimulus for innovation may come from marketing research. An insight into why customers are dissatisfied with the existing offering may provide the initial idea for innovation. Once developed, new ideas may provide question marks to add to the business portfolio.
- **Operations**. Innovation may require project management to develop new products. It may require new skills and techniques to develop the idea. It may also require investment to enable the innovation to occur. Process innovation may enable more efficient or more accurate operations which can help competitiveness.

ASSESSMENT ACTIVITIES

(a) Knowledge check questions

1 State one possible benefit of being an innovative organisation.

2 State one possible problem a business might face in becoming an innovative organisation.

3 What is meant by product innovation? Give an example.

4 What is meant by process innovation? Give an example.

5 Is kaizen likely to require heavy investment? Justify your answer.

6 What is the difference between R&D and market research?

7 What is meant by 'benchmarking'?

8 What is the difference between entrepreneurship and intrapreneurship?

9 Can you patent a book you have written to protect your ideas? Explain your answer.

10 Is a patent free? Explain your answer.

(b) Short answer questions

1 Explain one reason why a car manufacturer aiming to increase competitiveness may invest more in R&D. (5 marks)

2 Explain one problem a manager may face when trying to introduce kaizen groups into a relatively successful business. (5 marks)

3 Explain one possible reason why attempts by a UK theme park to use benchmarking with Disney to improve customer service may prove unsuccessful. (5 marks)

4 Explain one potential benefit to a mobile phone business of patenting its technology. (5 marks)

5 Explain one way in which a major computing business such as Microsoft or Google might encourage intrapreneurship. (5 marks)

(c) Data response question

Valve

Valve is a software business that has developed games such as 'Half-Life', 'Portal', 'Dota' and the 'Left 4 Dead' series that are well-known for their quality and high sales. It is also the developer of 'Steam', which is game platform that distributes and manages thousands of games to 65 million players around the world.

At Valve everyone is regarded as equal. Employees sit where they want, choose what projects to work on and agree on each other's pay. Once a year everyone goes on holiday together. The company sees itself as a 'flat' organisation where no one reports to anyone else – they work together. Employees discuss their work with each other and people work on whatever project interests them and where they can add value. There are no fixed work areas. All the workstations have wheels and staff can move to sit next to whomever they wish.

The company attracts able, creative people who like working with others who are similar. There is a strong sense of collective engagement with people working towards the same goal. The founder of the company, Gabe Newell, says that recruiting the right people is 'more important than breathing'. Once employed, staff are able to take risks and fail on some projects without the fear of being punished – the company says that many of its biggest breakthroughs have occurred due to learning from mistakes.

The company is very meritocratic. Staff working on the same project rank each other's technical skills, productivity, team-playing abilities and other contributions. This information is then used to create a rank order of performance which then helps to determine pay.

Questions

1 Explain one benefit of the way employees are rewarded at Valve. (6 marks)

2 Analyse why innovation is important at Valve. (9 marks)

3 To what extent do you think the success of innovation at Valve depends on the way it treats its staff? Justify your answer. (15 marks)

(d) Essays

1 To what extent do you think that finance is likely to be the major barrier to greater innovation within public limited companies in the UK? (25 marks)

2 To what extent do you think that the ability of a large, well-established pharmaceutical business to be innovative depends mainly on its culture? (25 marks)

Chapter 13

Assessing internationalisation

Introduction

In previous chapters we have examined two forms of strategic methods, namely growth and innovation. In this chapter we consider another option which a business can pursues instead of, or as well as, growth and innovation; this third strategic methods is internationalisation and involves doing business abroad. Many businesses buy in materials, raise finance and employ staff from abroad; they also export to other countries or have businesses there. We will consider the factors that affect the desire to do business abroad, and how greater internationalisation can create opportunities and threats for a business.

What you need to know by the end of this chapter:

- the reasons for targeting, operating in and trading with international markets
- the methods of entering international markets including export, licensing, alliances and direct investment
- how to analyse factors influencing the attractiveness of international markets
- how to analyse reasons for producing more and sourcing more resources abroad
- how to assess decisions regarding producing overseas, including off-shoring and re-shoring
- how to analyse ways of entering international markets and assess the value of the different methods
- that targeting overseas markets may include being a multinational
- the influences on buying, selling and producing abroad
- that managing international business includes managing the pressures for local responsiveness and the pressures for cost reduction
- how to analyse how international businesses are managed using Bartlett and Ghoshal's model of international, multi-domestic, transnational and global strategies
- how to analyse the impact on internationalisation for the functional areas of the business.

Strategic methods: internationalisation

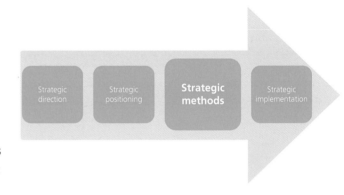

Figure 13.1 Strategic methods

The world in which we live is one where there is a great deal of international trade – far more than was the case in the past. You can buy goods and services from almost any country you care to mention, both in the shops and online. You have more ability to travel to, work in or sell to other countries than ever before. In recent years the value of world trade has increased to nearly $30 trillion a year – that's over a third of the value of the total income generated in the world. We are living in very international times and that is significant for businesses and for us as consumers and employees. What we are experiencing is greater internationalisation (sometimes called globalisation). This means that countries are becoming more linked through markets and production. There is increasing mobility of resources including flows of money, goods and services around the world.

This is important for managers because it means they need a broader vision than in the past. They have more markets in which to recruit, a greater cultural diversity in their workforce, a broader customer base and more market opportunities around the world. They also have more potential threats and face more competitive markets now that there are fewer barriers to trade globally. Managers, therefore, need to think about their business strategy in relation to international opportunities and threats rather than just domestic ones – where will they source their inputs from? Where will they actually produce? Where will they sell to? Who will they be competing against? Even if managers eventually decide to source locally, produce domestically and sell only in the UK, they need to consider their options at each stage and be clear why they are making these choices rather than being more international.

A good example of how international business has become is Facebook. Facebook highlights how interlinked countries and people all over the world now are and shows the similarities that there are in some aspects of our lifestyles, whether we live in Germany, the UK or the US. Facebook has over 1 billion users per month, i.e. more than one in eight people in the world. Although originally an American business, around 70 per cent of its users now live outside the US and speak more than 70 languages.

Greater internationalisation creates many opportunities for business –such as new markets and new places to source components and products – but brings the challenges that arise from greater competition.

What has caused greater internationalisation?

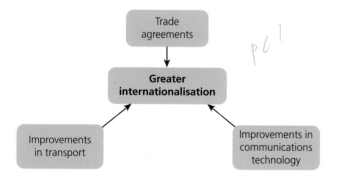

Figure 13.2 The causes of greater internationalisation

The increase in world trade and the greater openness of markets around the world for businesses have come about because of factors such as:

Trade agreements

Governments generally understand the benefits of trade. Trade enables businesses in one country to focus on producing the goods and services which they are relatively good at (this is called comparative advantage) and buy in the items which can be produced more efficiently abroad. The result should be that the country and its consumers as a whole benefit from a wider range of products than it could produce domestically. Consumers should also benefit from better value for money as items can be purchased from the best and most efficient producers in the world. Producers equally have access to the best suppliers in the world.

> ## Key terms
>
> **Free trade** occurs when there is trade between countries without barriers such as tariffs and quotas.
>
> A **tariff** is a tax placed on foreign goods and services.
>
> A **quota** is a limit on the number of imported goods and services.
>
> A **customs union** occurs when there is free trade between member countries but an agreed tariff on non-members.

However, not everyone favours **free trade**. For particular domestic industries that cannot compete effectively globally, more openness may lead to closure and redundancies; producers that are worried about their competitiveness may try to put pressure on governments to protect them. However, worldwide governmental organisations such as the World Trade Organisation (WTO) exist to reduce the amount of protectionism around the world and encourage governments to have more free trade. There have also been numerous trade agreements in recent years either establishing or extending areas in which there is free trade between member countries so businesses can easily produce or sell there. This means they remove the taxes of foreign goods (called **tariffs**) or limits on the amount of foreign goods that can be imported into a country (called **quotas**). The EU, for example, is a **customs union**, which means there are agreed restrictions on non-member countries trying to sell to the EU but there is free trade amongst the member countries themselves.

Other free trade agreements include NAFTA (North American Free Trade Area, which includes North America, Canada and Mexico) and ASEAN (Association of South East Asian Nations, which include Brunei, Cambodia, Malaysia, Myanmar, Singapore, Thailand and Vietnam).

Figure 13.3 EU members in 2015

Figure 13.4 NAFTA members in 2015

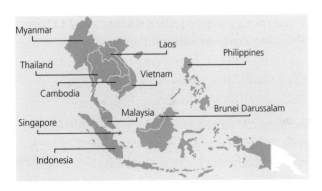

Figure 13.5 ASEAN members in 2015

Technology

As technology, particularly information and communications technology, has improved it has become easier and cheaper for businesses to operate around the world. The price of an international phone call, for example, has fallen dramatically in the last 20 years, making communication with overseas offices and staff affordable. It is now usually possible to pass the huge amounts of data required to run a business around the world quickly and efficiently via the internet. Developments in communications technology are also bringing people around the world closer to each other in terms of what they watch, read and listen to. There are films, bands and TV formats that are successful in many countries around the world. The internet, newspapers, radio and TV are making people more similar in their tastes, creating global markets. Theodore Levitt, a famous business writer said in 1983 that changes in technology, and particularly the dramatic changes taking place in communication, was effectively shrinking the world and was, he argued, having the effect of driving consumer tastes to a 'converging commonality' leading to standardised products across the world. With better technology citizens in one country can easily see what is happening in another, immediately enabling them to identify trends and access products more easily.

Transportation costs

Transportation costs have fallen dramatically in the last 50 years. It is now much cheaper to move items by air or sea, for example, and this makes global trade more attractive. One of the major breakthroughs for global markets in physical products was the development of containerisation. By standardising the size and design of containers, they can be fully loaded, quickly lifted off or onto a lorry, put onto a boat and stacked efficiently. In 1965, before containerisation, employees working at the docks could move only 1.7 tonnes per hour onto a cargo ship; five years later they could load 30 tonnes in an hour. Think of the impact of this massive increase in productivity on unit costs.

Figure 13.6 Container ships provide low-cost transportation of goods around the world.

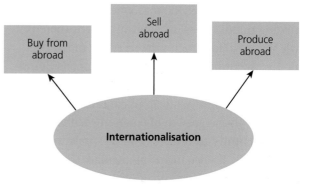

Figure 13.7 Opportunities of greater internationalisation

Greater internationalisation and the opening up of borders create opportunities for business in relation to:

- selling products abroad
- buying inputs from abroad
- producing abroad.

Business in focus: BRIC emerging economies

A recent survey on the emerging economies of Brazil, Russia, India and China (BRIC) by PWC consultants identified the reasons why major businesses wanted to do business in BRIC economies.

The chief executives were asked which of the following reasons were important considerations when doing business in each of the BRIC emerging economies (see Table 13.1).

	Brazil	China	India	Russia
Reducing costs	20%	48%	39%	18%
Increasing capacity	30%	38%	35%	28%
Accessing new customers	76%	75%	74%	62%
Serving existing customers	56%	50%	46%	48%
Accessing a highly talented skills pool	11%	22%	35%	12%

Table 13.1 Reasons for doing business in each of the BRIC emerging economies

Source: PWC

Questions

1. Summarise the key findings of the data in Table 13.1. Why do you think it varies from country to country?

2. Discuss the significance of the data in Table 13.1 for the strategies of UK businesses.

Selling in overseas markets

One aspect of international business involves selling in overseas markets. Selling abroad may be attractive because of:

- **a large target population**. For example, the UK has a population of around 60 million; China has a population of over 1 billion – providing a much bigger potential customer base. Brands such as Jaguar LandRover, Burberry and Mulberry have been extremely successful in overseas markets in recent years and targeting bigger economies has allowed them to achieve much higher sales than they could within the UK. Expanding overseas provides opportunities for fast growth in particular in emerging economies – these are countries such as China and India, which have relatively low incomes per person at the moment but which have been growing fast. Products such as microwaves, organic foods or dishwashers may be in the growth phase in emerging economies where there is a growing middle class, whereas in the UK there is little potential for much growth as the market is mature. According to the management consultants McKinsey, by 2025 there will 1.8 billion more people in the world with significant purchasing power due to the growth of emerging economies.

- **the opportunity to reduce risk.** By spreading sales more globally if sales in one market fall, they may be compensated by rising sales elsewhere. Using Ansoff's matrix, entering an international market may be an example of market development if the products are essentially the same as those being offered in domestic markets, or diversification if the products are new. Both these strategies involve the risk of

entering a new market but help spread risks at the same time by operating in new areas. The economic crisis of 2008 showed how whole areas of the world can be affected and the benefits of spreading risks and not being totally dependent on one region.

	Existing products	**New products**
Existing markets	Market penetration	New product development
New markets	Market development	Diversification

Figure 13.8 The Ansoff matrix

Business in focus: Unilever

Unilever is one of the world's largest companies with many well-known brands such as Dove, Magnum, Walls and Persil. It has four divisions which are: food, personal care, home care and refreshment. Unilever has a clear strategy to focus on emerging economies. In these countries there are rapidly growing numbers of middle-class consumers that Unilever can target. The company has more than 2 billion customers worldwide every day. Its products are sold in more than 190 countries with 57 per cent of its sales now in emerging economies.

The company divides the world into those who 'have lots' of income, those who have a reasonable amount of income and those who do not have much income. Its analysis of the changing nature of the world's population is shown in Table 13.2.

	2010 (bn)	**2020 (bn)**
Have lots	1.9	3.0
Haves	2.0	2.7
Have nots	2.9	1.9
Total	**6.8**	**7.6**

Figure 13.2 How Unilever divides the world's population

Questions

1. Summarise the changes in the number of people in each group shown in the data in Table 13.2 and explain why these changes might be occurring.

2. Discuss the significance of the data in Table 13.2.

Methods of entering international markets

There are different ways of entering overseas markets to sell in. These involve differing degrees of commitment and risk:

- **Exporting**. This occurs when a business continues producing domestically but sells (exports) some of its products abroad. This represents a relatively low level of commitment to overseas sales in terms of finance and management times. It is relatively low risk.
- **Licensing**. This occurs when a business sells the right to an overseas business to produce and/or sell its products. This provides a business with a local presence. Licensing can provide valuable insights into the business environment of the country and provide much needed networks and market links. The risk is mainly taken by the firm that buys the

licence; this is because it takes responsibility for generating the sales abroad.

- **Alliances/ventures**. These occur when a domestic business works in a partnership with an overseas business – perhaps they share the investment and the risk together in terms of building a brand and market presence. This gives the UK business access to local expertise and contacts and shares the risk, but does involve sharing the profits too.
- **Direct investment**. This involves the greatest level of commitment from the domestic business. It involves investing overseas, perhaps to establish outlets or production facilities. This usually requires relatively high funds and is quite a high-risk decision. When a business has its own operations abroad it is called a multinational.

Figure 13.9 Ways of entering international markets

Key term

A **multinational company (MNC)** has operations based in overseas markets.

Multinationals

Multinational companies (MNCs) are organisations that have production bases in more than one country.

MNCs may be welcomed by overseas governments because they can:

- bring skills and expertise
- bring employment
- bring investment
- increase demand for local goods and services
- increase tax revenue.

However, some MNCs have been criticised for:

- exploiting local resources and not sharing the rewards of the business with the local economy
- keeping senior jobs for their staff and employing local employees for low-level jobs
- keeping the majority of the profits for their own head office and not investing locally

- finding ways to avoid paying high levels of tax
- being involved in corruption to win contracts.

For the business itself, being a multinational:

- gives it direct access to local markets; this may help it overcome trade barriers against 'foreign' businesses because it operates with the country
- means its production is closer to local customers. This may improve the speed of responses, may fit well with a desire to buy locally-produced products and may reduce the environmental impact of transporting items around the world. It will almost certainly cut transporation costs.
- may involve subsidies and tax incentives from the local government which is eager for this investment. This can reduce costs.
- spreads the risks of being dependent on one country or one production base by having more than one around the world. If there was a natural disaster or industrial action at one car factory, for example, another may still be able to produce. If demand in one market fell, there may still be growth in another market.

However, being a multinational may:

- bring management challenges, as it may be more complex to manage a business with bases in different countries. There are the practical issues of communication (for example, if they are in different time zones and if travel between sites is time consuming), but also issues such as cultural differences and differences in labour markets, government regulations and ways of doing business.
- bring criticism from some groups if the business is said to be abusing its power in any way or if there is pressure to buy local brands not global ones.

Business in focus: China – guanxi

In China it is very important to know who you are dealing with and what connections they have with others in business or government. The term 'guanxi' refers to these social relationships. The importance of guanxi is partly because this was a society which, in the past, had little experience of business law as almost everything was run by the state. (If you cannot rely on contracts to enforce agreements, then it becomes very important to trust the people you are doing business with.) When doing business in China it is vital, therefore, to get to know your partners and to build a relationship with them before actually doing business. Westerners are often

surprised by the time it takes to actually start working together and the emphasis put on the social relationship as well as the business one. This is because Chinese business people are trying to find out more about who you are, your status and whether or not they can do business with you.

Questions

1. Why do you think that 'guanxi' is less important in the UK than in China?

2. What do you think is the consequence of 'guanxi' for UK businesses?

Factors influencing the attractiveness of markets

When deciding which markets, if any, to target abroad managers will consider a range of factors such as:

- **The size and growth of the market**. How does this compare to alternatives and what profit might it bring?
- **The expected costs of entering the market**. Also, how long it is likely to take to recover this initial investment.
- **The macro environment**. Managers may undertake a PEST-C analysis to evaluate the possible opportunities and threats in a given market. For example, under the political heading the managers will assess whether or not it is easy to do business in the country. Are the laws similar to UK laws? Is the country politically stable? Are there high levels of corruption?
- **How culturally similar the country is to the UK**. Will managers feel they understand the market and customers relatively easily or will this require extensive research and cultural understanding? Many businesses first expand abroad to a nearby region because they feel they know it best. Interestingly, most European businesses trade within the EU, most Asian businesses trade within Asia and most American businesses trade within the American continent. Although business is more global, the business writer Rugman highlights that the majority of it still remains quite localised – for example, UK firms are more likely to export to EU countries than to Asia – perhaps because it is easier to organise or control but also, perhaps, because culturally these regions seem more familiar.
- **The degree of competition**. Also, the likely reaction of these existing businesses. Managers may undertake a five forces analysis (Porter) to assess the competitive environment.
- **The perceived risk involved**. If it went wrong, what is the potential downside – for example, in terms of money and reputation?
- **The fit with the overall strategy of the business and its competences**.

- **The extent to which the business has to be adapted for local requirements**. What are the costs, rewards and risks of this?
- **The impact on the business of overseas growth**. For example, in terms of the ease with which the growth can be managed.

When discussing businesses targeting overseas markets this does not just mean UK businesses aiming at overseas customers. This is the opportunity created by international business. However, businesses based overseas can also expand and target UK customers. This is the threat created by international business. Tata, for example, is originally an Indian company but it has expanded greatly in recent years into western markets; Tata now owns Tetley tea and Jaguar cars. Another example of a business based abroad but growing fast in western markets is Huawei. Huawei is a Chinese telecommunications and mobile phone brand that is growing fast and is now challenging more established businesses such as Apple. It is one of many Chinese businesses now attacking global markets. By 2025, it is estimated that China will have more large companies than either the US or Europe, and more than 45 per cent of the companies on Fortune's Global 500 list of major international companies will come from emerging markets compared with just 5 per cent in 2000.

This is not the first time that western businesses need to be watching emerging economies closely. For example in the 1970s and 1980s, many US and European businesses rapidly lost market share to Japanese companies that offered better quality and more innovative products. In the last decade, South Korean companies such as Hyundai and Samsung have attacked a range of industries from automobiles to personal electronics. Nowadays, new competitors can come from many countries across the world and set up much more rapidly. The shift in the global economy towards emerging markets, and the emergence of nearly 2 billion consumers who, for the first time, will have incomes sufficient to support significant spending is likely to create companies in these markets which will then expand globally. Western companies need to be careful and plan for this ever-increasing threat!

Business in focus: McDonald's

Figure 13.10 Indian McDonald's – the Chicken Maharajah Mac

McDonald's operates in markets all over the world. Although a major competitive strength of McDonald's is its consistency so that customers know what they are getting, the company does adjust its offering for different markets. For example, when entering the India market McDonald's had to avoid having any pork or beef on its menu. (Nearly half of Indians are vegetarians usually for religious reasons.) In most countries the best-selling product in McDonald's is the Big Mac, but in India it is the Chicken Maharajah Mac.

The Indian market is very different from the US. For example, when researching the market in 2003 McDonald's found that out of 100 meals eaten a month only three were eaten out. As a result, the company set the price of its basic 'burger' at 20 rupees (20p). This burger was made of mashed potatoes and peas and flavoured with Indian spices. Eating out in India is now around 9 to 10 times per 100 meals and McDonald's has over 320 million customers. Another difference with the US is that the main customers in India are young people aged between 19 and 30 years with no children as opposed to families.

To set up in India was a major challenge for McDonald's as the required infrastructure did not exist. For example, there was no supply chain in place for lettuce, which meant that the company had to set up its own. McDonald's now tries to source as many of its inputs locally (including equipment for the stores). The company has over 350 stores in India and plans to open another 1,000 given that there are over 1.2 billion people in the country.

Questions

1. Do you think it is a good idea for McDonald's to target India?
2. What do you think are the arguments for and against McDonald's changing its approach in different countries?

Business in focus: UK exports

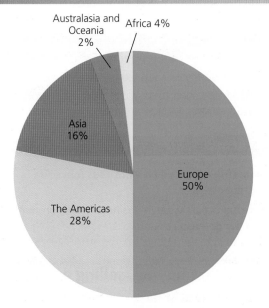

Figure 13.11 Percentage contributions to total UK exports of services, 2013

Source: Office for National Statistics (ONS)

According to the British Chambers of Commerce (BCC), in April 2014 the UK services sector's export sales and orders were at record high levels. The BCC's Chief Economist, David Kern, warned however that 'Investment and exports must play a larger contribution to our economic future, or else there is a risk that our recovery could stall.'

Questions

1. Figure 13.11 shows the latest data on the UK exports of services. Why do you think most UK services are exported to Europe?
2. Do you think it is easier to export goods or services?

Reasons for buying from abroad

Internationalisation may involve targeting overseas markets. It may also involve using suppliers based abroad. Most companies buy some of their supplies from abroad or even have the whole product produced abroad and then import it.

Reasons for using overseas suppliers include lower costs and better quality and technology. By sourcing products internationally, a business really can find the best in the world in terms of efficiency and effectiveness of production. Certain producers overseas will be the best in their field or the best value for money, and globally sourcing items enables companies like Apple to find them and benefit from good quality at relatively low costs.

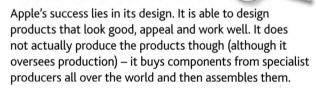

Business in focus: Apple

Apple's success lies in its design. It is able to design products that look good, appeal and work well. It does not actually produce the products though (although it oversees production) – it buys components from specialist producers all over the world and then assembles them.

For example, components in the Apple iPhone include:

- applications hardware: Samsung, South Korea
- wireless telephone technology: Infineon, Germany
- Flash memory: Toshiba, Japan
- gyroscopic chip: AT Microelectronics, Switzerland
- central processing chip: ARM, UK
- steel case: Catcher Technology, Taiwan
- multi-touch display: TPK Balda, China

Apple's profit margin on the finished product is much higher than the profit margin of the individual suppliers.

Questions

1. Why do you think Apple buys from all these different suppliers rather than producing all the components itself?
2. How does Apple manage to earn a much higher profit margin than its own suppliers?

Reasons for producing abroad

Overseas countries are not just appealing as potential markets or sources of suppliers; they are also a potential place to produce.

Businesses may want to produce abroad because:

- it costs less. For example, labour is significantly cheaper in many other countries around the world than it is in the UK.

- it may be nearer to resources. For example, a mining business will want to locate nearer natural resources; an oil business will need to locate near the source.
- it may be more efficient to produce locally in overseas markets and sell there, for example due to lower distribution costs, than to produce domestically and export.
- there may be particular skills or expertise in a given area. For example, film production in Hollywood or computing expertise in Silicon Valley.
- it may overcome barriers to trade such as tariffs (taxes on foreign goods) and quotas (limits on the number of foreign goods entering a market). Some governments introduce these barriers to protect local firms. However, by being based within the country these restrictions may not apply.

Outsourcing and re-shoring

If production is moved abroad, this is known as 'outsourcing'. This has been fairly common in recent years as UK businesses have sought to maximise the benefits of overseas production.

However, there have also been some instances of re-shoring when production has been moved back to the UK. This may because of:

- problems maintaining quality abroad.
- problems with delivery from overseas. Local production may be more flexible to demand.
- a fall in the cost differential. For example, if wages overseas rise faster than domestically.
- a desire to be seen to support domestic production and create jobs locally.

Key terms

Outsourcing occurs when a business moves its production overseas.

Re-shoring occurs when a business moves production back to the domestic country.

Influences on buying, selling and producing overseas

Influences to produce or sell abroad include the following:

- **The pressure for growth.** For example, from investors. If fast growth is required, it may be that the domestic market does not offer enough opportunities and overseas expansion is the key.

- **The pressure for lower costs**. Managers may be forced to search globally for the lowest cost resources or production sites.
- **Location**. The need to be closer to overseas markets may affect location decisions.

- **The availability of suitable resources locally**. For example, it may be necessary to source inputs overseas if they are not available locally.
- **Politics/economics**. The political and economic situation may affect the ease with which business can be undertaken overseas.

Business in focus: American Apparel

American Apparel is a leading clothing brand mainly targeting the young. It is known for cutting-edge advertising and its 'Made in Downtown LA' brand. It designs, produces and sells clothes which are made in the US.

Employees in its US garment factories earn around $30,000 a year, plus benefits such as health care. (In contrast, in Bangladesh, a garment worker is paid around $600 a year.) American Apparel aims to create jobs that motivate and enable employees to have a career. It seeks to promote from within the business and ensure employees have an input into decisions.

The company believes there are significant benefits from integrating its retailing and manufacturing in the

US. It aims to pay employees fairly and sell its garments profitability. It wants everyone to benefit: customers, workers and shareholders.

It believes that a reliance on low wages by other businesses is not actually sustainable and that it will increasingly be seen as exploitation and be opposed.

Source: American Apparel's website, www.americanapparel.net/aboutus/

Questions
1. Why do you think American Apparel produces in the US?
2. Do you think American Apparel would ever produce overseas?

Managing international businesses

When operating overseas managers will want to consider the best ways of managing these international operations. Should the overseas divisions have a high degree of independence, for example, and be able to make decisions about what to sell and how to sell it in their own region? Should the products be kept similar to those in the domestic market or be adapted to meet local requirements? These decisions will depend on various factors:

- The extent to which the local markets differ in terms of customer requirements.
- The costs of adapting products to local needs.
- The cost benefits (economies of scale) from standardising products and selling the same products all around the world.
- The ease of managing the business centrally from one location.

The strategic options open to managers can be shown using the Bartlett and Ghoshal (1991) matrix. In this matrix the choice of which strategy to adopt depends on the pressures for local responsiveness – that is the extent to which local tastes differ and the need to adapt to this – compared to the pressures to adopt an integrated approach globally; for example, the pressure for the cost reductions that might occur from operating as one global business and the extent to which these economies of scale exist.

	Low pressure for local responsiveness	High pressure for local responsiveness
High pressure for global integration	Global	Transnational
Low pressure for global integration	International	Multi-domestic

Figure 13.12 The Bartlett and Ghoshal matrix

The four strategic options in the matrix are:

1. International

In this approach the business is mainly focused on its domestic operations. The development of new technology and products, for example, will tend to be from the head office in the domestic country. Although the business operates abroad and there will be some independence, the decisions are mainly made from the home base. The products developed at home are sold abroad with some but not much adaptation. In this strategy the international business is seen essentially as less important than the domestic business. Products are designed for the domestic market and international markets are seen mainly as a way to boost sales.

2. Multi-domestic

In this approach the different parts of the business operate fairly independently in their own regions. The overall business is essentially a collection of separate units that operate alone. Each one adapts to its local environment in terms of what it offers and runs itself. This is relatively common in industries such as processed food, publishing and fashion where there can be significant differences in the tastes and requirements of each market. Each region essentially runs itself so the overall organisation is a collection of different local businesses (multi-domestic). The disadvantage of this approach is that resources are not shared between the separate companies.

3. Global

In this approach the businesses abroad are subsidiaries that are heavily dependent on the domestic business for resources and skills. This is relatively common in industries such as aerospace, computers and chemicals where demand is similar across the world. The pressure for this approach comes from the existence of major economies of scale and there is a major focus on efficiency. Firms sell standardised products across particular regions or even the world. For example, Caterpillar produces construction equipment that is used and sold all over the world with little adaptation.

4. Transnational

This approach aims to maximise responsiveness and integration across all the divisions around the world. Knowledge, technology and components are developed at different centres around the world and shared globally across the business. Staff are moved between centres to help unite the business globally. The business responds to local requirement whilst sharing the benefits of being a global business. It no longer thinks of itself as a 'UK' or 'US' business, for example.

The approach adopted by a business will depend on many factors, but one of these will be the nature of the industry it is in. It may be easier to adopt a global approach in oil, for example, than in publishing where there may need to be significant variations for different markets.

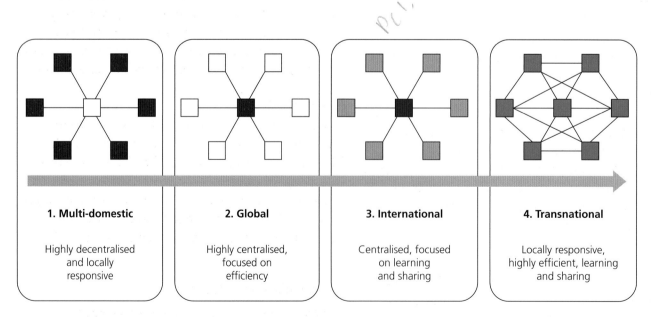

1. Multi-domestic

Highly decentralised and locally responsive

2. Global

Highly centralised, focused on efficiency

3. International

Centralised, focused on learning and sharing

4. Transnational

Locally responsive, highly efficient, learning and sharing

Figure 13.13 The four approaches in the Bartlett and Ghoshal matrix

- A global approach may be more likely for construction and mining machinery, chemicals and engines.
- A multi-domestic approach may be more suitable for food and household appliances. (Just think how plug sockets and voltages differ around the world!)

- A transnational approach may suit pharmaceuticals, computers and cars.
- An international strategy may suit publishing and textiles.

Business in focus: One Ford Strategy

In 2006 Alan Mulally took over as Chief Executive at Ford. He introduced a number of strategic changes. These included a major shift towards using:

- common 'platforms'. This means that the basic structure ('platform') of the car would be the same for several different models – what would differ was what was placed on top.
- common parts rather than designing specific parts and components for each model.

The aim of this strategy was to maintain variations for different parts of the world and consumers, but at the same time have as much 'communality' as possible to reduce costs. In 2007, Ford produced less than 30 per cent of its global output on common platforms. There were 27 different platforms. By 2016, the company

plans to produce 99 per cent of its vehicles on just eight global platforms.

The company is also aiming to develop more global cars, that is models that can be sold in many different markets.

This whole approach is known as the 'One Ford Strategy'.

Questions

1. Why do you think Mulally wanted the One Ford Strategy?
2. Do you think cars are a fairly standardised product across the world? Can you think of three other products that are standardised globally and three that are not?

The risks of internationalisation

Whilst the potential benefits for a company of greater international business are huge, the risks of undertaking it should not be underestimated. These risks arise for various reasons:

Cultural differences

Whilst greater internationalisation and globalisation may mean lifestyles converge in some ways (think of how pervasive global brands such as Coca Cola, Facebook and McDonalds are), there can still be significant differences in language, attitudes, customs and religion, which can make doing business abroad challenging and more demanding than operating in the local market. For example, in Japan it is common for employees to gather together first thing in the morning, sing the company song and even exercise together. This is less common in the UK. Even McDonald's adapts its menus in different countries recognising the differences in tastes that exist.

Differences in negotiating and decision-making style

In some countries, such as the US, managers tend to get straight to business. They want to reach a clear decision and agreement in a meeting. A handshake usually means that an agreement has been made. In other countries

managers may take longer to reach a decision. Meetings may at first be more social as they get to know and trust each other. A handshake may mean that they are going away to think about the decision, not that a decision has actually been made. The Japanese decision-making approach, for example, tends to involve a great deal of consultation and involvement of different staff – this does lead to a consensus but can be very slow, whereas the US style tends to listen to fewer voices but be quicker. Managers operating globally need to be conscious of these differences or they may get frustrated and cause offence.

Ethical standards

What might be seen as unethical or even illegal in one country, may be seen as acceptable or inevitable in others – in fact it may be regarded as the way that business is done. Levels of bribery and corruption vary considerably from country to country. If your managers do not bribe and domestic ones do give incentives to individuals in order to win contracts, this can make competing more difficult.

Anti-globalisation feelings

In recent years there have been various pressure groups and protests against businesses operating globally. Although the reasons behind the criticisms of globalisation vary, they include the views that:

- local cultures and businesses are destroyed by large multinational companies. Visit any major city in the world and you will most likely find Starbucks competing with small, locally-owned coffee houses. Critics argue that these big multinationals are destroying local business and making the world too similar.
- the big multinationals are exploiting local employees and businesses. For example, they produce in a country and make use of its natural resources, but the profits do not remain in the country – they are exported overseas.

Differences in the stability of the country

Compared to other countries, the UK is very stable politically and economically. Elsewhere there is a possibility of the government being overthrown, of military rule or of uprisings in parts of the country. Similarly, the currency can change dramatically in value or inflation can be in the hundreds, even thousands, of per cent. Listen to the news any week you choose and you will hear of major political and economic problems around the world. Even in the UK there are disagreements about government policy and uncertainty about what will happen at the next election – the state of the economy is far from predictable. This uncertainty makes it more difficult to plan ahead and do business.

Business in focus: Challenges of globalisation

When chief executives were asked in a recent PWC survey what they thought were the biggest challenges of globalisation, they said (in order of importance):

1. overregulation
2. trade barriers/protectionism
3. political instability
4. social issues
5. loss of intellectual capital
6. currency issues
7. corruption
8. terrorism
9. anti-globalisation movement.

Questions

1. Explain the significance of any three of the above challenges.
2. Do these challenges mean that global trade is not worth it?

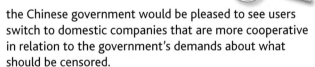

Business in focus: Google in China

In 2015, Google's email service was allegedly blocked in what seemed to be another attempt by the Chinese government to limit or even block access to Google's services.

Google said that its investigations had shown that China's government had blocked Google IP addresses in Hong Kong used by people on the mainland to access Gmail services.

The Chinese government has been accused of taking steps before to limit Google's search and email services because it has wanted to limit Chinese citizens' access to information on the internet. It has not publically admitted that it has taken these actions. It said that China always welcomes and supports foreign investors and wants to provide an open, transparent environment for foreign businesses. However, there is a sense that

the Chinese government would be pleased to see users switch to domestic companies that are more cooperative in relation to the government's demands about what should be censored.

Google closed its mainland China search engine in 2009 because it refused to cooperate with the government's demands for certain sites to be censored and access to them blocked. This was after hacking attacks aimed at breaking into the company's operating code were traced to China.

Questions

1. Why do you think the Chinese government might want to make it difficult for Google to do business in China?
2. Do you think Google should be willing to operate in China?

Impact of internationalisation on the functional areas of business

Any decision regarding the internationalisation of a business will have an impact on the different functional areas of that business. For example, it can affect the following:

- Market research activities, as a business wants to find out more about new markets and new segments to target.
- R&D, as a business develops new products or modifies existing products for an overseas market.
- The purchasing of supplies. Businesses now have access to far more suppliers all over the world. Communications technology enables them to identify them, contact them and manage their relationship with them more effectively. Lower transport costs make it more feasible to buy in from abroad in terms of costs and speed of delivery.
- Production. Businesses may look to produce overseas to benefit from lower costs, better skills and technology or the availability of resources.
- Marketing decisions, such as how to promote and price products and also how to distribute them.
- HR, in terms of how and where to recruit, the rewards offered and how best to manage people.

By operating internationally a business may be able to gain many benefits, such as lower costs of resources and greater access to customers, labour, technology and suppliers.

The precise impact of internationalisation will depend on the overall decisions made. Two examples, a decision to offshore production and a decision to target new overseas markets, are discussed here.

Decision to offshore production

A business's decision to offshore production may lead to:

- a relocation of production facilities and the development of the operation abroad (operations)
- a reduction in staff domestically and the recruitment of employees overseas (HR issues). Managing staff abroad may be very different due to differences in the labour market, the skills and expectations of the workforce, cultural differences and employment legislation
- marketing being affected if the business can build on the regional strengths of where the product is produced (for example, 'German engineering', 'Japanese quality' or 'French cuisine'). However, there has been some movement for businesses to focus on local produce and local suppliers and so moving production overseas may cause problems for the brand
- lower costs due to lower labour or material costs; this may increase profit margins (financial issues).

Decision to target new overseas markets

A decision made by a business to target new overseas markets may lead to:

- changes to the way products are produced (for example, they may need to be adapted for new markets) and changes to the way they are promoted, priced and distributed (marketing issues)
- changes to the operations process to be able to produce products suitable for the new market (operations issues)
- changes to HR decisions. If the business will be operating overseas, it will need to recruit and train staff abroad
- changes to finances. There may be initial costs and investments to establish a presence overseas; however, long-term overseas sales may lead to higher profits.

ASSESSMENT ACTIVITIES

(a) Knowledge check questions

1 State three reasons why the amount of international business worldwide is increasing.

2 What is the name for a tax on foreign goods and services?

3 What do the initials WTO represent and what does this organisation aim to achieve?

4 What is meant by an 'emerging economy'?

5 According to Ansoff, what is the name for a strategy that targets a new market with an existing product?

6 Explain one reason why a business might want to sell overseas.

7 Explain one reason why a business might want to produce overseas.

8 State two factors that might determine the attractiveness of an overseas market.

9 State what is on the axis of Bartlett and Ghoshal's matrix of international business.

10 State two possible problems of entering an overseas market.

(b) Short answer questions

1 The tobacco company BNA has found that sales of cigarettes have fallen in recent years in the UK given social change and changes in the laws about smoking. Explain why the business might want to target overseas markets.   (5 marks)

2 Albion Apparel, a clothing producer and retailer, has been under increasing pressure to lower its prices and offer better value for money. Explain one reason way Albion might wish to shift production overseas.   (5 marks)

3 The Frantic Advertising Agency is eager to expand its operations overseas. Explain one factor it might consider when deciding which country to target.   (5 marks)

4 The Gillter Bicycle Company is one of the few remaining bicycle producers in the UK. It would like the government to protect it. Explain one reason why Gillter might need government protection from international competition in order to survive.   (5 marks)

5 The Marson Food company sells fast food around the world. Explain one factor that might determine which of Bartlett and Ghoshal's strategies it might adopt.   (5 marks)

(c) Data response question

Airbnb

Airbnb is a marketplace to link those who have accommodation to rent with those who want somewhere to stay. The company was founded in August of 2008 and is based in San Francisco, California. Owners of property can list their facilities on Airbnb and those seeking somewhere to stay can search and book. It lists 34,000 cities in over 190 countries and has over 25 million users. Airbnb charges around 15 per cent for its service.

In 2015 the company added Cuba as a destination. This was made possible by an easing of restrictions on trade with Cuba by the US government. However, Airbnb was only able to allow US residents to make a booking in Cuba and to do this the visitors needed a business licence. People outside of the US could see the properties but not rent them. Airbnb started with 1,000 properties ranging from around £10 a night to £695 a night for the whole of a five bedroom chalet in Havana.

However, there are some possible difficulties of this new service. Firstly, Cuban households may be reluctant to offer 15 per cent to a US business to arrange for people to stay with them; many have been renting out their properties privately through friends and relations anyway. Secondly, an online service faces the problem of a slow and unreliable internet service within Cuba. It means enquirers may have to wait a while to get a reply! (That is assuming the renters have access to the internet. Internet penetration is estimated at about 2.8 million, or about 26 per cent of the country's population of 11.3 million.)

However, Airbnb is one of the first into a market that is likely to grow, especially if trade restrictions are relaxed even further. Travel companies have started offering services in Cuba, including flight and hotel site Kayak and the airline Sun Country, which began charter flights from New York to Havana through Cuba Travel Services.

Now that Airbnb is operating in Cuba there are relatively few countries where it does not offer properties; these include Iran and North Korea.

Netflix

The entertainment streaming site Netflix also announced it would begin services in Cuba, despite the slow internet speeds and the fact that its fee represents almost half of the average monthly salary of a Cuban.

Questions

1 Explain one factor that is likely to influence demand for Airbnb's services in any one country. (6 marks)

2 Analyse how Airbnb adds value for its customers. (9 marks)

3 To what extent do you think Netflix's decision to expand into Cuba is a good one? (16 marks)

(d) Essays

1 Is it better for a US producer of household electrical goods, such as washing machines and dishwashers, to target overseas markets than local ones? Justify your answer. (25 marks)

2 With reference to Bartlett and Ghoshal's model, is it better for a car manufacturer to operate as a multi-domestic or a transnational business? Justify your answer. (25 marks)

Assessing greater use of digital technology

Introduction

In the last three chapters we have considered different strategic methods: growth, innovation and internationalisation. In this chapter we consider a fourth option which is the use of digital technology. Digital technology seems to be driving many aspects of business these days through developments such as e-commerce, social media marketing and greater interconnectedness between businesses, products and customers. These developments in digital technology are creating opportunities and threats for businesses. Here we will consider what these changes involve and their potential impact on businesses.

What you need to know by the end of this chapter:

- the pressures to adopt digital technology
- that digital technology should include e-commerce, big data, data mining and enterprise resource planning (ERP)
- how to assess the value of digital technology
- the impact of digital technology on the functional areas of the business.

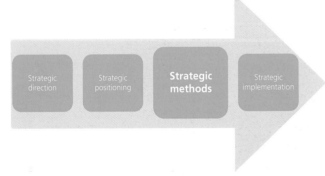

Figure 14.1 Strategic methods

Key term

E-commerce involves the buying and selling of goods or services or the transmitting of funds or data over an electronic network.

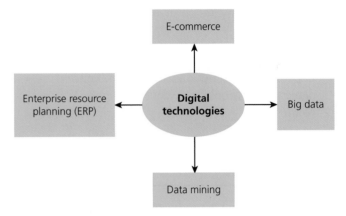

Figure 14.2 Digital technology

Digital technology involves the use of digital resources to find, analyse, create, communicate and use information digitally. Technically speaking, digital is a particular form of technology that stores data using binary codes; this means it combines 0s and 1s (also called bits) to represent words and images.

The term 'digital technology' covers a wide range of technologies and applications.

E-commerce

E-commerce refers to commercial transactions conducted electronically on the internet. It involves the buying and selling of goods and services, or the transmitting of funds or data over the internet.

E-commerce can involve:

- business-to-business (B2B), that is one business selling to another
- business-to-consumer (B2C), that is a consumer buying direct from a business such as Amazon
- consumer-to-consumer (C2C), this is consumers trading directly with each other, for example via e-Bay.

E-commerce has been growing as more people and businesses are connected online and as connection becomes easier and faster. The growth in mobile and tablet devices has added to this growth in recent years. For example, online retail sales have been growing at over 14 per cent a year and are now well over 10 per cent of all retail sales. Innovation is also removing barriers. For example, services such as click and collect delivery lockers and the integration of stores and online ordering for collection and returns have made online shopping a more attractive, easier-to-use proposition for shoppers than it used to be.

E-commerce can bring many advantages for a business such as:

● access to markets worldwide, 24 hours a day

● a new way in which customers can shop. This can be part of a multi-platform strategy whereby customers have many different ways of accessing the products such as in store, click and collect and online delivery

● relatively cheap start-up costs compared to establishing a high-street presence across the country. This enables businesses to compete in markets relatively quickly and enter markets that might not have been possible in the past

● greater access to suppliers and greater ease of comparing prices.

However, a move to e-commerce by a business does need to be considered carefully, since it may bring

Business in focus: Online retail sales

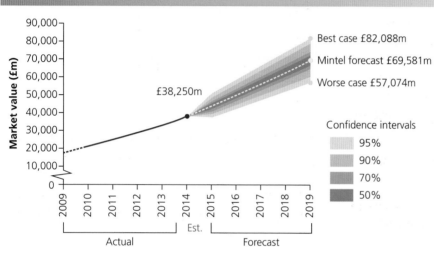

Figure 14.3 Online retail sales, UK, 2009–2019

Source: Office for National Statistics / Mintel E-commerce, July 2014

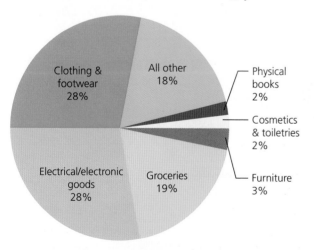

Figure 14.4 The composition of online retail sales, 2014

Source: Data from Mintel E-commerce, July 2014

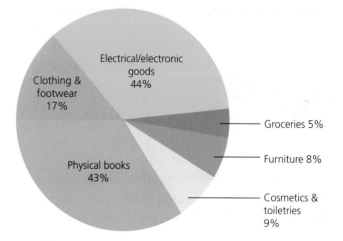

Figure 14.5 Online sales as a percentage of total sales, 2014

Source: Data from Mintel E-commerce, July 2014

Questions

1. Analyse why online retail sales are increasing.
2. Discuss the significance of the data in Figures 14.3–14.5.

additional costs in terms of spending in warehouses and the operating costs of the delivery system if the business produces physical products. Businesses must also consider the balance between having a physical presence and moving online. In the case of retailers, for example, will online sales enhance sales from retail outlets or just cannibalise their sales?

In the case of buying products online, there remain some barriers to e-commerce growth such as:

● the customer's inability to use and touch the products
● having to wait for delivery
● delivery costs
● worries about how to return products.

Study tip

Remember, there are many ways digital technology can affect a business so be careful to analyse the exact requirements of any question. For example, is the question focusing on the use of digital technology internally or in relation to marketing specifically?

What do you think?

Do you think all businesses will end up online in the future?

Key terms

Enterprise resource planning (ERP) is a software application that enables a business to effectively manage its activities, including inventory, manufacture, marketing, sales, etc. Bringing this information together should aid decision making.

Data mining is an analytical process that aims to analyse data in order to identify patterns and relationships between variables.

Big data refers to the huge amount of data that can now be mined from multiple sources to find links.

Enterprise resource planning

Enterprise resource planning (ERP) is a business management software system that allows a business to manage data relating to many of its activities, such as inventory management, manufacturing, marketing, shipping and sales. It manages the data that links all the different parts of the business together and,

therefore, enables managers to make well-informed, and therefore better, decisions.

ERP should give managers an overview of all the different activities within a business; often with real-time data, that is measuring changes as they actually happen. ERP systems are used to follow and track resources – for example, they measure the flow into and out of the business of cash, materials, products – and are able to identify at any moment the position of the business in terms of production, orders waiting to be fulfilled and inventories. ERP systems should also track customer orders and repeat purchases. ERP is, therefore, a very useful management tool that helps decision makers track what is happening and the effect of any changes they make.

ERP should help improve the:

● productivity and efficiency of the business by ensuring resources are used fully and are not idle
● flexibility of the business and response time by being able to coordinate parts of the organisation more effectively.

However, in order to be effective an ERP system will require:

● investment in systems and technological infrastructure
● training of staff
● planning to ensure the requirements of the ERP system are fully thought through before the technology is developed and implemented to ensure it has the functions required.

Figure 14.6 Enterprise Resource Planning (ERP)

Data mining

Data mining is an analytic process designed to explore data to try and find patterns within it and/or identify systematic relationships between variables. Data mining looks for possible relationships, for example, between different items a customer buys or how different market segments might respond to promotional offers. One global drinks company brings together daily weather forecast data from a meteorological office and incorporates this in its demand and inventory-planning processes. By analysing data such as temperatures, rainfall levels and the number of hours of sunshine on a given day the company is able to reduce inventory levels while improving its forecasting accuracy by about 5 per cent. Some airlines try to identify links between customer profiles and the likelihood of them not showing up for a flight, so they know how many seats they can oversell by.

Big data

Big data is linked to data mining, but refers to the fact that technology has developed so much now that huge amounts of data can be mined from multiple sources to find links. More than 2.5 exabytes of data are created each day, and this number is doubling every couple of years. More data crosses the internet every second today than was stored in the entire internet just 20 years ago.

Businesses are therefore able to work with much bigger datasets than they used to – hence the term 'big data'. For instance, it is estimated that Walmart collects more than 2.5 petabytes of data every hour from its customer transactions. A petabyte is one quadrillion bytes, or the equivalent of about 20 million filing cabinets' worth of text. An exabyte is 1,000 times that amount, or 1 billion gigabytes. This greater access to data, the greater speed of analysis and the falling costs of storage and interrogating the data means that analysts can gain incredible insights into business issues such as consumer behaviour. For example, MIT Media Lab used location data from mobile phones to infer how many people were in the car park of the world famous retailer Macy's on Black Friday – the start of the Christmas shopping season in the US. This made it possible to estimate the retailer's sales on that critical day even before Macy's itself had recorded those sales!

Big data takes the form of messages, updates, and images posted to social networks; readings from sensors; GPS signals from mobile phones, and more. Many of the most important sources of big data are relatively new. The huge amounts of information from social networks, for example, are only as old as the networks themselves; Facebook was launched in 2004, Twitter in 2006. The same holds for smartphones and the other mobile devices that now provide

Business in focus: Pace of technological change

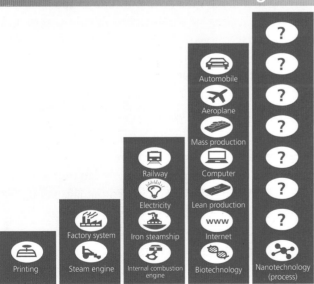

16th and 17th centuries | 18th century | 19th century | 20th century | 21st century

Printing — Factory system — Steam engine — Railway — Electricity — Iron steamship — Internal combustion engine — Mass production — Computer — Lean production — www Internet — Automobile — Aeroplane — Biotechnology — Nanotechnology (process)

The pace of technological change is now quite staggering, as can be seen in Figure 14.6 which shows some of the major innovations in different centuries. Consumers are adopting technological advances ever more quickly. The telephone took 76 years to reach half of all US households. The smartphone achieved the same level of penetration in less than 10 years. Just look at the incredibly rapid adoption of smartphones and tablets. In the UK, for example, 61 per cent of consumers are expected to be 'digital natives' (that is those who are actively using social media and several different devices) by 2020, up from 19 per cent in 2013. Facebook's membership – at 1.19 billion – is now nearly as big as the population of India.

Questions

1. Why do you think the rate at which digital technology is being adopted is so fast?

2. What do you think are the implications of such rapid change for businesses?

Figure 14.7 The pace of innovation

Source: Data from PWC 17th Annual CEO Survey

enormous streams of data that link people, activities and locations. Because these devices are seemingly everywhere now it is easy to forget that the iPhone was only launched in 2007 and the iPad in 2010.

What do you think?

Do you think that having access to more data is bound to improve decision making?

The impact of digital technology

Digital technology is creating huge changes in the business world. Digital technology has improved the way businesses produce and operate. It has also disrupted markets by enabling new businesses to enter and bypass the competitive advantage of established (also called 'incumbent') businesses. There was a time when having a chain of high-street outlets was a strength – in the world of retail, estate agency, travel agents or banking, for example; now it is often a burden because of high fixed costs compared to new entrants who operate just online. Digital technology can revolutionise industries, create new markets (such as downloadable books, specialist online auctions, online gambling and online dating) and destroy or severely damage others. It can also change the shape of industries – the postal service across the world has seen a decline in the posting of letters due to email but an increase in the delivery of parcels due to more online ordering. You may be reading this book in a physical form, but publishers are increasingly developing their digital offerings.

The importance of digital technology is growing at an ever-increasing speed and businesses must consider how this affects their activities. For example, 20 years ago less than 3 per cent of the world's population had a mobile phone and less than 1 per cent was on the internet. Today, more than two-thirds of the world's population has access to a mobile phone, and one-third can communicate on the internet. As information flows continue to grow and new waves of disruptive technology emerge, businesses can now start and gain scale with extraordinary speed with relatively little funding. Several of you reading this book may well be self-made millionaires from online businesses before the age of 40! Given the increased significance of digital technology, a number of businesses are

now appointing specialist staff to manage their digital operations.

The impacts of digital technology on a business include the following:

- significant improvements in the ease with which different stakeholders can communicate and monitor the performance of a business
- better management
- enabling new ways to do business
- changes in HR issues.

Improvements in communications and availability of information

Communication is now easier and faster so there is much greater transparency all round. Information is readily available to customers, for example, when searching for alternatives or trying to find out about the products and behaviour of an organisation. Information can also be available in several different formats (for example, via websites, video, social media) and can be tailored more readily to the specific needs of different groups (so you get to know what you want and need to know rather than being overwhelmed by data). More access to information can put more power into the hands of buyers, increasing buyer power in Porter's five forces model. How many times do you now look at customer reviews before buying anything? You have the chance to ask and learn from others' experiences before buying to a much greater extent than in the past. Managers need to be careful, therefore, how they and others behave, how the business is performing and how it reacts because every action is now taken on a very visible stage.

Better management

There is a famous phrase in business that you cannot manage what you cannot measure. The existence of more data and more analytical tools can enable better decision making and more focused management. Think about book retailing. In the past, a bookshop could measure what was sold; if it had a loyalty programme it might also be able to link sales to some particular features of the customers such as their postcodes and ages. However, with online shopping the business can now measure what particular types of products individual customers have bought, what they looked at (and for how long) and how they responded to different promotions or reviews. Managers' understanding of customers is now so great that they can predict what they are likely to want to read next when they are shopping. They can also get direct feedback from the reader on what they thought of the book. Better data within the business should then lead to better decision making and better performance. According to the management consultants McKinsey, the more data driven businesses are, the better they perform on objective measures of financial and operational results. In particular, companies in the top third of their industry in terms of the use of data-driven decision making are, on average, 5 per cent more productive and 6 per cent more profitable than their competitors. This performance difference is statistically significant and economically important and is reflected in measurable increases in stock market valuations.

Enabling new ways of doing business

Digital technology is enabling new ways of doing business. For example, businesses can access finance from the general public using crowdfunding and they can use customers and suppliers for new ideas or to advise each other. For example, Telstra, a mobile phone business, crowd sources customer service, so that users support each other to resolve problems without charge. At Chocomize, you can develop your own personalised recipe of chocolate; this can then be bought by others earning you points that can be put towards the price of your next order. Customers are now becoming very closely involved in the whole operations process.

Weblink

For more information about Chocomize, visit:
www.chocomize.com

Changes in HR issues

Digital technology involves the replacement of labour in many digital businesses. For example, of the 700 processes in banking (opening an account or getting a car loan, for example) about half can now be fully automated. Even in knowledge-intensive areas, such as health care, diagnosis software is being developed so that staff will not be needed to do this given the ability to scan and store massive amounts of medical research and the results of previous diagnoses. A key challenge for senior managers is to reallocate the money saved from automating the business into the development of talent required to move their businesses forward with new strategies and more effective use of digital techniques.

Study tip

Remember to think carefully about the particular situation facing any business – some lead the way in exploiting the opportunities of digital technology, some are catching up and some have been left way behind. Don't assume digital is good for all. Also think carefully about the implications of digital. Selling all over the world from your website may seem appealing for example, but how do you develop your website for each market, how do you process the transactions and how do ensure rapid delivery? You need to be able to take a critical view of digital technology.

Business in focus: ASOS

ASOS is an online fashion retailer.

Its mission is to be the world's leading fashion retailer for 20–30 year olds. It wants to lead its field in the same way that Google and Facebook lead theirs.

To achieve this, the company measures its success through its share of online traffic, the number of followers on social media sites as well as sales.

The company says that it aims to provide inspiration but also conversation for fashion lovers. It wants them to be part of the ASOS world talking to each other, sharing and providing ideas. It invests heavily in mobile and digital innovation to ensure people can access this information

and these conversations, but also to ensure that what you receive is personalised and therefore relevant to you. It buys fashion from all over the world to ensure its customers can stay right up to date with what is happening. It is speeding up its supply chain to ensure customers receive what they want quickly.

According to ASOS, the next challenge it faces is sorting out payment methods. For example, not every customer in every country likes using (or indeed has) credit cards – the security and processing systems vary and these need to be accounted for. Also, the websites need to be available in different languages. The company also needs to have more distribution centres around the world to speed up delivery globally.

ASOS is also working on improving quality – it hopes soon to have quality checked 100 per cent of its own label products rather than a sample. It is also aiming to check these as soon as they are made rather than when they arrive at the ASOS warehouse, as this means it can take action on sub-standard products faster.

Questions

1. What do you think is the value to ASOS of having a clear statement of its mission?
2. Outline the future challenges ASOS believes it faces.

Figure 14.8 The ASOS website

Business in focus: Flight arrivals

In the airport industry every single second counts. Managing the process of inward and outward flights is a hugely complex process in which timings are clearly critical. When a plane is coming in to land the ground staff need to be ready. If the plane is later than expected, then expensive resources are sitting idle. So estimating land time precisely is important in terms of efficiency. Typically, airports have relied on pilots' own estimates of their estimated times of arrival (ETA). A study then showed that at least 10 per cent of flights actually arrived 10 minutes earlier or later than expected. Thirty per cent were up to five minutes later or earlier than expected. A new system was therefore introduced taking

the pilot's estimate plus a whole range of other factors into account, including the weather, data from radar stations, flight schedules and progress of other planes in the air and what happened on previous occasions when planes landed under similar conditions. The result of using this new system was that the airport essentially eliminated the difference between the estimated time of arrival and the actual arrival time.

Questions

1. What are the benefits of knowing exactly when a plane is going to land?
2. How else might big data benefit an airline?

The challenges of digital technology

Although digital technology does bring with it many opportunities, it also creates challenges. These include the following:

● **Leadership**. Just because digital technology exists does not automatically mean that businesses will become more competitive. In fact, it may well be a threat to some organisations. Morrisons, the retailer, was slow to go online, for example, and lost market share as a result. The successful businesses will be those where the managers see the opportunities digital can provide and have the necessary leadership skills to guide the business so it can capitalise on them. This may involve significant change and investment; for example, when moving

more of a business online, leadership will be needed to provide the vision and to push forward the implementation. At the BBC, for example, the management have had to push the business to think more digitally so that, for instance, news content is shared and available anywhere any time on any device. There is also a danger with digital technology that investment happens but does not bring the required results because it is not thought through or used effectively; leadership may be needed to ensure 'going digital' provides a competitive advantage. For example, simply gathering more data about customers does not in itself ensure better decisions are made; the right questions have to be asked and the data has to be interrogated and interpreted correctly.

● **Culture change**. Digital technology enables decisions to be based on data. This means managers can ask key questions such as 'what do we know?' rather than 'what do we think?' For some, this is a culture change because they have been used to acting on instinct. In many organisations managers still tend to pretend to use data or try to find data that supports what they want to do anyway. Technology should enable them to make logical decisions but they have to be prepared to approach decision making in this way. Actually analysing data may well challenge some assumptions and some established ways of doing things. This may not always be popular!

- **The rate of change**. The importance of anticipating and reacting to the rapid change of digital is rising dramatically. That means managers need to monitor trends, engaging in regular planning exercises to predict future trends, and be sure they can respond rapidly when competitive conditions shift. For example, few of the traditional mobile phone manufacturers protected themselves against Apple's disruption via the iPhone. What will be the next big challenge?

Business in focus: Connected devices

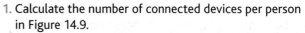

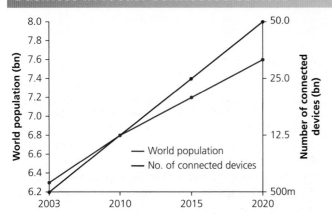

Figure 14.9 World population and number of connected devices

Source: PWC, 17th Annual CEO Survey

Questions
1. Calculate the number of connected devices per person in Figure 14.9.
2. Consider the significance of the data in Figure 14.9.

The pressures to adopt digital technology

The pressures to adopt digital technology include the following:

- **The need to keep up with the market**. If customers are researching online, for example, and don't find a particular business when they search, then that business will miss out on sales. If customers are expecting an online presence and a company don't have one, it can expect to be overlooked. E-commerce provides part of a multi-platform strategy; without it a business may be fighting with one hand tied behind its back.
- **The need to keep pace with competitors' decision making and strategy**. If competitors are gathering and using data more wisely to make their strategic decisions, then they are likely to be more efficient and effective, and a less effective business may struggle to compete.

- **The need to keep costs down**. By operating online rather than on the high street, for example, costs can be reduced. This can be a very strong driver for small businesses entering a market.

The threats of digital technology for businesses

According to McKinsey, the management consultants, there are a number of pressures on businesses as a result of digital technology.

Downward pressure on prices and on profit margins

As we know, digital technology is making it easier for potential buyers to compare prices, levels of service and the performance of different products. Customers can find alternatives and switch accounts more easily, increasing rivalry in the market. The level of competition is further increased by new businesses bringing together information to make it even easier for consumers to compare offerings and prices of different businesses. In South Korea, for example, OK Cashbag has a mobile app that brings together product promotions and loyalty points from more than 50,000 retailers. In the UK, there are websites such as GoCompare and Expedia. These forces push both prices and profit margins downwards. In the energy industry there has been a slowness by customers to shop around for the best prices, which has allowed the energy companies to earn what some regard as unusually high profits; online sites should reduce the perceived difficulty of finding the best deal, reducing what are known as switching costs' and putting more pressure on providers to be competitive.

New unexpected competitors

Digital technology removes many of the old barriers to entry to a market and enables new competitors to come from unexpected places. Setting up an insurance company or bank now no longer requires physical distribution networks. New competitors can often be smaller companies that can do a lot of damage to established firms. In the retailing industry, for instance, new businesses can focus on niche markets, attacking the edges of the more mainstream retailers.

Competition is made easier by the fact that it is becoming increasingly easy to buy and integrate aspects of an online business from other providers. Amazon, for instance, offers businesses logistics, online retail 'storefronts' and IT services. This enables other businesses to start up easily and be functioning quickly with relatively little investment, making use of the services Amazon provides. New businesses can tap into different portals and add other services to create their own business.

Keeping up with change

Change is increasingly rapid and is changing the shape of industries. Major players can quickly find themselves offering the wrong product. Look at the music industry, where the business model has shifted from selling tapes and CDs (and then MP3s) to subscription models, like Spotify. In transport markets digital technology (including a combination of mobile apps, sensors in cars and data in the cloud) has created a business model for companies such as Zipcar, where people pay to use cars when they need them rather than owning them. Driverless vehicles are increasingly being tested in cities around the world, again moving the transport industry forward and bringing in new competitors. We may buy Google cars not Ford cars in the future. This affects not just the producers but related industries – what happens to car insurance companies if we end up in driverless cars that don't crash?

Study tip

Whilst digital technology can create many opportunities for a business, it can also bring threats. Be careful to assess whether the business is leading and engaging with change, whether it is reacting to it or whether it is getting left behind.

Business in focus: Netflix's long-term view

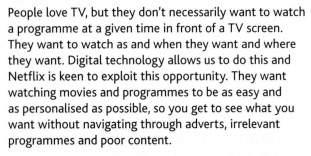

People love TV, but they don't necessarily want to watch a programme at a given time in front of a TV screen. They want to watch as and when they want and where they want. Digital technology allows us to do this and Netflix is keen to exploit this opportunity. They want watching movies and programmes to be as easy and as personalised as possible, so you get to see what you want without navigating through adverts, irrelevant programmes and poor content.

To ensure it remains competitive, Netflix is spending over $3 billion on content and is developing its systems so that customers are offered something that matches their viewing profile, whether that be blockbusters, children's cartoons or Brazilian soaps, immediately. The company is also investing in developing its own content,

that is it is producing its own shows, and, because of the way people watch, they can choose to watch the whole series in one go.

The challenges facing the company are other businesses that are competing for viewers' time – there are, after all, many other things you could do instead of watch Netflix – and competitors for content, so other programme makers you might watch instead of Netflix.

Questions

1. How is digital technology changing the entertainment industry?
2. What do you think determines the ability of a business like Netflix to compete effectively?

The impact of digital technology on the functional areas of the business

As with any major change in a business, adopting digital technology will have an impact on the functional areas. The precise effect will depend on the change being made but could include the following:

- **Human resources**. There may be changes to the skills required as greater information technology skills are needed. In particular, in a world of more data, the ability to analyse and ask the right questions of the data are increasingly important. The nature of jobs may change, focusing more on using data (rather than intuition) and it may be that some jobs are affected more than others, for example in traditional print advertising or publishing.
- **Marketing**. Digital technology enables far more data on customers to be gathered and to be linked to them as individuals. This can lead to far more personalised and efficient marketing. There should be 'less noise' for customers (so fewer irrelevant messages) and a closer fit between what the business offers and what is wanted.
- **Finances**. This will depend on what aspect of digital is being considered. Going online, for example, may lead to cheaper transaction costs than having a retail outlet, but a distribution network will need to be established which can be expensive.
- **Operations**. The impact will again depend on which aspect of digital technology is being considered. ERP, for example, will provide more data on different aspects of the business and should enable greater efficiency, better cash flow and less wastage. The use of big data should enable operations to be more flexible to demand and, therefore, reduce time lost and inventory being wasted.

Business in focus: Kickstarter

Digital technology affects all aspects of business. For example, it has enabled businesses to raise finance by appealing directly to investors online. This is called crowdfunding. One crowdfunding site is called Kickstarter. Kickstarter enables creators of films, games, music, art and technology to raise finance. Since it was launched in 2009, 8.3 million people have invested more than $1.6 billion, funding 82,000 creative projects. The creators of the project set a target for funding and a deadline by which the money needs to be raised. The site adopts an 'all or nothing' approach to funding. Either all the money needed is raised or, if the target is not met, then none of the money is invested. So far 44 per cent of projects have reached their funding targets.

Questions

1. What do you think are the advantages of crowdfunding?
2. What are the benefits of an 'all or nothing' approach to funding?

Weblink

To find out more about Kickstarter, visit:
www.kickstarter.com

ASSESSMENT ACTIVITIES

(a) Knowledge check questions

1 What is meant by data mining?

2 What is B2B e-commerce?

3 What is B2C e-commerce?

4 What is meant by 'big data'?

5 Which of the following do the initials ERP stand for?

 (a) Enterprise reality planning

 (b) Enterprise resource peripherals

 (c) Enterprise resource planning

 (d) Employment register permit

6 Explain how digital technology provides an opportunity for business.

7 Explain one reason why digital technology may be a threat to a business.

8 Explain one reason why digital technology might lead to better decision making.

9 Explain one way digital technology might affect the marketing function of a business.

10 Explain one way digital technology might affect the human resources function of a business.

(b) Short answer questions

1 Explain one benefit to a retailer of investing more in e-commerce.   (5 marks)

2 Explain one disadvantage to a retailer of the growth of e-commerce.   (5 marks)

3 Explain one way data mining might benefit an airline.   (5 marks)

4 Explain one way that ERP might benefit a car manufacturer.   (5 marks)

5 Explain one way that digital technology is changing the TV industry.   (5 marks)

(c) Data response question

Alibaba

Alibaba is a giant online Chinese business. It has an 80 per cent share of the Chinese online commerce market. The company's first business was alibaba.com set up by the company's founder Jack Ma in 1999. It started with 18 people and is now a worldwide company employing 22,000. It accounts for 80 per cent of all online retail sales in China.

The company has many different activities:

● www.alibaba.com – a website that helps to connect exporters in China (and other countries) with companies in over 190 countries around the world. The site allows a business in the UK to find a manufacturer in China and order items to be produced and shipped.

● www.taobao.com – China's largest shopping website.

● www.tmall.com – another website that offers a wide selection of branded goods to China's emerging middle class.

● www.aliplay.com – an online payment system like Paypal.

● A large stake in Sina Weibo, China's version of Twitter.

● The online video provider, Youku Tudou, which operates like YouTube.

● An online marketing, cloud computing and logistics operation.

Being so big in the Chinese market is no mean achievement. China now has over 600 million internet users, out of a population of 1.3 billion people. That compares with 277 million internet users in the US and 546 million in Europe. China accounts for $3.43 billion of Alibaba's sales.

In 2015, Alibaba was floated and sold $25 billion of its shares. The flotation valued the company at £223 billion. One of the appeals of the company to investors is not just its scale but the profit margins it achieves of over 50 per cent. Its revenue is mainly through selling advertising space rather than taking commission on sales. The company has 279 million active buyers and 8.5 million active sellers use Alibaba's online services every year. With over 14.5 billion orders annually, its appeal to advertisers is clear.

The flotation is seen as the first step towards attacking western markets. Companies such as Facebook, Amazon and eBay should beware.

Most recently, Alibaba bought a stake in Snapchat, investing approximately $200 million (£133 million) in the messaging application. That values the four-year-old firm at nearly $15 billion (£10 billion), making it one of the world's most valuable start-ups. Snapchat allows users to send text and picture messages which disappear in ten seconds. The $15 billion valuation puts the business in a league with taxi service Uber and Xiaomi, the Chinese smartphone maker. Snapchat says its users send 700 million snaps daily and the company recently started generating revenue from advertising.

Other developments include a move into the banking sector.

However, there are some problems facing Alibab. For example, the company is criticised by China's State Administration for Industry and Commerce (SAIC) for not doing enough to prevent the sale of goods that infringe trademarks.

Questions

1 Explain one possible problem Alibaba might have faced when growing. (6 marks)

2 Analyse what determines competitiveness in the markets in which Alibaba operates. (9 marks)

3 To what extent does Alibaba pose a threat to the established firms in the West, such as Facebook, Amazon and eBay? (15 marks)

(d) Essays

1 To what extent is digital technology inevitably an opportunity for a start-up business? Justify your answer. (25 marks)

2 To what extent is adopting digital technology essential to be competitive in the retail sector? Justify your answer. (25 marks)

Case study: Unit 9 Strategic methods

How to pursue strategies: Amazon

Since it was founded in 1994, Amazon, the online retailer, has pursued growth relentlessly. It has gone from originally offering books to now offering a huge range of different products. It has also developed the Kindle, Kindle Fire and its own smartphone, as well as expanding into cloud computing, e-books, video streaming and music downloads. Throughout all of its activities Amazon has gathered data on its customers to try and understand everything it can about their tastes and shopping habits. Amazon has incredible computing power to gather and analyse data. It also has one of the world's most impressive physical distribution systems.

Amazon's aim from the beginning has been to gain market share. It believes that if it achieves scale in its chosen markets, profits will follow in the long term. In achieving growth the company has been extremely innovative. At one time customers were worried about paying for items online until Amazon managed to reassure us that it was safe to do so. Amazon also helped develop the role of customer reviews in influencing customer purchases. From the start it asked buyers to rate and review books. Nowadays almost everything is rated by customers.

Amazon has managed to disrupt several industries it has entered. For example, it revolutionised the way books are bought and sold. Then it dramatically changed publishing with the launch of the Kindle in 2007. There were other e-readers at that time but these were not reliable or user-friendly. By comparison, the Kindle was easy to use, worked well and allowed instant delivery to the device rather than via a PC.

Amazon also pioneered a new business approach to cloud computing. In 2006 it began renting out computer capacity by the hour. The option to rent rather than buy computing power greatly reduced the cost and complexity of launching a new company. Amazon's cloud services have been used by start-ups including Netflix, Instagram, Pinterest, Spotify and Airbnb.

Amazon's approach has been focused on the long term throughout. Whilst shareholders are usually obsessed with short-term dividends, with Amazon they get long-term growth of the business. Amazon is happy to operate with low profit margins and pursue scale. Given a choice between making a profit and investing in new areas, it will always choose the latter. Unlike other technology companies, Amazon does not sit on huge amounts of cash because it has many ideas on how to use it instead. Perhaps surprisingly investors seem to like this as its share price is extremely high. It rewards its staff mainly with shares rather than high salaries to keep them focused on moving the share price upwards.

However, Amazon has been criticised for some aspects of its behaviour. It is accused by some of:
- not paying enough tax because it uses legal tax avoidance techniques to declare its profits in low tax countries
- being a tough employer
- competing very aggressively against its rivals
- damaging small business, such as local bookshops.

There is also a concern that Amazon is becoming so powerful that it may abuse its market power; when rivals leave the market, for example, will Amazon start to increase its prices?

Questions

1 Analyse the factors Amazon might consider before deciding which markets to move into next. (10 marks)

2 Analyse the benefits to Amazon of being innovative. (10 marks)

3 To what extent do you think Amazon should keep targeting new markets? (16 marks)

4 To what extent do you think Amazon should worry about criticisms of its behaviour? (20 marks)

5 To what extent is pursuing growth always a good strategy for a business? (24 marks)

Unit 10

Managing strategic change

Chapter 15

Managing change

Introduction

Businesses operate in an ever changing environment. Change can come from outside the business or from within. The ability to anticipate, prepare for and respond to change is essential for a business to remain competitive. In this chapter we consider the causes of change. We also consider why there might be resistance to change within a business and how managers might seek to overcome this. We also analyse how managers might seek to build a flexible organisation to enable a business to cope with the threats and exploit the opportunities of change.

What you need to know by the end of this chapter:

- the causes of, and pressures for, change
- the different types of change including internal change, external change, incremental change and disruptive change
- that managing change includes Lewin's force field analysis
- the value of change
- how to analyse the value of a flexible organisation
- that flexible organisations include: restructuring, delayering, flexible employment contracts, organic vs mechanistic structures and knowledge and information management
- how to analyse the value of managing information and knowledge
- how to analyse and evaluate the barriers to change
- how to use Kotter and Schlesinger's four reasons for resistance to change
- how to overcome barriers to change including Kotter and Schlesinger's six ways of overcoming resistance to change.

Managing strategic change

Sign up to any news feed and you will see how much is changing in the business environment. Some changes are:

- **external** – they happen outside of the business. For example, in recent years a political dispute between Europe and the US and Russia over the Ukraine has led to sanctions on trade with Russia. Meanwhile, the EU and the US have been in discussion recently to allow freer trade between these two huge trading areas. These changes are out of the control of any individual business but, nevertheless, are very significant for any organisation trying to trade in these areas.
- **internal** – this is obviously change that happens within the business. For example, over time staff may have ideas to change the way things are done.

Change may be:

- rapid and unexpected, such as sudden bad weather conditions disrupting supplies. This can be a big issue in industries such as coffee and agricultural products.
- long term, such as the shift in economic power towards economies in India and China or ageing populations in the UK and Japan. These are shifts that are predictable in terms of how they are developing and, therefore, managers have more time to prepare but they are nonetheless very significant.
- incremental – this means step-by-step change. Most businesses will gradually improve their processes over time. Staff or customers will have suggestions of small changes that over time can build and move the business forward quite significantly.
- disruptive – this refers to 'game changing' developments in an industry. Think of Dyson launching a bagless vacuum cleaner or the Dyson Airblade hand-dryer, the impact of digital cameras on traditional camera makers, the impact of email on the postal service, the effect of smartphones and GPS on the sales of maps and street atlases and navigation-product makers like TomTom, Garmin and Magellan. More recently, think of how Amazon has challenged the book retailing industry, how Tesla, the electric car producer, is

challenging our understanding of what a car might be and do, how Uber has completely changed the taxi industry, how Airbnb is threatening hotels, how Dropbox has changed the way we save and share files, how Spotify has changed the way we access music and how Skype has changed the way we communicate – new businesses, new technologies and new ways of meeting customer needs are creating changes that are so significant they are disrupting whole industries. These changes are dramatic for the industries involved and, if a business is on the wrong side of them, can prove to be quite overwhelming.

Business in focus: Changing industries

Uber

Uber has completely changed the taxi industry, even though it itself is not a taxi business. It owns no taxis and has no taxi drivers as employees, and yet is an increasingly large provider of taxi services. The company matches what the customer wants in terms of a taxi ride to a driver and car and then takes 20 per cent of the fare for organising this. Customers use the Uber app to call a taxi; they can see from the app the nearest one and find information on the car, the driver and the ratings this driver has received from previous passengers. The value of Uber to the customer is the convenience of finding a car of their choice easily and the fact that Uber screens the taxis and drivers to ensure safety and comfort.

Figure 15.1 Uber app – the new way to hail a taxi

Tesla

Tesla is an automobile company that produces electric cars. They have brought massive innovation to car design and look like making low-emission electric cars mainstream purchases. Not only that, but Tesla keeps innovating and changing our view of what a 'car' actually is. All Tesla cars are now equipped with the ability to drive themselves! It looks like the autopilot feature in cars will go from something drivers use to take an occasional break, to something drivers use frequently. And then, seemingly overnight, the car's software, rather than its owner, will become the driver! Tesla cars can communicate with other cars, calculate appropriate speeds for the road conditions and choose the optimal route at any given moment given traffic conditions. All of these developments rely on software, whereas innovations in cars in the past traditionally came from developing more aspects of the physical product. This means the software developers become the key to car design and this could seriously threaten existing car manufacturers whose experience in this area is limited. Tesla thinks more like Apple than like General Motors.

Questions

1. What do you think the effect of Uber and Tesla will be on more established companies in these industries?
2. Can you think of any other disruptive businesses?

Future disruptive change is expected. For example:

- The development of new applications that collect, report and respond to information from our own bodies. Apps will track our health and flag when and what action is needed, thereby affecting the health care industry. Already we are beginning to wear more technology, for example Apple Watches, and this technology will learn more about what we do, what exercise we do and our physical condition. This will be able to report back to us or others on our health. Not surprisingly, Google is looking carefully at health care businesses.

- 3D or additive manufacturing is the process of making three-dimensional solid objects from a digital file of data. In an additive process, an object is created by laying down successive layers of material until the entire object is produced. With traditional production you need to set up the production equipment and tools to produce a particular design. Having to set up these tools, which is an expensive process, a business has to produce on a relatively large scale to spread the costs. This 'tooling up' is not needed in an additive process where the 'printer' simply prints (manufactures) what is designed. This will speed up product development time and provide much greater flexibility. With 3D printing, businesses can make one-off personalised products. The lower set-up costs of 3D printing also makes it easier for there to be new entrants to the industry, which could transform the competitive structure. In fact, you may even be producing some products and some replacement parts for your equipment at home. If designs become readily available and are shared and printing costs continue to fall rapidly, our homes could become mini factories.

- The Internet of Things – this is technology in which everyday items became fitted with the ability to collect, send, and receive information. The idea behind this is to connect any device to the internet and to each other. This includes everything from mobile phones, coffee makers, fridges and washing machines. This also applies to components of machines, for example a jet engine of an aeroplane or the drill of an oil rig. The analyst firm Gartner says that by 2020 there will be over 26 billion connected devices. In this increasingly connected world wherever you go, whatever you do, you may be connected! Your printer will know it is running out of ink and will reorder for you, your car might know it is due a service, your heating system knows to change the temperature, billboards will change their adverts as you drive past and your TV will recommend what you should be watching and find an appropriate film for you. Imagine you are on your way to a meeting and your car realises that due to traffic conditions ahead you will be late and sends a message to the person you are meeting, whilst simultaneously changing the route you are taking to try and avoid some of the delay. Imagine you set the alarm for 7 a.m. which automatically sets the heating to come on at 6 a.m., the kettle to switch on at 6.55 a.m. and, when you make the tea and use up all the milk, the fridge reorders milk from the shop for you.

Business in focus: Twitter

To see how disruptive technologies can emerge using existing technology, look at Twitter. Twitter began its life in 2007 having been developed at a hackathon the year before. Its developers wanted to test sending standard text messages to multiple users simultaneously; this required an experiment that needed almost no new technology. The company now boasts well over 200 million active users and more than half a billion tweets a day. Twitter has changed the way we communicate in a remarkably short space of time.

To see how disruption often comes from somewhere unexpected, think about map making. For years map making was a mature industry dominated by a few companies and the not-for-profit automobile clubs. Competition started with free internet sites for route directions, such as MapQuest and Yahoo Maps. Then came standalone and dashboard devices such as Garmin and TomTom that use GPS satellite data to generate real-time routes and turn-by-turn spoken directions. The big disruption, however, came from the smartphone and, yet, this was never intended to compete with traditional navigation aids. The Google Maps app, for example, offers virtually all the features of high-end GPS devices and it costs nothing – it's just another add-on for the free Android operating system. Garmin lost 70 per cent of its market value in the two years after navigation apps were introduced; TomTom lost nearly 85 per cent.

Questions

1. Do you think Twitter will continue to grow?
2. What could producers such as Garmin and TomTom do in response to the changes in their industries?

Lewin's force field analysis

Managers should be constantly monitoring the changes that are relevant to their industry, as well as facing internal pressures for change such as employees wanting to implement new plans. However, managers are often too busy with their 'day job' to appreciate exactly what is happening and just because there are pressures to do something differently does not mean this will automatically happen. Often ideas and plans have been talked about for months or even years without anything actually changing. Just think how long the discussion over where to put a new runway in the UK has been going on. This is because whilst some forces may be pushing for change, other forces will be pushing back to keep things as they are. At any moment a business is likely to be in a position of equilibrium – staying as it is.

This is illustrated in Lewin's force field analysis model.

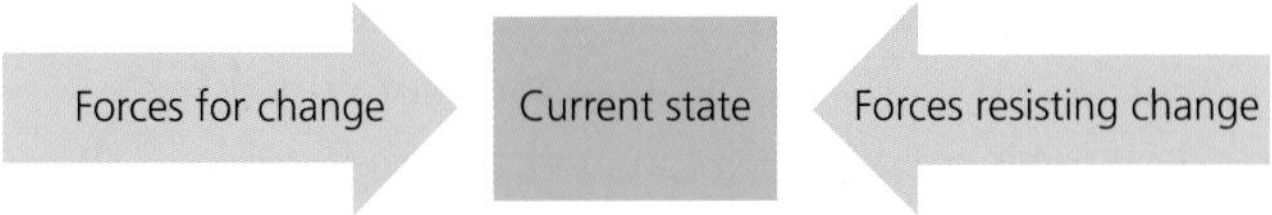

Figure 15.2 Lewin's force field analysis model of change

In Figure 15.2 the forces pushing for change might include:

- the need to keep up with the competition
- an increasing number of customer complaints
- new owners wanting higher returns
- a poor performance.

The forces resisting change might include:

- a lack of finance for investment
- a reluctance on behalf of existing staff to change the way they do things
- resistance from certain stakeholders groups that might be worse off following the change.

For change to actually occur, the balance of these forces must alter:

- The drivers for change may get stronger. For example, if the business falls ever further behind its rivals, this clearly makes the need for change stronger.
- The forces resisting change may be reduced. For example, employees may begin to see the need to change more clearly and, therefore, become more open to the idea, or the financial position of the business might improve providing the money needed to invest in changing its approach.

The pressures for change may be:

- **internal** – for example, managers or other employees may be eager for things to be done differently. They may have experienced new ways of doing things in other organisations or have been involved with different products in other organisations and feel it is essential to match this. Alternatively, they may simply be anticipating change in the outside world and want to get the business ready for this.
- **external** – this occurs with change in the external environment – for example, political, economic,

social, technological changes as well as changes in factors in the competitive environment. External changes such as changes in the value of currencies, the price of oil, the cost of borrowing money, market conditions, new businesses starting up and new laws are hugely significant to business and create new opportunities and threats.

When a business changes its strategy this means there has been a shift in the balance of the drivers for change and the forces resisting it. In some cases, managers will want to lead this strategic change by changing the different forces.

Study tip

If change is occurring in a business, stand back and try to identify why this is happening. Is it because there is now more pressure for change or that the resistance to change has been reduced? It is important to understand why change is happening to be able to analyse whether it is needed, what would happen if it did not occur, what the definition of success might be and the likely issues involved in making it successful.

The value of change

Change can be scary and frightening. If a business is not keeping up with the changes that are occurring elsewhere, if other organisations seem to be pushing forward and leading the change and a business is simply feeling the effect of these changes, then change can rightly be seen as threatening.

However, this is not the case for all change and for all individuals or all organisations. For example:

- Some change can bring positive benefits – think of an economic recovery or higher levels of customer confidence leading to more spending.
- Some change may be foreseeable and, therefore, managers can prepare for it – it is clear that the population is ageing in the UK, for example, and this creates opportunities for businesses that build retirement homes if they act appropriately.
- Some businesses may lead the change. Companies such as Uber, Snapchat and Dyson deliberately try to change the types of products we use and the way we work – change for them creates new possibilities and is not something to fear but is there to be embraced.

Change, whether it is internal or external, is going to happen and so managers need to look ahead, anticipate and be ready to lead it or react to it. It may bring threats, but it also brings many opportunities if organisations have the necessary resources and competencies and the right strategies in place. The very successful businesses around us are the ones that have exploited the opportunities that change brings; the ones that have performed badly have failed to manage change well. Kodak and Nokia failed because they missed the changes in their markets. Whitbread succeeded by realising that beer may not be an attractive market long term and so moved into Costa Coffee and Premier Inns, building on its strengths in the service industry.

Of course, reactions to change will vary within an organisation. At any moment some divisions or regions may be doing well and benefiting from changes in their environment, whilst others may be suffering.

Study tip

Do remember that change can be positive. In any change situation some people may welcome it because they might benefit. When considering resistance, therefore, think carefully about who is likely to resist and the impacts (good and bad) on a wide range of stakeholders.

What do you think?

Does change always present potential opportunities for businesses?

The value of a flexible organisation

The ability to prepare for or respond to change depends on the flexibility of the organisation. Managers seek to build a business that is agile, that is one that can adapt and reshape to internal and external change as opposed to one that is sluggish. However big the organisation, it needs to be able to adapt when change is needed. Rosemary Moss Kanter wrote a book called *Teaching Elephants to Dance* that highlighted the importance of big businesses trying to be nimble.

To be flexible a business may need to restructure, delayer, use flexible employment contracts, develop an organic rather than a mechanistic structure and emphasise knowledge and information management.

Restructuring

It may be that an organisation is initially organised on functional areas, such as marketing, operations and finance. However, as the organisation expands internationally, it may be more logical and appropriate to reorganise and base the structure on different geographical regions. By doing this, the regional managers can focus on and respond more quickly to local changes, making the business more flexible to these demands. It may be that a business does not want a traditional structure anyway as it finds this too limiting.

Delayering

If layers of hierarchy do exist, it may be that a business needs to remove levels of hierarchy if costs need to be cut and if it needs to reduce the distance from the top to the bottom of the organisation. Harriet Green did this when she took over Thomas Cook in 2012 as she felt the communication between customers and senior managers had to go through too many levels of hierarchy. This has cut management costs but, importantly, may lead to faster decision making and more decision making by those who are closer to their customers.

Using flexible employment contracts

Flexibility can be helped by having broadly defined employment contracts rather than defining very precisely what an employee has to do. This enables the business to move employees around as and when they are needed; they can be switched from one task to another or moved from one location to another as demand patterns change or as the requirements of the business alter. By comparison, if contracts are very tightly defined, then it may be difficult for managers to adjust to different situations as employees can argue that 'it is not my job'. Flexible employment structures also include the use of temporary employees and contract or agency workers. This enables a business to increase or decrease its labour force as and when needed. There has been much debate in recent years about zero hours contracts, for example; these are contracts in which someone is employed by a business but is not guaranteed any work. When the business needs the employee it asks them to work, when it does not need them it doesn't allocate the employee any hours or any pay. These contracts have been greatly criticised in that they provide no security for the employee; however, from a business perspective they provide great flexibility and make wage costs variable costs rather than fixed.

Developing an organic structure rather than a mechanistic structure

A mechanistic structure is one that is very formal. There are clear rules and procedures, there are many levels of hierarchy, there is close control over employees and the result is that the business performs in a known, predictable manner and delivers known, consistent outputs. This may be desirable in some situations – for example, you may want all insurance claims to be processed in the same logical, fair and objective manner.

Organic structures tend to have more fluid teams that are created for specific projects and then end with new teams being set up for new challenges. There is no fixed set of reporting relationships – these change according to who is needed for what and according to what particular projects are being undertaken. Organic structures tend to involve people based on their ability to contribute to a task rather than based on their job title and level of seniority.

The writer Gary Hamel argues that employees should be more self-managing, creating their own teams when they need them, bringing together the expertise required as and when but not working within a formal structure which is too traditional and limits creativity. Concepts such as span and hierarchy are totally out of date in the knowledge, creative-type businesses that are so successful – 'structure, if there is such a thing, needs to be far more fluid'.

Study tip

Remember that the right structure depends on a range of factors – for example, whether or not you want the outcomes to be predictable. If so, then you want tight control and quite a mechanical structure. If you want more innovation and can live with uncertainty, then an organic structure may be required.

Business in focus: Valve

Valve is a computer games developer. It has a very interesting approach to managing people – essentially it expects employees to manage themselves. Employees are expected to follow through their ideas by talking with colleagues, working out what is needed and then trying it. Valve is not a world of hierarchy. In its staff handbook it says 'Welcome to Flatland'!

The company says that, whilst hierarchy is good for predictability and control, in Valve's world which is full of intelligent, innovative, creative people and where ideas are needed and valued, hierarchy does not work. Valve is 'flat' which means there is no hierarchy and nobody reports to anyone else. As it says: 'You have the power to green light projects. You have the power to ship products.'

Questions

1. Why do you think Valve has this approach to organisational design?
2. Do you think Valve's approach would work for every organisation?

Emphasising knowledge and information management

The ability to be flexible depends largely on managers knowing what is happening and what needs to be done and on all employees knowing what the strategy is and what their role in the plan is meant to be. This involves gathering data effectively and ensuring that the relevant information is available in the right format, at the right time, for the right people. Within any organisation there is a huge amount of knowledge about customers, suppliers, systems, processes, what works well, what does not work and who can or can't do what. Gathering this knowledge and making sure it can be tapped into and shared, especially across a large organisation, is a significant challenge. An organisation's ability to manage data effectively will influence its ability to understand what it needs to be doing in a changing environment and to help employees to do things successfully.

The value of managing information and knowledge

Information is a key resource these days. Developments in technology have made much more data available to businesses. Through online sales, data from tills, data from loyalty cards as well as access to hundreds of other databases about issues such as the economy, companies and population patterns, businesses can pull together vast amounts of data. By managing data effectively managers can:

- identify changes before or as they happen
- develop suitable strategies to respond to or prepare for change
- evaluate the effectiveness of the strategies adopted.

If a business does not manage information effectively, it will be making decisions in the dark whilst everything around it is changing rapidly – a dangerous approach! Managers need to capture the information that exists and find ways of sharing knowledge between employees. This often involves investing in information systems and systems to store and access knowledge databases.

Business in focus: McKinsey

A challenge facing many businesses is how to gather, store and share information between employees who may be in completely different divisions and even parts of the world. This is extremely important in many organisations. Think of the world of management consultancy, for example, where employees may have worked on similar projects before and, therefore, their expertise would be incredibly valuable.

At the management consultancy McKinsey, for example, the company has developed The McKinsey Knowledge Network. This includes nearly 200 staff who work alongside consultants to gain insights into key management issues. These members of staff help to develop, codify, sanitise and manage McKinsey's global knowledge portal, which includes more than 50,000 documents and is at the heart of the company's knowledge management system which forms the firm's backbone. The access to knowledge is a key competitive weapon in the consultancy business.

Questions

1. What difficulties might there be in storing and sharing knowledge in a global business such as McKinsey?
2. McKinsey is a management consultancy. Why do think knowledge management is so important to McKinsey?

Resistance to change

Whilst some employees may welcome change, others will almost inevitably resist.

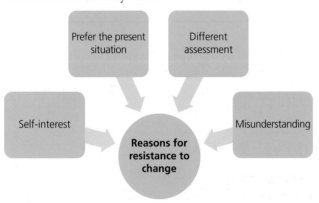

Figure 15.3 Reasons for resistance to change

According to Kotter and Schlesinger, resistance to change occurs for four main reasons:

1. **Self-interest**. People wish to protect their own self-interest. Some may resist change because they think they will be worse off. They may lack the knowledge or skills required in the new world or they may be worried they will lose their bonuses, their jobs or their status within the business.

2. **Preference for the present situation**. People prefer things the way they are. Some may not have particularly strong feelings about change except for the fact that they prefer to leave things as they are. Change may be seen as a hassle and people may prefer to stay within their comfort zone of doing things the way they have always been done. Some people don't like change simply because it means doing things in a different way.

3. **Differing assessment of the situation**. People do not agree with the change. Some may resist the change because they do not think it is the right plan. They may think they have a better idea of how the change should occur, or they may simply disagree with the strategy and think it will fail.

4. **Misunderstanding**. People may not understand why change is needed. Employees may not appreciate there is a need for change and think that everything is fine as it is.

What do you think?

Do you think all change in business will face some opposition?

Overcoming resistance to change

There are many ways in which managers may try to overcome resistance to change. According to Kotter and Schlesinger, these include the following:

1. **Education and communication**. Managers need to explain to employees why the change is occurring, why it is needed and why it will work. This can bring about effective change because, if it works, employees will understand the reason and ethics of change and can become ambassadors for it. However, it can be slow to bring about.

2. **Facilitation and support**. This is when managers ensure employees have the support they need to cope with the change. This could be the equipment they need, the training or the emotional support they require to cope with the change.

3. **Participation and involvement**. To ease change managers may involve employees so they know what is happening and when, and so they can have some input into the process. The degree of involvement may vary in terms of how much employees can actually influence decisions, but by getting participation from staff there may be more commitment to the change. The problem of this approach is that managers and employees may disagree on how much involvement is appropriate. Although participation may lead to insights into how to make the change more effective, it may also lead to delays and obstacles to the process.

4. **Manipulation and co-option**. Managers may identify the key people who are likely to resist the change and bring them into the process. For example, they could be on the relevant committees and be given roles involved in bringing about change. The aim is to win over key influencers and get them to help win over other employees.

5. **Negotiation and bargaining**. This occurs when managers do a deal with employees. For example, they get employees to agree to higher productivity in return for higher wages. Rewards can be used to benefit those who agree to go along with the change.

6. **Explicit and implicit coercion**. If managers feel they cannot persuade employees to accept the change, or where fast change is essential, managers may simply force change through. This will not in itself change the minds of employees but, if the change then proves to be successful and helps the business, they may then accept it and eventually agree with it. Coercion may take the form of threats such as redundancies or pay cuts. These threats may be explicitly made or it may just be implied that opposition would have negative consequences.

Figure 15.4 Overcoming resistance to change

How a business overcomes resistance to change depends on what the underlying reason or reasons for resistance are. For example, if employees are worried about their ability to cope, then training and information may be important. If people resist change because they fear they will be worse off or simply do not like change, then rewards for changing (if appropriate) may help. If people think they have a better plan, then participation to listen to the alternatives and find the best solution may be useful.

Study tip

Remember that the best way to overcome resistance to change depends on what caused the resistance in the first place. It also depends on how much time you have, how important it is to have agreement amongst employees and other stakeholders and the extent to which the change is resisted.

Business in focus: A new old town

In 1988, William Samuelson and Richard Zeckhauser, economists at Boston University and Harvard, wrote about a case in which the West German government needed to relocate a small town so that it could mine the minerals beneath it. The authorities suggested many options for what the new town could look like, but the citizens chose a plan that looked 'extraordinarily like the layout of the old town – a layout that had evolved over centuries without (conscious) rhyme or reason.' This shows how reluctant we are to change – even when given the option to build any town we want, we stick with the one we know!

Questions

1. Why do you think people wanted to keep their town exactly the same when they had the opportunity to design it any way they wished?

2. If the people in the town were reluctant to move, how might the government get them to change their minds?

ASSESSMENT ACTIVITIES

(a) Knowledge check questions

1 Give one example of internally driven change.

2 Give one example of a recent political change that can affect business.

3 Give one example of a recent technological change that can affect business.

4 Give one example of a social change in recent years that can affect business.

5 State one way in which the competitive environment of a business might change.

6 According to Kotter and Schlesinger, state four reasons why people resist change.

7 State four ways of overcoming resistance to change.

8 Removing levels of hierarchy in an organisation is known as _____.

9 Outline Lewin's model of force field analysis.

10 Explain one difference between an organic and mechanistic structure.

(b) Short answer questions

1 Explain why a new chief executive may face resistance to a new strategy that involves delayering. (5 marks)

2 Explain how managers of a retail chain could overcome resistance to move most of the business operations online. (5 marks)

3 Explain how the effective management of information can help the managers of a cinema business to be successful. (5 marks)

4 Explain one reason why the employees of a failing business might welcome a change of management. (5 marks)

5 Explain one way in which the managers of a large multinational business might make the business more flexible and responsive to change. (5 marks)

(c) Data response question

BP

In 2015, the multinational giant oil business BP announced that it is going to incur restructuring costs of about $1 billion in the next year or so. These charges would occur as BP tries to streamline its business operations. The company will also be reviewing its capital expenditure plans given the major fall in oil prices in 2015.

Over the last 18 months the company has sold off businesses worth more than $43 billion. Its Chief Executive said it needed to focus on its core businesses and, without diverting attention from safety and reliability, the goal was to make the business stronger and more competitive. This is seen to be essential given a tougher trading environment and, in particular, the excess supply of oil that has occurred recently. The US has become a net exporter of oil rather than an importer due to the success of fracking; at the same time, demand has been falling due to the slow growth of economies such as China and this has weakened demand. The low price makes many projects that the company had planned on undertaking unprofitable. It usually assessed projects using a price of around $80 a barrel; by the end of 2014 the price of oil was at its lowest for five years at $65 a barrel. BP has also announced that it would continue to be reducing the number of jobs at the company. BP employs almost 84,000 people worldwide, including 15,000 in the UK. The company's share price has fallen by 24 per cent in the last six months.

The restructuring charge will mainly involve redundancy costs. The group has been divesting parts of its portfolio in recent years and is a third smaller than it was four years ago. It plans a further $10 billion of asset disposals by 2016 and analysts are expecting cuts in exploration spending and possible project deferrals.

Rail and bus operator Stagecoach, meanwhile, warned of 'challenges' ahead as cheaper fuel costs tempt passengers off its buses and into their cars next year.

Questions

1   Explain why the price of oil is low.   (6 marks)

2   Analyse the effects of the changes being made by BP on its stakeholders.   (9 marks)

3   To what extent are the changes such as those BP is planning to make bound to face employee resistance?   (15 marks)

(d) Essays

1   You are the new Chief Executive of a business and want it to pursue much faster growth. Is it best for you to force through this change in strategy? Justify your answer.   (25 marks)

2   To what extent do you think resistance from employees is inevitable when a business is restructuring itself? Justify your answer. (25 marks)

Managing organisational culture

Introduction

In this chapter we consider the culture of a business. This refers to the values and attitudes of the employees within an organisation. The culture of a business can influence how employees make decisions, what risks they are prepared to take, how they treat customers and what they prioritise. Culture can be a very powerful driver of strategy and a major determinant of the success or failure of a business. In this chapter we consider what influences the culture of a business, why the culture is so important, how managers might attempt to change the culture and the problems they may facing when doing so.

What you need to know by the end of this chapter:

- the importance of organisational culture
- how to analyse culture using cultural models, including Handy's task culture, role culture, power culture and person culture and Hofstede's national cultures
- how to analyse and evaluate the influences on organisational culture
- how to analyse the reasons for, and problems of, changing organisational culture.

Organisational culture

The culture of an organisation refers to the values, attitudes and beliefs of its employees. This determines what employees prioritise, what they think is important, how they react in different situations and how they respond to change. The culture is clearly very important in terms of how people behave and how the business performs. Lou Gertsner was a highly successful chief executive of IBM. When asked about managing a business successfully he said, 'Corporate culture is not part of the game: it *is* the game.'

The culture of a business will be demonstrated in many different ways for example:

- **The stories**. In any organisation there will be stories about great employees of the present and past – these stories are very revealing and show what the organisation values. Is it customer service? Profit, regardless of how it is earned? Is it innovative behaviour or those who basically did as they were told? Think of your school – which students are featured in the school's newsletter? What type of achievements are recognised and celebrated most?
- **Rituals**. Any organisation will have certain events and certain ways of doing things. These, again, demonstrate what is important within the business. Does your school have an assembly? What does this involve and what does this tell you about the culture of the school? Are the assemblies religious? Are they mainly student led? Do they focus on current issues in the news?
- **The rewards system**. Does your school have an awards day? What is rewarded? Good behaviour? Exam performance? Sporting achievement? The awards on offer show what is valued within your school. Similarly, the types of rewards and what they are given for tell us about the culture of the business. Are sales people rewarded for sales or customer satisfaction? (These may not be the same thing as a customer may be dissatisfied in the long term if you sell them something that doesn't really solve their problem.) Is the sales team paid on individual bonuses or group bonuses? This shows whether or not the business really does value team performance.
- **The physical environment**. The decorations on the wall, the facilities and where the investment goes and the layout of the offices, again, reveal how people within the business think. Was the last investment in your school in science labs or sports facilities?

Business in focus: Culture in a US football team

In 1979, Walsh took over an American football team that had won 2 games and lost 14 the previous season. During the entire first year as coach, Walsh spent a lot of time teaching football players how to wear coats and ties on buses. His view was that if they wanted to win they had to be professional about everything they did and that included how they dressed before games, how they presented themselves to the media and how they arrived at opposing stadia. According to Walsh, it's essential to get the culture right and what you wear is an outward sign of this. Two years later, his team won the Super Bowl – the biggest US football competition there is.

In the UK, Clive Woodward took over the Lions team and focused amongst other things on what they wore, where they stayed, what they ate and how they trained. He made sure they had first-class accommodation, first-class transport and started to think of themselves as winners. Again, it was all part of getting the culture right.

Questions

1. If you play in or support a sports team, how would you describe its culture?
2. Do you think wearing smart team clothes is an important part of being a winning team?

Types of culture

There are, of course, many types of culture; every organisation's employees have their own set of values and beliefs. Areas where organisational cultures may differ include the following:

- **The focus on profit**. Is profit regarded as the key to everything? Is profit seen as the most important objective for the business – something that is more important than anything else?
- **The focus on safety**. Is safety seen as a priority? How much is the business willing to invest in safety? Does safety come before or after profit in people's minds? This can be extremely important in industries such as oil, transport and private health care.
- **Task vs people**. To what extent is getting the job done regarded as important? Is the task regarded as more important than the welfare and happiness of staff? If an employee had problems at home, would managers try to understand and work around this or is it an unfortunate distraction that is seen as getting in the way of work?

It is important to remember that there are, in fact, as many cultures as there are organisations. It may be possible to group some of them under various headings such as those above (for example, task focused or people centred), but each business has its own particular culture with its own approach to planning, rewarding, managing, innovating, dealing with customers, and so on. In addition, cultures will vary within organisations. Just as you may find that the cultures of

the science and art departments or the sixth form and lower school vary, so do cultures vary between sites, between divisions and between departments within a business. The marketing team may see themselves as different from the finance team, who see themselves as different from the legal team, for example. Whilst having short cuts such as 'a caring culture' or a 'profit-focused culture' may help us to get a sense of what happens within a business, culture is in fact much more complicated than that. To make matters worse, we cannot really know a culture unless we are part of it. We can guess or draw conclusions by listening to the stories, looking around the facilities, reading the promotional material and talking to staff, but you will only really understand a culture if you are part of it, that is an employee of the business in question.

Study tip

Remember, there is no 'right' culture. Cultures vary and need to vary given their owners, their employees, the nature of the business and the business and social environment in which they operate. However, there are strong and weak cultures, that is in some organisations the same values and beliefs are held by the majority of employees, whereas in other organisations there are considerable differences in what people believe.

What do you think?

How would you describe the culture of your school? How does this affect its performance?

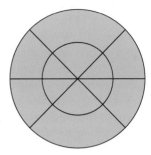
As a computer games developer, Valve encourages creativity. It believes it is important to give able people the freedom to get on with things and so allow them to be willing to try things and not worry about failing. It recognises that some of the best ideas come out of failure, so trying things is important. The company actively seeks creative risk takers.

Questions

1. Why do you think this sort of culture might be appropriate for Valve?
2. Do you think this culture is suitable for a) an insurance company, b) a hospital or c) an advertising agency?

There are many ways of categorising culture. Here we will look at Handy's models of culture and Hofsteds's national cultures in detail.

Handy's models of culture

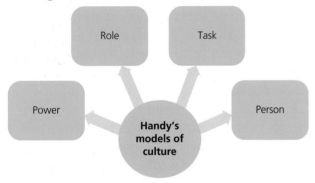

Figure 16.1 Handy's models of culture

Charles Handy is a well-known management writer. He identified four types of culture:

1. **Power culture**. This occurs when there are a few key people at the centre of the organisation. These people make all the major decisions. Other employees refer issues to the centre to get a decision made. This culture is very common in small businesses, especially where the founder is still heavily involved and wants to keep close control over all the decisions being made. The positives of this culture are that those at the centre have an overview of everything that is done and this can lead to quick decision making and a consistent approach. However, as the business expands this puts greater pressure on those at the centre. An overload on the key managers can lead to slow decision making and stress. This culture may only be effective,

therefore, in relatively small departments or organisations.

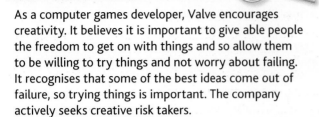

Figure 16.2 Power culture

2. **Role culture**. In this culture individuals have a clear role within the organisation. They know who they report to and who they are responsible for. They understand which part of the business they belong to and identify with a particular function or department of the business. This type of culture is commonly adopted as a business moves from being a power culture and starts to formalise processes and procedures more and adopt a functional organisational structure. It creates order, structure and certainty in a business.

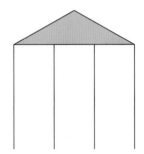

Figure 16.3 Role culture

3. **Task culture**. In this type of culture individuals identify with the task that they are working on. The importance of an individual depends on their ability to contribute to a particular project regardless of their age, seniority or length of service. This culture is common in a business where there are many projects – for example, advertising agencies, design businesses or consultancies.

Figure 16.4 Task culture

4. **Person culture**. In this culture individuals have their own space; they are given their own parts of the business to make decisions on and to control. For example, this culture can exist in hospitals where surgeons have a great deal of independence and in universities where lecturers have considerable freedom deciding what to do in relation to the modules they run. It respects the individual's expertise but means there is not necessarily consistency of approach, and the very senior managers are placing a high level of trust in others within their organisation.

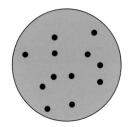

Figure 16.5 Person culture

Hofstede's national cultures

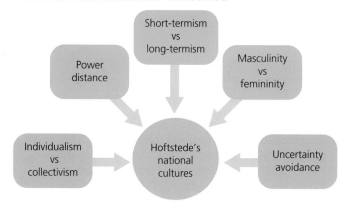

Figure 16.6 Hofstede's national cultures

Hofstede's original study was based on his research of employees of IBM to see how cultures may differ around the world within the same organisation. His studies have identified a number of areas in which cultures appeared to differ including:

- individualism vs collectivism
- power distance
- short-termism vs long-termism
- masculinity vs femininity
- uncertainty avoidance.

Individualism vs collectivism

Some societies value the individual; others value the team player. Imagine a football team with a striker who is a bit greedy but highly talented and a defender

who is less 'flash' in the way he plays but very good at passing the ball to others; which of these players is the most valued by the manager? Similarly, in business, is the individual star sales person praised and celebrated (encouraging others to push themselves forward) even if they win sales at the expense of their colleagues, or is more value placed on the sales team that works best as a whole? This will affect your behaviour at work – are you trying to help others or prove that you are better than them?

Power distance

Is the society one where there is a clear sense of rank and status? For example, in the family are the elders valued and the younger ones expected to respect them? Or is it a more fluid society where respect has to be earned according to what you actually *do* rather than *who* you are? In a business this will influence everything from how meetings are run to how decisions are made. For example, are 'juniors' expected and allowed to challenge the views of their superiors or are they expected to 'do as they are told' until they have been there enough years and have a job title that is senior enough to allow them to contribute? In Japan, for example, it is still the case that you are expected to adopt a different form of the language when talking to someone superior to you. This could be your boss or simply a student in the year above you. This reflects a society where seniority matters – for example, promotion depends on the number of years of service rather than who is 'best' at the job. This is a very hierarchical society that rewards loyalty, status, seniority and age. The positive side of this is that it avoids fighting and unproductive competition, but it will not appeal to those who want to rise quickly within an organisation.

Short termism vs long termism

Different societies seem to have different approaches to time. In some countries individuals tend to plan for only a few years ahead; in other countries people seem to plan many years ahead. This may be linked to factors in society such as the political system. For example, in the UK the government is only in power for five years at most before a re-election and, therefore, the planning horizon for any government tends to be relatively short term; there is not much incentive to plan for the long term if you will not be in power then. This might influence the way everyone thinks in the UK. In other societies such as China the government assumes it will be in power forever. This might encourage more long-term thinking throughout society. In business this will impact on investment decisions. Some managers may look three years ahead whilst others are willing to take longer term risks.

Masculinity vs femininity

This refers to the decision-making style people adopt. According to Hofstede masculine traits include focusing on the self, work, being competitive, winning and material rewards. By comparison femininity refers to an approach that is more relationship centred, consultative, caring and involving, and focused on a work–life balance. Put these different approaches together and there can be conflict. For example, those with a masculine approach may be seen by others as overly aggressive.

Uncertainty avoidance

This refers to the extent to which individuals are comfortable with uncertainty. In some societies people

Business in focus: Cultural differences

Hofstede's work analyses the cultural differences between countries and finds some significant differences. Managers should consider these when dealing with their counterparts abroad.

On a scale of 1–100, Hofstede's findings are shown in Table 16.1.

Questions

1. Analyse the possible implications for the culture of businesses in the UK shown by the data in Table 16.1.
2. Discuss the significance of the data in Table 16.1.

	China	UK	US	Japan
Power distance	80	35	40	54
Individualism vs collectivism	20	89	91	46
Masculinity vs femininity	66	66	62	95
Uncertainty avoidance	30	35	46	92

Table 16.1 Cultural differences between countries

Source: The Hofstede Centre

Business in focus: Short-term culture

Businesses in the UK have often been criticised for having a short-term culture. The major shareholders in UK listed public limited companies are usually banks and pension funds. These investors want share price increases and dividends in the short term to pay out to their own clients. This means the investors are not necessarily interested in how the business is going to perform long term; they are more focused on making sure they get quick returns. If they don't, they will sell their shares and invest elsewhere. This puts pressure on managers to focus on projects that deliver short-term returns and avoid projects that might take longer to deliver. This differs from the situation in some countries such as Germany and Japan where the shareholders tend to be other stakeholders such as suppliers and distributors; these partners are interested in the long-term success of the business and are willing to wait for longer term rewards. Another factor is that managers tend to change jobs every few years in the UK – this is seen as an important part of building your career. The consequence of moving jobs so often is that managers will be less eager to undertake long-term projects because they may not be there to see the results.

However, this is not to say that short-termism is always a problem. Between 1990 and 2013 the US economy, usually seen as a very short-term country, grew by 24 per

cent, whereas Japan, usually seen as a long-term country, stagnated.

It is possible that, if a business takes too long term a view, managers will avoid tackling the immediate issues facing them. Nokia, the Finnish mobile phone business, left Olli-Pekka Kallasvuo in place as Chief Executive for four years despite growing protests from investors; some say he should have been replaced much earlier. By the time he was replaced in 2010 the company was very seriously damaged. Arguably the pressure from investors to report every quarter ensures problems are brought into the open and is, therefore, desirable. Also, short-term pressure may ensure managers focus on the performance and avoid letting problems emerge, otherwise, if they do not, shareholders will sell bringing the share price down. The solution may be a mixture of short- and long-term views depending on the context. In relatively stable industries, for example, a long-term approach may be beneficial but in industries undergoing rapid change such as social media a more short-term approach may be required.

Questions

1. Analyse why there might be a short-term culture in the UK.
2. Do you think a short-term or long-term approach is better for business?

are used to receiving very precise instructions. It is a world of lists, plans and detail; people know exactly what they are expected to do and when. In other societies people are comfortable with broader outlines and do not need to be told or shown how to do things. They prefer to be told the destination and be free to work out how to get there themselves. Put these two groups together and there can be potential problems. Those who dislike uncertainty want specifics; those who are happy with uncertainty may find too many instructions in what to do quite restrictive.

Influences on organisational culture

There are many influences on the culture of an organisation:

- **The history of the business**. Some businesses will look back to when they first started and what worked then and what the founders thought was important. Often stories are told of the early days and what the founders believed in and valued.
- **The present leadership**. The current leaders will set an example in terms of what is valued and what is expected. Leaders will create the vision of what people within the organisation are trying to create.
- **Society in general**. What is valued and is held to be important will be influenced by what employees

want and what customers and investors expect; this, in turn, is influenced by the values of society as a whole. We can see how a greater focus on environmental issues, for example, has influenced many organisations and changed what they produce and how they produce it.

- **Experience and the performance of the business**. If a business is doing well, this will tend to reinforce the existing culture – whatever you are doing now seems to work so why change it? On the other hand, if the business is struggling, this may well be a time to question your assumptions about how to do things.
- **Ownership**. The ownership of a business will influence what employees value. If it is a government-owned organisation, for example, there may be more emphasis on social responsibility and providing a service to society more than profit. If it is a family business, then the feelings and welfare of family members may dominate. If it is a public limited company, it may mean that maintaining a high share price and dividend payout may dominate.

What do you think?

What do you think has influenced the culture of your school or college?

Business in focus: W. L. Gore

W. L. Gore is a highly innovative business that is constantly developing new products. This is due to its culture and structure.

The company was set up in 1958 and has always worked in teams and avoided layers of hierarchy. It does not have an organisational chart because it thinks this limits conversations. Instead, it encourages people to talk to whoever they need to anywhere in the business to get things done. Individuals create teams and invite others to join their projects. You may be a team leader on one project and a team member on another. Employees (who are called associates) are employed for general work areas rather than specific jobs. They then work with sponsors who guide them until they are able to start working on their own projects. The company values autonomy, initiative and creativity.

The key principles of being an associate are:

- to be fair to each other and everyone you are in contact with
- to have the freedom to help other associates develop in their knowledge and responsibilities
- to make your own commitments and keep them
- to discuss issues with other associates before doing anything that would affect the company's reputation.

Questions

1. What do you think the W. L. Gore approach to organisational structure tells you about the culture of the business? *Task culture*
2. What do you think might have been the influences on the culture at W. L. Gore? *Society.*

Business in focus: RBS and HBOS

Royal Bank of Scotland

In 2011 the Financial Services Authority (FSA) undertook a study into the behaviour of the Royal Bank of Scotland (RBS). RBS had made a number of unsound financial decisions, including the purchase of the Dutch bank ABN AMRO for which it overpaid significantly. In the end, the UK government had to bail out RBS because it was in such a dangerous financial position. The government had to take 80 per cent ownership of RBS to prevent it collapsing. The FSA report stated that:

'The directors... relied for their due diligence during the disastrous takeover (of ABN AMRO) on two ring-binder folders and a CD. ...The decision to make a bid of this scale on the basis of limited due diligence entailed a degree of risk-taking that can reasonably be criticised as a gamble.'

Source: *The Failure of the Royal Bank of Scotland*, Financial Services Authority (FSA) Board Report, *December 2011*.

Questions

1. What do you think created cultural problems within the banks?

HBOS

In 2013, the FSA undertook a study of HBOS to try to understand what had led to excessive risk taking at this bank. The report found that:

'The strategy set by the Board from the creation of the new Group sowed the seeds of its destruction. HBOS set a strategy for aggressive, asset-led growth across divisions over a sustained period. This involved accepting more risk across all divisions of the Group. ...the strategy created a new culture in the higher echelons of the bank. This culture was brash, underpinned by a belief that the growing market share was due to a special set of skills which HBOS possessed and which its competitors lacked.'

Source: House of Lords, House of Commons, *Changing banking for good*, Report of the Parliamentary Commission on Banking Standards, Vol. 1, HL Paper 27-I

2. How might you try to change the culture within the banks?

Business in focus: The Enron Corporation

Remember, just because an organisation states it has a particular type of culture does not mean it really does.

The Enron Corporation was an American energy, commodities and services company based in Texas. Before it went bankrupt on 2 December 2001, Enron employed 20,000 staff and was one of the world's biggest electricity, gas, communications and paper companies. It claimed to have revenues of nearly $111 billion, but it was shown that there had been massive fraud and false accounting. In the lobby of the company's headquarters its values were displayed:

- Integrity
- Communication
- Respect
- Excellence

In reality, employees had been guilty of falsifying accounts and pursuing ever-faster growth in return for huge bonuses.

Questions

1. Why do you think the actual culture of the organisation might differ from the stated culture?

2. Why do you think people might become involved in falsifying accounts?

Reasons for changing organisational culture

The reasons for changing culture relate directly to the influences on culture. There may be pressure for change for a variety of reasons. For example:

- If there is a new leader who has their own way of doing things and wants to do things differently from the way things have been done before.

- If society's values change, for example the attitude towards different ethical issues. Over time in the UK, there have been major changes in customers' expectations about how suppliers are treated. This has led to the growth of initiatives such as Fair Trade.

- If the performance of the business suffers, managers will consider whether the culture had affected the performance and look to see if cultural change is needed.
- If there are new owners who might have different objectives from the old ones. This is often the case with a takeover and can lead to clashes.

Business in focus: Facebook

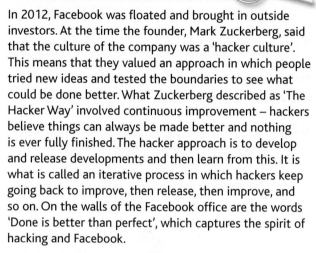

In 2012, Facebook was floated and brought in outside investors. At the time the founder, Mark Zuckerberg, said that the culture of the company was a 'hacker culture'. This means that they valued an approach in which people tried new ideas and tested the boundaries to see what could be done better. What Zuckerberg described as 'The Hacker Way' involved continuous improvement – hackers believe things can always be made better and nothing is ever fully finished. The hacker approach is to develop and release developments and then learn from this. It is what is called an iterative process in which hackers keep going back to improve, then release, then improve, and so on. On the walls of the Facebook office are the words 'Done is better than perfect', which captures the spirit of hacking and Facebook.

Hacker culture is also very meritocratic. The best idea wins regardless of who developed it. Your age, your years of service, your qualifications do not matter – your code does. To show the importance of code, all new engineers – even those who will not be writing code in their job – go to Facebook's Bootcamp to learn about its coding and approach.

Questions

1. Why do you think Facebook has had a hacker culture?
2. Do you think becoming a public limited company might change the culture of Facebook? Why?

Problems changing organisational culture

Managers may want to change the culture of their organisation but many problems can exist:

- Change may be challenging the existing assumptions of employees of how things should be done and what matters. Employees may well resist such changes believing that what they did before

was right. This is particularly true if employees appeared to do well with the old approach; change will be seen as a threat.

- What you are trying to change are people's beliefs. These can be deeply held and attempts to change them may question the way in which we view the world. Getting people to think in a different way can be a long task.
- Changing culture may involve extensive training and education. This can require heavy investment.

Changing culture will be particularly difficult if:

- there are large numbers of people involved in many different locations
- the values being questioned are very deeply held.

Study tip

Remember, you cannot just adopt a culture or change a culture. It requires a change in the way people think and in what they believe. This can take a very long time to bring about, especially if you are looking for a major realignment in people's attitudes.

Business in focus: Ford

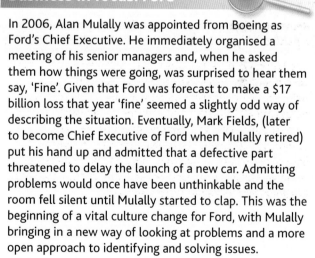

In 2006, Alan Mulally was appointed from Boeing as Ford's Chief Executive. He immediately organised a meeting of his senior managers and, when he asked them how things were going, was surprised to hear them say, 'Fine'. Given that Ford was forecast to make a $17 billion loss that year 'fine' seemed a slightly odd way of describing the situation. Eventually, Mark Fields, (later to become Chief Executive of Ford when Mulally retired) put his hand up and admitted that a defective part threatened to delay the launch of a new car. Admitting problems would once have been unthinkable and the room fell silent until Mulally started to clap. This was the beginning of a vital culture change for Ford, with Mulally bringing in a new way of looking at problems and a more open approach to identifying and solving issues.

Questions

1. Why do you think the managers at Ford failed to admit to any problems when asked?
2. How might Mulally have developed a more open culture at Ford?

Business in focus: Johnson & Johnson's Credo

The values of Johnson & Johnson are set out in what is called 'Our Credo'. This Credo (that is set of beliefs) determines the way people behave, make decisions and are appraised. The Credo sets out the groups that employees need to put first beginning with the doctors, nurses and patients who they produce their products for. The company's investors are some way down the list – the belief is that if you do the right thing for others, the profits will happen as a result.

Our Credo was written by Robert Wood Johnson, who was Chairman of the company from 1932 to 1963 and a member of the company's founding family. This was long before anyone talked about 'corporate social responsibility'. The company believes it is Our Credo that has kept the business strong.

The Johnson & Johnson Credo clearly reflects a certain culture. The company seems to think it has played an important role in its success.

Figure 16.7 Johnson & Johnson products

Questions

1. How do you think the Credo might have influenced the success of the Johnson & Johnson business?

2. Do you think Johnson & Johnson will ever change its culture?

ASSESSMENT ACTIVITIES

(a) Knowledge check questions

1 What is meant by 'organisational culture'?

2 Explain one reason why the culture of an organisation matters.

3 State Handy's four types of culture.

4 State three aspects of national culture identified by Hofstede.

5 State two influences on organisational culture.

6 Explain one reason why managers may want to change the culture of an organisation.

7 Explain one reason why changing culture may be difficult.

8 What is meant by 'short-termism'?

9 What is meant by 'individualism'?

10 State one way in which you might identify the culture of a school if you visited it.

(b) Short answer questions

1 Explain how the culture of Google might be important to its success.   (5 marks)

2 Explain why a newly appointed chief executive of a failing business may want to change its culture.   (5 marks)

3 Explain the factors that might influence the culture of Facebook.   (5 marks)

4 Explain the type of cultural differences a multinational business may find in the different locations where it operates.   (5 marks)

5 Explain why a power culture may not be appropriate to a rapidly growing business. (5 marks)

(c) Data response question

Stafford hospital

Between January 2005 and March 2009 it is estimated that 400–1,200 patients died as a result of poor care at Stafford Hospital, a small district general hospital in Staffordshire. Conditions in the hospital were appalling. Patents were neglected with some having to drink the water from flower vases because no nurses were looking after them. Life-threatening decisions were being made by unqualified staff and complaints were ignored.

The horrific neglect of patients has led to a tremendous amount of scrutiny to find out what happened and to find ways to ensure it does not happen again. The second of two public inquiries completed its report in 2013. Inevitably, there was a range of factors at the root of the problems but, undoubtedly, what developed at Stafford was a culture of patient neglect. The inquiry found the culture was one in which:

- there was a lack of openness to criticism
- there was a lack of consideration for patients
- individuals were defensive about their work and actions
- staff looked inward not outward and did not learn from what was happening outside of the hospital
- there was an acceptance of poor standards
- there was a failure to put the patient first in everything that was done.

Part of the cause was that the hospital trust was under financial pressure and made savings that were harmful to patient care. Staff were expected to follow the system put in place by the Trust, even if this did not serve patients well, and the culture was not one in which people spoke up. Good news was rewarded and bad news ignored. There were no effective systems in place to deal with complaints. There was also a failure to appreciate the damage that was done to 'corporate memory' when staff left – they took with them an understanding of how things were done which was difficult to replace quickly.

Questions

1 Explain how the culture at Stafford Hospital affected patient care.   (6 marks)

2 Analyse the possible reasons why the culture that developed at Stafford Hospital was so negative.   (9 marks)

3 To what extent do you think the culture of an organisation such as Stafford Hospital could be completely changed for the better?   (15 marks)

(d) Essays

1 To what extent do you think the organisational culture of a retailer determines the success of the business? Justify your answer.   (25 marks)

2 To what extent do you think it is possible to take the culture from a successful business and introduce it into a less successful business to turn it around? Justify your answer.   (25 marks)

Chapter 17

Managing strategic implementation

Introduction

Deciding on the right strategy for a business is a very important decision for managers. They need to decide on which markets to compete in and which products to offer (strategic direction), how to compete (strategic positioning) and how to pursue the strategy (strategic methods). However what is also essential is to implement the strategy effectively. An idea is not much use in itself unless it is put into action. In this chapter we consider how to implement a strategy including how to manage projects effectively. As part of this analysis we consider the importance of having the right organisational structure for the chosen strategy.

What you need to know by the end of this chapter:

- how to implement strategy effectively
- how to analyse the value of leadership in strategic implementation
- the value of communications in strategic implementation
- how to analyse the importance of organisational structure in strategic implementation
- that organisational structures include functional, product-based, regional and matrix structures

- how to analyse the value of network analysis in strategic implementation
- that network analysis includes understanding and interpreting network diagrams, amending network diagrams and identifying the critical path and total float.

Implementing strategy

Having a good strategy in the first place may be important, but putting it into practice is also key. If anything, managers may spend too long planning and not enough time making sure that the plan actually works. There are always various projects in the news that have overrun, gone over budget or not worked as well as expected – whether it be a new train line, a new sports stadium, a restructuring, a major IT project or a relocation. These are examples of poor implementation.

Implementing a project effectively requires good planning skills. Managers need to work out what has to happen when, who is going to do what and which resources are needed. They then need to plan all of this and bring together the resources and monitoring systems to make sure it happens.

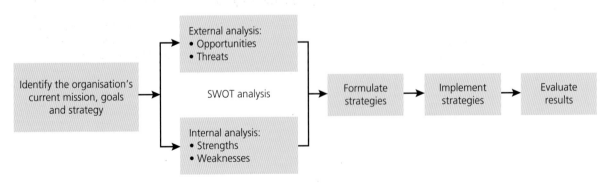

Figure 17.1 The strategic planning process

Business in focus: Saatchi & Saatchi

Kevin Roberts, Chief Executive Worldwide of Saatchi & Saatchi, has said that given that change now happens so fast strategy is dead, what matters now is getting on with plans and executing them. If you take too long planning, you will find you have lost the opportunity that was there and your competitors have 'eaten your lunch'. In the past, he says that managers spent 50 per cent of their time assessing the situation, 30 per cent discussing the options and then it was left to others to implement. He argues that now 20 per cent of the time needs to be spent assessing, two minutes to decide and then the vast majority of the time should be spent executing the plan and making sure it is put into action properly.

Questions

1. Do you agree with this view that execution is what really matters?
2. What are the implications of this view of change for management?

Implementing strategy effectively

Effective strategic implementation involves:

- planning what and who is needed where and when
- setting clear standards of what is expected so that all those involved understand what they need to deliver
- organising the resources required to do the job properly
- coordinating what has to happen
- ensuring the right people are in charge of the various parts of the strategy
- establishing clear points at which progress can be measured and reviewed.

Leadership and implementation

The leader of a team, department or division should provide the vision of where the business is heading. They should be able to gain followers and help them to understand the reason for the strategy. However, they are also responsible for ensuring the strategy is implemented effectively.

Whilst a leader cannot personally make every decision and check every aspect of strategy implementation, they are ultimately responsible for whether it works and their role is to lead others properly. This means a leader needs to:

- make clear what is being done and why
- gain the support of other senior, middle and junior managers who will have to put the strategy in place
- ensure the required resources are in place; for example, that budgets are in place
- ensure effective communications systems are in place
- ensure that reward and appraisal systems are designed to ensure employees are aligned to the strategy
- design systems to check quality is being achieved and the system is on target
- overcome any resistance to the strategy being implemented
- ensure there are clear stepping stones marking progress; it should be clear who is in charge of what and what success looks like at each point.

The leader is the one who will be:

- representing the business. They will be the 'ambassador' presenting the strategy to others, explaining it to key stakeholders and hopefully generating enthusiasm and momentum to ensure it happens and is implemented successfully.
- negotiating if there are serious obstacles to progress. The leader needs to make sure such barriers are overcome or worked around. They need to be good at bargaining and problem solving.

Study tip

Remember to always consider how a strategy is going to be put into effect. The way a strategy is implemented is as important (if not more so) than developing the strategy in the first place.

Business in focus: Mintzberg

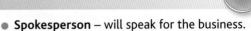

A famous management writer Henry Mintzberg published his Ten Management Roles in his book, *Mintzberg on Management: Inside Our Strange World of Organizations*, in 1990. The ten roles of a manager are:

- **Figurehead** – represents the business to others – for example at ceremonies and public events; others will look up to the manager.
- **Leader** – has to provide the vision.
- **Liaison** – will act as an intermediary between different individuals and groups internally and externally.
- **Monitor** – will review progress of projects and monitor the teams and the external business environment.
- **Disseminator** – will give out information about plans and progress.

- **Spokesperson** – will speak for the business.
- **Entrepreneur** – will have ideas and initiative to create change.
- **Disturbance handler** – will resolve any disputes.
- **Resource allocator** – decides what resources are needed by, and are available for, different departments and teams.
- **Negotiator** – will need to negotiate deals and what has to be done by when.

Questions

1. To what extent do the roles above describe the activities of your head teacher or principal?
2. To what extent do you think these roles require different skills? Do you think these skills can be learned?

The importance of communication when implementing a new strategy

As we saw in Chapter 15, people often have a resistance to change. They fear or oppose change for a number of reasons such as a fear they will be worse off.

Communications can play an important part in making a strategic change successful. For example:

- It can help win support from stakeholders. Effective communication can explain to the banks, for example, why funding is necessary and why the project is worth investing in. Similarly, good communication can help overcome resistance from the local community – for example, if they are concerned about the impact of any building plans it may make sense to consult them and involve them in the planning process.

- It can help to reduce distrust and highlight the benefits to those involved in the process, thereby winning over the people who have to live with and make a success of the new plan. By communicating effectively managers may also learn from others about possible flaws in the plan or how to undertake some aspects most effectively.

Communication can provide a sense of direction and purpose. Employees may feel more ownership of the strategy and, therefore, be more cooperative and engaged with it.

Once the project is underway communication is important to track progress and identify any possible problems, hopefully before they occur.

What do you think?

Why do you think many strategies are implemented badly?

Business in focus: Business strategy and workforce

A recent study by consultants PWC showed that:

- in most cases, 95 per cent of the workforce do not understand the strategy of the business
- in general, there is a lack of trust in the company's strategy from both internal and external stakeholders.

Questions

1. Why do you think the workforce generally does not understand the strategy of the business they work in?
2. Why do you think there is a lack of trust in the strategy of many businesses?

Organisational structure in strategic implementation

The structure of an organisation is the result of decisions in several areas:

- What specific jobs are involved? For example, are they widely or narrowly defined?
- How are jobs grouped together? (This is called departmentalisation.)
- How many people does a superior oversee? This is known as the span of control. The span of control measures the number of subordinates directly responsible to a superior.
- How many levels of authority are there? This is known as the number of levels of hierarchy. The wider the span of control, the fewer supervisors will be required and the lower the number of levels of hierarchy are likely to be.

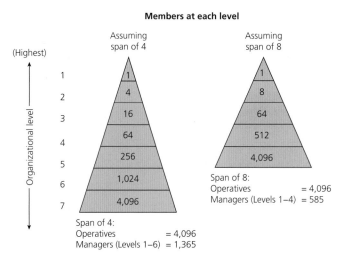

Figure 17.2 Hierarchy and span

- What authority do different jobs have? For example, is the business centralised whereby decision making is mainly the right of senior managers, or is it decentralised whereby individuals at lower levels are able to make relatively significant decisions for themselves? The more centralised a business, the more that authority is kept at the centre. A centralised business brings with it some advantages – for example, decision makers will have an overview of the business as a whole and are likely to be experienced. However, a decentralised organisation may engage employees more (because they feel greater responsibility for what happens as they are making decisions themselves); it may also

be more flexible in relation to local conditions. In a decentralised national retail chain, for example, local managers can adjust prices and stock to meet the demand in that particular region.

Advantages of centralisation	Disadvantages of centralisation
Decisions made by people with experience and overview	May lack flexibility in relation to market conditions
Decisions made by those with access to resources	Decision making may be slow if centre becomes over loaded with decisions to be made
May reduce some risks by having experienced decision makers	May be demoralising for those locally who are not making decisions

Table 17.1 Advantages and disadvantages of centralisation

Forms of organisational structure

When businesses are relatively small the organisational structure is often quite informal. There are relatively few people, the jobs are often loosely defined and there are no clear 'departments' or 'divisions'. However, as a business grows and there are more people and more decisions to be made it is usual to start to group jobs within their different functions and to develop a more formal organisational structure.

The different forms of organisational structures, that is the different ways jobs are defined, grouped and organised include functional, product-based, regional and matrix structures.

Functional structure

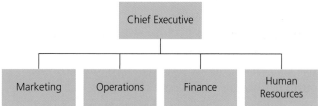

Figure 17.3 Functional structure

In a functional structure the marketing team forms one part of the business, the finance team another, operations another, and so on. There is a logic to this approach in that members of each department have the same job area – they can share expertise, they can help problem solve and they talk the same business language. However, the danger can be that people identify more with the department than with the business as a whole. They become the IT team who are battling against everyone else, the finance team who no one else understands, or the marketing team who could achieve amazing things if only the other departments didn't hold them back and were more cooperative. Each department can develop its own culture and its own way of seeing things. This can lead to the 'silo effect'; this occurs when people view the business from their own departmental perspective and regard themselves as somewhat separate from the other parts of the organisation. They lack empathy with other departments and do not try hard to imagine what it is like from their perspective.

Product structure

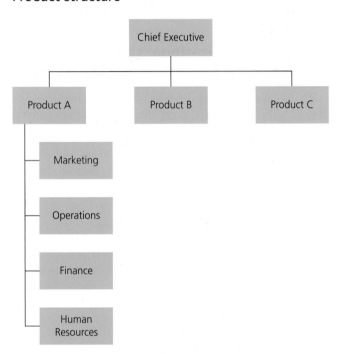

Figure 17.4 Product structure

A product oriented approach occurs when a business has very clear product lines that have different customer bases and different challenges and opportunities – a travel business may run a coach division, a camping division and a weekend break division. A bank may have a section for high-street customers, a section for small businesses and a section specifically for high income individuals. This product approach can make sense if the demands of the different customers vary significantly. The millionaire considering whether to move their fortune to a Swiss bank account needs different advice from the average home owner who has gone overdrawn at Christmas, or the small business owner who needs a loan to expand.

Creating divisions (or departments or sections or even separate companies) to meet very different customer needs is logical because it groups together those with the specific expertise and skills for that group of customers. Once again, though, it does lose a sense of overview of the business as a whole – the divisions may see themselves as competing against each other rather than looking for opportunities to cooperate. A product-oriented structure can also involve a duplication of resources. For example, IT systems, designers and HR teams are duplicated within each product division. Where possible, senior managers should look to share resources and centralise some functions such as payroll, HR, legal advice, printing and purchasing of supplies.

Regional structure

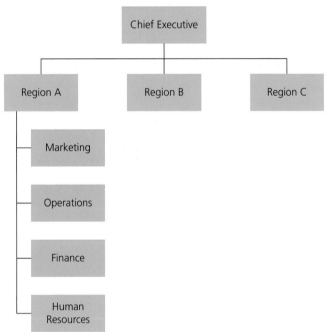

Figure 17.5 Regional structure

A regional structure (for example, grouping jobs under sections such as the north, the south east and the west) makes sense if the strategy of a business involves competing in very distinct regions of a country or around the world. This structure is common, for example, in global businesses such as automotives, tobacco and soft drinks. The reasons are similar to the product approach – the specific issues and demands in the regions may vary, and so having jobs focused on one region may lead to much more in-depth market knowledge, better matching of what is offered to what markets want and more efficient decision making as the business environment is better understood. This approach is common as a business expands nationally and internationally and wants to develop a focus on particular parts of the country or world.

Matrix structure

In a matrix structure individual job holders have more than one boss. The business is organised in such a way that managers report to at least two superiors. For example, in the car industry it is important to understand the region in which the company operates – what is demand doing? What is the legal environment? How are sales of all the company's products doing? What are the trends within the market as a whole? However, if a job relates specifically to one brand – let's say the Ford Mondeo – then the employee must be interested not just in how the Mondeo is doing in their country but also how that brand is performing all over the world. The employee will want to share understanding and learn from those other managers involved with the Mondeo in other regions. In this case, the employee's superiors would be the regional manager and the global Mondeo manager.

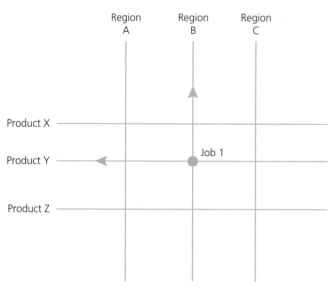

Job 1 reports to Region B manager AND Product Y manager.

Figure 17.6 Matrix structure

The advantage of the matrix approach is that it tries to avoid the silo effect that can otherwise occur within organisations by bringing in different perspectives. At the same time, it can create difficulties as employees have two managers who may have different priorities. For example, the global Ford Mondeo manager may want to

keep this a relatively premium brand, whilst the regional manager may want to discount to sell more to hit local sales targets.

Of course the whole concept of a formal structure may not be appropriate in some organisations that want to encourage creativity and interactions between individuals across the organisations. Some organisations would be against formal organisational charts, for example, because they feel they might restrict and limit communications to some predetermined channels, thereby stifling debate, initiative and new thinking.

The right form of organisational structure

The way that jobs are grouped will affect the performance of the business. The structure needs to fit with the business's overall strategy.

The right form of organisational structure will:

- provide sufficient flexibility to meet local needs without losing the benefits of centralisation
- be cost efficient
- enable decision making to be suitably fast and decisions to be made by those suitably qualified to make them.

What is an appropriate organisational structure will depend on factors such as:

- the market conditions – does the business serve very different segments? In which case, a product structure might be appropriate.
- the global scale of the business – if it operates in very different geographical markets, then a regional approach may be suitable.

What do you think?

Do you think that organisational structures in general need to become more organic?

Maths moment

Imagine you have 4,000 frontline staff to organise. If the span of control is four, how many levels of hierarchy would be required to have this many people supervised on the front line? What if the span was eight?

Network analysis

Managing the implementation of a strategy involves planning the different elements that need to be implemented and working out the order in which these can be carried out. Managers will want to identify all the key activities and identify the order in which they must occur in order to get the plan implemented as efficiently as possible. They will also want to allocate the appropriate resources to ensure the different tasks are completed within the set time and to a suitable standard. In addition, managers will want to think about appointing others to be responsible for their part of the project.

Key term

Network analysis occurs when a network diagram is used to analyse the activities involved in a project and to identify the fastest way of completing the project to a given standard.

To help them in organising and implementing a strategy, managers may use **network analysis** (which is also called critical path analysis). Network diagrams aim to identify the activities which must be completed on time to complete the strategy in the shortest possible time. The order of different activities is shown on a network diagram.

Network diagrams organise the different activities involved in a strategy in order to find the most efficient means of completing and implementing it. The aim is to complete the implementation in as short a time as possible. To do this, managers will determine the exact order in which activities have to be undertaken and identify which ones can be undertaken simultaneously to save time.

To undertake network analysis and produce a network diagram managers must:

- identify all the different elements of the strategy
- estimate the expected length of time each element of the strategy will take to complete
- determine the order in which the different elements of the strategy must be completed. For example, in some cases, specific elements cannot be completed until another one has taken place first (these are known as 'dependent' activities). In other cases,

activities can be undertaken simultaneously (these are known as 'parallel' activities because they can be undertaken at the same time as each other – 'in parallel').

A network diagram is a diagrammatic representation of all the activities involved in the strategy, the order in which they must be undertaken and the time each one is estimated to take.

When drawing a network diagram the following features are used:

- a circle (called a 'node') represents the start and end of an activity
- a straight line represents the activity itself.

A line showing an activity is labelled in the following way: above the line the name of the activity is given; below the line the length of time the activity is expected to take is shown – this is known as the expected duration of the activity. In Figure 17.7 activity B is expected to last ten days; activity A is expected to last four days; activity B can only be started when activity A is completed (that is why it only begins once activity A is complete).

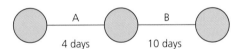

Figure 17.7 Activities and durations

In Figure 17.8 activities C and D can only be started after activity B has been completed and can be done in parallel. Activity E can only start when C and D are finished.

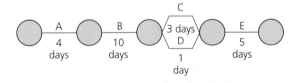

Figure 17.8 C and D can be done in parallel.

In Figure 17.9 we have added in some more activities. You can see that:

- activity F can start immediately
- activity G can start once activity F is completed
- activity H can start once activities E and G are completed.

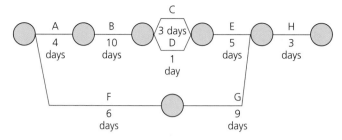

Figure 17.9 A network diagram

All this information is shown in Table 17.2.

Activity	Preceded by	Duration (days)
A	–	4
B	A	10
C	B	3
D	B	1
E	C and D	5
F	–	6
G	F	9
H	E and G	3

Table 17.2 Activities, dependencies and durations

We now have a whole network diagram. Remember the following rules when constructing a network diagram:

- The lines showing different activities must never cross.
- The lines showing activities should always begin and end at the mid-point of the nodes.
- The diagram must begin and end with one node.
- When drawing the activities and nodes, do not put the end node on any activity until you are sure what comes next and whether anything else must also be completed before the following activity takes place.

Adding earliest start and latest finish times

Key terms

Earliest start time (EST) is earliest time that a given activity can begin.

Latest finish time (LFT) is the latest time a given activity can finish without delaying the project as a whole.

Critical path shows the activities which have zero float. These activities determine the fastest a project can be completed. Any delay in these critical path activities causes a delay to the project as a whole.

Float time is how long an activity can overrun without holding up the whole project.

The next stage in producing a network diagram is to show various information that can be calculated from the duration of each activity. This information is shown inside the node and to do this we now draw nodes in the following way:

- The left-hand side shows the number of the node; this is used simply for reference and is done by numbering the nodes left to right.
- The right-hand side of the node is used to show two other pieces of information known as the **earliest start time (EST)** of the next activity and the **latest finish time (LFT)** of the activity before.

Earliest start times

The EST is exactly what it says: it is the earliest time a particular activity can begin. This piece of information is shown in the top right of the node at the beginning of an activity.

As you can see in Figure 17.10, the earliest times have now been added. To calculate these figures you take the earliest start time of the activity before and add on the duration of that activity.

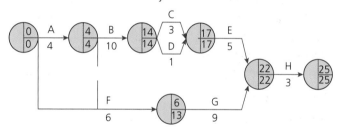

Figure 17.10 A network diagram with ESTs and LFTs added

The earliest time activity A can start is day 0 (this is the first activity in the project); this activity takes four days so the earliest time that activity B can start is day 4. Activity B takes ten days so the earliest that activities C and D can start is day 14.

Activity E can only start when activities C and D are both finished. C takes longer than D so the project must wait for this activity to be completed before moving on; the earliest that activity E can start is therefore day 17.

If you have a choice of numbers to add on to calculate the earliest start time, choose the bigger number; the projects cannot continue until all previous dependent activities are finished, so you must wait for the longest one to be completed. Before activity H can start, for example, it must wait for both activities E and G to be completed, which means it cannot start until day 22.

By identifying the earliest start times a firm can see when materials are likely to be needed. This means that components and supplies can be ordered to arrive just in time to be used rather than arriving too early and sit around taking up space and costing money, or arriving late and delaying the whole project. Materials and resources for activity E, for example, do not need to be ready until day 17.

Calculating the earliest start time is therefore an important part of developing a lean approach to a project and ensuring people and materials are coordinated and ready at exactly the right moment.

Latest finish times

The bottom-right space of a node is used to show the LFT of an activity. Again, this shows exactly what it says – the latest an activity can be finished without holding up the whole project.

Activity H must finish on day 25 – the day the whole project can be completed; since H takes three days it means the activities before must be finished by day 22 if the project is to be completed on time. Activity E, therefore, must be completed at the latest by day 22. Since E takes five days this means the activities before (C and D) must be finished by day 17. Given that activity C takes three days (which is the longer activity out of C and D), if this stage is to be completed by day 17 the stage before must be finished by day 14.

To work out the latest finish times, therefore, you work right to left, deducting the duration of a particular activity from its latest finish time to get the latest finish time of the one before. If there are two or more activities involved (such as C and D), choose the longer duration.

Rules when calculating ESTs and LFTs:

- To calculate the EST of an activity, work left to right and add on the duration of the next activity to the previous EST; if there is a choice, choose the largest number to add on.
- To calculate the LFT of an activity, work right to left and deduct its duration from the previous LFT; if there is a choice of numbers, choose the largest number to deduct.

Total float time

Using the ESTs and the LFTs it is possible to calculate the total **float time** of an activity. The total float time shows how long an activity can overrun without holding up the whole project.

To calculate the total float time use the equation:

Total float time = latest finish time – duration – earliest start time

For example, if activity D has to be finished by day 17, can start on day 14 and lasts one day then the total float is 2 days (17 – 1 – 14 = 2). This activity has two days' slack – it could overrun by two days and the project would still finish on time. By comparison, if activity B has to be finished by day 14, can start on day 4 and lasts ten days, its float is 0 days (14 – 10 – 4 = 0). There is no float – it must be completed on time or the whole project will be delayed. B is therefore known as a 'critical' activity because it has no total float. By identifying all of the critical activities the firm can see which activities must be finished on time; this is known as the **critical path**.

The critical path for the project in Table 17.2 (on page 267) is ABCEH because these activities have no total float time. If they are delayed, the whole project will be late and will not be finished in 25 days.

By identifying the activities on the critical path managers can see exactly which activities are the priority in terms of making sure they stay on time; the critical path also shows the shortest time in which a project can be completed.

Benefits of network analysis

When undertaking network analysis managers:

- must consider exactly what activities are involved in a strategy. This is a useful exercise in itself because it should help to make sure that nothing is forgotten. It also means that managers are likely to consult all the different departments and functions involved and this can help to improve everyone's understanding of the issues and challenges involved in getting the strategy completed.

- can calculate the earliest time by which the strategy should be implemented. This can be important information for customers – for example, the firm can announce a release date of a new product or the opening date of new stores. It can also help the managers decide whether or not a deadline can be hit.
- can identify the 'critical' activities that must be completed in time to get the whole strategy implemented as quickly as possible. This means that they can focus on these specific activities and make sure they do not overrun. At the same time, the amount of float time on non-critical activities can be calculated. While managers cannot ignore these activities entirely it may not matter so much if they overrun (provided they do not use up all their float time); it may even be possible to transfer labour and other resources from non-critical activities to critical ones to ensure the latter are completed promptly.
- may be able to produce items or develop products more quickly than the competition, providing the business with a possible competitive advantage. By seeking to reduce the time taken for a strategy, network diagrams are an important element of time-based management.
- can implement just-in-time (JIT) ordering. Network analysis shows the ESTs for each activity. Using these the firm can order materials and supplies to arrive exactly when they are needed and not before. This saves storage costs and also the opportunity cost of having money tied up in stock. This can improve the firm's liquidity and free up cash which can be used elsewhere in the organisation.
- can use network analysis as a control mechanism to review progress and assess whether the strategy is on target. If there have been delays, the effects of the ESTs and LFTs can be reworked to see the effect on the completion of the strategy.

Although some of the estimates of the likely durations may prove to be wrong, and although external factors may cause delays, this does not mean that network analysis is unnecessary. On the contrary, by having a network diagram the effects of any delays can be relatively easily calculated in terms of the impact on the final completion date. Network analysis enables managers to understand the significance and likely dangers of any delay. Strategies may still overrun, but managers should be able to predict if this is going to

happen as soon as a problem emerges (rather than being taken by surprise) and, if possible, take action to get the strategy back on track.

Maths moment

$$\frac{1+b}{c} = 3$$

Activity	Preceded by	Days
A	–	2
B	–	7
C	B	18
D	A	1
E	C, D	5
F	–	30
H	E, F	2
I	H	14
J	–	5
K	I, J	16

Table 17.3

Construct a fully labelled network diagram based on the information in Table 17.3. Identify the critical path.

Limitations of network analysis

Although network analysis can help business decision making, it can have a number of drawbacks and limitations.

- It relies on the estimates for the expected duration. If these prove to be inaccurate, the calculations for ESTs and LFTs, and thus the critical path analysis, may be wrongly identified. The estimates may be incorrect because some managers may exaggerate how long an activity takes to make it easier for them to complete within the agreed time. On the other hand, some managers may be too optimistic, particularly if these activities have not been carried out before. A more complex version of network analysis, called **programme evaluation and review technique (PERT)**, includes a range of estimates for the durations of different activities; PERT produces a number of network diagrams based on optimistic, pessimistic and most likely durations of activities to take account of the fact that estimates cannot be completely relied on.
- If JIT is used for the delivery of materials, the ability to complete the project on time will depend on the reliability of suppliers. If they are late, this will prevent the next activity starting on time.

- Network analysis simply shows the quickest way to complete a project; it does not guarantee that this is the right strategy to be undertaking in the first place. It may be that the firm's resources could be used more effectively elsewhere.
- All strategies must be managed properly if they are to be completed on time. Drawing up a network diagram is only the starting point. Managers must agree on who is responsible for each stage of the strategy. They must be given the resources and budget to complete in the time agreed. There must be an effective review system to make sure the strategy is on schedule and to agree what action to take if it is not. A network diagram can provide a valuable focal point for the management system, but it is up to the managers to make sure that everything is implemented correctly and that each activity is completed on schedule.

Key term

Programme evaluation and review technique (PERT) involves network analysis of a project using a range of possible estimates for the durations of activities, enabling the business to produce optimistic and pessimistic completion dates.

Other issues in using network analysis

Before a strategy is started managers must agree on a definition of success. They must set out exactly what they want to achieve, otherwise subordinates may cut corners to get the strategy implemented on time. The result may be that the strategy is implemented quickly but that the quality is poor.

Managers must also agree on what resources and spending they are willing to commit to during the project. Obviously, the quickest way of implementing a strategy will depend on what facilities and resources are available and how much the firm is willing to invest into getting it completed. With more people, more money and more machines, implementation of the strategy could probably be speeded up. Whether particular activities can be conducted simultaneously will often depend on whether the firm has or is willing to invest in the necessary resources.

Managers will also be interested in the utilisation of resources throughout the strategy. It may be that certain activities could be undertaken simultaneously, but that as a result some periods would require very high levels of personnel, whereas at other times very few people would be needed. If it adopted such an approach, a firm may have to bring in extra staff for the busy periods and pay its existing staff to do little in the other less busy period. Rather than have such fluctuations in staffing levels managers may want to shift activities around; this may mean that the strategy takes a bit longer to implement but it may nevertheless be more desirable if it means that its full-time staff are fully employed throughout.

Study tip

When analysing a network diagram remember to consider how the estimates of the time needed were calculated and by whom. Consider also the resources involved – it may be possible to reduce the time an activity takes if more resources are allocated to it.

ASSESSMENT ACTIVITIES

(a) Knowledge check questions

1 The number of people reporting directly to a superior is called _____.

2 A level of authority in an organisation is called a level of _____.

3 Explain one benefit of the functional structure.

4 Explain one disadvantage of the functional structure.

5 What is meant by a matrix structure?

6 What is meant by the earliest start time of an activity in a project?

7 What is meant by the critical path?

8 What is meant by total float time?

9 Explain one reason why leaders are important when bringing about change.

10 What is meant by centralisation?

(b) Short answer questions

1 Explain why the role of leader may be important when implementing a strategy of retrenchment. (5 marks)

2 Explain one way a network diagram may help with the implementation of a strategy of new product development. (5 marks)

3 Explain one benefit of having a centralised structure at a school. (5 marks)

4 Explain one benefit of having a decentralised structure for a retailer. (5 marks)

5 Explain one potential difficulty of using network analysis when entering a new market. (5 marks)

(c) Data response question

Derby velodrome

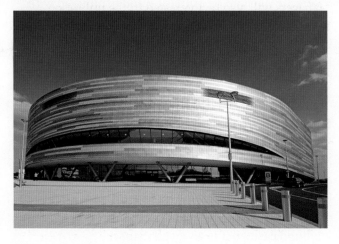

Figure 17.11 Derby velodrome

The velodrome for cyclists in Derby opened three months late in 2015.

Pride Park is a 250 metre cycle track and also includes a 12-court sports hall, gym, group exercise space and a café. It holds an audience of 5,000. The £28 million venue has been built at a time of major cuts in council spending and so has generated criticism as being unnecessary in times of austerity. The venue will host high-level cycling events, basketball and volleyball games, as well as being a concert venue and community leisure facility.

Work on the arena – one of only five such venues in the UK – began in April 2013. The delay in opening the venue was said to be down to 'getting things right'. The council says that this type of project is very complex and requires a great deal of work which is difficult to coordinate. Local cycling shops are disappointed at the delay as they think its opening will boost sales and so wanted it to be ready as soon as possible. They also hope to use the venue to allow potential customers to try out new bikes as part of promotional events.

The velodrome is expected to make a loss of around £2 million over its first three years. This has led to further criticism. However, the council believes that it will eventually pay for itself.

The council said it was still in negotiations with potential sponsors over a new name for the velodrome.

Key facts about the velodrome
- The velodrome has a footprint of 14,500m² or 156,000 sq ft.
- The structure incorporates 1,700 tonnes of steel – that's equal to 200 London buses.
- If all the wood for the track was put end to end, it would reach from Derby to Leicester.
- 265,000 nails were hand-driven into the 250 metre track, over a six week construction period.

Questions

1 Explain one possible reason for the delay of the velodrome at Derby. (6 marks)

2 Analyse how network analysis would have helped with the Derby velodrome project. (9 marks)

3 To what extent are complex projects such as the velodrome almost certain to overrun? (15 marks)

(d) Essays

1 Do you think that for a business trying to launch a new product the implementation of the strategy is more important than the planning? Justify your answer. (25 marks)

2 To what extent is the structure of an organisation key to the strategic success of a business that is growing internationally? Justify your answer. (25 marks)

Chapter 18

Problems with strategy and why strategies fail

Introduction

So far we have examined how strategies are chosen, developed and implemented. This might appear to be a relatively straightforward process but in reality many strategies go wrong. In this chapter we consider why strategies can fail. Sometimes business fail to adapt their strategy to changing conditions; on other occasions they fail to implement their strategies successfully. Here we consider the value of strategic planning, analyse the difficulties of strategic decision making and then assess the possible reasons why business strategies sometimes prove unsuccessful.

What you need to know by the end of this chapter:

- how to analyse the difficulties of strategic decision making and implementing strategy
- the difference between planned vs emergent strategy
- the reasons for strategic drift
- how to analyse the possible effect of the divorce between ownership and control
- that the effect of the divorce between ownership and control includes corporate governance
- how to evaluate strategic performance
- how to assess the value of strategic planning
- how to assess the value of contingency planning.

Problems with strategy

Developing a strategy requires an insight into where markets are headed and an understanding of the strengths and weaknesses of the business.

It requires the ability to:

- identify what really matters and ask the key questions
- make judgements on the relative importance of issues and the priority that should be given to different elements of a plan
- persuade others that the plan is right and then to make it happen.

All of this is likely to be happening in a changing environment with a high level of uncertainty when others are likely to be criticising and coming up with what they think are better ideas. Making strategic decisions involves, almost inevitably, upsetting some people because the road to change can be bumpy and unpleasant for some; others will not be sure where you are headed or will not want to go there.

Furthermore, the results are unlikely to be immediate – strategies take time to unfold and prove themselves. Making a strategic decision is like sending off a container ship in a particular direction. You hope you have it right because it will be very difficult to stop once it gains momentum and you won't be able to turn it around easily if it is going off course.

Difficulties of strategic decision making

Strategic decisions are unfamiliar. They are major decisions, involving a large degree of risk and a very high level of uncertainty. This particular decision will not have been made before. Even if a business's managers have done a takeover before, they won't have done this one; even if they have entered a new market before, they won't have entered this one. However experienced managers are, strategy is scary and strategic decisions are difficult. Managers cannot easily refer back to what they did last time, they do not have any easy points of reference and they cannot 'try it and see'. It may take many years to be sure whether the right decision has actually been made. The decision may involve millions of pounds and affect thousands of people, as well as many other linked businesses. Such decisions are therefore stressful and complex.

Strategic decision making is also difficult and often flawed because managers naturally have their own perspectives. The way we look at things is inevitably influenced by our backgrounds and experiences. When analysing data this means managers' interpretation of

Business in focus: Knowns and unknowns

'There are known knowns; there are things we know we know.

We also know there are known unknowns; that is to say we know there are some things we do not know.

But there are also unknown unknowns – the ones we don't know we don't know.'

Donald Rumsfeld, Secretary of State, USA

Questions

1. What do you think are business examples at the moment of known knowns?
2. What do you think are business examples at the moment of known unknowns?

information is likely to be biased and this can lead to flawed decision making. To avoid this problem of bias many organisations deliberately try to recruit people with differing perspectives. Also, when they form teams they give some members the role of challenging any proposal that is put forward to ensure it is thoroughly tested.

Study tip

Remember that just because a strategy does not work does not mean it is wrong – almost inevitably strategies will hit problems and the key is often how managers work through these difficulties.

Figure 18.1 It's a question of perspective: do you see an old or a young woman in this picture?

Why do strategic decisions go wrong?

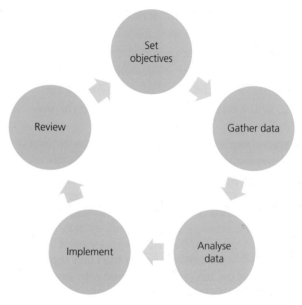

Figure 18.2 The decision-making process

The decision-making process is shown in Figure 18.2. The possible reasons for decisions going wrong are as follows:

● **The wrong objectives are set**. The managers may have set the wrong targets.
● **The data may not be easily available**. Strategic decisions often involve unfamiliar decisions and managers may not have all the information they need or want. Market conditions may be changing so fast that managers are missing the changes that are occurring around them.
● **Data may be badly analysed**. This is particularly likely with strategic decisions which involve unfamiliar situations and one-off decisions.
● **The implementation can go wrong**. There may be resistance or delays, for example.
● **The progress of the plan is misread**. For example, there may be a culture in which managers have

some success and then believe they are invincible. They then ignore any signs of problems assuming that they cannot fail because they have succeeded in the past.

Planned vs emergent strategy

The **planned strategy** is the one the managers intend to implement. The **emergent strategy** is the one that develops over time. If all goes according to plan, the planned and the emergent strategies will be the same. However, in reality, what actually emerges often has elements of the strategy that was planned but is not quite the same. This is because along the way some elements of the plan prove to be too difficult to implement and/or because changes in the external or internal environment help reshape the plan. You may have an idea now of what you will be doing in ten years' time. You may end up doing exactly what you predict but, more likely than not, you will do something in this area though not exactly what you predict at this moment. In the next ten years various things will happen to shape your journey with the result that in some cases you will end up doing something completely different from what you imagined you would be doing.

Key terms

The **planned strategy** is the strategy the managers intend to implement.

The **emergent strategy** is the strategy that actually develops over time.

Business in focus: Accidental success

The success of the Japanese motorbike manufacturers to conquer the US market was long regarded as an amazingly successful and well-planned strategy. The Japanese producers were up against well-established US bikes, such as Harley Davidson. Japanese bikes were regarded with suspicion. Rather than take the US producers head on, the Japanese entered with a small 50cc bike called the Supercub. This won many fans and gradually the Japanese producers traded up, producing and selling bigger and bigger motorbikes until they ended up dominating the market... or so the story goes.

In reality, the Japanese producers, led by Honda, entered the US market with big motorbikes competing directly against Harley Davidson. However, their sales were poor. US bikers did not like the electric start and the Japanese bikes proved unreliable at high speeds and on long distances. The strategy looked doomed to failure.

However, the Japanese sales representatives had been riding on the Honda 50cc Supercubs between locations. These were spotted by buyers at the major US chain, Sears, who asked to stock them. The Supercubs turned out to be a great success, therefore establishing the Honda brand in the us motorbike market. Gradually, Honda introduced more and bigger bikes and other Japanese producers followed. The trading up strategy which proved so successful was an accident and not what was intended at all!

Questions

1. Explain the difference between the planned and emergent strategies for Honda with reference to the Supercub example.
2. What does the above example suggest in terms of managers making a strategy successful?

Reasons for strategic drift

Strategic drift occurs when the strategy of the business no longer matches with the environment in which it operates. What might have been appropriate at one time may become out of date and inappropriate as the environment changes. The drift occurs because the strategy has failed to adapt to differing environmental conditions. Business strategy often develops incrementally, that is step by step, and remains based in what has been done in the past; sometimes this means that strategy simply does not change fast enough to keep pace with what is happening outside of the business. It is likely that with faster change in some markets, for example with rapid technological change, that strategic drift is becoming more common.

Strategic drift may be due to a failure to identify the changes that are occurring and/or a failure to react quickly enough. The failure to react could be because the pressures against change are so great – employees do not want to change, the resources are not available to change or other stakeholders resist. In some cases, managers will actually deny that there is a problem. They might assume the environment will change back again or that the business will somehow survive. In other cases, the business might be in a serious position because it has fallen so far behind what is needed; managers may be worried by the extent of the drift and panic. This can lead to them reaching out for major changes including changing the Chief Executive.

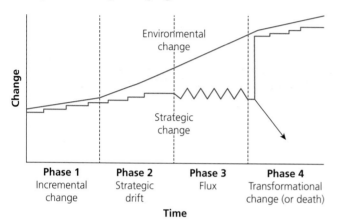

Figure 18.3 Environmental change and strategic drift

Key term

Strategic drift occurs when the strategy of the business no longer matches with the environment in which it operates.

The possible effect on strategy of the divorce between ownership and control

In the case of a sole proprietor the owner is also the manager. However, in the case of companies it may be that the owners (the shareholders) are different from the managers. In many ways this is a good thing. It means people with money can invest and hand over the day-to-day running of the business to the managers. However, it can bring problems in that the owners are not necessarily involved in detailed decision making. They rely on the senior managers telling them what the options are and keeping them informed about the major issues in the business. This means there is a **divorce between ownership and control**. This can cause difficulties. For example, the managers may pursue their own interests at the expense of the

owners'. For example, managers may decide they want the business to grow because it would make them look more successful, even if it is not actually in the interests of the shareholders. The shareholders may not have the full picture of the growth option and may believe the information given to them by managers is correct and, therefore, approve the wrong strategies.

In order to ensure managers pursue the interests of the owners it is fairly common these days to make shares part of managers' reward packages so that they focus on issues such as the share price and the dividends.

Key terms

The **divorce between ownership and control** occurs when the owners of a business do not control the day-to-day decisions being made.

Corporate governance refers to the systems and processes that are in place to monitor and control how a business is run.

Study tip

It is always worth analysing the ownership of a business because this is likely to affect the culture and the objectives. You will not be able to assess whether a strategy is successful unless you are clear what the owners actually want. You should not impose your views of what success means unless it is your business.

Corporate governance

In recent years there has been much greater concern over how businesses are regulated and how their owners know what is happening within them. **Corporate governance** refers to the systems and processes that are in place to monitor and control how a business is run. For example, who are the directors of a business? Are they all managers as well, in which case the people who are supposed to be protecting the shareholders' interests may also be trying to protect their own jobs as managers. Companies are advised to have non-executive directors so that they have some 'outside eyes' on what they are doing to ensure that managers are acting in the best interests of the owners. According to the government, 'The purpose of corporate governance is to facilitate effective, entrepreneurial and prudent management that can deliver the long-term success of the company'.

Business in focus: UK Corporate Governance Code

The UK Corporate Governance Code (the Code) was written in 1992 by the Cadbury Committee. According to this Code, boards of directors are responsible for the governance of their companies. The shareholders' role in governance is to appoint the directors and the auditors and to ensure that an appropriate governance structure is in place. The board has to set the company's strategic aims, provide the required leadership to put them into effect, supervise the management of the business and report to shareholders.

For a board to function effectively there must be constructive and challenging dialogue between members. What must be avoided is 'group think', whereby individuals start agreeing with each other and become reluctant to challenge an established way of thinking.

Diversity on a board should also be encouraged – this in itself should help avoid group think and should also lead to better quality decision making. Diversity may relate to gender and race but also experience and approach.

When appointing directors the processes need to be transparent and rigorous. Directors need to have sufficient time to allocate to their duties. The board needs to have its performance evaluated regularly and members should have to stand for re-election at appropriate intervals. No director should be involved in deciding their own rewards.

Questions
1. Why does group think occur?
2. Why does diversity matter?

Evaluating strategic performance

Evaluating strategic performance means assessing whether or not the strategy worked. This can only be done if you are clear what it was trying to achieve, the resources it had and the conditions it was operating under. Coming fifth in the league may not seem to make you very successful, but if you had an injured squad, falling crowds, no money for investment and were expected to be relegated, you may actually have done a good job. Equally, you may have been pleased to have come second but if the expectation was that you would win you may be in trouble.

It is essential, therefore, to understand what the objectives are, how the managers expect to be measured and also how they are expected to behave. Achieving sales targets but breaking the businesses' codes of conduct (for example through bribery) may be worse than not achieving the targets. 'Success' therefore means different things in different businesses and, in most cases, there will be a number of indicators – did the business achieve its growth target, for example

whilst staying within budget, behaving ethically and improving the brand reputation? Is a small family business that provides jobs and security for a few family members, that helps bond the family together and create a shared sense of achievement, any less successful than the giant billion dollar profit-making multinational? Not necessarily. In the same way, an unhappy single millionaire may not be more successful in life in the broadest sense than the care worker who earns less but gives a lot back to the community, has a happy family and a sense of job satisfaction. Think carefully before judging 'success' based on too narrow a range of indicators and on your own perceptions of what is valuable – that may not be what the other organisation values. Also think about the time frame. A business may not be profitable in the short term, for example, but be building its reputation and relationships for longer term growth. Equally, a business may have a one-hit success with a games app but have no other products in the pipeline and therefore not be sustainable.

Business in focus: GlaxoSmithKline, China

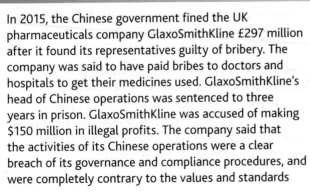

In 2015, the Chinese government fined the UK pharmaceuticals company GlaxoSmithKline £297 million after it found its representatives guilty of bribery. The company was said to have paid bribes to doctors and hospitals to get their medicines used. GlaxoSmithKline's head of Chinese operations was sentenced to three years in prison. GlaxoSmithKline was accused of making $150 million in illegal profits. The company said that the activities of its Chinese operations were a clear breach of its governance and compliance procedures, and were completely contrary to the values and standards

expected from GlaxoSmithKline employees. The company produced a statement of apology which was published on its website.

Questions
1. Why do you think GlaxoSmithKline employees behaved so badly in relation to the company's values?
2. What might the long-term implications of such illegal behaviour be for the company?

The value of strategic planning

Much of what we have described in relation to strategy has seen the process of developing strategy as a logical, rational process. We have outlined the idea of managers analysing the existing position of the business and the outside environment and then developing a strategy to match the two appropriately. This approach to strategic planning has great merits:

- It bases its plans on data. This should avoid irrational and badly thought through decisions being made.
- It can provide a strategy that sets out for managers what the business is doing and how to do it. This plan can unify and motivate employees and provide everyone with a sense of direction.

However, it must be remembered that:

- the environment can change so fast that strategic plans may need reviewing regularly and, at times, may need a complete overhaul. The management writer Pascale said that, as observers, we often want to find coherent and rational behaviour when there may not be any! According to Pascale, it is often how a business deals with miscalculation, mistakes and events outside its field of vision that determines its success over time, that is flexibility and adaptability may be as important as long-term plans. The great military writer von Clausewitz said that the Prussian general staff did not expect a plan of operations to survive beyond the first contact with the enemy. The same may be true of a business plan – it will change as soon as it starts!
- it may be that a strategy evolves over time and is actually the result of a series of decisions that gradually moved the business forward in a series of small steps. Looking back, it may be possible to describe this as strategy but at the time it may not have been entirely clear where it was headed!
- the level of detail in a strategic plan may need to be considered. Some argue that because things do change so fast there is little point trying to anticipate detail too far in advance. Better perhaps to focus on the overall direction and work out the detail as it is needed.

The value of contingency planning

Contingency planning occurs when managers plan for what might happen. In many cases managers are planning for events that are unlikely but would be very significant if they did occur. For example, a business might plan for what would happen if the Chief Executive suddenly left or fell ill, or if the business was subjected to a takeover bid or if a major supplier suddenly closed down.

In one sense, contingency planning may be a waste of resources because the things that are being planned for may never happen. However, if they do occur, then, in theory, the business will be ready and able to react quickly. In the case of a school, for example, it will have a plan for what might happen in case of fire and will regularly have fire drills to make sure the plan works. The hope is that this plan will never be needed in reality but, if a fire does happen, then the staff and students will be trained and able to react more effectively than if the school had not had a contingency plan.

Obviously a business cannot plan for every eventuality, so managers must decide what the key issues to focus on are. The issues a business chooses to prepare for will depend on the perceived likelihood of them happening, the likely impact on the business if they did happen and the costs of planning.

ASSESSMENT ACTIVITIES

(a) Knowledge check questions

1 Planning for unlikely future events is called
_____ planning.

2 What is meant by 'strategic implementation'?

3 State four aspects of effective strategic
implementation.

4 Explain one reason why implementing a strategy
may prove difficult.

5 What is meant by 'strategic drift'?

6 Explain one reason why strategic drift might occur.

7 What is meant by the divorce between ownership
and control?

8 The way in which the activities of managers are
overseen and regulated by the owners is called
_____.

9 Explain one benefit of strategic planning.

10 Explain one difficulty of planning strategically.

(b) Short answer questions

1 Explain the benefits of planning for the departure
of the Chief Executive of a major UK cosmetics
business. (5 marks)

2 Explain how strategic planning can help the new
Chief Executive of a failing business. (5 marks)

3 Addt, a bicycle manufacturer, has grown and
become a public limited company. At the same
time, a divorce between the ownership and
managers of the company has developed. Explain
why this might matter. (5 marks)

4 The family that owned the Tortellin Cake
Company recently sold their shares and floated the

company. Explain one possible effect of this on the
strategy of the business. (5 marks)

5 The Beta Games App Company made millions
of pounds with its one game called 'BETA
BLOCKERS'. However, sales have been slowing
in recent months. The new Chief Executive of
the Beta Games App Company has asked all team
members to contribute to the writing of a strategic
plan for the business for the next five years.
Explain one benefit for the business of producing a
strategic plan. (5 marks)

(c) Data response question

Tesco failure

Having been the superstar business of the UK, Tesco
seems to have been stumbling in the last few years.
Its profit margins have been squeezed and it has lost
market share to discounters such as Aldi and Lidl.
It has also faced accounting scandals and has been
accused of bullying suppliers.

A former Chief Executive of Tesco, Sir Terry Leahy,
has said that in his view many of the problems were
due to a failure of the leadership of Philip Clarke.
Leahy claimed that people tried hard to do the
right thing under Clarke but it simply did not work.
Ultimately, the leader must take the blame. (Sir Terry
Leahy was widely credited with building Tesco
into one of the world's largest and most successful
retailers, presiding over 14 years of growth in profits
and sales. Leahy stood down in 2011 and handed
over to Clarke.)

According to Leahy, the problems facing Tesco have
been due to a failure to maintain its reputation for
low prices. Consumers lost trust as a result. People
had got used to Tesco providing the lowest prices
and not having to check around for the best deals;
when this was no longer the case the brand was
severely damaged. Faced with competition from the
discounters, Tesco seemed to lose its way and it had
no clear positioning between the more upmarket
supermarkets, like Waitrose, and the discounters.
There were price promotions but Tesco was no longer
consistently the lowest price business.

Leahy argues that too many experienced people left
when Clarke took over and this meant that Tesco was
not able to respond appropriately in these difficult
times. Leahy also claims that the culture changed
under Clarke. Tesco employs nearly half a million

people and if they aren't working towards the same goal and don't understand the goal this can clearly damage performance.

In his defence, Mr Clarke argues that people had to leave the company as he addressed the challenges the business faced. According to Clarke, the real challenge facing him was to reduce the number of new UK supermarket openings in order to divert company cash into price promotions and facelifts for existing stores which had been neglected as the business had concentrated too much on overseas stores. Clarke argued that there had been a 'race for space' in which Tesco acquired more and more land

to build bigger stores at a time when customers were ordering more online and needed local stores to top up their weekly online shopping. Mr Clarke had £1 billion to restructure the business. However, he failed to deliver results quickly enough.

In 2014 Philip Clarke left Tesco and was replaced by Dave Lewis of Unilever. The company's profits had again been below expectations. Mr Clarke had worked his way up from the shop floor and had been at the company for 40 years. The board felt they needed someone with a fresh perspective to move the company forward.

Questions

1 Explain one difficulty caused for Tesco by having an unclear position in the market.   (5 marks)

2 Analyse one reason for the success of the discounters in recent years.   (9 marks)

3 To what extent is the failure of a business such as Tesco due to leadership?   (16 marks)

(d) Essays

1 Strategic plans often fail to work out exactly due to changes in the environment. To what extent do you think this means strategic planning is a waste of time? Justify your view.   (25 marks)

2 To what extent is effective leadership the key to the successful implementation of a significantly new strategy? Justify your view.   (25 marks)

Case study: Unit 10 Managing strategic change

Microsoft

Figure 1 Satya Nadella (centre) with Bill Gates (left) and Steve Ballmer (right)

In February 2014, Satya Nadella took over from Steve Ballmer as Chief Executive at Microsoft. Ballmer had worked at Microsoft for years and was known for his passion and energy when it came to preaching about the virtues of the company. He had been Chief Executive since Bill Gates, the founder, stood down in 2000. When Ballmer got the job he made an emotional speech in which he declared his love of Microsoft. Nadella is quieter in his approach than Ballmer but in his first few months he reassured investors with his new strategy and Microsoft's share price rose by nearly 25 per cent as a result. Nadella's strategy is to make Microsoft a mobile first and cloud first business.

The company's success was huge when desktops dominated and almost every computer had Microsoft Windows installed, but it lost out to smartphones and needs to improve its position in the cloud and smartphone markets. Under Nadella Microsoft is fighting back. Nadella joined Microsoft in 1992 and since mid-2013 he has been running the company's cloud computing and business platforms. Cloud computing has become increasingly important to software companies, as people connect to the internet with many different kinds of devices – PCs, mobiles and tablets – and share resources and files online. One criticism of Nadella's appointment was that he was another company man. Some said that Microsoft needed new blood from outside, although Nadella seems ready to focus the business in a new direction.

At the same time Nadella has to restore morale in the business. In 1999, the company was worth $616 billion (£385 billion) – the most valuable company North America had ever known. It had a 98 per cent market share of the PC market. But over the past decade, Microsoft has made several high-profile mistakes – such as the Zune MP3 music player, which quickly became obsolete as smartphones were used to store music on the move, and Windows Vista, which was heavily criticised by developers and PC owners. The company's market capitalisation dropped to $380 billion and its market share fell to 56 per cent. Employees have lost some faith in the company as they have watched the success of Google and Apple and the less steady progress of Microsoft. Several senior Microsoft executives have left in recent years and Nadella needs to stop this loss of talent.

Having said this, Nadella does inherit one of the world's most famous brands and its software, Windows, is still used by 1 billion users. Microsoft also continues to have Xbox and Skype in its portfolio.

Under Nadella Microsoft has bought and rebranded Nokia's mobile phone business. Nadella has announced that he intends to cut 18,000 of Nokia's 127,000 staff and focus more on cheaper smartphones (which is the fastest growing segment of the market). The new phones will use exclusively Windows Phone, Microsoft's own operating system.

On the cloud side of the business Microsoft is already doing well. Companies and consumers are buying more software and services by online subscription; businesses are doing more computing in Microsoft's data centres (or in their own with Microsoft's help). The company is also pleased that the demand for PCs seems to have bottomed out as companies replace old machines. Microsoft is now focusing on dual users – that is people using technology at work and at home. Some engineers have been redeployed to avoid such a big split between consumer and business-to-business units.

Nadella also promises a leaner Microsoft with fewer layers of management as part of his efficiency drive.

Questions

1 Analyse the possible reasons why the share price of Microsoft may have increased in the first few months with Nadella as Chief Executive. (10 marks)

2 Analyse the possible reasons why employees might resist Nadella's attempts to make Microsoft leaner. (10 marks)

3 To what extent was recruiting a new Chief Executive internally likely to have been a good move for Microsoft? (16 marks)

4 To what extent do you think the leadership of Nadella will be the main factor determining the success of Microsoft's new strategy? (20 marks)

5 To what extent is pursuing growth always a good strategy for business? (24 marks)

Acknowledgements

The Publishers would like to thank the following for permission to reproduce copyright material:

Photo credits: **front cover** © peshkov – Fotolia; running heads: Canary Wharf © fazon – Fotolia; The Gherkin © Alex Yeung – Fotolia; **p. 1** © Rido – Fotolia; **p. 3** © Tommy Trenchard / Oxfam; **p. 9** © BEN STANSALL / AFP / Getty Images; **p. 11** © Roger Bamber / Alamy; **p. 15** © Kiyoshi Ota/Bloomberg via Getty Images; **p. 45** @ Angelo Giampiccolo – Fotolia; **p. 53** © dolphfyn / Alamy; **p. 70** © Jeffrey Blackler / Alamy; **p. 89** © Startraks Photo/REX Shutterstock; **p. 103** © redbrickstock.com / Alamy; **p. 118** © Foster + Partners; **p. 131** © Microsoft; **p. 159** © peshkova – Fotolia; **p. 162** © LEON NEAL / AFP/Getty Images; **p. 163** © Charles Pertwee/Bloomberg via Getty Images; **p. 165** © Urbanmyth / Alamy; **p. 169** © Keenretail / Alamy; **p. 172** © Netflix. All Rights Reserved.; **p. 173** © David Askham / Alamy; **p. 175** © Andrew Paterson / Alamy; **p. 176** © Kathy deWitt / Alamy; **p. 178** © JOHANNES EISELE/AFP/Getty Images; **p. 179** © chungking – Fotolia; **p. 183** © Shchipkova Elena – Fotolia; **p. 184** © Art Directors & TRIP / Alamy; **p. 190** © Jerod Harris / ACMA2012 / Getty Images for ACM; **p. 197** © Mark Elias / Bloomberg via Getty Images; **p. 199** © Action Press/REX Shutterstock; **p. 201** © Bryn Lennon/Getty Images for Jaguar; **p. 205** © Long Wei / Photoshot; **p. 211** © mbolina – Fotolia; **p. 215** © David Pearson / REX Shutterstock; **p. 230** © Tim Goode / EMPICS Entertainment / Press Association Images; **p. 237** © Sondem – Fotolia; **p. 239** © Victor J. Blue / Bloomberg via Getty Images; **p. 256** © Richard Levine / Alamy; **p. 269** © Chris Whiteman / Alamy; **p. 271** © The Granger Collection, NYC / TopFoto; **p. 278** © ZUMA / REX Shutterstock

Acknowledgements:
Permission for re-use of all © Crown copyright material is granted under the terms of the Open Government Licence (OGL):
p. 5, Figure 1.3 'Mission, vision and other statements for England's National Health Service', from A Guide to Our Vision and Purpose, NHS England; **p. 10**, Figure 1.7 'Changes in consumer expenditure in real terms between 2013 and 2014', Office for National Statistics (ONS); **p. 11**, Figure 1.9 'Emigration, immigration and net migration for the UK, 1970–2014', ONS; **p. 22**, Figure 2.2a 'Average household finances, 2004–13', ONS; **p. 22**, Figure 2.2b 'Debt-to-income and savings for households in the UK, 2004–19', Office for Budget Responsibility (OBR); **p. 64**, Figure 4.2 'Self-employment data for the UK, 1975–2014', Report on Self-Employment in the UK, ONS; **p. 69**, Figure 4.3 'Investment in infrastructure in the UK, 1997–2013', ONS; **p. 71**, Figure 4.5 'How the UK's electricity will be generated during the period 2013–30', Department for Energy and Climate Change; **p. 74**, quote, Department of Trade and Industry; **p. 85**, Figure 5.3 'Changes in the UK's real GDP in the UK, 2003–14', ONS; **p. 91**, Figure 5.6 'The UK's rate of inflation, 2010–15, as measured by the CPI', ONS; **p. 93**, Figure 5.8 'Corporation tax rates for the G20 group of 20 major economies, 2015', HM Treasury, A Guide to UK Taxation; **p. 95**, Figure 5.9 'The UK's actual and forecast budget deficit/surplus, 2003–19', ONS /

Office for Budget Responsibility (OBR); **p. 98**, Figure 5.12 'Public expenditure as a percentage of GDP', OBR, Economic and Fiscal Outlook, July 2015; **p. 114**, Figure 6.1 'The UK's population size and rate of annual change, 1964–2013', ONS; **p. 133**, Figure 6.15 'Data relating to the size of the UK's capital stock and its trend in labour productivity', ONS; **p. 133**, Figure 6.16 'A comparison of UK labour productivity rates with selected countries, 2013', House of Commons Library Briefing Paper Number 06492, Productivity in the UK, 3 July 2015; **p. 135**, Figure 6.17 'UK migration, 2004–14', ONS; **p. 203**, Table 12.2 'Types of intellectual property and protection', Intellectual Property Office; **p. 204**, Table 12.3 'Patents applied for and those granted', 2012 and 2013', Intellectual Property Office; **p. 204**, Table 12.4 'Patents granted to top 10 companies, 2013', Intellectual Property Office; **p. 215**, Figure 13.11 'Percentage contributions to total UK exports of Services', ONS; **p. 225**, Figure 14.3 'Online retail sales, UK, 2009–2019', ONS; **p. 254**, quote (left), The Failure of the Royal Bank of Scotland, Financial Services Authority (FSA) Board Report, December 2011; **p. 254**, quote (right) House of Lords, House of Commons, Changing banking for good, Report of the Parliamentary Commission on Banking Standards, Vol. 1, HL Paper 27-I, © Parliamentary Copyright House of Lords and Commons 2013.

The Publishers would like to thank the following for permission to reproduce copyright material: **p. 2**, quote top right, www.johnlewispartnership.co.uk/work/our-commitments.html; **p. 2**, quote bottom right, www.bbc.co.uk/corporate2/insidethebbc/whoweare/mission_and_values; **p. 3**, quote top left, from The Power of People Against Poverty: Oxfam Strategic Plan, 2013–2019; **p. 3**, quote bottom left, Retrieved from http://www.tateandlyle.com/aboutus/Pages/Aboutus.aspx. Used by permission from Tate and Lyle.; **p. 4**, Chanel quote, www.facebook.com/media/set/?set=a.10150306753849535.413584.104810759534&type=3; **p. 8**, Figure 1.5, 'The price of iron ore, 2014–15', data from The Steel Index (TSI) via the International Monetary Fund; **p. 17**, quote from the Ford website, www.gusjohnsonford.com/our-mission-statement/; **p. 24**, Table 2.1 'Ted Baker plc balance sheet as at 25 January 2014 and 26 January 2013 (summarised)' and **p. 30**, Table 2.3 'Summarised group income statement for Ted Baker plc', adapted from Ted Baker plc's Annual Report & Accounts, 2013–14, www.tedbakerplc.com/~/media/Files/T/Ted-Baker/results-and-reports/report/2014/TedBaker_AnnualReport_07_may_2014.pdf; **p. 44**, Figure 3.2 Public performance data for the Britain's rail industry, 2002–15', http://www.networkrail.co.uk/about/performance/; **p. 47**, Figures 3.4a and b 'HR data on engagement and diversity and inclusion for BP plc, 2009–13', BP Strategic Report, 2013, www.bp.com/content/dam/bp/pdf/investors/Strategic_Report_2013.pdf; **p. 48**, Figure 3.5 'UK sales of organic products, 2012–14', Soil Association website, https://securepayment.soilassociation.org/page/contribute/organicmarketreport2015; **p. 49**, Table 3.3 'Mothercare plc UK and international sales figures, financial years ending 2012–14', Mothercare plc Annual Report, 2014, www.mothercareplc.com; **p. 51**, Table 3.4 'A selection of environmental data for Rio Tinto plc, 2011–14', adapted from Rio Tinto Annual

Report 2013, http://www.riotinto.com/annualreport2013. Used by Permission from Rio Tinto; **p. 53**, Figure 3.7 'Global market share for search engines, January 2015', data source Netmarketshare, https://www.netmarketshare.com; **p. 53**, Business in focus text source: Google, www.google.co.uk/about/careers/lifeatgoogle/; **p. 55**, Figure 3.9 'R&D investment by industrial sector based on the world's top 2,500 companies, 2013', http://europa.eu/rapid/press-release_MEMO-14-2347_en.htm, © European Union, 1995–2015; **p. 56**, Table 3.5 'Customer satisfaction ratings for the UK's gas and electricity suppliers', adapted from the Independent, 21 January 2015, data from *Which?*; **p. 59**, Figure 3.11 'The balanced scorecard – its use and level of satisfaction, 1996–2012', Bain & Company, Insights – Management Tools, 5 June 2015, http://www.bain.com/publications/articles/management-tools-balanced-scorecard.aspx, Used by permission from Bain.; **p. 62**, Table 3.7 'A selection of Novo Nordisk performance data, 2012–14', adapted from Novo Nordisk Annual Report, 2014, www.novonordisk.com/; **p. 65**, Business in focus text, Business is Great Britain website, www.greatbusiness.gov.uk/cooking-up-a-growth-business/; **p. 68**, Business in focus text, adapted from the Ofgem website, www.ofgem.gov.uk; **p. 72**, Figure 4.6 'Percentage changes in the volume of global exports and value of GDP, 2005–12', World Trade Organisation, www.wto.org/english/res_e/statis_e/its2013_e/its13_highlights1_e.pdf; **p. 74**, quote, Department of Trade and Industry White Paper, Productivity and Enterprise, (Cm. 5233, July 2001); **p. 92**, Business in focus text and Figure 5.7 'The UK's index of shop prices, 2012–15', adapted from the 'UK shop price deflation deepens as food costs fall', *The Guardian*, 4 March 2015. Copyright Guardian News & Media Ltd 2015; **p. 97**, Figure 5.11 'The major elements of UK government expenditure, 2015', UK Public Spending website, www.ukpublicspending.co.uk; **p. 102**, Table 5.6 'A selection of economic data from 2013–15', data from the Trading Economics website, www.tradingeconomics.com; **p. 104**, Figure 5.14 'Merchandise exports and GDP, 1980–2014', 'A troubling trajectory', *The Economist*, 13 December 2014; **p. 105**, Figure 5.15 'World trade, containerisation and other trade data', 'The humble hero', *The Economist*, 16 May 2013; **p. 105**, Figure 5.16 Some of Asia's prominent multinational companies and their export sales', 'The fear factor', The Economist, 29 May 2014; **p. 106**, Table 5.7 'Jaguar Land Rover's sales have become more global as incomes have risen.', Jaguar Land Rover Annual Report, 2014; **p. 114**, Figure 6.2 'Global population forecasts for the remainder of the 21st century', 'World population to hit 11bn in 2100 – with 70% chance of continuous rise', *The Guardian*, 18 September 2014, Copyright Guardian News & Media Ltd 2015; **p. 115**, Figure 6.3 'The world's annual average rates of population change', adapted from a World Bank data set: http://web.worldbank.org/WBSITE/EXTERNAL/0,,contentMDK:22547097~pagePK:50016803~piPK:50016805~theSitePK:13,00.html; **p. 116**, Figure 6.4 'Flow of migrants between the world's countries and regions, 2005–10', Guy Abel, https://gjabel.wordpress.com; **p. 116**, Figure 6.5 'Some consequences of the rapid urbanisation that has taken place globally', PWC Megatrends, www.pwc.co.uk; **p. 116**, Table 6.1: 'Urbanisation rates for a selection of countries, 2000 and 2013', World Bank, http://data.worldbank.org. Used by permission from World Bank; **p. 120**, Figure 6.7 'Global spending on foods intended to promote health and well-being, 2007–17', Euromonitor International, http://blog.euromonitor.com; **p. 120**, Figure 6.8 'Average weekly discretionary incomes and annual changes in discretionary income for the UK, 2008–14', Centre for Economics & Business Research, 2015; **p. 122**, Figure 6.9 'The share of the retail market held by online businesses in selected European countries in 2014 and 2015', Centre for Retail Research, Nottingham; **p. 123**, Figure 6.10 'The number of retail stores in the UK, 1950–2012', Centre for Retail Research, Nottingham;

p. 127, Figure 6.12 'The framework for McDonald's corporate social reporting', from McDonald's Corporate Social Responsibility & Sustainability Report, http://www.aboutmcdonalds.com/content/dam/AboutMcDonalds/2.0/pdfs/2014_sustainability_report.pdf, Used with permission from McDonald's Corporation; **p. 129**, 'Numbers of smartphones shipped by manufacturers 2009–2019', drawn from data from Statista.com; **p. 129**, Table 6.4 'Forecast sales of global smartwatches, 2014 and 2015', Strategy Analytics; **p. 144**, Business in focus text and Table 8.1 'The payback period for students taking MBAs at a selection of UK universities' adapted from e-financial careers website, http://news.efinancialcareers.com/; **p. 149**, Business in focus text and Table 8.3 'Investment by the UK's oil and gas industry, 2010–14', 'Oil industry investment plunges after commodity price tumble', The Telegraph, 26 February 2015; **p. 157**, Table 1 'Selected financial data for M&S, 2013–14', M&S Annual Report, http://annualreport.marksandspencer.com/. Used by permission from M&S; **p. 158**, Table 2 'Some key facts about M&S, 2014', M&S website, http://corporate.marksandspencer.com/. Used by permission from M&S; **p. 175**, Business in focus text, adapted from Halfords' website, www.halfordscompany.com/strategy; **p. 200**, Figure 12.5 'World's top 50 companies by their total R&D investment (£m) in the 2014 Scoreboard', European Commission fact sheet, World trends in R&D private investment – Facts and figures, Brussels, 4 December 2014, http://iri.jrc.ec.europa.eu, © European Union, 1995–2015; **p. 211**, Table 13.1 'Reasons for doing business in each of the BRIC emerging economies', adapted from PWC data; **p. 212**, Figure 13.2 'How Unilever divides the world's population', adapted from the Unilever website, www.unilever.com/Images/ir_Introduction-to-Unilever-Nov-2014-update_tcm244-421552.pdf; **p. 225**, Figure 14.3'Online retail sales, UK, 2009–2019', Figure 14.4 'The composition of online retail sales, 2014' and Figure 14.5 'Online sales as a percentage of total sales, 2014', Mintel E-commerce, July 2014; **p. 227**, Figure 14.7 'The pace of innovation', PWC 17th Annual CEO Survey; **p. 231**, Figure 14.9 'Connected devices around the world', data from PWC, 17th Annual CEO Survey; **p. 253**, Table 16.1 'Cultural differences between countries', The Hofstede Centre, http://geert-hofstede.com/.

In compiling the Business in focus and Case study texts within this book, the authors referred to a great number of newspaper articles including the following:

p. 14, 'BT returns to mobile phones with £12.5bn takeover of EE', *The Independent*, 5 February 2015; **p. 22**, 'The balance-sheet boom – Household wealth, and debt, is forecast to swell in 2015', *The Economist*, 3 January 2015; **p. 57**, 'Ryanair's charm offensive pays off in December', *Financial Times*, 5 January 2015; **p. 77**, 'Free banking in the firing line as competition inquiry launches', *The Guardian*, 6 November 2014; **p. 94**, 'Amazon UK boycott urged after retailer pays just £4.2m in tax', *The Guardian*, 9 May 2014; **p. 101**, 'UK business concerned about exposure to interest rate rise', Commercial Risk Europe, 22 January 2015; **p. 111**, 'Japan Tobacco International stubs out UK's last cigarette factory', *The Daily Telegraph*, 8 October 2014; **p. 121**, 'UK health and fitness wearable tech users to double in 2015 as interest sparks', *The Drum*, 16 October 2014; **p. 125**, 'Ending the race to the bottom: why responsible companies should pay taxes', *The Guardian*, 22 July 2014; **p. 133**, 'If Britain cannot get more from its legion of cheap workers, the recovery will stall', *The Economist*, 12 March 2015; **p. 138**, 'Suppliers scared to blow the whistle on supermarkets', *The Guardian*, 5 February 2015; **p. 151**, 'Dyson invests $15m in technology that may double smartphone battery life', *The Guardian*, 16 March 2015; **p. 178**, 'Aston Martin battles to reinvent itself', BBC News website, 5 March 2015; **p. 194**, 'One in six B&Q stores to close as UK boss departs in major shakeup', *The Guardian*, 31 March 2015.

Index